ABOUT THE BOOK

This book establishes a base of scholarly research, both conceptual and empirical. This base can be used to guide the formulation of educational policies, standards, and practices in schools and classrooms so that improved student learning and other positive outcomes of schooling are likely to result. From diverse perspectives, the chapter authors — each a nationally recognized expert — systematically assemble and interpret the evidence on what is objectively known about increasing educational productivity. Each chapter also contains a discussion, criticism, and extension of the material by a second expert.

The volume is organized into three parts. Part One addresses the ways in which the characteristics, behaviors, interactions, and roles of administrators, teachers, pupil-personnel staff, and students are associated with higher levels of learning productivity. Part Two concerns management and instructional strategies, educational media, and extra-curricular activities. This part explores how the organization of activities and resources in and outside the school are associated with higher levels of learning. Part Three discusses facilities, climate, and community. It covers the qualities of the educational milieux or contexts in which learning takes place.

This work brings together topics of research that are ordinarily investigated and considered in isolation from one another. This synthesis, combining the work of specialized scholars with a wealth of material, which includes extensive references to primary research, should prove helpful to educational policy makers and practitioners concerned with formulating or revising educational standards and increasing educational productivity.

Improving

Educational Standards

and

Productivity

THE NATIONAL SOCIETY
FOR THE STUDY OF EDUCATION

Series on Contemporary Educational Issues
Kenneth J. Rehage, Series Editor

The 1982 Titles

Improving Educational Standards and Productivity: The Research Basis for Policy, Herbert J . Walberg, editor
Schools in Conflict: The Politics of Education, Frederick M. Wirt and Michael W. Kirst

The National Society for the Study of Education also publishes Yearbooks which are distributed by the University of Chicago Press. Inquiries regarding all publications of the Society, as well as inquiries about membership in the Society, may be addressed to the Secretary-Treasurer, 5835 Kimbark Avenue, Chicago, IL 60637. Membership in the Society is open to any who are interested in promoting the investigation and discussion of educational programs.

Improving
Educational Standards
and
Productivity

The Research Basis for Policy

Edited by

Herbert J. Walberg

University of Illinois
at Chicago Circle

McCutchan Publishing Corporation
2526 Grove Street
Berkeley, California 94704

ISBN 0-8211-2260-6
Library of Congress Catalog Card Number 81-83251

Printed in the United States of America

Cover design by Terry Down, Griffin Graphics
Typesetting composition by GraphicType Inc.

Series Foreword

The National Society for the Study of Education is grateful to the many authors who contributed the papers that have enabled us to present this report of an interesting project undertaken by the Georgia State Department of Education. We are especially grateful to Professor Herbert J. Walberg, who assumed responsibility for editing the papers and organizing the material for presentation in book form.

As Professor Walberg has pointed out in the introduction to the volume, this book is an extension of work undertaken previously and reported in two volumes published in this series in 1979: *Research on Teaching* and *Educational Environments and Effects*. Taken together, these three volumes represent the Society's commitment to produce publications of interest to those concerned about research on improving practice in the important enterprise of education.

Kenneth J. Rehage

for the Committee on the Expanded
Publication Program of the National
Society for the Study of Education

Preface

A book of this size, scope, and complexity is a product of many hands that deserve acknowledgment and gratitude. This published work grew out of a large and unprecedented project in the State of Georgia intended to base public school standards on disciplined empirical research in education on the question of what makes for productive growth in student learning and self-concept. Ronald Luckie, then Assistant Superintendent in the Division of Planning, Research, and Evaluation, and Bernard A. Kaplan, consultant to the project, made many contributions to the formulation and execution of the work in Georgia. I have asked them to prepare an appendix describing the background, purpose, and activities of this work.

I am grateful to Messrs. Luckie and Kaplan as well as to several members of the Committee on the Expanded Publication Program — Robert J. Havighurst, Daniel U. Levine, and Harriet Talmage — for extensive suggestions on the draft chapters. The chapter authors and discussants were diligent in making many revisions of their drafts. Kenneth J. Rehage, Series Editor for the Society, participated graciously and extensively in planning and producing the book.

Herbert J. Walberg

Contributors

David C. Berliner, Department of Educational Psychology, University of Arizona, Tucson

Gary D. Borich, Instructional Systems Laboratory, College of Education, University of Texas, Austin

Roald F. Campbell, University of Utah, Salt Lake City

Miriam Clasby, Boston University, Massachusetts

Mario D. Fantini, School of Education, University of Massachusetts, Amherst

Edwin L. Herr, Department of Counseling and Educational Psychology, Pennsylvania State University, University Park

Larry W. Hughes, Department of Administration and Supervision, College of Education, University of Houston, Texas

Bernard A. Kaplan, Educational Consultant, Marcellus, New York

Marilynn M. Kash, Southwest Educational Development Laboratory, Austin, Texas

Stephen J. Knezevich, School of Education, University of Southern California, Los Angeles

Leon Lessinger, Superintendent of Schools, Stockton, California

James M. Lipham, University of Wisconsin, Madison

Ronald Luckie, Consultant, JRB Associates, Atlanta, Georgia

Carroll W. McGuffey, University of Georgia, Athens

Martin L. Maehr, Institute for Child Behavior and Development, College of Education, University of Illinois, Urbana-Champaign

Lewis Miller, Research and Planning Division, Ontario Educational Communications Authority, Toronto, Canada

O. K. O'Fallon, School Planning Laboratory, College of Education, University of Tennessee, Knoxville

Luther B. Otto, Research Division, Boys Town Center for the Study of Youth Development, Boys Town, Nebraska

Richard J. Riordan, Counseling and Psychological Services, Georgia State University, Atlanta

Louis J. Rubin, College of Education, University of Illinois, Urbana-Champaign

William H. Schubert, University of Illinois, Circle Campus, Chicago

James Stanton, Institute for Responsive Education, Boston, Massachusetts

Julie Stulac, Georgia State University, Atlanta

Herbert J. Walberg, College of Education, University of Illinois, Circle Campus, Chicago

Garry R. Walz, Counseling and Personnel Services Clearinghouse, University of Michigan

Gene Wilkinson, University of Georgia, Athens

Ann C. Willig, Institute for Child Behavior and Development, College of Education, University of Illinois, Urbana-Champaign

L. Douglas Young, School Planning Laboratory, College of Education, University of Tennessee, Knoxville

Contents

PREFACE   ix

1   **Introduction and Overview,** Herbert J. Walberg   1

PART I: EDUCATIONAL STAFF AND STUDENTS

2   **Administrators and Supervisors,** James M. Lipham   13
      Discussion, Larry W. Hughes   40

3   **Teachers,** Marilynn M. Kash and Gary D. Borich   49
      Discussion, David Berliner   72

4   **Pupil Personnel Staff,** Garry R. Walz   85
      Discussion, Edwin L. Herr   99

5   **Students,** Martin L. Maehr and Ann C. Willig   111
      Discussion, Julie Stulac   124

PART II: EDUCATIONAL PROCESSES AND RESOURCES

6   **Management Strategies,** Stephen J. Knezevich   133
      Discussion, Roald Campbell   154

7   **Instructional Strategies,** Louis Rubin   **161**
       Discussion, Leon Lessinger   **176**

8   **Educational Media,** Gene L. Wilkinson   **181**
       Discussion, Lewis Miller   **211**

9   **Extracurricular Activities,** Luther B. Otto   **217**
       Discussion, William H. Schubert and Herbert J. Walberg   **228**

PART III: EDUCATIONAL CONTEXTS

10   **Facilities,** C. W. McGuffey   **237**
       Discussion, O. K. O'Fallon and L. Douglas Young   **281**

11   **Educational Climates,** Herbert J. Walberg   **289**
       Discussion, Richard J. Riordan   **303**

12   **Community,** Mario D. Fantini   **313**
       Discussion, Miriam Clasby and James Stanton   **321**

APPENDIX: **The Georgia State Department Project on Public School
           Standards,** Bernard A. Kaplan and Ronald Luckie   **341**

INDEX   **347**

1

Introduction and Overview

HERBERT J. WALBERG

This book is both an extension and culmination of two earlier volumes in the Series on Contemporary Educational Issues of the National Society for the Study of Education: *Research on Teaching* (Peterson and Walberg, 1979) and *Educational Environments and Effects* (Walberg, 1979). In the introduction to the second of these, I wrote of the difficulties of basing prescriptive educational policies and practices on psychology and the social sciences in the ways that medicine, agriculture, and engineering are based on the natural sciences. Educational decisions about valued outcomes and costly resources must be based to some extent on wisdom, tradition, guesswork, and authority rather than completely on systematically applied scientific principles. Despite these difficulties, however, I wrote:

It still seems reasonable in a democratic society to raise skeptical questions about the effectiveness and efficiency of our public agencies, including the schools, rather than to place complete trust in tradition or expert opinion. With respect to effectiveness, democracy assumes an educated citizenry; if education can be improved by objective means, so much the better for society and individuals. With

1

respect to productivity, if education is the largest industry in the United States (involving nearly all the people at some time during their lives and perhaps a quarter or third at any given time), then even small gains in productivity can bring about immense savings, including conservation of those precious resources, time and energy of both educators and students.

Public interest in educational effectiveness and efficiency has been growing since the 1970s. On November 14, 1977, *Time* reported that from 1962 to 1976 the cost per student in the public schools rose from $400 to an inflation-adjusted $750. During that same period the scores for national samples of students who took a college entrance examination, the *Scholastic Aptitude Test,* fell from 470 to 430 on the verbal section and from 500 to 470 on the mathematics section. One week earlier, on November 7, *Newsweek* also noted the decline in scores on the *Scholastic Aptitude Test,* and reported that, for the period from 1972 through 1977, the total professional staff in all public schools in the United States increased by 8 percent and the cost per student rose 21 percent with correction for inflation, while the number of students and the number of schools had fallen 4 percent. I do not mean to imply that scores on the *Scholastic Aptitude Test* should be considered the only outcome of interest or that cost per student is the best indicator of efficiency. What I am suggesting is that raising questions about the effectiveness of schools seems not only reasonable but timely [Walberg; 1979, p. 3].

Thus, the previous two books and the present one are concerned about raising educational productivity in response to the public's concerns about the schools. The present volume, however, differs from the other two in its focus on specific policies, practices, and standards that are likely to increase educational productivity and the marshalling of research evidence related to the educational staff in the school, to educational processes and resources, and to those educational settings that are conducive to learning. The subsequent chapters in this volume also differ from those in the first two books; these analyze and evaluate a large amount and a wide variety of research rather than report details of primary research findings (citations to primary studies, of course, are given for interested readers).

The chapter authors have been asked to assemble the evidence relevant to their topics with respect to what can be done within and outside the school to increase learning. The purpose of this book is to make explicit what is objectively known about increasing educational effectiveness so that these findings — along with such other factors as wisdom, tradition, and public opinion — can be used to formulate educational policy.

Educational research, I think, has a large but not unlimited contribution to make to the formulation of such policy. Our federal and state governments as well as private foundations have provided more funds for educational research and evaluation in recent decades than they did in the past; a vast amount of material lies in primary research reports and other documents for the scholar and practitioner to review. This material, unfortunately, is so voluminous and scattered that it is difficult for educational scholars outside their particular specializations to acquaint themselves with a substantial body of it. I hope, therefore, that this volume, which presents the research syntheses of specialized scholars on a single educational problem — increasing educational productivity and improving standards — will be of value to the many educators and citizens who are concerned with these problems today.

The reader may note, however, that in many of the chapters there is a shortage of research on some topics and a lack of clarity or consensus on other topics. A second opinion — in the form of a discussion by another scholar — follows each of the eleven chapters in this book. In these discussions, the authors agree or disagree with points made in the chapters, cite additional research, or reinterpret some of the findings and conclusions. Although the chapter authors have attempted to report the degree of validity of the conclusions, the discussions convey the consensus, controversy, or uncertainty with respect to factors that make for productive learning.

Although the parts and chapters overlap somewhat, Part One is chiefly concerned with the people within the school — their characteristics, behaviors, interaction, and roles that are associated with higher levels of learning productivity. Part Two concerns the organization of activities and resources within and outside the school that are associated with higher levels of learning. Part Three covers qualities of the educational milieux or contexts in which learning takes place.

Like any means of organization, the parts and chapters simplify, abstract, and fracture experience. The topics of the chapters, although physically separated in the parts of the book, are implicitly related. To start, for example, with the primary purpose of education — learning, which all the chapters address — students most directly and immediately control the process. They in turn are controlled or influenced by instructional strategies, educational media, and extracurricular activities provided by teachers. The efforts of these educators are organized, coordinated, and managed by administrators and supervisors whose influences on learning are less direct but nonetheless aimed at maintaining and improving the process. The productive relations and interactions among students and staff take place, of course, within the influential contexts of the physical facilities of the school, the educational climate, and the community.

Thus, the book brings together topics of research that are ordinarily investigated and considered in isolation from one another. For example, the relations of instructional strategies and student motivation to learning are usually investigated separately by instructional and individual psychologists. Educational media and extracurricular activities similarly are neglected by instructional and individual psychologists in most research efforts in educational psychology.

Because they influence learning indirectly, the influences of administrators on learning productivity, moreover, are less often considered, but they provide the incentives and conditions for learning to take place. The educational facilities, climate, and community are also seldom considered important influences on learning, yet the absence of lighting in the building or an extreme climate can make it difficult for students to concentrate on learning.

Educational research today cannot specify the necessary or sufficient conditions that directly cause or indirectly influence school learning. The research discussed in the chapters, nevertheless, has pointed with varying degrees of consistency and causal knowledge to factors that are positively associated with and that probably influence school learning. Educators and other policy makers, therefore, who wish to increase the productivity of schools can find useful insights and information in all of the chapters and are likely to succeed to the extent that the factors in all domains rather than in a single one are used optimally.

PART ONE: EDUCATIONAL STAFF AND STUDENTS

The first chapter in Part One, "Administrators and Supervisors" by James M. Lipham, employs systems theory to analyze the impact of material and human resources on the processes of schooling that lead to both staff and student growth. He considers the organization of the school as well as leadership, decision making, and staff roles and morale that may lead indirectly to student outcomes.

In his discussion of Lipham's chapter, Larry W. Hughes agrees that additional research is necessary on administrative and supervisory productivity, using especially such methods as ethnography and case studies to add to the experimental and correlational research that has been conducted. He adds that the work of Rensis Likert further illuminates some of Lipham's points about morale: general and employee-centered supervision lead to both productivity and higher morale rather than high morale causing productivity. Hughes further points out specific examples of school reorganization in case studies that suggest more effective and direct roles of administrators and supervisors in education.

In "Teachers," Marilynn M. Kash and Gary D. Borich review research on teacher effectiveness. Time engaged in learning, direct instruction, questioning, and the use of praise, evaluation, and feedback are some of the factors that research suggests lead to greater levels of student learning. The teacher's organization and management of classroom tasks are also associated with higher levels of student learning.

In his discussion, David C. Berliner questions the validity of some of the observer judgments that have been employed in research on teacher effectiveness, although he concurs with Kash and Borich that engaged learning time is associated with learning. The implication that he questions is that engaged time and direction may be taken to such extremes that the tasks become boring and tedious. In further response, Berliner emphasizes that effective teaching is like music in that the combination, sequence, and pacing of elements is as important as the quality and the quantity of the elements.

In "Pupil Personnel Staff," Garry R. Walz reports a scanning of 200,000 documents for research on staff effectiveness that yielded only 106 citations, most of which are severely limited in research and practical application. Ten national trends in pupil personnel services, however, can be identified, and a number of implications for reorganization, investigation, and evaluation can be drawn. In addition, research studies show that counseling programs can contribute to the improvement of achievement in school and self-concept.

In discussing Walz's chapter, Edwin L. Herr agrees that research on the total effectiveness of the pupil personnel program is somewhat limited. He goes on, nonetheless, to present a number of documented guidelines for effectiveness that can be derived from studies of counselors and their influences on student achievement, self-concept, mental health, and career planning.

In Chapter Five, "Students," Martin L. Maehr and Ann C. Willig ask to what degree the student should be expected to initiate and control the teaching-learning process. They describe a number of studies by psychologists that suggest trade-offs between short- and long-term learning, between teacher authority and student autonomy, and between competition and cooperation in the classroom. Research on animals and adult humans as well as on students in classrooms suggests that highly aversive environments and tasks inculcate helplessness, which prevents learning of even simple tasks. Maehr and Willig also present research that examines learning beyond that measured on readily administered direct, immediate tests of classroom lessons.

Julie Stulac finds the Maehr and Willig chapter lacks a firm stance on any of the alternative positions presented. She cites several studies of educational expectations of boys and girls of various social classes that she believes may suggest improvements in school productivity and standards.

PART TWO: EDUCATIONAL PROCESSES AND RESOURCES

In "Management Strategies," Stephen J. Knezevich treats five major topics: management and utilization of professional resources; instructional program management; school climate, communications, and conflict management; planning; and policy development. While noting a number of useful implications for school management, Knezevich also regrets the limitations of research on these and related topics.

Roald F. Campbell, in his discussion, agrees with Knezevich's assessment and review in general and notes seven topics such as mastery learning and student tutoring that he feels deserve greater emphasis. In addition, Campbell points out both the difficulty and value of research on indirect organizational effects of management on learning.

In "Instructional Strategies," Louis Rubin describes recent ferment in the field of research on teaching, the utility of esthetic judgments and ethnography, and studies of student engagement on academic tasks and strategies to increase it. Rubin also points to the difficulties of establishing widely applicable generalizations about the causal links between teaching strategies and student outcomes.

In his discussion of Chapter Seven, Leon Lessinger notes that limited evidence exists for the effectiveness of various teaching approaches. He summarizes Mayrhofer's analysis of strategies and tactics in teaching and several related topics that suggest implications for teaching strategy for policy makers and practitioners.

In "Educational Media," Gene L. Wilkinson, after a brief characterization and history of research on educational media, describes the results of the comparisons of alternative media, the characteristics of different media, and research on school media centers. Notwithstanding the misconceptions and defects of much of the research, Wilkinson draws five reasonable conclusions.

Lewis Miller, in his discussion, supplements Wilkinson's review by considering the situation of the school district officer responsible for expending scarce public funds for media and other goods and services. Although nearly any usual medium can be used for instructional purposes, according to Miller, there is little evidence on which is the most effective. Accordingly, the tasks to be accomplished as well as the costs of alternative media should be the chief considerations in decision making.

In "Extracurricular Activities," Luther B. Otto retraces the early history and impact of research on such activities to educational policy and practice. He explores statistically controlled empirical associations between the amount of participation in extracurricular activities, especially athletics (the field in which the most research has been conducted), and academic performance, aspirations, adult achievements, and other consequences. Otto concludes with a series of possible causal explanations of the empirical associations between these two domains.

In discussing Chapter Nine, William H. Schubert and Herbert J.

Walberg point to a great number of curriculum writings that argue for the value of extracurricular and nonschool activities as educational means and ends in the usual academic areas as well as in nonacademic fields. They roughly estimate from a budget of the typical child's time that perhaps 6 percent of the time potentially devoted to education is actually employed in productive curricular activities, which leaves extensive time for expanding intramural and extramural, curricular and extracurricular activities and accomplishments. Moreover, they point to the need to study the implicit curricula in the lives of students outside of school as an extension of extracurricular phenomena.

PART THREE: EDUCATIONAL CONTEXTS

In "Facilities," C. W. McGuffey divides the research in his review into that concerning variables in the physical environment, such as light and heating levels, and in building configuration, such as the amount and openness of space. From considering the interaction of these two sets of variables on educational outcomes, he concludes with a list of general recommendations.

In their discussion, O. K. O'Fallon and L. Douglas Young supplement McGuffey's review by presenting conclusions of additional reviews of studies on thermal, lighting, seeing, and hearing factors. They find McGuffey's conclusions warranted on the basis of research and professional opinion.

In "Educational Climates," Herbert J. Walberg considers five types of productive educational climates — classroom, school, open, teaching, and home — from a social-psychological viewpoint. He argues that the consistent, controlled, and moderate to large correlations of factors in these climates with educational outcomes help justify their encouragement either as means to both measurable and immeasurable ends or as ends in their own right.

Richard J. Riordan discusses the work of the Schmucks on humanizing climates, McGee and others on climate interventions, Brookover on sociological aspects of school climates, and Barclay on climate measurement. He agrees that educational climates influence learning and concludes that research efforts in this area are increasingly sophisticated and give hope that climate intervention programs can be effectively mounted.

In "Community," Mario D. Fantini considers citizen participation, particularly parent involvement, in the educational process. He finds the evidence on parental participation as a cause of increased educational productivity scanty, but discusses several studies that demonstrate such participatory effectiveness. Although the general research basis is admittedly questionable, Fantini believes that, under certain conditions, parental involvement is effective in promoting learning.

Miriam Clasby and James Stanton take issue with Fantini because of incompleteness in the research description and weaknesses in his analysis of governance-related participation. They present a series of alternative perspectives on community participation and formulate several policy guidelines for developing more effective strategies.

TWO CAVEATS

The wealth of material in this book, including the references to primary research, should prove useful to educational policy makers and practitioners concerned with formulating or revising educational standards and increasing educational productivity. Two caveats, nonetheless, should be mentioned. The first is that many valuable qualities of individual students lie outside the boundaries of educational and psychological measurement. Educational achievement in the usual school subjects (language, mathematics, social studies, science, physical education, and, to a lesser extent, art and music) can be measured with reasonable reliability and validity. The same is true for self-concept and attitudes toward learning. Good citizenship, creativity, morality, and other qualities, however, are now immeasurable. Much of the research reviewed in this book concerns the measurable set of outcomes, and thus the implications of the research are limited in this respect. On the other hand, students are unlikely to attain the less tangible, long-term qualities unless they have mastered the basic school subjects and have attained as well the discipline and other individual and social skills required for their mastery. Nor is there persuasive evidence that one set must be traded for the other.

Much of the research reviewed in this volume, to turn to the second caveat, is correlational in that it shows the association of factors within and outside the school with higher levels of student learning. Educational researchers, practitioners, and policy makers must retain some skepticism about such correlational relationships even when they are statistically controlled, just as medical researchers and physicians continue to retain at least a small doubt about the causal connection between smoking and lung cancer, notwithstanding statistical control for age, social class, and local air pollution. Thus more definitive research and evaluation is in order, both that which addresses local school problems and innovations as well as that which is more extensive and general.

Decision makers, however, cannot wait for definitive results and must face the challenge of increasing of educational productivity as a day-to-day effort. On the basis of the research cited in this volume, improvements in a number of aspects of school organization and student experience are likely to increase both the effectiveness and the efficiency of learning. For example, doubling the time that students actually concentrate on their lessons and study might nearly double learning, and improvements in instruction and morale might redouble it.

Agriculture, industry, and medicine made great strides in improving human welfare as doubts arose about traditional, natural, and mystical practices. Productivity grew as the measurement of the results intensified, as experimental findings were replicated, accumulated, and synthesized, and as their theoretical and practical implications were forcefully implemented. Education is no less open to humanistic and scientific inquiry and no lower in priority when about half the workers in modern nations are in knowledge industries. Although we need more and better educational research, it now points toward improvements that seem likely to increase educational effectiveness. As I noted in my conclusion to the introduction to *Eductional Environments and Effects,* science can help educators by subjecting insights to empirical tests and by providing records of the results that are open for examination. The record of research is imperfect, but, in the end, it remains the best resource for making educational practice more systematic and productive.

Part 1

EDUCATIONAL STAFF AND STUDENTS

2

Administrators and Supervisors

JAMES M. LIPHAM

This review of research summarizes and synthesizes the current state of our knowledge regarding the impact of administrative and supervisory personnel on the outcomes of the school — particularly those outcomes related to students' cognitive achievement and affective development. Some researchers (March 1978) take the skeptical view that attempting to improve American education by changing the structure of the school or the behavior of the administrators and supervisors is unlikely to produce dramatic or even perceptible results. It is, of course, naive to assume that a particular kind of organizational structure or a specific type of leadership behavior will raise students' achievement or self-esteem, yet each of us undoubtedly can cite particular superintendents, principals, and other school personnel who either directly or indirectly influenced the quality of our lives. Without subscribing specifically to the "great person" theory of leadership, one must consider the leadership behavior of administrators and supervisors (Goodlad 1977, Trump 1972, Lipham and Daresh 1979) as one influential factor since most organizations, including the school, tend to change more from the top down than they do from the bottom up (Griffiths 1959).

To place the following review of research into an appropriate theoretical context, I first present a general systems framework, which provides a perspective for presenting current theoretical and empirical findings regarding the administration of the schools. Then, I report the results of research on administrative roles, organization of the school, decision-making structures and processes, and leadership behaviors of administrators and supervisors. After drawing conclusions for each of these topics, I conclude with a brief enumeration of persistent problems regarding present and future research in the field of educational administration.

THE SCHOOL AS AN OPEN SYSTEM

Recognition that the school is an open system enables one to analyze the impact of administrative and supervisory personnel on the outcomes of the school. Systems theory — holistic, interdisciplinary, methodical, and analytical — is concerned with the organizational boundaries, environments, structures, inputs, processes, and outputs of the school (Immegart 1969). In the systems view the school is seen as a dynamic, interactive organization, as shown in Figure 2-1.

Figure 2-1
The School as a System

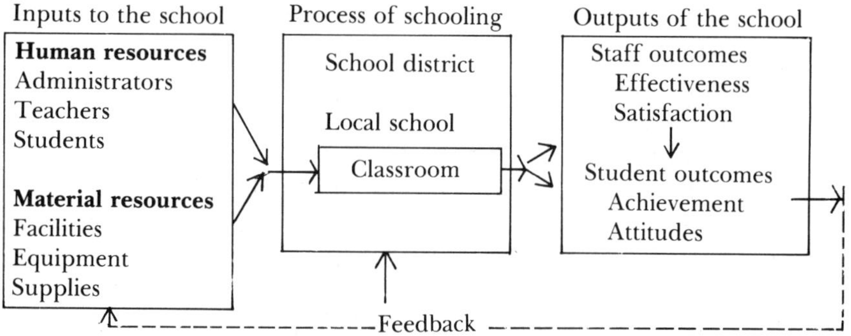

Inputs to the school	Process of schooling	Outputs of the school
Human resources Administrators Teachers Students **Material resources** Facilities Equipment Supplies	School district Local school Classroom	Staff outcomes Effectiveness Satisfaction ↓ Student outcomes Achievement Attitudes

Feedback

Source: Adapted from James M. Lipham and J. A. Hoeh, Jr., *The Principalship: Foundations and Functions* (New York: Harper & Row, 1974), p. 34.

As the figure shows, inputs to the school are both human and material. Analysis of material resources is beyond the scope of this review, but school facilities, equipment, supplies, and other financial resources obviously have an impact on the quality of the outcomes of the school. In terms of human resources, the characteristics of the students entering the school also affect system outputs. In fact, research by Coleman (1966) has shown that the home, community, and other factors may be much more powerful determinants of student achievement than is the entire process of schooling. Similarly, teacher characteristics and behaviors are presumed to have a more direct impact on students than do those of administrators and supervisors — the subjects of this analysis.

The classroom is a subsystem of the school, which is a subsystem of the school district. Thus, the school superintendent's behavior can be expected to pervasively influence the district, the principal to influence the local school, and the teacher to influence the classroom. Hence, in analyzing the relationship of administrative and supervisory behavior to student outcomes, one must first focus on the relationship of administrative behavior to the staff outcomes of productivity and morale (as shown by the route of the solid arrows in the output category in Figure 2-1). The productive and motivated teacher is assumed to influence positively and significantly both student achievement and student attitudes. Following the model in Figure 2-1, let us now turn to the summary of relevant theory and recent research findings, beginning with administrative and supervisory roles in education.

ADMINISTRATIVE AND SUPERVISORY ROLES

During the past decade substantial research has been conducted concerning the roles of administrators and supervisors in education. These studies have drawn heavily on social systems theory, which is described next and is followed by a synthesis of recent research findings.

Social Systems Theory

First and foremost, the school is a dynamic, interactive social system consisting of three basic dimensions. The first is the normative or sociological dimension of the institutional roles and expectations designed to accomplish the goals of the school (Getzels and Guba 1957, Getzels, Lipham, and Campbell 1968). Roles, representing dynamic aspects of positions, offices, or statuses within the school, are complementary or interlocking and in the school are quite flexible. Roles are defined in terms of expectations, which are the normative rights and duties of a role incumbent — superintendent, supervisor, principal, teacher, student, and so forth. When role incumbents put these rights and duties into effect, they perform their roles. The extent to which the behavior of a role incumbent is congruent with the expectations held for that role is the measure that is used in evaluating the effectiveness of one's role behavior.

The second basic dimension of a social system is the personal or psychological dimension consisting of the individual personalities with their unique abilities, interests, and needs. The school emphasizes this dimension, which is concerned with accomplishment of the goals of the individual. The people in the schools stamp the roles they occupy with their own personalities. The extent to which the behavior of an individual is congruent with the individual's unique pattern of needs is a measure of personal efficiency.

Social behavior within the school derives simultaneously from the normative and the personal dimensions. Behavior in a social system is a function of the interaction between a given institutional role, defined by the expectations attached to it, and the personality of a particular role incumbent, defined by one's needs. That is, social behavior results from an individual's attempts to cope, in ways consistent with the individual's own pattern of needs and dispositions, with expected patterns for one's behavior. The extent to which the demands of the organizational role and the requirements of the individual personality are congruent is a measure of satisfaction — the role suits or fits the individual and vice versa.

The institution and the individual are embedded in a cultural milieu that conditions and shapes both the institutional roles and the individual personalities, and thereby influences social behavior. The culture may be described in terms of its prevailing ethos and values. A value is "a conception, explicit or implicit, distinctive of an individual or characteristic of a group, of the desirable which influences the selection from available modes, means, and ends of action" (Kluckhohn 1951, p. 395). Therefore, the basic values and the educational values held by the community, the staff, the students, and others bear directly on the school and all the individuals within it.

In summary, the three dimensions of institutional roles, individual personalities and cultural values are the primary determinants of social behavior in the school. This model is particularly valuable as the basis for conducting research on role expectations and behavior of administrators and supervisors in schools.

Research on Administrative and Supervisory Roles

Many authorities in education (Brieve 1972, Gross and Herriott 1965, Hansen 1974, Lipham and Hoeh 1974) and numerous researchers (Bert 1976, Espalin 1976, Pitts 1976, Traugott 1976) have examined the major tasks, or role functions, required of superintendents, supervisors, principals, and other administrators. From these studies we can conclude that the major role tasks, particularly of line administrators, include five functions.

1. *Curriculum and instruction.* Although administrators typically do not accord the instructional program the emphasis they feel it should receive, instruction is the foremost function of the school. Typically administrative tasks in this area include assessing the community context for education, stating educational objectives, planning and organizing curricula and cocurricular programs, implementing instructional activities, and evaluating educational outcomes.

2. *Staff personnel.* Because of the increased unionization of teachers, the function of personnel today is assuming increasing importance — primarily because staff negotiations can curb change, as well as restrict management rights. The traditional staff personnel tasks of the administrator include the recruitment, selection, orientation, assignment, supervision, motivation, development, negotiation, arbitration, evaluation, transfer, and termination of staff.

3. *Student personnel.* Typical role expectations in the area of student personnel include student scheduling, attendance, guidance, health, and discipline. In fulfilling these functions, administrators are assisted by counselors, psychologists,

nurses, social workers, and others. Even so, student personnel concerns demand continued attention, particularly on
the part of principals and assistant principals. Hence administrators must be skilled in working effectively with students.

4. *Financial and physical resources.* At a time of accountability and
declining enrollments, the administrator must give attention
to the appropriate use of the human and material resources
available to the school. Traditional tasks in this area include
planning, programming and budgeting; accounting for
school monies (both curricular and cocurricular); maintaining inventories; supervising school construction, remodeling, and maintenance; and supervising school lunches,
transportation, and other auxiliary services. Administrators
sometimes spend more time on these matters than they
desire.

5. *Home, school, and community relations.* Today, parents and
citizens are demanding a stronger voice in the administration and operation of their schools. These demands increase
the importance of tasks in home, school, and community
relations, which include assessing community values, needs,
and aspirations; analyzing the composition, relationships, and demands of community groups; working with
parents and parent organizations, community leaders, and
agencies; and informing the community and involving it in
determining the purposes, programs, progress, and plans for
the improvement of the school.

Conclusions Regarding Administrative Roles

In addition to defining the major expectations for administrative and supervisory roles in education, the research on roles leads
to the following conclusions:

1. There is often a substantial difference between the role functions actually performed by administrators and those ideally
desired (Traugott 1976). For example, most administrators
would prefer to give greater attention to educational leadership, curriculum planning, and staff supervision and less
attention to administrative routines, such as financial management and school plant operations (National Association

of Elementary School Principals 1970, Knezevich 1971).

2. Administrators and supervisors experience considerable role conflict — conflict among roles, role conflict among and within groups, and self-role conflict (role-personality relations) (Gross, Mason, and McEachern 1958, Muse 1966, Getzels, Lipham, and Campbell 1968). Hence there is a need to increase role clarity and complementarity in education.

3. Agreement on role expectations and the adequate fulfillment of role expectations by administrators and supervisors result in a positive school climate (Halpin and Croft 1963, Berends 1969); increased staff motivation and morale (Campbell 1959, Lipham and Hoeh 1974); and improved student attitudes toward self and others (Christiansen 1953, Becker 1970).

THE ORGANIZATION OF THE SCHOOL

Much of the recent research regarding the formal organization of the school is based on axiomatic organizational theory. This theoretical approach to the analysis of the school is considered first, followed by a summary of the related research.

Axiomatic Organizational Theory

Schools and school systems are, of course, bureaucracies governed by standard concepts of hierarchy, authority, organization, management, and control. Based on the earlier analyses of bureaucracy by Weber (1947), Barnard (1946), and Thompson (1961), a general axiomatic theory of organizations, which has generated considerable research on the formal organization of the school, was developed by Hage (1965). He outlined eight variables related to organizations — four "means" and four "ends." The means are those variables in an organization's structure, and the ends represent performance, or outcome, variables. In this theory, the structural variables are termed complexity, centralization, formalization, and stratification; the outcome variables are termed adaptiveness (flexibility), job satisfaction (morale), production (effectiveness), and efficiency (cost). Brief descriptions of the structural variables follow.

Complexity. The complexity of an organization represents the extensiveness and intensiveness of knowledge in the organization and is measured by two indicators — the number of occupational specialties and the level of training of persons in the organization. In schools, personnel generally have a high degree of initial professional preparation, supplemented by in-service staff development activities, such as attending workshops and conferences, involvement in professional organizations, and reading current educational literature.

Centralization. Centralization refers to the distribution of power to make decisions and is measured by two indicators — the extent to which organizational members at different levels participate in decision making and the number of areas in which decisions are made. The lower the proportion of members that participate in decision making, the fewer the areas in which they can make decisions, then the higher the centralization of the organization.

Formalization. Formalization relates to the codification of jobs and to the explicitness by which performance is directed through rules and regulations. The greater the discretion allowed to members in performing their responsibilities, then the lower the formalization.

Stratification. Stratification refers to the extent to which formal and informal rewards are distributed equitably in the organization, as well as to perceived status differences among personnel. The greater the difficulty in earning status or rewards, then the more stratified is the organization.

Axiomatic theory proposes that the structure of the school and the outcomes of the school are interrelated and that an increase in one variable will result in a decrease in other variables. For example, if the stratification in the school is high, then job satisfaction and morale of teachers will be low. Although it would be interesting to examine each of the propositions, it is even more instructive to consider two extreme types of organizations suggested by the variables — the organic organization, which emphasizes adaptiveness, and the mechanistic organization, which emphasizes production. Each is the converse of the other:

Organic organization	*Mechanistic organization*
High complexity	Low complexity
Low centralization	High centralization
Low stratification	High stratification

Low formalization	High formalization
High adaptiveness	Low adaptiveness
Low production	High production
Low efficiency	High efficiency
High job satisfaction	Low job satisfaction

To what extent is the school organic or mechanistic? Which structural variables are helpful in predicting certain organizational outcomes? Several researchers have sought answers to these questions.

Research on the Organization of the School

A considerable body of research on the organization of the school has been conducted during the past five years in schools that have changed from a traditional organizational structure to one that includes team planning and teaching. In such schools, Pellegrin (1969) found teacher satisfaction to be higher than in traditional schools on the following items: (a) progress toward one's personal goals in present position, (b) personal relationships with administrators and supervisors, (c) opportunity to accept responsibility for one's own work and the work of others, (d) seeing positive results from one's efforts, (e) personal relationships with fellow teachers, (f) present job in light of one's career expectations, and (g) availability of pertinent instructional materials and aids.

A major study of the relationship between the overall structure of the school and its adaptiveness in utilizing innovative instructional and learning activities was conducted by Walters (1973). He discovered a significant and direct relationship between the structural properties of the school and organizational adaptiveness. Specifically, schools using team teaching were significantly less centralized in their decision-making processes than were traditional schools. Moreover, the schools organized into teaching teams were significantly more innovative and adaptive in terms of both teacher activities and student activities than were traditionally organized schools.

A more recent study by Mendenhall (1977) examined the relationship of the structural aspects of the organization to the organizational outcome of teachers' job satisfaction. Using questionnaires, she gathered data on the structural dimensions of complexity, centralization, formalization, and stratification. Total and partial job satisfaction of teachers were measured in terms of satisfaction with administrators, co-workers, career future, pupil relations, and the like. Mendenhall found that if stratification and formalization in the schools was low, then teachers' job satisfaction was high. These findings were congruent with the propositions of axiomatic organizational theory that high formalization and high stratification would relate negatively to teachers' job satisfaction. Regarding stratification in schools, Mendenhall noted that sometimes informal and subtle rewards can be used to create an informal status system, and if these rewards are distributed only to a select few, then stratification increases and job satisfaction decreases. Regarding formalization, she noted that educators are members of a profession and, as such, they hold certain norms; highly codified job descriptions, rules, and regulations are not needed.

The relationship between organizational variables and teachers' motivation to perform was examined by Herrick (1974) in terms of axiomatic organizational theory. Herrick found that if centralization in decision making and stratification of social relationships were low, then job satisfaction and teacher motivation to perform were high.

To investigate the relationship of the organizational structure of the school to students' self-concepts as learners, Nelson (1972) compared responses from students in thirteen schools using team teaching with those of students in twelve traditional schools. Students in schools with team teaching scored significantly higher in their attitudes toward themselves as learners than did students in traditional schools.

Conclusions Regarding the Organization of the School

The following conclusions are based on research on the organization of the school:

1. Schools differ in the extent to which they are mechanistic or organic organizations (Pellegrin 1969, Walters 1973). It is possible to change the school from a traditional bureaucracy to a less bureaucratic environment.
2. The more organic the organizational structure of the school, the higher will be the following outcomes: innovation and adaptiveness (Walters 1973); staff satisfaction and motivation (Mendenhall 1977, Herrick 1974); and students' attitudes toward themselves as learners (Nelson 1972).

DECISION MAKING

Decision making is the primary responsibility of the administrator. After an overview of important theoretical constructs concerning the decision-making process, I present some significant findings of recent studies concerning the decision-making behavior of school administrators and supervisors in relation to the outcomes of the school.

Decision Theory

Decision making is a complex phenomenon involving intricate interrelationships of situational, organizational, and personal variables, which makes it difficult to develop a comprehensive and concise explanatory model. Even so, the importance of decision making has been recognized, and many researchers (Gregg 1957, Griffiths 1959, Dill 1964, Phi Delta Kappa 1971) have attempted to describe and delineate its significant elements in applying decision-making concepts to educational practice.

Decision making has been defined as a rational process wherein "awareness of a problematic state of a system, influenced by information and values, is reduced to competing alternatives, among which a choice is made, based upon estimated outcome states of the system" (Lipham 1974, p. 84). In examining decision making as a rational process, one must give attention to the dimensions of content, stages, and involvement.

Decision Content. In regard to content, each decision in the school may be classified by what the decision deals with — the administrative functions of curriculum and instruction, staff personnel, student personnel, finance and business management, school plant services, or home, school, and community relations. The content of most decisions differs according to the various levels of the organization. Since the school is a system, some decisions are most relevant at the classroom level; others, at the local school level; and still others at the district level. Hence, in analyzing the decision-making process, one finds it instructive to examine the scope of the content covered in terms of its appropriateness within, between, and among the several levels of the organization, since all major decisions in education are shared.

Decision Stages. Regardless of content, consideration must be given to how a decision is made — the several steps or stages in rational decision making. Although described differently by various authors (Barnard 1938, Bross 1953, Cyert and March 1963, Simon 1960), the six stages of decision making include the following: (a) identifying the nature of the problem, (b) clarifying and defining the problem, (c) formulating and weighing alternatives, (d) making the decision choice, (e) implementing the decision solution, and (f) evaluating the effectiveness of the decision.

Decision Involvement. Who participates in making a decision, how often they participate, and the level of their participation constitute the elements of involvement in decision making. The major groups and individuals within the school system who can participate include the board of education, school superintendent, central office personnel, principal, teachers, and students. Outside groups may include parents and citizens in the local community. Theoretically, any educational decision may either directly or indirectly involve many individuals and groups that are either closely linked or loosely coupled, since schools are dynamic social systems (Getzels, Lipham, and Campbell 1968).

The second aspect of decision involvement relates to how often groups or individuals participate in making a particular decision. Such frequency of involvement may range from frequent to rare or always to never. Excessive involvement leads to a state called "decision saturation" whereas infrequent involvement — particularly when the individual is informed and wishes to be involved (Bridges 1967, Alutto and Belasco 1972) — leads to a condition called "decision deprivation."

The third aspect of decision involvement refers to the level, extent, or degree of participation in decision making. As conceptualized in the study of decision point analysis (Eye, Lipham, and Netzer 1965), one's level of decision involvement may range from high to low according to the following scale: (a) no involvement in the decision, (b) provide information, (c) help in formulating alternatives, (d) suggest specific alternatives, and (e) make the decision.

The dimension of involvement in decision making includes consideration of who is involved, how often they are involved, and the level of their involvement. Recent studies of decision making in the schools have paid attention to these three important variables in the involvement as well as to the other two major dimensions of content and stages.

Research on Decision Making

Two basic research approaches have recently been used to examine decision making in the schools. The first is the empirical approach wherein decision-making instruments have been developed and utilized across a wide sample of schools. The second is the field study approach wherein observations of decision making have been made in selected case schools.

Empirical Studies of Decision Making. Based on the earlier work of Eye, Lipham, and Netzer (1965), Wright (1976) developed the Decision Involvement Index to measure both the actual and the desired level of involvement of staff members in making decisions in each of the functional content areas of decision making in schools with programs of Individually Guided Education (IGE). The functional content items were factor analyzed to reveal items at the classroom level, the local school level, and the district level. The instrument was administered in seventy-seven randomly selected schools in thirteen states. Wright discovered that teachers were moderately to highly involved in making important decisions affecting their classrooms, had some involvement in making decisions affecting the school, and had little involvement in making decisions with an impact on the district. He found that teachers desired greater involvement in making decisions at the school and district levels, since many of them felt that administrators were making more decisions than was ideal, particularly on matters relating to curriculum and instruction.

In a subsequent study of schoolwide decision making, Feldman (1977) adapted Wright's Decision Involvement Index, adding a question to obtain information about the outcome of staff satisfaction with the decision-making process itself, ranging from "very satisfied" to "very dissatisfied." He found the actual level of involvement of teachers in decision making to be significantly and positively related to the overall and partial job satisfaction of teachers. Moreover, teachers' satisfaction with the decision-making process itself also was significantly and positively related to job satisfaction.

Similar results were found by Nerlinger (1975) in an empirical analysis of participative decision making in elementary schools. In addition to using Wright's Decision Involvement Index, she obtained measures of the perceived effectiveness of their classroom instruction.

In a study of decision making in secondary schools, Speed (1979) discovered that teachers generally desired increased participation in decision making — particularly on schoolwide decisions. He also found that teachers' involvement in making decisions (whether deprived, at equilibrium, or saturated) related significantly and directly to their overall and partial job satisfaction.

Observational Studies of Decision Making. Using the comparative case study mode, researchers have observed the decision-making process in both elementary and secondary schools.

In analyzing decision making in elementary schools, Holmquist (1976) conducted an intensive on-site observational study to ascertain qualitative descriptions of the decision-making process by examining primary documents, observing meetings, and interviewing all the staff members in three selected schools. Regarding the content of decisions, he found considerable sharing of decisions regarding curriculum and instruction and student personnel, but some reluctance of central office administrators and school principals to share decisions whose content concerned staff personnel, finance and business management, school plant, and even home, school, and community relations. Regarding the stages of decision making, Holmquist discovered that great attention was given to the initial stages of problem articulation, posing and weighing of alternatives, and making the decision, but little attention was given to the subsequent stages of implementation and evaluation of decisions. He also discovered excessive reliance on total group participation for making many decisions. Such personal variables as expertise, experience in the school, and informal influence plus such organizational variables as legal requirements, formal position, and access to information frequently rendered the actual decision-making process in the schools to be more social or political than rational.

Other observational studies of decision making in elementary schools were recently completed by Kawleski (1977) and Moyle (1977). In schools implementing programs of individualized schooling, they found that teachers were dynamically involved — making and implementing many decisions regarding instructional programming, curricular materials, and evaluation of students. Even though the scope of such decisions occasionally was constrained by the central office staff or the principal, teachers generally were able to share information, expertise, and input to making, implementing, and evaluating decisions on instructional programming. Concerning the stages of making decisions, however, they found, as did Holmquist (1976), a tendency to overuse the total group participation mode. The process, moreover, often was unduly influenced by such variables as position, organization, and personality. Regarding decision involvement, the researchers concluded that teachers generally were satisfied with both the frequency and the level of their involvement. As Wright (1976) had ascertained earlier, however, teachers desired an increase in the scope of their involvement, particularly at school and district levels, since some of the decisions they viewed as their prerogatives were still constrained by district and school policies and procedures.

In an observational study of the decision-making process in secondary schools, Watkins (1978) examined the philosophies, structures, processes, and groups engaged in decision making; the involvement of personnel in the decision-making process; and the satisfaction of school personnel with the structures and processes and their involvement in decision making in six comprehensive high schools. He found a clearly articulated, understood, and internalized philosophy of education to be essential as a basis for policy, managerial, and instructional decision making. Moreover, an articulated policy for making decisions was essential to the successful implementation of an innovative instructional program. In the schools examined, many of the major educational decisions were shared. The staff considered their level of participation in making decisions to be generally satisfactory. Even so, the principal still performed a major role in determining the decision-making policy and in implementing the decision-making structures and processes — authority-guided participation.

In regard to the schoolwide organization for decision making, those structures that were highly satisfying to the staff facilitated intradepartmental and interdepartmental exchange of information, ideas, and opinions; accelerated decision making at the teaching-learning level; and afforded access to administrators. Regarding districtwide decision-making structures, secondary school staffs felt frustrated in their efforts to provide input to and have an influence on districtwide decisions, which increasingly concerned curricular, staff, and student personnel and financial operations of the local school. In sum, appropriate decision-making structures had not yet been developed to articulate school concerns with district concerns. Although centralization of decision making in the several schools ranged from high to low, staff satisfaction remained high because the level of staff participation in the decision-making process was appropriate.

Conclusions Regarding Decision Making

Based on the foregoing research, the following conclusions can be drawn regarding the decision-making process in the schools.

1. The philosophy and organization of the school affect decision making (Wright 1976, Feldman 1977, Moyle 1977). Hence, schools should be structured to provide opportunities for those affected by a decision to participate in making it.
2. There is an increased desire on the part of teachers and other staff members to become involved in the decision-making process on matters of schoolwide and districtwide scope, as well as on matters concerning classroom (Moyle 1977, Kawleski 1977).
3. Appropriate involvement of staff in making decisions is significantly and positively related to the outcomes of staff satisfaction (Feldman 1977, Speed 1979) and teaching effectiveness (Nerlinger 1975).
4. In schools, there is excessive reliance on the total group decision-making mode (Holmquist 1976, Kawleski 1977, Moyle 1977). Administrators and supervisors should increase their theoretical understandings and leadership skills regarding the decision-making process.

EDUCATIONAL LEADERSHIP

The leadership of administrators and supervisors is an important factor in the successful implementation or improvement of any program in the school. Such aspects as leadership frequency, potency, scope, style, and quality are particularly crucial to achieving successful school outcomes. In this section, a brief overview is given of leadership theory as a background for reporting recent research conducted on educational leadership.

Leadership Theory

In analyzing leadership, one must give attention to the definition, locus, frequency, potency, scope, and style of leadership. There are many ways to define leadership. In education, I have defined leadership as "that behavior of an individual which initiates changes in goals, objectives, configurations, procedures, inputs, processes, and ultimately the output of a social system" (Lipham 1973, p. 6).

The locus for leadership involves the issue of the focal social system in which leadership occurs. It considers, for example, whether the leadership being analyzed occurs in the classroom, school, school district, or entire community. The frequency of leadership, or how often a leader engages in certain behaviors, is also important. On the one hand, leaders may attempt too many acts of leadership too often without actually accomplishing anything; on the other hand, some people rarely attempt any active leadership. There is no consensus as to what constitutes the optimal balance.

Linked to the concept of frequency of leadership is the variable of potency, which refers to "the extent to which an initiated change by a leader represents a significant departure from that which exists, that is, the magnitude of an initiated change" (Lipham and Hoeh 1974, p. 186). Scope of leadership refers to whether leadership is viewed as functionally diffuse (the individuals in a relationship are bound to one another in such a way that their mutual responsibilities and obligations are unlimited) or functionally specific (obligations and also the breadth and depth of the leadership role are limited and the functions ascribed to a person in the role of leader are circumscribed).

Leadership style has been conceptualized in many ways. In an early study, Lewin, Lippitt, and White (1939) described leadership as being autocratic, democratic, or laissez faire. Halpin and Winer (1957) viewed leaders' behavior as composed of two basic dimensions, initiating structure and consideration, which are defined as follows (1957, p. 4):

1. Initiating structure: behavior which delineates the relationship between the leader and members of the work group and endeavors to establish well-defined patterns of organization, channels of communication, and methods of procedure.
2. Consideration: behavior which indicates friendship, mutual trust, respect, and warmth in the relationship between the leader and the staff.

House (1971) used three terms for describing leaders' behavior: instrumental, participative, and supportive behavior. They are defined as follows:

1. Instrumental leadership: behavior which delineates the relationship between the leader and members of the work group and attempts to clearly define patterns of the organization without autocratic or punitive control.
2. Supportive leadership: behavior which indicates friendship and warmth toward the work group from the leader.
3. Participative leadership: behavior which allows subordinates to influence decisions by asking for suggestions and including subordinates in the decision-making process.

Another approach to describing leadership was developed by Bowers and Seashore (1966), who viewed leadership behavior as consisting of goal emphasis, work facilitation, support, and interaction facilitation. These four dimensions are defined as follows:

1. Work facilitation: behavior which helps goal attainment by scheduling, planning, and coordinating.

2. Support: behavior which enhances someone else's feelings of personal worth and importance.

3. Interaction facilitation: behavior which encourages members of the group to develop close, mutually satisfying relationships.

4. Goal emphasis: behavior which stimulates enthusiasm for meeting the group's goals or achieving excellent performance.

These descriptive classifications are those most recently used by researchers to examine and explain leadership behavior exhibited by administrators and supervisors and how their behavior affects the school.

Research on Educational Leadership

Most of the recent research on educational leadership employs an empirical approach wherein various measures of leadership states are administered and the results correlated with a wide variety of schooling process or outcome variables (Bandy 1977, Baily 1978, Frick 1979, Lubinsky 1976). These studies typically focus on the leadership behavior of the school principal, although some note the leadership behavior of school superintendents (Frick 1979). Only a sampling of the leadership studies are here summarized as they relate to the school outcomes of educational change and staff job satisfaction and morale.

Leadership and Change. Several studies have shown that the leadership behavior of administrators is significantly related to organizational change, innovation, and adaptiveness. Carlson (1962), for example, found higher levels of innovation in school districts led by school superintendents who were informed, upwardly mobile, and cosmopolitan.

At the individual school level, Goodridge (1975) sought to answer the question, "Who are the individuals in the school who make the initial decision to adopt an innovation?" In examining elementary schools that had recently adopted a major educational innovation, he found that principals were the major decision makers in the decision to adopt. In the majority of schools, moreover, this decision was shared with teachers in the school. Superintendents, central office personnel and parents typically were minimally involved in the decision to make a major change. School boards often let others make decisions about the adoption of educational programs if no additional costs were involved.

At the secondary school level, a recent study of the changes was completed by Neiner (1978), who looked at six comprehensive senior high schools that had switched to individualized schooling. Data were collected through nonparticipant observations, documentary analysis, and in-depth analysis of semistructured, open-ended interviews. A major finding of the study was that the nature and quality of the leadership behavior provided by administrators appropriate to the various phases of the implementation was essential as was continuity in leadership by administrators. Those schools experiencing greatest difficulty had a high rate of

turnover in administrative posts. In addition, the following components were necessary to implement change: a shared decision-
making structure, the creation of a personable environment,
adequate in-service training of staff, and a program of continuing
curricular development.

Leadership and Staff Satisfaction. A signal empirical study of the
relationship between the leadership behavior of school principals
and teacher job satisfaction was conducted by Mendenhall (1977).
She used Bowers and Seashore's four dimensions — work facilitation, support, goal emphasis, and interaction facilitation — in
having teachers describe the predominant leadership styles of their
principals. Teachers also indicated their overall job satisfaction and
their satisfaction with various facets of their jobs. She found that
when the principal exhibited leadership behavior high in work
facilitation support, interaction facilitation, and goal emphasis,
then staff job satisfaction was high. She concluded that the leadership behavior of the principal was important in promoting the
outcome of increased job satisfaction in the schools.

Moyle (1977) also examined principals' leadership behavior in
relation to the effectiveness of decision making in the schools. He
used interview and observation techniques to characterize and
describe their leadership by following the instrumental, participative, and supportive leadership dimensions of House (1971). Decision-making processes were described according to their perceived
effectiveness and the extent to which members felt satisfied with
how and what decisions were made. He found that instrumental
leadership was exercised with caution by principals, but other staff
members viewed such behavior by principals as a positive attribute
of leadership. Supportive leadership was also critical to teachers'
job satisfaction and effective decision making in the school. Even
so, additional responsibilities frequently kept principals from providing support to the extent desired by themselves and others.
Principals also exhibited participative leadership by accepting information, input, and advice of staff members. From these findings Moyle concluded that the leadership behavior of the principal
was a critical factor in the effective functioning of the school.

Another empirical study (Smith 1972) investigated the relationship between the principal's initiating structure and considera-

tion behavior and the satisfaction of the staff with the planning and decision-making structure within the school. Smith found that while initiations by the principal were important, planning and decision making were more effective if the principal considered the comfort, well-being, status, and contributions of the staff.

Gramenz (1974) examined the relationship between the leadership behavior of the principal and teachers' perceived effectiveness of the instructional program. Using the leadership dimensions developed by House, he found that when principals exhibited instrumental, supportive, and participative leadership, then the instructional program of the school was evaluated as effective. He concluded, therefore, that principals should indicate instrumental leadership by clarifying expectations, specifying procedures to be followed, and assigning specific tasks. They should also provide support by being friendly and approachable, looking out for the personal welfare of staff members, and helping make work pleasant and should encourage participation by consulting with staff members before taking action, allowing them to influence decisions, and asking them for suggestions.

Conclusions Regarding Educational Leadership

From the foregoing, and other studies, the following conclusions can be drawn regarding the leadership behavior of administrators and supervisors:

1. The leadership behavior of administrators is a powerful factor that influences the adoption and institutionalization of an educational change (Carlson 1962, Goodridge 1975). Different styles of leadership may be necessary at different stages of changes (Neiner 1978).

2. The nature and quality of leadership provided by administrators and supervisors is directly and positively related to the following outcomes of the school: perceived effectiveness of the decision-making process (Moyle 1977, Kawleski 1977, Smith 1972, Watkins 1978), perceived effectiveness of instruction (Gramenz 1974), and staff satisfaction and morale (Mendenhall 1977).

IMPLICATIONS OF THE RESEARCH

Based on the previously delineated conclusions, several implications can be drawn for improving the administration and supervision of the schools, immediately and in the years ahead. The implications relate both to research and practice.

Implications for Research

Future research on educational administration may be improved by paying attention to a number of substantive and methodological issues, including paradigms, approaches, instruments, analyses, and resources utilized.

Regarding research paradigms in administration, Halpin, as early as 1957, observed that the attempt to relate such outcomes of the school as student achievement directly to specific administrative behaviors is practically impossible. He said, in effect, that you can't get there from here. That is, the host of intervening societal, financial, legal, community, home, institutional, organizational and individual variables and the interrelationships among them must be taken into account. Thus, in an era of academic specialization, if any grand study attempted to analyze everything, it would probably produce nothing. Even the general systems model presented in Figure 2-1, although limited, does show the complexity of the input, process, and output variables of the school as a general system. Returning to our opening theme, therefore, one should view with healthy skepticism those simplistic studies that measure or correlate — not to mention ascribe — student outputs to administrative inputs.

During the past two decades, the bulk of the research on administration has been based on administrative and behavioral science theories and has used the empirical survey approach. Again, Halpin (1960) reminded us that there are alternative "ways of knowing," and this theme has recently been reiterated by Greenfield (1978). The recent phenomenological, ethnographic approaches, utilizing the case study methods of observation, interview, records analysis, and other reality-derived data, are encouraging and perhaps fruitful, as can be surmised from reading the findings from such studies reported in this chapter.

Implications for Practice

The implications for improved practice on the part of school administrators and supervisors, based on the research reported here, are multitudinous. They relate to the requisite knowledge, skills, and attitudes likely to be required of administrative personnel, both now and in the future.

In regard to administrative knowledge, it is obvious from the research that administrators and supervisors must possess a thorough understanding of both administrative functions and theories. Programs for the preparation of administrators and supervisors must continue to include the study of curriculum and instruction, staff and student personnel, finance and business management, and home, school, and community relations, since these are basic to the effective functioning of the school. Most administrators and supervisors are probably not as knowledgeable as they should be about organizational, decision-making, leadership, and other theoretical concepts — not to mention theories of politics, economics, psychology, and other fields of social science. In the setting of standards for the preparation of future administrators, emphasis should be placed on increased requirements in these social science domains (Lipham 1975).

Opportunities must be provided whereby prospective school leaders can experience, practice, and learn those behaviors conducive to personal growth and the development of other members of the school organization. In addition to current case study, simulation, and other approaches utilized to prepare administrators, apprenticeship, internship, and other ways of preparing educational administrators are needed. Just as student teaching is the best way for preparing future teachers, so also is the administrative internship a valuable way, within our present resources, for preparing educational leaders of quality.

REFERENCES

Alutto, Joseph A., and Belasco, James A. "A Typology for Participation in Organizational Decision Making." *Administrative Science Quarterly* 17 (March 1972): 117–25.

Baily, Martha F. G. "A Study of the Relationship between Teachers' Self-Concept and Teachers' Evaluation of Their School Principals' Leadership Behavior." Doctoral dissertation, Auburn University, 1978.

Bandy, Lynn S. "Relationships of Perceived Administrative Styles of Selected Elementary School Principals to Predetermined Situational Variables." Doctoral dissertation, American University, 1977.

Barnard, Chester I. *The Functions of the Executive.* Cambridge, Mass.: Harvard University Press, 1938.

Barnard, Chester I. "Functions and Pathology of Status Systems in Formal Organizations." In *Industry and Society,* edited by William F. Whyte. New York: McGraw-Hill, 1946.

Becker, G. "Issues and Problems in Elementary School Administration." Doctoral dissertation, Oregon State University, 1970.

Berends, Eugene H. "Perceptions of the Principal's Personality: A Study of Relationship to Organizational Climate." Doctoral dissertation, Michigan State University, 1969.

Bert, G. "A Study of Administrative Competencies for Beginning School Principals in Northern Illinois." Doctoral dissertation, Northern Illinois University, 1976.

Bowers, David G., and Seashore, Stanley E. "Predicting Organizational Effectiveness with a Four-Factor Theory of Leadership." *Administrative Science Quarterly* 11 (September 1966): 238–63.

Bridges, Edwin M. "A Model for Shared Decision Making in the School Principalship." *Educational Administration Quarterly* 3 (Winter 1967): 49–61.

Brieve, Fred J. "Secondary Principals as Instructional Leaders." *NASSP Bulletin* 56 (December 1972): 11–15.

Bross, Irwin D. J. *Design for Decision.* New York: Macmillan, 1953.

Campbell, Merle V. "Teacher-Principal Agreement on the Teacher Role." *Administrators' Notebook* 7 (February 1959): 1–4.

Carlson, Richard O. *Executive Succession and Organizational Change.* Chicago: University of Chicago Press, 1962.

Christiansen, Winfield S. "The Influence of the Behavior of the Elementary School Principal upon the School He Administers." Doctoral dissertation, Stanford University, 1953.

Coleman, James S., and others. *Equality of Educational Opportunity.* Washington, D.C.: U.S. Government Printing Office, 1966.

Cyert, Richard M., and March, James G. *A Behavioral Theory of the Firm.* Englewood Cliffs, N.J.: Prentice-Hall, 1963.

Dill, William R. "Decision Making." In *Behavioral Science and Educational Administration.* Sixty-third Yearbook of the National Society for the Study of Education, Part 2, pp. 199–222, edited by Daniel E. Griffiths. Chicago: University of Chicago Press, 1964.

Espalin, Charles A. "Skills Characteristic of Successful Inner-City School Administrators." Doctoral dissertation, University of Southern California, 1976.

Eye, Glen G.; Lipham, James M.; and Netzer, L. A. *Decision Point Analysis Instrument.* Madison: Department of Educational Administration, University of Wisconsin, 1965.

Feldman, R. H . *Involvement in and Satisfaction with Decision Making Related to Staff and Student Behavior in IGE Schools*. Technical Report no. 408. Madison: Wisconsin Research and Development Center for Cognitive Learning, 1977.

Frick, Robert A. "Installation of an Educational Innovation: The Relationship to Selected Characteristics of School Districts." Doctoral dissertation, Temple University, 1979.

Getzels, Jacob W., and Guba, Egon G. "Social Behavior and the Administrative Process." *School Review* 65 (Winter 1957): 423–41.

Getzels, Jacob W.; Lipham, James M.; and Campbell, Roald F. *Educational Administration as a Social Process*. New York: Harper & Row, 1968.

Goodlad, John I. "Principals Are the Key to Change." *AIGE Forum* 2 (Spring 1977): 74–78.

Goodridge, C. G. *Factors That Influence the Decision to Adopt an Educational Innovation: IGE*. Technical Report no. 376. Madison: Wisconsin Research and Development Center for Cognitive Learning, 1975.

Gramenz, G. W. *Relationship of Principal Leader Behavior and Organization Structure to the IGE/MUS-E to I and R Unit Effectiveness*. Technical Report no. 320. Madison: Wisconsin Research and Development Center for Cognitive Learning, 1974.

Greenfield, Thomas B. "Reflections on Organization Theory and the Truths of Irreconcilable Realities." *Educational Administration Quarterly* 14 (Spring 1978): 1-23.

Gregg, Russell T. "The Administrative Process." In *Administrative Behavior in Education*, edited by Roald F. Campbell and Russell T. Gregg, pp. 269–317. New York: Harper & Row, 1957.

Griffiths, Daniel E. *Administrative Theory*. New York: Appleton, 1959.

Gross, Neal, and Herriott, Robert E. *Staff Leadership in Public Schools*. New York: Wiley, 1965.

Gross, Neal; Mason, Ward S.; and McEachern, Alexander W. *Explorations in Role Analysis*. New York: Wiley, 1958.

Hage, Jerald. "An Axiomatic Theory of Organizations." *Administrative Science Quarterly* 10 (December 1965): 289–320.

Halpin, Andrew W. "A Paradigm for Research on Administrative Behavior." In *Administrative Behavior in Education*, edited by Roald F. Campbell and Russell T. Gregg. New York: Harper & Row, 1957.

Halpin, Andrew W. "Ways of Knowing." In *Administrative Theory as a Guide to Action*, edited by Roald F. Campbell and James M. Lipham. Chicago: Midwest Administration Center, University of Chicago, 1960.

Halpin, Andrew W., and Croft, Don B. *The Organizational Climate of Schools*. Chicago: Midwest Administration Center, University of Chicago, 1963.

Halpin, Andrew W., and Winer, B. James. "A Factorial Study of the Leadership Behavior Description Questionnaire." In *Leader Behavior: Its Description and Measurement*, edited by Ruth M. Stogdill and Alvin E. Coons. Research Monograph no. 88. Columbus: Bureau of Business Research, Ohio State University, 1957.

Hansen, J. Merrell. "Administration: Role and Function in Education." *NASSP Bulletin* 58 (December 1974): 82–89.

Herrick, H. S. *The Relationship of Organizational Structure to Teacher Motivation in Multiunit and Non-Multiunit Elementary Schools.* Technical Report no. 322. Madison: Wisconsin Research and Development Center for Cognitive Learning, 1974.

Holmquist, A. M. *A Definitional Field Study of Decision Making in IGE/MUS-E Schools.* Technical Report no. 377. Madison: Wisconsin Research and Development Center for Cognitive Learning, 1976.

House, Robert J. "A Path-goal Theory of Leader Effectiveness." *Administrative Science Quarterly* 16 (September 1971): 321–88.

Immegart, Glenn L. "The Systems Movement and Educational Administration." In *Systems Approach to the Management of Public Education,* edited by G. G. Mansergh, pp. 2–4. Detroit: Metropolitan Bureau of School Studies, 1969.

Kawleski, S. J. *Decision Making of the Instruction and Research Unit in IGE Schools: Functions, Processes, and Relationships.* Technical Report no. 420. Madison: Wisconsin Research and Development Center for Cognitive Learning, 1977.

Kluckhohn, Clyde, and others. "Values and Value-Orientations in Theory of Action." In *Toward a General Theory of Action,* edited by Talcott Parsons and Edward A. Shils. Cambridge, Mass.: Harvard University Press, 1951.

Knezevich, Stephen J. *The American School Superintendent.* Washington, D.C.: American Association of School Administrators, 1971.

Lewin, Kurt; Lippitt, Ronald; and White, Ralph K. "Patterns of Aggressive Behavior in Experimentally Created 'Social Climates'." *Journal of Social Psychology* 10 (May 1939): 271–99.

Lipham, James M. "Competency/Performance-Based Administrator Education (C/PBAE): Recent Development in the United States." In *Administering Education: International Challenge,* edited by Meredydd G. Hughes. London: Athlone Press, University of London, 1975.

Lipham, James M. "Improving the Decision-Making Skills of the Principal." In *Performance Objectives for School Principals,* edited by Jack A. Culbertson, Curtis Henson, and Ruel Morrison. Berkeley, Calif.: McCutchan, 1974.

Lipham, James M. "Leadership: General Theory and Research." In *Leadership: The Science and the Art Today,* edited by Luvern L. Cunningham and W. J. Gephart. Itasca, Ill.: Peacock, 1973

Lipham, James M., and Daresh, J. C. eds. *Administrative and Staff Relationships in Education: Research and Practice in IGE Schools.* Madison: Wisconsin Research and Development Center for Individualized Schooling, 1979.

Lipham, James M., and Hoeh, James A., Jr. *The Principalship: Foundations and Functions.* New York: Harper & Row, 1974.

Lubinsky, Roberta. "Machiavellianism, Values, Administrative Effectiveness, and Self-Reported vs. Colleague-Reported Perceptions of Public School Principals." Doctoral dissertation, Bowling Green State University, 1976.

March, James G. "American Public School Administration: A Short Analysis." Unpublished paper, Stanford University, 1978.

Mendenhall, D. R. *Relationship of Organizational Structure and Leadership Behavior to Teacher Satisfaction in IGE Schools.* Technical Report no. 412. Madison: Wisconsin Research and Development Center for Cognitive Learning, 1977.

Moyle, C. R. J. *Decision Making of the Instructional Improvement Committee in IGE Schools: Functions, Processes, and Relationships.* Technical Report no. 416. Madison: Wisconsin Research and Development Center for Cognitive Learning, 1977.

Muse, Ivan D. "The Public School Principalship: Role Expectations by Alter Groups." Doctoral dissertation, University of Utah, 1966.

National Association of Elementary School Principals. *The Assistant Principalship in Public Elementary Schools, 1969: A Research Study.* Washington, D.C.: National Association of Elementary School Principals, 1970.

Neiner, G. A. *Analysis of Planned Change within Comprehensive Senior High Schools That Individualize Instruction.* Technical Report no. 456. Madison: Wisconsin Research and Development Center for Individualized Schooling, 1978.

Nelson, R. G. *Learning Climate in IGE/MUS-E Schools.* Technical Report no. 213. Madison: Wisconsin Research and Development Center for Cognitive Learning, 1972.

Nerlinger, C. M. *Participative Decision Making in IGE/MUS-E Schools.* Technical Report no. 356. Madison: Wisconsin Research and Development Center for Cognitive Learning, 1975.

Pellegrin, Roland J. *Some Organizational Characteristics of Multiunit Schools.* Working Paper no. 22. Madison: Wisconsin Research and Development Center for Cognitive Learning, 1969.

Phi Delta Kappa, National Study Committee on Evaluation. *Educational Evaluation and Decision Making.* Itasca, Ill.: Peacock, 1971.

Pitts, John H. "A Study of Urban Administrators' Perceptions of Emphasis Placed on Selected Administrative Competencies." Doctoral dissertation, Indiana University, 1976.

Simon, Herbert A. *The New Science of Management Decision.* New York: Harper & Row, 1960.

Smith, K. B. *An Analysis of the Relationship between Effectiveness of the Multiunit Elementary School's Instructional Improvement Committee and Interpersonal and Leader Behavior.* Technical Report no. 230. Madison: Wisconsin Research and Development Center for Cognitive Learning, 1972.

Speed, N. E. *Decision Participation and Staff Satisfaction in Middle and Junior High Schools that Individualize Instruction.* Technical Report. Madison: Wisconsin Research and Development Center for Individualized Schooling, 1979.

Thompson, Victor A. *Modern Organization.* New York: Knopf, 1961.

Traugott, William M. "A Study of the Difference Between School Administrators' and Teachers' Perceptions of Administrators' Actual and Ideal Priorities of Reponsibility." Doctoral dissertation, Kansas State University, 1976.

Trump, J. Lloyd. "Principal Most Potent Factor in Determining School Excellence," *NASSP Bulletin* 56 (March 1972): 3–9.

Walters, J. E. *The Relationship of Organizational Structure to Organizational Adaptiveness in Elementary Schools.* Technical Report no. 276. Madison: Wisconsin Research and Development Center for Cognitive Learning, 1973.

Watkins, A. N. *Decision-Making Processes in Senior High Schools that Individualize Instruction.* Technical Report no. 460. Madison: Wisconsin Research and Development Center for Individualized Schooling, 1978.

Weber, Max. *Theory of Social and Economic Organization.* Translated by A. M. Henderson and Talcott Parsons, New York: Oxford University Press, 1947.

Wright, K. W. *Development of an Instrument to Measure Real and Ideal Decision Structure and Involvement in IGE Schools.* Technical Report no. 374. Madison: Wisconsin Research and Development Center for Cognitive Learning, 1976.

Discussion

Larry W. Hughes

The "science" of teaching, as well as the science of management, has received attention. If children were orderly learners with uniform backgrounds, one might predict a well-skilled and easily evaluated product from practices in teaching and management, impaired only by incomplete research and knowledge about the psychology of learning. Alas, humans are not orderly learners and learner backgrounds are diverse indeed. The problem may be in the art, not in the science, of teaching. How does the administrator organize the school so as to unleash the art of teaching? That is really the subject of Lipham's chapter.

An important contribution by Lipham is his admonition to conduct better research on the topic under discussion and to make better use of such research methodologies as ethnography, case study, phenomenology, and documentary analysis. One can only applaud this. We do not know much about how leader behavior affects learners, and thus we can not know as much as is necessary about the training, selection, and evaluation of administrators. It is about time we did.

Research indicates a relationship between administrator behavior and teacher satisfaction. Are teacher satisfaction and high morale sufficient to show a relationship between principal behavior and learner outcomes? We can not be certain, although Lipham tries hard to make the link. Are happy teachers necessarily more highly skilled teachers? It would seem that it ought to be so; they certainly would be more pleasant to be around. One might conclude that there would be at least some kind of salutary effect on learning by pupils.

ORGANIZATIONAL CLIMATE

Lipham writes extensively about the organizational climate of schools and about how teachers are organized to teach. If we know little else, we know about the impact of the executive on organizational climate and we know that one of the things under the executive's control is working arrangements such as time allocations and who is scheduled to work with whom and when.

The research of Halpin and Croft (1963) on the organizational climate of elementary schools lends a needed perspective. Their studies focused on aspects of principal and teacher behavior in describing the personality of a school and in determining the degree to which the school was "open" or "closed." They posited that an open school climate indicates an effective school and a closed climate indicates an ineffective school. An open climate is one in which there is attention to both task achievement by members and the social needs of members. The closed climate is defined as one in which group members obtain little satisfaction with respect to either task achievement or social needs. In short, it is a situation in which the leader is ineffective in directing the activities of the staff and is not inclined to look out for their welfare.

Halpin and Croft (1963) characterized the principal of an open (and thus effective) school as follows:

The behavior of the principal represents an appropriate integration between his own personality and the role he is required to play as principal. In this respect his behavior can be viewed as "genuine." Not only does he set an example by working hard himself (high *thrust*) but, depending on the situation, he can either criticize the actions of teachers or can, on the other hand, go out of his way to help a teacher (high *consideration*). He possesses the personal flexibility to be "genuine" whether he is required to control and direct the activities of others or be required to show compassion in satisfying the social needs of individual teachers. He has integrity in that he is "all of a piece" and, therefore, can function well in either situation. He is not *aloof*, nor are the rules and regulations which he sets up inflexible and impersonal. Nonetheless, rules and regulations are adhered to, and through them, he provides subtle direction and control for the teachers. He does not have to *emphasize production*; nor does he need to closely monitor the teachers' activities, because the teachers do indeed produce easily and freely. Nor does he do all the work himself; he has the ability to let appropriate leadership acts emerge from the teachers. Withal, he is in full control of the situation and he clearly provides leadership for the staff [pp. 61–62].

The productive environment clearly requires more than smiling faces. It requires opportunities for emerging situational leadership on the part of staff and organizational and personal certitude, as well as considerate actions, on the part of the executive.

Missing from Lipham's paper and appropos to this discussion is the work of Rensis Likert. Likert, a pioneer in the field of modern supervision and administration, headed the Institute for Social Research at the University of Michigan, where he and his associates conducted a myriad of studies in government, industry, and public services, including schools. The major findings of his research (Likert 1953) include the following:

1. Employee-centered supervisors tend to be higher producers than production-centered supervisors.
2. Close supervision tends to be associated with lower productivity and more general supervision with higher productivity.
3. Within a particular organization there is little relationship between an employee's overall attitude toward the organization and productivity. (There is, however, a relationship between the overall attitude toward the organization and the absentee rate: those with a favorable attitude are absent less often.)
4. High morale (defined as the total satisfaction a worker gets on the job) does *not* necessarily mean high productivity. However, the kind of supervision that results in high productivity also tends to result in high morale.

Such findings are consistent with Blake and Mouton (1964), McGregor (1960), and Herzberg (1966), among others. For specific applications of Likert's findings to school supervision, the reader is also directed to Sergiovanni and Starratt (1971, pp. 15–24) and Sergiovanni and Carver (1973, pp. 55–118).

I would call particular attention to the last point in the summary of Likert's findings, especially in light of Lipham's great reliance on "high morale" as a way to infer teacher-learner effectiveness. High morale does not mean high productivity, but may only describe a management style that Blake and Mouton characterize as showing great consideration of workers with little attention to organizational goal accomplishment, a style which they label the "country club." People probably go home at night tired from all that good morale, but with no discernible product. High morale thus could be seen as an outcome, rather than being a cause, of an already productive environment.

Research by Fiedler (1967, 1971) helps to clarify why the issue addressed by Lipham is such a difficult one. Fiedler's model clearly reveals the situational nature of effective leadership and helps to explain why some studies have shown that a directive, task-oriented leader may promote effective group performance while other studies have revealed that a nondirective, human-relations orientation is desirable for effective group performance (Fiedler 1967). From a large number of studies Fiedler has concluded that three dimensions are crucial factors in leader effectiveness:

1. *Leader-member relations* — the leader's feeling of being accepted by his or her subordinates.
2. *Task-structure* — the degree to which the subordinates' jobs are routine and precisely defined, as opposed to being relatively unstructured and loosely defined.
3. *Power position* — the power inherent in the leadership position, including the means available to the leader to grant or withhold rewards and support of the leader by those in upper management and official authority, among a number of other similar characteristics.

Fiedler's research indicates that effective leadership — leadership that relates to high productivity — varies according to the nature of these factors in a given work environment.

Generally, one can assume the teacher's job to be relatively unstructured. (See Hughes and Ubben [1978, pp. 12–14] for a model of organizational latitude.) Job descriptions are not highly prescriptive and wide latitude is permitted in individual decisions affecting classroom activities. Table 2-1, borrowing from Fiedler's research (1967, 1971), offers the following summary:

Table 2-1.

Group Work Environment

Leader-Member Relations	Task Structure*	Power Position	Leadership Style Correlating with Productivity
Good	Unstructured	Strong	Directive
Good	Unstructured	Weak	Permissive
Moderately Poor	Unstructured	Strong	Permissive
Moderately Poor	Unstructured	Weak	Directive

*Note: Situations which can be depicted as a "structured" task result in a different array of productive leadership styles *(Fiedler 1971)*.

The relationship between leader behavior and productivity is complex. If a leader can be effective in some situations and not in others, even though performing in exactly the same way that led to a former success, it becomes more difficult to examine the relationship between leadership and school productivity. Fiedler's model provides a means to better research on the subject, however, because certain characteristics or combinations of characteristics may well predict performance in certain situations. This is, of course, what the situational model suggests.

ADMINISTRATORS AND SUPERVISORS AS EDUCATIONAL ENGINEERS

Administrators and supervisors do set a tone and a standard for a school. Reporting a study of more than 300 elementary school principals representing every state, Goldhammer and others (1971) concluded: "In schools that were extremely good, we inevitably found an aggressive, professionally alert, dynamic principal determined to provide the kind of educational program he deemed necessary, *no matter what*" (p. 11). The Goldhammer study included wide-ranging interviews with principals and on-site reviews of the spectrum of conditions in elementary schools. They found that the poor schools invariably suffered from weak leadership. The buildings were in disrepair, teacher and student morale was low, and fear was the main motivator. "The schools were characterized by unenthusiasm, squalor. The principals were just serving out their time" (Goldhammer and others 1971, p. 2).

Such conclusions about administrator influence are not limited to the Goldhammer study. In a 1970 report about innovation in American schools, Stanley Peterfreund Associates (1970) detailed many of the same findings; over 1,200 schools were involved in the study. The kind of leadership demonstrated by building principals was among a number of conditions that correlated with innovativeness. They concluded that "the school system must have principals who are in tune with the district's objectives and who are skilled at involving and motivating their teachers" (1970, p. 9). In further describing this conclusion, the authors stated: "Innovative principals identify their role in terms of educational leadership, of creating an environment for learning. They are less concerned with traditional administrative routine. Leadership implies good communication with the staff, the students and the community, and these principals have a communication system which allows information and ideas to flow up and down the line" (p. 10).

Two other studies deserve mention. In an investigation of inner-city elementary schools, Doll (1967) identified two major factors responsible for a successful learning environment: the method of grouping students and the principal. He concluded that the principal is the single most important influence on the learning environment. His analysis shows that the successful principal is flexible and personnel oriented and prone to act independently of bureaucratic directives. Such a principal sees his or her primary task as helping teachers teach.

Marcus (1976) reported that students' achievement was likely to be improved in schools where leadership in instruction was most effective. This conclusion included the importance of the principal in helping to select basic instructional materials and making decisions about instructional practices. Marcus also reported that teachers' perceptions of the principal's leadership style were significantly related to student achievement.

CONCLUDING COMMENTS

We do not know as much as we need to about how administrators and supervisors directly affect learners. Studying administrators' and supervisors' effects on learners is complex and is made more so by such environmental variables as desegregation, diverse student populations, location of the school (urban, rural, suburban), ex-

pectations of the community, resource allocation, teacher turnover, teacher expectations, and transience of student population,
among others. More ethnographic and phenomenological research is needed.

We do know how principals can affect teacher behavior, and we
know how leaders can affect production in a work group. If the
"product" of teachers is a learning, growing, healthy child, then
Fiedler's research may be useful in conducting inquiries in what it
takes to be an effective administrator or supervisor. We know
school environments differ not only because administrators differ
but because of a host of intervening variables from inside and
outside the school organization.

Given these intervening variables and the differing intensity of
their force in any given school community, it is not surprising that
it is difficult to determine how supervisors and administrators
should behave to be most influential in students' growth.

Characteristics of our complex society are communities that are more generally
reflective of cultural pluralism. The fact is that many people . . . will not derive
their normative behavior from a white, middle-class heritage — and by extension,
of course, neither will the student body nor the teaching staff. Responses to
traditional control and decision systems in the school and community may vary
from hostile acquiescence to open challenge. Teachers and administrators must
learn to cope with this great diversity, for as the salesmen in Meredith Willson's
The Music Man tell us, [to be successful] "You gotta know the territory" [Hughes
1976, p. 19].

The territory to be known is complex indeed. Adjusting administrative and supervisory behavior and adjusting organizational structure and decision-making processes to be compatible
with the needs of the territory requires a leader who is a well-
trained, intelligent, and humane individual with a repertoire of the
necessary human, conceptual, and technical skills to lead teachers
and children into rich educational adventures.

REFERENCES

Blake, Robert R., and Mouton, Jane S. *The Managerial Grid.* Houston: Gulf
    Publishing, 1964.

Doll, Russell C. "Variations among Inner-City Elementary Schools: An Investigation of the Nature and Causes of the Differences." Kansas City: Research Center for the Study of Metropolitan Problems in Education, University of Missouri, 1967.

Fiedler, Fred E. *A Theory of Leadership Effectiveness.* New York: McGraw-Hill, 1967.

Fiedler, Fred E. *Leadership.* New York: General Learning Press, University Program Module Series, 1971.

Goldhammer, Keith, and others. *Elementary School Principals and Their Schools: Beacons of Brilliance and Potholes of Pestilence.* Eugene: Center for the Advanced Study of Educational Administration, University of Oregon, 1971.

Halpin, Andrew W., and Croft, Don B. *The Organizational Climate of Schools.* Chicago: Midwest Administration Center, University of Chicago, 1963.

Herzberg, Frederick. *Work and the Nature of Man.* New York: World, 1966.

Hughes, Larry W. *Informal and Formal Community Forces: External Influences on Schools and Teachers.* Morristown, N.J.: General Learning Press, 1976.

Hughes, Larry W., and Ubben, Gerald C. *The Elementary Principal's Handbook: Guide to Effective Action.* Boston: Allyn & Bacon, 1978.

Hughes, Larry W., and Ubben, Gerald C. *The Secondary School Principal's Handbook: Guide to Executive Action.* Boston: Allyn & Bacon, 1980.

Likert, Rensis. *Motivation: The Core of Management.* Personnel Series No. 155, New York: America Management Association, 1953.

McGregor, Douglas. *The Human Side of the Enterprise.* New York: McGraw-Hill, 1960.

Marcus, Alfred C. "Administrative Leadership in a Sample of Successful Schools from the National Evaluation of the Emergency School Aid Act, 1974-1975." Paper presented at the annual meeting of the American Educational Research Association, San Francisco, April 23, 1976.

Sergiovanni, Thomas, and Carver, Fred D. *The New School Executive: A Theory of Administration.* New York: Dodd, Mead, 1973.

Sergiovanni, Thomas, and Starratt, Robert J. *Emerging Patterns of Supervision: Human Perspectives.* New York: McGraw-Hill, 1971.

Stanley Peterfreund Associates. *Innovation and Change in Public School Systems.* Englewood Cliffs, N.J.: Stanley Peterfreund Associates, 1970.

3

Teachers

MARILYNN M. KASH
AND GARY D. BORICH

The research on teacher effectiveness to be considered here represents the state of the art at the present. Conceptually, this research is based on a model that consists of observing and recording identified teacher and pupil behaviors in a classroom. The achievement levels of the students are assessed before and after the observations; the correlations are reported. These are the bare bones of the process-product model of teacher effectiveness research.

Methodologically, we will deal with few experimental studies. Our data base includes ethnographic or ecological analyses of the classroom, program evaluation techniques, and correlational research. All of these methodologies result in correlational data. A reading of previous reviews suggests that we can now draw conclusions based on an emerging consensus of replicated results from a variety of relatively comprehensive sources. We will report findings, which can then be described as representative of those sources.

Rather than burden the body of this discussion with extensive references, we present a table at the end of the chapter relating specific findings (identified by number) to those references from which they were drawn (identified by authors). In constructing this table we often had to forego the creativity of variable-namers and to condense similar variables into one category.

Discussions following the summaries of findings are based primarily upon those major studies that represent the sum of identified teacher behaviors that we considered valuable. Other studies offering insights pertinent to the discussions are also in Table 3-1, but not all findings of those studies may appear. Theories and interpretations will be cited in the body of the text and appear in the References.

TIME IS IMPORTANT

Summary of findings:

1. *Time spent actively engaged in learning is positively correlated with pupil achievement.*
2. *Amount of allocated time for academic subjects is positively correlated with pupil achievement.*
3. *Length of school day or year is positively correlated with pupil achievement if it is a factor in allocating time per subject.*

The most intensely researched questions in terms of breadth and scope, with the most substantiated results in terms of confirmation and mutuality across circumstances, address the relationship of time to academic achievement. The three basic questions are:

1. What is the relationship between the length of the school day and the level of academic achievement?
2. What is the relationship between time allocated to specific subject content and achievement levels in that subject?
3. What is the relationship between pupil-engaged time within the time allocated to a subject and achievement levels in that subject?

We have selected three research studies that address at least two of these questions in different geographical circumstances. The first study is one undertaken by the International Association for the

Evaluation of Educational Achievement, which has been operating for over a decade. This study included twenty-one countries, seventeen of which are classified as "developed" and the remaining four as "developing" countries. It evaluated the achievement of student populations ranging from age ten to the final year of secondary education, in six subjects (Farrell 1977). The results of this study, specific to the research questions, are: (a) while there was considerable variance in the length of school days and the number of days per year across countries, these variables did not predict academic achievement; however, (b) the amount of time allocated to a specific subject did predict levels of academic achievement. The more time pupils spent on a subject, the more they achieved.

All of these factors — length of school day, allocated time, study time, and measurable differences in program characteristics between schools — come together in the next study.

The Follow Through Classroom Observation Evaluation (Stallings and Kaskowitz 1974) was designed to investigate the differential effects of in-school programs that were based on different theories of development and education. These programs, extensions of preschool programs, were designed to consolidate and maintain the academic gains made by pupils enrolled in Head Start and similar projects. Seven programs, representing among them the theories of Dewey, Piaget, the English Infant School, and reinforcement, were selected for evaluation, along with non-Follow Through comparison populations. The thirty-five selected project sites covered all geographic areas of the United States, rural and urban locations, and several racial and ethnic minorities at first- and third-grade levels. The study focused on reading and mathematics instruction and achievement.

The length of the school day and the average time spent by the pupil engaged in reading or mathematics were related at both first- and third-grade levels to higher reading and mathematics scores. Since the length of the school day varied by as much as two hours among the schools in this study, the amount of time allocated to specific subjects varied.

The ability level of each of the pupils in this study was assessed at entry into kindergarten or first grade by the Wide-Range Achievement Test (WRAT). Stallings and Kaskowitz (1974) concluded that classroom instruction predicted as much or more of the outcome score variances than did test scores of children entering school. Based upon these findings, they concluded that what occurs within a classroom does contribute to achievement in basic skills, good attendance, and desired child behaviors.

The Beginning Teacher Evaluation Study, Phase II (Fisher and others 1978) identified the following correlates of gains in achievement in reading and arithmetic: (1) The amount of time that teachers allocate to instruction in a particular subject is positively associated with pupil learning in that subject, and (2) the proportion of time that students are engaged in studying is positively associated with student learning.

Data on allocated time and pupil-engaged time were collected over a one-year period in twenty-five second-grade and twenty-one fifth-grade classes. Once again the wide variation in the amount of time allocated to subject content at both grade levels and the positive relationship between time allocated to subject content and pupil achievement were confirmed. The amount of allocated time limits the time spent with a particular subject and thus limits the time a pupil is actively engaged in learning. In the fifth-grade reading sample of this study the range of average allotted time varied from approximately 60 to 140 minutes per day.

In examining the relationship of allocated time to engaged time, an equally large variance in the proportion of engaged time appeared from class to class and pupil to pupil. Some classes had an average engagement rate of 50 percent while others reached an average approaching 90 percent.

The length of the school day does not predict pupil achievement in specific content areas because it does not reflect the time allocated to a specific subject. However, it does restrict the amount of time that can be allocated to subject content within a school day. The amount of allocated time per subject reflects the priorities of those who make the allocations. The amount of time students spend on assignments reflects both the effectiveness of the teaching occurring in the classroom and the pupils' values, or motivations, as well as their aptitudes and abilities.

Time is an ever-constant factor in systematized learning. It is used to classify pupils as fast, average, or slow learners as defined by a ratio of learning content over time. On the average, nine months allocated to specific curriculum content constitutes a grade level.

Pupils who, because of their rate of learning, do not cover the assigned curriculum objectives in the allocated time may benefit from more time assigned to the same curriculum objectives. Pupils who can cover the assigned curriculum in the set time may benefit from an increase in allotted time and an increase in curriculum objectives. These are, to date, the essential elements of both individualized instruction by self-paced curriculum materials and ability grouping by teachers.

The issue of time — in school, in the classroom, allocated, and on-task — seems too obvious to warrant much more attention, yet the most solid research results and specific policy implications concern this issue. Since time is finite, the relative allocation of school time must inevitably involve trade-offs between and among different activities. The research conclusions, which strongly suggest that more time spent in reading and mathematics classes by pupils in the lower elementary grades leads to increased achievement in those subjects, have the following implications.

First, we must assume that such an increase in reading and mathematics time will lead to less time spent on other subject matter or on social, esthetic, and recreational activities of a broader educational nature, further emphasizing cognitive rather than affective experiences in the classroom.

Second, we must also raise the question of whether or not, within time spans specifically allocated to these subjects, there are still more or less effective teacher behaviors. That is, nothing suggests that we should not continue the search for effective teachers.

Third, we need to remember that these results strongly emphasize the central role of the pupil in investing the school and the teacher with the power to teach. The basic issue is the time pupils spend studying. With all other conditions optimal, students determine whether they will or will not be engaged in the learning tasks prepared for them. In the research a number of different procedures have measured such pupil behavior, all of which are inadequate in at least one sense. One pupil skill which will forever elude any but the most sensitive and sophisticated observer is the ability to appear to be working, intently poring over textbook or work sheet, while actually dreaming of things far away.

PUPILS' ATTENDING BEHAVIORS AND TEACHER EFFECTIVENESS

Summary of findings:

4. *Pupils' attending and cooperating behaviors differentiate more-and less-effective teachers across pupil socioeconomic status (SES) and grade levels.*

"Teachers are assigned to meet with groups of students for designated periods of time and to conduct activities that involve all students and have some educative justification. At a proximate level, the teacher's task engendered by this arrangement is to secure the cooperation of students in classroom activities. Complications in gaining cooperation arise from the fact that students vary in their abilities to accomplish academic tasks and in their inclinations to participate in classroom activities" (Doyle 1979, p. 4). As Doyle notes, by attending to the teacher, pupils indicate that they may be vesting the teacher with the power to teach and, by accepting the pupil role as defined by the teacher, they indicate at least a respect for adult, or teacher, authority. Less-effective teachers of early elementary pupils of low socioeconomic status (SES) have more deviant, disruptive pupil behavior in their classrooms. In classrooms of students with high SES, pupil behaviors labeled as withdrawn and passive were negatively correlated with academic achievement. These behavior patterns could be interpreted as cues that, at best, these pupils did not fully understand their role and, at worst, that they did not accept or value it.

As demonstrated by observed pupil behavior, more-effective teachers of pupils of low SES in the lower elementary grades have pupils who value teacher authority, the teacher-defined role and the perception of self as an active learner, or teacher approval.

In terms of observed pupil behaviors, both more and less effective teachers of middle and high SES pupil populations have less deviant and disruptive behaviors in their classrooms. From this evidence we can infer that when classrooms are characterized by students' attention and cooperation and significant increases in learning are not taking place, other factors related to teacher practices or pupil characteristics must be more salient in these classrooms.

DIRECT AND INDIRECT TEACHING METHODS

Summary of findings:

5. *Direct teaching methods are positively correlated with pupil achievement of lower-order cognitive objectives.*
6. *Direct teaching, with slower placing of learning objectives, is positively correlated with achievement of low SES pupils.*
7. *Indirect teaching is negatively correlated with achievement at lower elementary grade levels and across SES levels.*

Two methods of teaching that incorporate characteristics of teacher-centrality and pupil-centrality, with regard to the style in which a lesson is communicated, are described as direct teaching and indirect teaching, respectively.

Direct teaching employs a stimulus-response model with immediate evaluation of response, elements that are incorporated in conditioning, programmed learning, and contingency models. It is considered to be a highly appropriate and effective method when the cognitive objective is convergent (focused on the one and only "right" answer, as in learning number facts or learning to spell), or involves decoding or recalling (associating sounds and letter symbols, using phonemes and word recognition in reading).

The appropriateness of this method appears to be substantiated by research results indicating that pupil gains in academic achievement, at the basic skills acquisition level, are positively correlated with teachers' direct teaching styles. Low SES pupils have made gains in achievement when direct teaching was used and when subject content was presented in smaller amounts at a slower pace. Tallmadge (1974) has also identified direct teaching as an effective method in remedial education, where basic skills acquisition is again the primary learning objective.

In applying the first teaching mode to the presentation of subject content, the pupil role could be interpreted with equal narrowness and be confined to drill, drill, and more drill in the tasks following presentation. However, a creative use of materials as instructional aids and more individual interaction with the teacher (or other adults in the classroom) and discussion about the subject content can broaden the pupil's participation and increase the opportunities for a positive perception of self as doer, learner, and knower. Such a perception gives a positive concept of themselves as students.

Indirect teaching, a style considered to be more appropriate for divergent learning tasks (developing and applying mathematical concepts to problem solving, analyzing context for word meaning, finding relationships to form generalizations and discover principles) and requiring higher-order cognitive functioning, has a limited role at the early elementary level. In the context of higher-order questioning, higher-order cognitive functions have a negative association with the achievement of pupils in elementary grades.

The fact that lower elementary subject content is characterized by lower cognitive learning objectives does not mean that concept development is not occurring at, or even below, these grade levels. There is every reason to infer from the research and from knowledge of curriculum content that there is a role for indirect teaching practices that relates to learning at these grade levels, but the effects cannot be measured by standardized achievement tests.

Tests administered to both Follow Through project pupils and control pupils produced significant information regarding the effects of teaching practices on pupils' self-perceptions. The cognitive level and subject content for all the pupil populations was essentially the same. However, in those programs where pupil roles were broadened to allow some pupil initiative and access to a wider variety of activities and exploratory materials, pupils "learned to see the relationship between parts and wholes" (Stallings 1976, p. 47). Pupils in these programs also showed more independent and more cooperative behavior.

TEACHER QUESTIONING PRACTICES:
PUPIL QUESTIONING RESPONSE BEHAVIORS

Summary of findings:

8. *Higher-order questioning is negatively correlated with pupil achievement across SES, elementary grade levels, and subject order.*

9. *Lower-order questioning is positively correlated with pupil achievement across SES, elementary grade levels, and subject content.*

10. *More-effective teachers of high SES pupils permit pupils to take the initiative in asking for help.*
11. *More-effective teachers of low SES pupils persist in questioning pupils and help them to respond.*
12. *More-effective teachers of both high and low SES pupils gauge questions at an appropriate level of difficulty.*

Questioning is one of the classroom teacher's most potent teaching skills. Through asking questions the teacher can tell whether presentations are understood, whether procedures are clear, and whether the level of learning is acceptable. The students' answers reveal to the teacher which pupils are having trouble and which pupils proceed with tasks.

The widely held belief that higher-order questioning contributes to pupil gains in learning was not substantiated by the research that we examined. Higher-order questions were negatively correlated with pupil academic gains across all SES groups, grade levels, and subject content.

Lower-order questions gauged at an appropriate level of difficulty for pupil ability and subject content were positively correlated with pupil gain across all SES groups, grade levels, and academic subjects. An appropriate level of difficulty was defined as one that was challenging to pupils rather than simply drawing upon well-known information. The practice of calling on volunteers also correlated with pupil achievement across pupil populations.

More-effective teachers of low SES pupils persisted with their questioning when pupils could not answer and supplied cues to help pupils respond. Such teachers also tended to ask questions in rotation, providing opportunities for all students to recite.

More-effective teachers of high SES pupils tended to ask more product questions (requiring short answers) than process questions (requiring long explanations). Rather than persisting when pupils failed to answer, these teachers either asked other pupils for correct answers or supplied the correct answers themselves.

Student-initiated questioning correlated with pupil achievement gains across all SES and grade levels and academic subjects. High SES pupils tended to ask their teachers questions; low SES pupils did not. High SES pupil response behaviors of "calling out" were positively correlated with pupil achievement in mathematics; this same behavior for the same group was negatively correlated with pupil gain in reading.

These data on teacher questioning processes support the general contention that early elementary pupils show gains when questions are kept straightforward and relatively simple because the material to be learned is straightforward and convergent. The consistent finding that higher-order questions correlate negatively with achievement may be interpreted as an argument against the use of such questions. However, this finding may reflect the fact that the use of higher conceptual level thinking is not easily measured or that pupils have not had the opportunity to develop such cognitive processes in school. Future research may resolve this question.

TEACHER PRAISE

Summary of findings:

13. *Teacher praise is positively correlated with the academic achievement of low SES pupils.*
14. *Teacher praise shows either no relationship or negative correlations with the academic achievement of high SES pupils.*

Investigators have presumed that students will respond to teacher praise with increased performance. Teacher praise, acceptance, and approval have often been studied. The results of these studies indicate that pupils respond differently to teacher praise.

One of the difficulties confronted in examining the research on teacher praise and pupil achievement has been the variety of definitions used for "praise." Some measures have included all possible forms under a global term and others have differentiated between the use of praise during instruction and the use of praise as a means of behavior control. As a specific teacher behavior, praise is correlated with pupil achievement. However, when pupil characteristics such as SES are used as discriminators, teacher praise is more highly correlated with the achievement of low SES pupils and shows either no relationship or a slightly negative relationship with achievement of high SES pupils.

These results suggest the nature of pupils' experiences with teacher praise and their individual values for it. It seems reasonable to suspect that pupils who receive a great deal of praise for their performances and products will become used to it and that pupils who are not performing and producing at an approved rate will be more impressed by a positive evaluation of their efforts. This may explain the patterns of research results. But there are additional findings that suggest a closer relationship between individual pupil values and the way they respond to praise. Among low SES pupils there was a positive relationship between teachers' praise of pupils' responses to questions asking for opinions, but a negative relationship with praise for responses to factual questions. Among low SES pupils, approval-seeking behaviors were also negatively correlated with learning gains. Hartup (1958) suggested that pupils who are dependent upon the teacher's praise and approval are more likely to be motivated by that praise and approval. He found a positive relationship between teacher praise and achievement of girls and of "dependent" boys.

Teachers' praise is most likely to motivate and encourage low SES pupils who value that positive reflection of their performances. It does not seem to affect the already positive self-esteem of high SES pupils.

EVALUATIVE FEEDBACK

Summary of findings:

15. *Teachers' use of evaluative feedback that directly relates to pupils' performances and products is positively related to increased academic performance by both high- and low-ability pupils.*

The point at which both praise and criticism come together for pupils is in evaluations offered by teachers. High achievers respond more positively to evaluative feedback that includes criticism of their work than they do to teachers' praise and approval. Pickup and Anthony (1968) reported that pupils with low expectations for the success of their work responded with more effort and higher achievement when they were given the benefit of the doubt (received credit for partially correct answers) that resulted in higher grades than were expected.

The kind of self-fulfilling prophecy that is often related to teacher expectations for pupils is also related to pupils' expectations of their own successes and failures. Students, too, are in a position to influence the outcomes of their performances, but those pupils who believe they will fail are likely to fail.

In a simple and practical experiment, Page (1958) investigated the effects of written teacher feedback practices on school tests and found that low-achieving pupils responded with better test scores on subsequent tests when teachers wrote evaluative and complimentary comments on their test papers. The effects of this practice were compared with giving only a number grade or letter mark and writing one-word comments like "excellent," "good," or "poor" on the papers. Teachers in this study expected their high achieving pupils to respond most favorably to the written comments, but the failing students showed the greatest gains on subsequent testing.

In an experimental study of pupils' expectations and their responses to negative and positive feedback (Crandall, Good, and Crandall 1964), pupils who expected to succeed but failed were more affected by failure than were those pupils who expected to fail and did fail. Similarly, pupils who expected to fail and succeeded were not as willing to attribute success to their own ability and did not raise their expectations appreciably. For them, success came from something outside of themselves but failure was their own responsibility. As far as expectations are concerned, the Crandall study showed that success cannot raise expectations as effectively as failure can lower them.

This study also reported that the effects of positive and negative feedback were more lasting, and varied in their effect on subsequent pupil performances. Pupils who received positive feedback while performing a task and who then performed the task without any feedback from an attending adult were inclined to interpret the lack of feedback as criticism. Pupils who first received criticism for their performances and then experienced silence while performing with an adult tended to interpret silence as approval.

This same phenomenon was found in another experimental

study (Meichenbaum, Bowers, and Ross 1969) in which pupils who had experienced a reduction in the amount of teacher criticism (and a reduction in the amount of teacher praise, as well) improved their academic scores. Pupils who received more teacher praise, but no reduction in the amount of criticism, improved their scores but not as significantly as those who experienced a reduction in criticism.

Pupils who are achieving seem to value teacher's feedback when it helps them solve problems that they have identified. Criticism motivates them to improve their work. Low achievers value teacher's praise and feedback as reflections of their progress and also as a positive reflection of their own personal contributions. Students who spend much of their time doing what they are told to do, in the way they are told to do it, should value the opportunity to make their own personal contributions. When teachers use too much praise, it can become meaningless and cannot be taken personally or used as a measure of a pupil's performance and products. Instead, praise becomes a characteristic of the teacher. Continued criticism probably has the same effect, and when it simply describes the miserable state a pupil is in, without any information as to how to get out of it, the pupil's most likely recourse will be either not to take it personally or not to listen.

TEACHER CONTROLLING BEHAVIORS

Summary of findings:

16. *Teachers' belittling of pupils is negatively correlated with pupil achievement across SES groups, grade levels, and subject content.*
17. *Teachers' treatment of the class as one unit in pressuring for peer control is negatively related to pupil achievement across SES groups, grade levels, and subject content.*
18. *Establishing reasonable rules for class deportment and following through with the application of consequences is positively correlated with pupil achievement at the elementary level.*

Teachers are in classrooms because they choose to be; pupils are there because they have to be, and that one small fact can loom large. Those pupils who arrive in the classroom ready to accept their role as students will pose few problems. Those who arrive unprepared or unwilling to accept that role will provide all the problems a teacher or a school can handle. It is no surprise that maintaining discipline is a major concern of classroom teachers and school principals. But how the pupil's role is defined and how teachers maintain discipline is the core of many of the problems of classroom discipline.

The majority of the pupils in public school classrooms are not deviant and disruptive, but they may still be subject to teachers' controlling behaviors that cause them embarrassment, humiliation, and loss of self-confidence. In a survey of college students who were asked to describe their most negative and growth-inhibiting experience, interactions with teachers were named as the primary sources of such experiences (humiliation, embarrassment, unfairness, destruction of self-confidence), even outdistancing parents and peers (Branan 1972).

In the research on teacher effectiveness, *belittling,* defined as berating a child before the class, is negatively correlated with pupil achievement across grade levels and subject content. Another controlling behavior found to be negatively correlated with pupil achievement is *oneness,* defined as the practice of treating the whole group or class as one in an effort to exert peer pressure to maintain control.

The classroom controlling behavior found to be positively correlated with pupil achievement is *consistency of message for control,* defined as giving a direction or threat and following through with it.

The two negatively correlated behaviors are those that require an adversary teacher-pupil relationship. Teachers who resort to belittling, shaming, disgracing, and humiliating pupils intentionally cannot hope to establish the relationship of trust necessary to promote learning. And teachers who institute a "hostage" system of control, making others pay for behavior they cannot control, cannot expect children to develop responsibility for their own behavior.

Teachers who set behavioral limits and establish classroom rules and who apply them fairly, rather than indiscriminately, promote self-sufficiency and pupil self-control.

TASK STRUCTURING FOR COGNITIVE DEVELOPMENT

Summary of findings:

19. *Structuring tasks for less direct cognitive control but with behavioral control is positively correlated with pupil achievement of higher-order cognitive objectives.*

Although direct instruction has been correlated with achievement in grades where pupils are engaged in lower-order cognitive tasks, there is evidence that teachers should not consider more to be better in using direct instruction. Too much direct teaching and too closely structured activities may limit learning and the development of higher-order cognitive skills.

Research indicates that direct teaching facilitates learning of lower-order cognitive objectives, but that less directness is indicated for higher-order cognitive objectives. In a comparative analysis of program effects of the Follow Through project, one model — highly structured in design and based on programmed learning and conditioning principles — that had previously ranked high on measures of pupil academic gain reversed its status when measures for high-level cognitive objectives and concept development were introduced.

Where creativity and higher-order concept development are the objectives of the learning task, pupils should have more freedom under supervision. Some of this freedom can be obtained by structuring tasks so that pupils can apply rules and directions. This not only offers an opportunity for the student to relate the impact of his or her skills to a task but also increases the opportunities to develop constructive, cooperative behaviors (Torrance 1971).

TEACHER TALK AND PUPIL TALK

Summary of findings:

20. *Teacher clarity is positively correlated with pupils' academic achievement.*

21. *Increased levels of the use of symbols by pupils and teachers (students' questions, discussion, time allocated to reading and mathematics, and reading time in other subjects) are positively correlated with pupils' achievement in reading and mathematics.*

Words and other symbolic representations of reality are the working tools of education, and not much of what we call formal education can take place without them. Progressing from the acquisition of basic skills to the application of those skills represents a move into a world where ideas, not just facts or concrete reality, exist (Bruner 1971).

Earlier research dwelt on the ratio of teachers' talk to pupils' talk. The results of this research were unrewarding, but the patterns of classroom interaction and communication were highly informative. Little of the research was done with the learning situation reported and, as a result, it was difficult to tell whether a high amount of a teacher's talk stemmed from presentation of material or from a tendency to control. Pupils' talk, unless it was related to subject content, revealed more about nonacademic behavior than about the relationship between their talking and achievement.

In the Follow Through studies that incorporated several different programs for early elementary education, verbal activities — including activities related to other subjects — were associated with students' gains in reading. Other research at the fourth- and fifth-grade levels found that discussion about subject content was also correlated with achievement for middle and high SES pupils.

In addition to the importance of feedback, teacher clarity in presenting information correlated with the academic achievement of pupils above the third grade. Moving to higher-order cognitive tasks with expanding applications of the basic skills to higher-order processes and concepts may reveal clarity of presentations as a differentiating characteristic of effective teachers in a way that is not discernible at lower elementary levels.

At every level, and increasingly so, education is a verbal experience. When pupils lack, and cannot acquire, this key to the system, it is highly unlikely that they will be successful in school.

CLASSROOM MANAGEMENT PRACTICES

Summary of findings:

22. *Small group instruction is positively correlated with pupil achievement in the basic skills in the first and second grades.*

23. *Instruction directed toward the whole class is positively correlated with pupil achievement in mathematics and reading at the higher levels of elementary education.*
24. *Pupil-to-pupil tutoring and unsupervised individual or small group work are negatively correlated with pupil achievement at the early levels of elementary education.*

What to do, how to do it, and when to do it describe the themes to be scripted by teachers, whether they are dealing with classroom management or structuring learning tasks. Research describing such themes is confined to a few of the elements that go into classroom management. One element that does appear regularly in the recent literature is the way pupils are grouped for instruction.

Whole Class Instruction. Students are organized for lesson presentation in small groups at primary levels; the whole class is addressed at the higher levels of elementary education. At the third-grade level, large group instruction was correlated with pupil achievement in both reading and mathematics; in the fourth grade, such instruction also correlated with greater gains in mathematics.

Studies examining differences in whole group and small group presentations also investigated feedback, use of additional material and workbooks, and audiovisuals in relation to effective whole class or large group instruction, but found no consistent relationships.

Small Group and Individual Instruction. Small group instruction was correlated with pupil gains in the first grade. Included in these conditions were more highly structured and more systematic instructional patterns, more teacher-pupil interaction, and immediate feedback and reinforcement of pupil responses. These instructional patterns applied to both reading and mathematics achievement at this grade level.

Individual attention, supervised desk work and small group work were also positively correlated with higher achievement when the pupils showed persistence in the assignments. Pupil-to-pupil tutoring and unsupervised small groups or individual desk work were negatively correlated with achievement.

At the early levels of instruction, pupils fare better with closer teacher supervision and help. Pupils at the upper levels have acquired at least sufficient classroom behaviors to be allowed more autonomy.

RELATING TEACHER PRACTICES TO PUPIL SELF-CONCEPT

Summary of findings:

25. *Pupils' roles that include opportunities for initiative and exploration, with access to a wider variety of activities and material, are positively correlated with measures of students' independence and spatial concept development.*
26. *Teachers' attitudes and beliefs expressed in classroom behaviors can positively or negatively affect pupils' performance and opportunity to learn.*

A successful school experience seems to have within it an image of self-control over what happens, a control that stems from understanding and knowing what to do, how to do it, and when to do it — all derived from the teacher who informs, reflects, and interprets the classroom environment. In the course of acquiring a successful experience, pupils are dependent upon teachers' evaluation and feedback of their progress and performances.

An unsuccessful school experience seems to be characterized by a self-image lacking control over classroom events, a lack of understanding as to what to do, how to do it, and when to do it. This results in less initiative, less goal-directed behavior, less participation, and poorer products. It also appears to result in more deviant and disruptive pupil behavior.

The problems involved in studying the relationship of self-concept development to teacher behaviors are far greater than those confronting research on cognitive pupil gains, and the problems are much farther from any resolution. No foundation of solid research applies to teachers' behaviors and their impact on pupils. But we have brought together the teacher behaviors identified here as associated with pupil achievement and self-concept that will allow us to consider the possible relationships.

Tests to both Follow Through project pupils and control pupils produced significant information regarding the effects of teaching practices on pupils' self-perceptions. The cognitive level and subject content for all the pupil populations were essentially the same. However, in those programs where pupil roles were broadened to allow some pupil initiative and to allow access to a wider variety of activities and exploratory materials, pupils "learned to see the relationship between parts and wholes" (Stallings and Kaskowitz 1974, p. 47). Pupils in these programs also showed more independent and more cooperative behavior.

Administration of a measure of pupil's acceptance of responsibility for their successes and failures (Crandall, Katkovsky and Crandall 1965) provided interesting results of program effects. Third-grade pupils in programs that spent more time in practice with subject content and with high rates of praise from their teachers (the conditions that produced the highest rates of performance and growth) tended "to accept responsibility for their *failures* but not for their success" (p. 45). Pupils in less structured and more flexible learning situations took responsibility for their *successes* but not for their failures. The only program in which pupils accepted responsibility for both their successes and failures was the program based on the principles of the English Infant School.

Pupils who accepted responsibility for their failures but not their successes may have perceived themselves only as approved or disapproved, and their responses as acceptable or unacceptable to the significant adult, the teacher. They view academic performance as a means of gaining approval; the power of approval and the standards for approval are vested in the teacher, an outside source. Failure, however, reflects the pupil's inability to gain approval, a condition directly attributable to the self.

Pupils who accepted responsibility for their successes and not for their failures may have acquired a more positive self-perception as having a positive impact on their environment through their behaviors, but may not yet have acquired a set of standards for academic behaviors. Therefore, failure in academic performance is defined by standards not yet acquired by the pupil.

Pupils who see themselves as responsible for both success and failure understand the behaviors that gain approval and success and know the standards to apply. They have a realistic concept of themselves as students.

The clearest and most constant image a pupil receives in the classroom is the self-image that is formed by the teacher's reflections and interpretations of the pupil's performances and products. The real experiences of pupils, successful and unsuccessful, are found in the nature of these reflections and interpretations and in the pupils' responses to them. The schooling experience is idiosyncratic, with no two pupils in the same room with the same teacher having exactly the same experience. Regardless of how many other students there are in the school or the class, school is interpreted as "my school," "my class," "my teacher," and, ultimately, "my education."

Two sources that have an impact on the nature of a pupil's schooling experience are teacher bias and teacher expectation. There is evidence in the research literature that pupils' experiences can differ because of their cognitive abilities, their sex, socioeconomic status, ethnicity, and race. The generally held belief that girls are more suited to the controlled environment of the classroom has been supported by research indicating that girls receive more approval, but boys receive more attention, both positive and negative. Boys' performances are more highly praised when they are correct, and boys' behaviors are more harshly criticized (Lahaderne 1975, Meyer and Thompson 1956, McNeil 1964, Good and Brophy 1972).

Palardy (1969) showed that teachers' beliefs can be translated into an effect on pupil performance and achievement. Palardy's study confirmed that teachers who believed boys learned to read more slowly than girls produced reading scores to confirm their beliefs; teachers who did not believe there was a difference in the learning rates of boys and girls were equally able to substantiate their beliefs through pupil scores.

The idea that teachers' expectations affect pupils' IQ scores has not been substantiated by research. However, there is evidence to support the hypothesis that teacher expectations affect their behaviors and, subsequently, the performance and achievement of their pupils. Teachers with low expectations for their pupils can reduce the subject content and limit the activities, thus influencing their students' performance.

The belief that all pupils will be negatively affected by academic failure and will have low self-esteem as a result is widely held by

Table 3-1.
Sources

Sources	Time is important			Pupil's attending behaviors	Direct & indirect teaching				Teacher questioning practices				Teacher praise		Evaluative feedback		Teacher con-trolling behavior		Task structuring cognitive development	Teacher talk and pupil talk		Classroom manage-ment practice			Teacher practices and pupil self-concept	
(Findings)	1	2	3	4	5	6	7	8	9	10	11	12	13	14	15	16	17	18	19	20	21	22	23	24	25	26
Brophy and Evertson 1974a, 1974b	X			X	X	X	X	X	X	X	X	X	X	X	X		X	X		X	X		X	X		
Fisher and others 1978		X	X	X	X											X	X	X			X	X				
Good and Grouws 1975	X				X			X	X	X		X	X	X	X					X			X			
Farrell 1977	X	X	X																							
McDonald and others 1975	X	X	X	X	X	X		X	X						X			X		X	X	X	X			
Stallings and Kaskowitz 1974	X	X			X		X					X	X		X					X	X	X	X	X	X	
Soar 1968 / Soar and Soar 1972							X	X	X										X							
Coker and others 1976	X			X	X					X		X		X	X	X										
Good and Brophy 1972																										X

educators whose values for education are reflected in that belief. There are, however, pupils who do not value education and are, therefore, not affected by academic failure. Pupils can have values for the self related to physical traits and abilities or for reference groups outside of school that are more important to them than a sense of self-esteem as students. The problems these pupils present for teachers are ones of influencing their value systems and creating a value for academic achievement.

CONCLUSION

As suggested by the research, the experiences of pupils in the early years may include a great deal of direct teaching. The question that must be raised with regard to this experience, and in the light of current research, is whether this process constitutes educating in the broad sense or training in the narrow sense. Careful attention should be given to the consequent achievement of pupils who successfully acquire basic skills through direct teaching practices. If their success in giving right answers does not increase their ability to make decisions, direct their own behavior, set their own goals and assume responsibility for their own successes and failures, then we will have failed to eliminate socioeconomic status as a predictor of academic achievement. The ordinary citizen must be equipped, now more than ever, to make informed decisions that deal with our national and global welfare. Daily decisions of the marketplace are not just matters of addition and subtraction but of judgments based on knowledge of risk and personal values.

REFERENCES

Branan, John M. "Negative Human Interaction." *Journal of Counseling Psychology* 19 (January 1972): 81–82.

Brophy, Jere E., and Evertson, Carolyn. *Process-Product Correlations in the Texas Teacher Effectiveness Study: Final Report.* Research Report no. 74–4. Austin, Tex.: Research and Development Center for Teacher Education, 1974a.

Brophy, Jere E., and Evertson, Carolyn. *The Texas Teacher Effectiveness Project: Presentation of Non-linear Relationships and Summary Discussion,* Research Report no. 74–6. Austin, Tex.: Research and Development Center for Teacher Education, 1974b.

Bruner, Jerome S. *The Relevance of Education*. New York: W. W. Norton, 1971.

Coker, H.; Lorentz, J. L.; and Coker, J. *Interim Report on the Carroll County CBTC Project, Fall, 1976*. Atlanta: Georgia State Department of Education, 1976.

Crandall, Virginia C.; Good, Suzanne; and Crandall, Vaughn J. "Reinforcement Effects of Adult Reactions and Nonreactions on Children's Achievement Expectations: A Replication Study." *Child Development* 35 (June 1964): 485–97.

Crandall, Virginia C.; Katkovsky, Walter; and Crandall, Vaughn J. "Children's Belief in Their Own Control of Reinforcements in Intellectual-Academic Achievement Situations." *Child Development* 36 (March 1965): 91–109.

Doyle, Walter. "Research on Teaching in Classroom Environments." Paper presented at the conference on "Exploring Issues in Teacher Education: Questions for Future Research," Austin, Tex., January 1979.

Farrell, Joseph P. "The IEA Studies: Factors That Affect Achievement in Six Subjects in Twenty-One Countries." *Teachers College Record* 79 (December 1977): 289–96.

Fisher, Charles W., and others. *Teaching and Learning in the Elementary School: A Summary of the Beginning Teacher Evaluation Study*. Report VII-I. San Francisco: Far West Laboratory for Educational Research and Development, 1978.

Good, Thomas L., and Brophy, Jere E. "Behavioral Expression of Teacher Attitudes." *Journal of Educational Psychology* 63 (December 1972): 617–24.

Good, Thomas L., and Grouws, Douglas A. *Process-Product Relationships in Fourth-grade Mathematics Classrooms*. Final Report, National Institute of Education Grant NEG-00-3-0123. Columbia: University of Missouri, 1975.

Hartup, Willard W. "Nurturance and Nurturance-Withdrawal in Relation to the Dependency Behavior of Preschool Children." *Child Development* 29 (June 1958): 191–201.

Lahaderne, Henrietta M. "The Feminized Elementary School: An Unpromising Myth to Explain Boys' Reading Problems." Paper presented at the annual meeting of the American Educational Research Association, Washington, D.C., March 1975.

McDonald, Frederick J., and others. *Final Report on Phase II of the Beginning Teacher Evaluation Study*. Prepared for the California Commission on Teacher Preparation and Licensing, Sacramento. Princeton, N.J.: Educational Testing Service, 1975.

McNeil, John D. "Programmed Instruction versus Usual Classroom Procedures in Teaching Boys to Read." *American Educational Research Journal* 1 (March 1964): 113–20.

Meichenbaum, Donald H.; Bowers, Kenneth S.; and Ross, Robert R. "A Behavioral Analysis of Teacher Expectancy Effect." *Journal of Personality and Social Psychology* 13 (December 1969): 306–16.

Meyer, William J., and Thompson, George G. "Sex Differences in the Distribution of Teacher Approval and Disapproval among Sixth-Grade Children." *Journal of Educational Psychology* 47 (November 1956): 385–97.

Page, Ellis B. "Teacher Comments and Student Performance: A Seventy-Four Classroom Experiment in School Motivation." *Journal of Educational Psychology* 49 (August 1958): 173–81.

Palardy, J. Michael. "What Teachers Believe — What Children Achieve." *Elementary School Journal* 69 (April 1969): 370–74.

Pickup, Anthony J., and Anthony, W. S. "Teachers' Marks and Pupils' Expectations: The Short-Term Effects of Discrepancies upon Classroom Performance in Secondary Schools." *British Journal of Educational Psychology* 38 (November 1968): 302–9.

Soar, Robert S. "Optimum Teacher-Pupil Interaction for Pupil Growth." *Educational Leadership* 26 (December 1968): 275–80.

Soar, Robert S., and Soar, Ruth M. "An Empirical Analysis of Selected Follow-Through Programs: An Example of a Process Approach to Evaluation." In *Early Childhood Education*. Seventy-First Yearbook of the National Society for the Study of Education, Part 2, pp. 229–59, edited by Ira J. Gordon. Chicago: University of Chicago Press, 1972.

Stallings, Jane A. "How Instructional Processes Relate to Child Outcomes in a National Study of Follow Through." *Journal of Teacher Education* 27 (Spring 1976): 43–47.

Stallings, Jane A., and Kaskowitz, David H. *Follow Through Classroom Observation Evaluation 1972-1973*. Menlo Park, California.: Stanford Research Institute, 1974.

Tallmadge, Karstin. *The Development of Project Information Packages for Effective Approaches in Compensatory Education*, Technical Report UR-25. Mountain View, Calif.: RMC Research, 1974.

Torrance, E. Paul. " 'Structure' Can Improve the Group Behavior of Five-Year-Old Children." *Elementary School Journal* 72 (November 1971): 102–6.

Discussion

David C. Berliner

Kash and Borich provide an excellent conceptual framework for understanding the literature on teacher effectiveness. This critique annotates some of their ideas and discusses some areas they did not cover.

THE VALIDITY OF OBSERVER JUDGMENTS

At one point in their chapter, the authors point out that students may be "on-task," but be coded as "off-task" or vice versa. After many hours of observation in classrooms, I have found that young students, particularly below fourth grade, have not learned to fool observers. When such students appear to be on-task, I think they are. Once the students abandon their task, it is obvious — they jump, dance, sing, leave for the restroom, and so forth. Older students, above the fourth grade, have learned different kinds of classroom behavior. Many times a student will be gazing out the window and will be coded as off-task when, in fact, the student has been processing the material at hand. At other times, students appear to be following the teacher and yet you sense that the student is really on Mars. I think that with young children, we do not have to worry about the validity of the observations. With older students, it probably is not an important issue because an observer probably makes as many judgments of off-task behavior that are invalid as judgments of on-task behavior that are invalid. Thus, when using a class mean in analysis, one can dismiss the invalidity of the observational system.

SUCCESS RATES AND ACADEMIC LEARNING TIME

There are some aspects of time that the authors did not discuss: time spent in activities with a high success rate and academic learning time.

Success Rate. Three rather broad categories were used to define levels of difficulty in the work of Fisher and others (1978) cited by Kash and Borich. One was "high success," in which the student understands the task and makes only occasional careless errors. A second was "medium success," in which the student has partial understanding, but makes some substantive errors. The third category was "low success," in which the student does not understand the task at all. These categories coincide with common-sense notions of easy, medium, and hard.

High Success Rate. The findings consistently point out the positive effects of school tasks yielding high success rates (easy materials, providing a low error rate). Other research on instructional design has stressed the importance of high success rates. High success rate in scholastic activities is one of the factors that contribute to high levels of a student's self-esteem.

The average student in the study by Fisher and others spent about half the time working on tasks that provided high success. Students who spent more time than the average in high success activities had higher achievement scores in the spring, better retention of learning over the summer, and more positive attitudes toward school. From these data, one might recommend that students spend 60–70 percent of their time on tasks they can carry out with high success.

The idea of success rate may be more understandable if one thinks about the cyclical nature of learning. Learning is a process of moving from not knowing to knowing. Most likely, when new material is introduced, the student will not understand completely and will make some errors. Guided practice or explanation helps the student to understand and thus make fewer errors. Eventually, the student will perform correctly, although probably with some effort. Learning will become well established and further work will be practice or review — a stage of consolidation. At some later point, the student knows the material so well that further practice is of minimal value, and he or she can move on to something new. The results of the study by Fisher and others suggest that for learning of basic skills in the elementary grades, the stage of *successful practice* (consolidation) is particularly important. Concepts and procedures must be thoroughly mastered. Some teachers do not devote sufficient time to this stage which is crucial for younger and slower students.

Although these data suggest the importance of giving students ample opportunity for successful practice, obviously students should not spend all of their time on tasks they can perform correctly. Common sense suggests that too high a rate of "high success" work would be deleterious (boring, repetitive, time wasting, and so forth). A working philosophy for a teacher should probably be to stress experiences with "high success" and simultaneously to try to maximize content coverage. By keeping these two possibly antagonistic notions in mind, a teacher stands a good chance of ensuring academic success for students.

Low Success Rate. When students worked with materials or activities that were categorized as "hard," yielding a low success rate, achievement was lower. In the study under discussion, no teacher assigned a high proportion of materials that were exceptionally hard for students. Nevertheless, students who were observed to spend more time on excessively difficult material generally learned less than other students. It is seldom, if ever, desirable for students to be given tasks where they experience low success.

Academic Learning Time. Academic learning time, the research variable of most interest in the study of Fisher and others (1978), is the time a student is engaged (on-task) with academic materials or activities that yield a high success rate. Thus, one component of ALT is the engagement rate of students. Another component is the level of difficulty of the material that a student is working on. Increases in academic learning time in relationship to achievement are illustrated in Table 3-2, using examples from the analysis of reading instruction in second grade. This table displays total reading scores in October, student engaged time with a high success rate (academic learning time) in reading over the period from October to December, and estimated total reading scores in December. The expected reading scores in December shown in the table are estimated from linear regressions that use the test scores in October and the intervening academic learning time. Total reading scores are given in terms of raw scores and percentile rank among students in this study.

The table shows that substantial increases in academic learning time are associated with important increases in achievement. Consider the student who started the period with a second-grade reading score that was average (50th percentile). If this student experiences the average amount of academic learning time (573 minutes total, or 23 minutes per day in reading), the student should show average reading achievement in December (50th percentile again). Note also that the "average" student with "average" academic learning time does show a considerable increase in predicted raw scores.

The table also indicates that if the average student (in terms of the October test score) experienced only four minutes per day of academic learning time (100 minutes total for the intertest period), that student would show almost no change in raw scores (36 out of 100 correct in October, 37 out of 100 in December) and would decline considerably in relative terms (50th percentile in October, 39th percentile in December). However, if the same student had a lot of academic learning time (52 minutes per day in this example),

Table 3-2.

Academic Learning Time and Student Achievement: Example from Second-Grade Reading

Reading Score at First Testing (October)		Student Engaged Time in Reading with High Success Rate		Estimated Reading Score, Second Testing (December)	
Raw Score (out of 100)	Percentile	Total Time Over 5 Weeks (Minutes)	Average Daily Time (Minutes)	Raw Score (out of 100)	Percentile
36	50	100	4	37	39
36	50	573	23	43	50
36	50	1300	52	52	66

Note: An average of twenty-five school days occurred between the first and the second testing. The values of all variables in this table are within the ranges actually obtained in the sample. The average engaged time with high success rate in second-grade reading for the intertest period was 573 minutes. The December reading scores are estimated via linear regression.

Source: From Charles W. Fisher et al., *Teaching and Learning in the Elementary School: A Summary of the Beginning Teacher Evaluation Study.* BTES Report VII-1. (San Francisco, Calif.: Far West Laboratory for Research and Development, 1978)

then he or she could be expected to answer almost 50 percent more items correctly on the December test than on the October test. Furthermore, the student would show considerable improvement in reading achievement relative to the other students in the study (50th percentile in October, 66th percentile in December). Thus, the student with large amounts of academic learning time benefits substantially.

This range from four to fifty-two minutes per day may appear unrealistically wide, but it actually occurred in the classes in the study. One can easily imagine how either four or fifty-two minutes per day of academic learning time might come about. If fifty minutes of reading instruction per day is allocated to a student who pays attention only about a third of the time and only about one fourth of the student's reading time is at a high level of success, then the student will experience roughly four minutes of engaged reading at a high success level. Similarly, if 100 minutes per day are allocated to reading for a student who pays attention 85 percent of the time, at a high level of success for almost two-thirds of that time, then that student will have about fifty-two minutes of academic learning time per day.

In summary, large differences in academic learning time are associated with very important changes in predicted achievement levels. These large differences in academic learning time are well within the range actually observed in that study. In addition, one can easily imagine how these differences in academic learning time could occur in realistic situations. Therefore, academic learning time is of considerable practical importance in terms of its relationship to achievement.

Academic Learning Time and Attitude. The data from this study also revealed that students with high and low rates of allocated and engaged time were equally likely to have positive or negative attitudes toward the subject matter and the school. Educators are naturally concerned about whether greater-than-average time in academic pursuits or greater-than-average rates of attending will result in negative attitudes; the study by Fisher and others did not find this to be true. The one consistent, positive trend in the data is that students experiencing high rates of success are somewhat more likely to have a positive attitude toward reading and school.

Increasing Time on Task. There are some research findings that might lead to higher rates of student engagement or higher rates of academic learning time. Crawford and others (1978) reviewed some of the same documents that Kash and Borich reviewed. In particular, they focused on four studies: Brophy and Evertson 1974, McDonald and Elias 1976, Soar and Soar 1973, and Stallings and Kaskowitz 1974. From these studies, it is possible to identify behaviors that reduce time wasted and increase academic learning time.

1. Teachers should have a system of rules that allows pupils to attend to their personal and procedural needs without having to obtain the teacher's permission (Stallings and Kaskowitz 1974, Brophy and Evertson 1974).

2. Teachers should move around the room to monitor pupils' seatwork and communicate to the pupils an awareness of their behavior (Stallings and Kaskowitz 1974, McDonald and Elias 1976).

3. When pupils work independently, teachers should ensure that the assignments are interesting and worthwhile and still easy enough to be completed by each pupil working without teacher direction (Stallings and Kaskowitz 1974, McDonald and Elias 1976).

4. Teachers should minimize such activities as giving directions and organizing the class for instruction by writing the daily schedule on the board, ensuring that pupils know where to go, what to do, and so forth (McDonald and Elias 1976, Soar and Soar 1973).

5. Teachers should make abundant use of textbooks, workbooks, and other paper-and-pencil activities, which are associated with higher pupil achievement. Games, toys, and machines are associated with lower pupil achievement (McDonald and Elias 1976, Stallings and Kaskowitz 1974, Brophy and Evertson 1976).

6. Teachers should avoid "timing errors," that is, they should prevent misbehaviors from continuing long enough to increase in severity or spread to and affect other children (Brophy and Evertson 1974).

All of these teaching practices, particularly for independent seatwork, are recommended on the basis of the findings of the correlational studies cited. They make good sense as well (see Gage and Berliner 1979).

DIRECT AND INDIRECT TEACHING

Kash and Borich try to deal with the notions of direct and indirect teaching — two vague terms. Contrary evidence exists for either side of the debate. Kash and Borich state that indirect teaching is negatively correlated with achievement at lower elementary grade levels and across levels of socioeconomic status. Another investigator, Gene Glass, a well-respected psychologist and methodologist, has reviewed the literature on indirectness and found a positive correlation of .26 between measures of indirectness and student achievement in the elementary grades. The correlation goes up to .32 if the upper-grade levels are used (Glass and others 1977). Thus, I would not accept the statement that indirect teaching is negatively correlated with achievement.

It is also worth noting that although more direct instructional methods seem to produce more positive relations with achievement, the differences between the direct and indirect methods are minimal. In a recent review of studies of formal and informal education, Peterson (1979) performed a meta-analysis of the extant literature and found a positive effect for formal instruction on many of the traditional outcome measures. She also found an effect for informal instruction on some affective outcomes. Differences between the formal and informal instructional situations on the more traditional outcome measures were really quite small. Thus, supposedly large differences in philosophy and beliefs about how children should be educated seem to produce only small differences on the traditional tests of achievement. I think it might be best if we all avoid worrying too much about formal and informal instruction, direct or indirect teaching, and so on, until we have terms that are more precise. This area is open to misinterpretation because of the sloppiness of the concepts. It is therefore hard to draw conclusions from these studies.

TEACHER QUESTIONING

Kash and Borich report that the research has not substantiated the fact that higher-order questioning contributes to pupil gains in learning. A recent meta-analysis of that research reaches a different conclusion. Students of mine, Redfield and Rousseau (in press), show a large positive effect size for questioning. Despite a paucity of significant differences favoring questioning treatments, when taken as a pool of replicates, the average effect size is substantial.

The amount of time allotted for a response is one aspect of questioning that teachers need to be concerned about. The research of Rowe (1974) has revealed that a teacher's pause after a question is asked is an important variable in classroom instruction. She has found that teachers should wait longer (at least three seconds) than they customarily wait (about one second) after asking a question before they repeat the question, call on another student, or say anything. Increasing this wait-time from one second to more than three seconds has several effects on student responses: (a) the length of response increases; (b) the number of unsolicited but appropriate responses increases; (c) failures to respond decrease; (d) confidence, as reflected in decrease of inflected (questionlike tones of voice) responses, increases; (e) incidence of speculative responses increases, (f) incidence of child-to-child comparisons of data increases; (g) incidence of evidence-inference statements increases; (h) the frequency of student questions increases; (i) responses from students rated by teachers as relatively slow increases; (j) the variety of verbal type moves made by students increases (Rowe 1974, p. 81).

FEEDBACK

Kash and Borich consider the positive effects of feedback. In the study by Fisher and others (1978), academic feedback proved to be a key teaching behavior. Higher amounts of academic feedback to pupils result in better pupil performance and achievement.

INDIVIDUALIZED INSTRUCTION

On the issue of small group and individualized instruction, addressed by these authors, I must note that the greatest problem is not with the theory of individualized instruction but with its practice. In studying engaged time in classes, I have found that some of those classes labeled "individualized" were the least efficient in terms of getting students to attend to tasks. It takes an exceptionally skilled teacher to perform well in an individualized instructional setting. The teacher has to move about the class rapidly; follow the work of a number of students, each of whom is doing a unique project; attend to classroom activities and behavioral difficulties simultaneously; have a higher tolerance for movement and noise than most other teachers; and so forth. The result is that many teachers claim to run an individualized class when in fact students are in three different groups, working in a set system for each group. A lot of individual seatwork occurs. Students are often alone and often unsupervised. But this is not individualized instruction.

STRUCTURING

Kash and Borich did not comment on structuring, which I believe to be one of the few variables that make a difference for children. Structuring includes giving directions, setting the stage, telling people what to do, and letting people know what is expected of them. The study by Fisher and others points out the importance of structuring behaviors. All too frequently in classrooms many children do not know what they are supposed to do. Good teachers give clear and concise instructions rapidly. Students need this kind of structuring.

CONTENT COVERAGE

Another variable in which I have faith but which is not given attention in the review by Kash and Borich is content coverage. In the recently completed study of instructional dimensions (Cooley and Leinhardt 1978), the variable "opportunity to learn" was extensively examined. Opportunity to learn is related to the issue of content coverage. In studies by McDonald and Elias (1976), Good and Grouws (1979), Borg (1979), and others, content coverage is a powerful variable. If students are not exposed to fractions, then students cannot do well on tests of fractions. If students do not learn to identify adjectives, then they cannot do well on a test asking for the identification of adjectives. It appears that teachers who can keep the content coverage high while, at the same time, keeping the success rate high are those who are most successful in elementary school. Cooley and Leinhardt (1978) note, "In summary, the major generalization with respect to classroom processes must be that the most useful construct in explaining achievement gain is the opportunity that the children had to learn the skills assessed in the achievement test" (p. 32). Opportunity is high when allocated time is high, engaged time in that content area is high, content coverage in that subject is broad, and the time and content choices match the depth and breadth of the achievement tests used in assessing instruction.

DISCUSSION

What Kash and Borich and many others have tried to do is to identify variables that can be useful for teacher training or teacher evaluation. The problem, as Gage and Berliner (1979) point out, is that when these variables are identified they are often thought of as single entities. And it is not the single variable that is important but the interplay of variables with each other. By dealing with the research on one teacher behavior variable at a time, we appear to be saying that the frequency of one kind of teacher behavior is crucial in teaching. But, just as in music, it is not the frequency of single behaviors (notes) that determines the whole effect (the melody). It is the combinations, sequences, rhythms, and pace of what the teacher does (and hence what the students do) that also makes a difference between effective and ineffective teaching.

At times . . . I feel that the teacher is being conceived almost as a swordsman who lays about the learner with his repertory of sharp-pointed skills, each of which will have a mechanical effect on learning outcomes. The expectation seems to be that if he pushes on the learner with a certain kind of question, then a certain kind of learning will pop out and we will be able to see it quickly and clearly. Such is not the nature of the interaction between learning environments and learners. It is very rare that any one skill (any single sword thrust) or any stylistic characteristic will stand out as the cause of the learning. Even where we find that increased learning is associated with the presence of a certain kind of skill or style in teaching, it is very likely that the reason is because that skill or aspect of style is an index of a much larger complex of behaviors that signals the presence of a certain kind of environment [Joyce 1975, p. 62].

Unfortunately, research workers are only beginning to invent ways of understanding teaching in more subtle, multivariate, and sophisticated ways. In the meantime, we are forced by what research is available to deal with teaching as if one dimension of teaching behavior could make a difference. That approach is not completely fruitless. We have strongly suggestive evidence that some single kinds of behavior are desirable and others are undesirable. Teachers should guide their interactions with students in classroom teaching in accordance with these findings, which are based on better research evidence than has previously been available.

REFERENCES

Borg, Walter R. "Teacher Coverage of Academic Content and Pupil Achievement." *Journal of Educational Psychology* 71 (October 1979): 635–45.

Brophy, Jere E., and Evertson, Carolyn M. *Process-Product Correlations in the Texas Teacher Effectiveness Study: Final Report.* Research Report no. 74–4. Austin: Research and Development Center for Teacher Education, University of Texas, 1974.

Cooley, William W., and Leinhardt, Gaea. *The Instructional Dimensions Study: Final Report.* Pittsburg, Pa.: Learning Research and Development Center, University of Pittsburgh, August 1978.

Crawford, John: Gage, N. L.; Corno, Lyn; Stayrook, Nicholas; Mitman, Alexis; Schunk, D.; and Stallings, Jane. *An Experiment on Teacher Effectiveness and Parent-Assisted Instruction in the Third Grade. Three Volumes.* Stanford, Calif.: Center for Educational Research, Stanford University, 1978.

Fisher, Charles W.; Berliner, David C.; Filby, Nikola; Marliave, Richard; Cahen, Leonard S.; Dishaw, Marilyn M.; and Moore, Jeffry L. *Teaching and Learning in the Elementary School: A Summary of the Beginning Teacher Evaluation Study.* BTES Report VII-1. San Francisco, Calif.: Far West Laboratory for Research and Development, September 1978.

Gage, N. L., and Berliner, David C. *Educational Psychology.* Chicago: Rand McNally, 1979.

Glass, Gene V; Coulter, D.; Hartley, S.; Hearsold, S.; Kahl, S.; Kalk, J.; and Sherritz, L. *Teacher "Indirectness" and Pupil Achievement: An Integration of Findings.* Boulder, Colo.: Laboratory for Educational Research, 1977.

Good, Thomas L., and Grouws, Douglas. "The Missouri Mathematics Effectiveness Project: An Experimental Study in Fourth-Grade Classrooms." *Journal of Educational Psychology* 71 (June 1979): 335–62.

Joyce, Bruce R. "Listening to Different Drummers: Evaluating Alternative Instructional Modes." In *Competency Assessment, Research, and Evaluation: A Report of a National Conference,* pp. 61–81. Albany, N.Y.: Multistate Consortium on Performance Based Teacher Education, 1975.

McDonald, Frederick, and Elias, Patricia. *The Effects of Teaching Performance on Pupil Learning, Beginning Teacher Evaluation Study: Phase II, Final Report.* Vol. 1. Princeton, N.J.: Educational Testing Service, 1976.

Peterson, Penelope L. "Direct Instruction Reconsidered." In *Research on Teaching: Concepts, Findings, and Implications,* edited by Penelope L. Peterson and Herbert J. Walberg, pp. 57–69. Berkeley, Calif.: McCutchan, 1979.

Redfield, D. L., and Rousseau, E. W. "A Meta-Analysis of Experimental Research in Teacher Questioning Behavior." *Review of Educational Research,* 51 (Summer 1981): 237–45.

Rowe, Mary B. "Wait-Time and Rewards as Instructional Variables, Their Influence on Language, Logic, and Fate Control: Part 1 — Wait-Time." *Journal of Research in Science Teaching* 11, no. 2 (1974): 81–94.

Soar, Robert S., and Soar, Ruth M. *Classroom Behavior, Pupil Characteristics, and Pupil Growth for the School Year and for the Summer.* Gainesville: Institute for Development of Human Resources, University of Florida, 1973. (Mimeograph.)

Stallings, Jane A., and Kaskowitz, David H. *Follow-Through Classroom Observation Evaluation 1972-73.* Menlo Park, Calif.: Stanford Research Institute, 1974.

4

Pupil Personnel Staff

GARRY R. WALZ

The search strategy adopted for this chapter was designed to provide comprehensive coverage of all relevant sources of data, documented and experiential, regarding guidance and pupil personnel services. To carry out this approach, we conducted a computerized search of ERIC and several other national data bases. In addition, we contacted personally a number of state directors of pupil personnel services and asked them to contribute documents and resources relating to pupil personnel services.

A dual analytical approach, comprising two strategies, is used here. The first strategy examines the materials identified by the search and extracts and synthesizes the major trends, developments, and findings from them. This examination provides an ideal base from which to draw inferences and generate recommendations. The second strategy considers the extent of coverage of different critical topics in an area and notes which areas are emphasized and which are neglected. This approach deals with the emphases present in the literature, rather than with the content of the material. Using the first approach, I address the extant findings regarding pupil personnel staffing; using the second, I discuss emphases and gaps in the literature on pupil personnel services. The combination of strategies gives a comprehensive overview of the scope and content of the literature.

NATIONAL DATA BASE SEARCH RESULTS

The search of the ERIC data base provided forty-six pages with a total of 106 citations and covered over 200,000 documents (the entire ERIC collection since 1967) and approximately 400 educational journals. The total number of citations may seem small, but analysis of them produced several interesting findings.

First, the literature on pupil personnel services abounds in opinion papers and articles based on personal viewpoints. Overviews of pupil personnel services and descriptions of various facets of pupil personnel services comprise the bulk of the literature.

Second, most articles under the general rubric of pupil personnel services actually deal with a particular pupil personnel service specialty, such as guidance and counseling, rather than with pupil personnel services overall. The focus is typically on the functions or role of the particular specialty rather than on the outcomes produced by a team of pupil personnel workers. Apparently, authors as practitioners identify most closely with their specialties within pupil personnel services, not with their roles as pupil personnel service team members.

Third, by far the best represented of these specialties is guidance and counseling. The number of articles and source materials obtained from the search in the area of guidance exceeds that of all other specialties combined.

Fourth, articles tend to focus on special high-priority educational needs (such as the prevention of drug abuse, dropouts, delinquency, and school violence or promotion of career development); different staff specialties are seen as interchangeable in responding to those needs. These articles identify the needs and discuss strategies for responding to them without much attention to who will respond.

Fifth, and perhaps most important of all for the purposes of this chapter, no identifiable research studies covered the overall efficiency of pupil personnel services or provided empirical data that could be used in responding to some of the central issues. Many of the questions of magnitude and importance raised in this inquiry cannot be answered by direct reference to definitive research studies conducted over a period of years. The research simply does not exist.

GENERALIZATIONS ABOUT GUIDANCE AND PUPIL PERSONNEL SERVICES

Listed here are generalizations regarding guidance and pupil personnel workers, staffing, and program models. They are the result of a synthesis of disparate sources of information and research.

1. In many situations pupil personnel specialists operate relatively independently of each other, with some located at the school level and others located at the system level.

2. There is great interest in implementing the "team approach," which usually involves the creation of a master plan for pupil personnel services, the presence of a systemwide pupil personnel services director vested with strong authority and responsibility, a sufficient budget (7–15 percent of the district budget), and extensive community linkages.

3. Pupil personnel specialists are increasingly expressing the desire to be more involved in the mainstream of the total education process, rather than serving the needs of small numbers of special students.

4. All pupil personnel specialists to some degree — and counselors in particular — seek to develop a more proactive, developmental approach, working toward prevention of problems both within students and within the system.

5. Current legislation, such as P.L. 94–142 (Education of Handicapped Children), is leading to increased emphasis on individualized learning designs and the involvement of parents in educational planning. This trend is influencing the work of all pupil personnel specialists, although specific responsi-

bilities vary considerably from program to program and
from state to state.

6. The functions of pupil personnel workers are increasingly
   performance-based, related to a specific set of objectives and
   evaluated against clearly established criteria.
7. Differential staffing has broadened the types of personnel
   involved in pupil personnel service.
8. The increased scope of function and the broadening of pupil
   personnel staff training have led to greater consultative and
   collaborative relationships with other specialists.
9. Educational technology and media are redefining the roles of
   pupil personnel workers, with greater emphasis on assisting
   students in planning and decision making.
10. Many pupil personnel service programs and activities are
    being controlled more by economic constraints than by sound
    professional and educational judgments, with a resulting ero-
    sion of financial support and resources.

SCHOOL PSYCHOLOGY

Writers and researchers in school psychology generally concur
that this psychological specialty is in ferment. One of the first
expressions of concern that set the tone for much subsequent
writing was the comment that "there is increasing evidence today
that school psychology practice has been weighed in the balance
and found wanting" (Barclay 1971, p. 257). The last decade has
witnessed numerous attempts to evaluate school psychology and
identify appropriate roles and functions, efforts which have been
hindered by a lack of clearcut empirical evidence. Sandoval and
Lambert speak to the problem: "It is ironic that school psychologists have not set the pace in educational evaluation, since they
have a greater range of research skills and broader knowledge of
evaluation than any other employee in most school districts." They
go on to despair current evaluation efforts: "School psychologists
are ubiquitously evaluated by tallies of their various activities.
Counts are made of such things as number of tests given each
month, number and type of people seen" (Sandoval and Lambert
1977, p. 172). Beyond these frequency counts, districts evaluate
psychologists via the principal's or administrator's ratings of the

quality of the psychologist's work, including such areas as punctuality, appearance, and friendliness.

Bardon has suggested that school psychology can be thought of as an "intermediate" specialty, trying to put into practice whatever might benefit schools. School psychology has been characterized primarily by experimentation with new methods and procedures and only secondarily by systematic evaluation of these methods and their relationship to specific outcomes. The result is that school psychology, despite the rigorous activity which has characterized the field, "still is a specialty in disequilibrium" (Bardon 1976, p. 785).

If empirical results for choosing one programmatic approach or practice over another are lacking, the process of making informed choices can still be aided by sifting and sorting the available data about the practice of school psychology. The evaluation of roles and performance of school psychologists can be accomplished through the use of internal or external perspectives. Internal evaluation uses observations of psychologists themselves regarding the efficacy of different programs and practices. External evaluation is implemented by obtaining the observations of professional persons outside the field.

Internal Evaluation

The differing roles of school psychologists form one area of investigation. In reviewing responses to two major roles (consultant and traditional), Fairchild (1976) discovered that he was more responsive to requests from school personnel when using the consultant role, but that teachers rated both roles highly and did not distinguish between them.

Interviews with school psychologists from fifty-eight school districts were conducted by Keogh and others (1975). Conclusions from the interviews indicated that school psychologists (a) are well credentialed, (b) express satisfaction with their work, (c) have been trained as teachers (over 50 percent), (d) maintain local rather than professional affiliations, (e) spend the majority of their time in individual testing and related activities, (f) use relatively few tests, (g) believe they have good relationships with other educators, and (h) feel (in a few instances) that additional training is desirable.

Internal evaluations of school psychology are heavily loaded with personal views and basically subjective appraisals. The effectiveness of school psychology depends upon the data and observations obtained from external evaluations.

External Evaluation

A number of studies provide evaluations of school psychology by school principals, teachers, and superintendents. Although these studies may be thought of as "perceptions" rather than measured outcomes, they provide interesting and useful data regarding expectations and judgments of various educators toward the roles and practices of school psychologists.

Teachers. Styles (1965) surveyed teachers' views about the training of school psychologists and its effect on working with children. Teachers tended to see school psychologists in a clinical light and as more knowledgeable about severe emotional disturbances than was actually the case. The results clearly showed that teachers were inaccurate in their judgments of specific tasks school psychologists should undertake. Teachers preferred that school psychologists help them by holding conferences regarding specific pupils and by preparing written reports. Styles concluded that teachers did not hold inappropriate or exaggerated expectations of school psychologists; however, he ascribes a clinical model for school psychologists.

Principals. Principals' ratings versus those made by psychological services supervisors were compared by Lesiak and Lounsbury (1977). Of twelve areas surveyed, eleven were identified as valuable by both groups, with "individual diagnostic" viewed as the most important. The supervisors gave higher ratings to research and the conducting of in-service and preventive programs than did principals. On the other hand, principals rated parental counseling and liaison between the school and the community as more important than did supervisors. Thus, although principals and supervisors agree on most items, some differences do exist between them regarding special emphases for school psychology.

Superintendents. A study by Manley and Manley (1978) compared the personal values and operative goals of school psychologists and school superintendents in Ohio. They found generally similar value systems between the two groups and high agreement on the goals of school psychologists. Notably, superintendents regarded values such as obedience, loyalty, and ambition as more important than did the psychologists. The superintendents also stressed the importance of goals relating to increased learning efficiency and community interaction. In contrast, school psychologists placed greater value on the development of an atmosphere of positive mental health in the school. Manley and Manley believe their study highlights the transitional role of the school psychologists.

Another survey of Ohio school superintendents was conducted by Kaplan, Chrin, and Clancy (1977), who surveyed school administrators' priorities for school psychologists. The superintendents rated psychological diagnosis and child study the highest and research and evaluation of curricula the lowest. These findings are generally in agreement with those of other investigations, but the emphasis on child study is unusual.

A particularly interesting study was conducted by Gilmore and Chandy (1973), who obtained perceptions of school psychologists from teachers, principals, and school psychologists. They found that experienced teachers favored traditional activities, such as testing for special class placement, while newer teachers preferred more novel interventions. The consultant role was viewed as more appropriate for principals and school psychologists than for teachers. School psychologists were valued least by highly experienced teachers.

Models for School Psychology

A different approach to evaluation was adopted by Gilmore (1974), who analyzed five models for school psychology: clinical, psychoeducational, educational programmer, systems-level problem solver, and preventive mental health. In reviewing the models, Gilmore made three points. First, there is a major split between models developed within school psychology, that is, clinical, and those adopted for other areas, that is, systems-level problem solving. Second, the models are practice-oriented. Third, the clinical model is most clearcut with regard to roles and functions. Gilmore strongly recommended further experimentation with all five models rather than a premature identification of one "best" model.

Implications of the Research

The previous review of the research provides a base for determining the most effective utilization of school psychologists.

1. No substantive data document the superiority of one model or approach to school psychology over another. The basis for choice is the congruence between prevailing values and goals of a school system and the selected model. A traditional school system, for instance, would likely find the clinical model closer to the expectations of school personnel and community than the systems-level problem solver or preventive mental health models. Thus, the wisest choice of a model is most likely to reside in the "closeness of fit" between the needs and expectations of a particular school system and the school psychology model.

2. There is a serious and continuing need for communication and planning regarding the role of school psychology, regardless of the model. While school personnel agree generally on appropriate activities for school psychologists, they frequently disagree about priorities. This disagreement stems from a lack of knowledge about what school psychologists do and uncertainty about the greatest school needs. In many cases school personnel cannot see the relationship between particular psychologist activities and school outcomes.

3. School psychologists are increasingly assuming the roles of consultants and system-wide educational program developers. This approach offers the promise of extending the expertise of the school psychologist to have an impact on more school personnel and more areas. Increased use of school psychologists' services, however, is not positively correlated with an estimation of the worth of the services (Gilmore and Chandy 1973). More work with educational personnel might result in less-favorable evaluations of school psychological services.

ELEMENTARY COUNSELING

Interest in the use of group counseling in elementary schools has increased in recent years. The goals for group counseling are varied. Studies on group counseling in elementary schools are grouped into five major areas: (a) improving the sociometric status of pupils, (b) enhancing the ability of pupils to set appropriate minimal goals, (c) assisting pupils in overcoming behavior problems such as low achievement, disciplinary difficulties, and poor verbalization, (d) evaluating the effectiveness of different group counseling methods, and (e) assessing the impact of a statewide elementary guidance and counseling program.

Improving the Sociometric Status of Pupils

Kranzler and others (1966) assessed the results of a combination of group and individual counseling with fourth-grade pupils over a period of eighteen weeks, using sociometric status as the criterion. Students were randomly assigned to one of three treatment conditions: counseling, teacher guidance, and control. The results indicated that pupils who received individual and group counseling became more accepted and liked by their classmates than noncounseled students, and that the measured differences persisted over a period of seven months.

Using similar procedures to those in the previous study but without including individual counseling, Mayer, Kranzler, and Matthes (1967) studied the effects of counseling and teacher guidance upon the peer relationships of fifth- and sixth-grade elementary students. The results showed that neither teacher guidance nor counseling significantly changed the sociometric status of the students. The difference between the Kranzler and the Mayer studies may be attributable to the short amount of counseling time provided in the latter study — a nine-week period versus an eighteen-week period — and it suggests that effective group counseling with school students must be of sufficient duration to have an impact on students.

Enhancing Goal Setting

Warner, Niland, and Maynard (1971) investigated the prevalence of goal discrepancy among elementary students in rural, urban, and suburban settings, as well as the effectiveness of model-reinforcement group counseling in helping students reevaluate their minimal goals. The results demonstrated no significant differences in the proportion of students with discrepant minimal goals in the three locations. The model-reinforcement group counseling approach was significantly more effective in reducing discrepant student goal setting than counselor-led group sessions.

Group Counseling to Help Students Overcome Behavior Patterns

Elementary school children who were persistent discipline problems were counseled in groups for ten weeks by Kelly and Matthews (1971). Change in behavior did not reach statistical significance on either teacher behavior ratings or self-ratings.

Lack of verbal participation by students in elementary classrooms was the object of a study by Tosi and others (1971). A significant increase in unsolicited verbal responses was demonstrated by the experimental subjects after four weeks of participation in behavioral group counseling. These authors also demonstrated that several approaches could effect change but that counseling interventions that focused most directly upon the desired behavior change had the greatest impact.

The effectiveness of group counseling in changing specific problem behaviors with elementary school children and the transference of those changes to the classroom were investigated by Hinds and Roehlke (1970). Their results justify the conclusion that specific behaviors can be changed using group counseling and that these changes will apply to the classroom. However, the resultant transferred changes are less marked than those present in counseling.

Several group counseling studies investigated the effectiveness of different group counseling methods with students. Moulin (1970) examined the effects of client-centered group counseling using play media on the intelligence, achievement, and psycholinguistic abilities of underachieving children in primary school. Results showed that client-centered group counseling was successful in significantly increasing nonlanguage functioning and some aspects of language usage. Crown (1971) compared three group counseling approaches (structured aural, structured visual, and unstructured) used with elementary students. Each of the three methods significantly increased the gains of the experimental subjects over the control subjects on a number of variables, including self-esteem, self-concept, and teacher-rated behavior, but had no significant influence on grades. The data did not clarify which of the three approaches would be most desirable to use with sixth-grade students.

Impact of Statewide Elementary Guidance

Between 1966 and 1976 Florida increased the number of elementary counselors from 9 to almost 800. The impact of elementary guidance in Florida was the focus of a study conducted by Peck and Jackson (1976). Seventy-five counselor units were studied over a period of three years. Among the results were the following: (a) boys tended to receive more counseling than girls; (b) students in the upper or intermediate grades received the most counseling; (c) students showed improvement in grades and a positive increase in self-concept, but not in amount of school attendance; and (d) parents and teachers expressed high support for the elementary counselor on a number of measures.

Conclusions

The following conclusions are warranted based upon the research reviewed.

1. Group counseling can bring about changes in elementary students. Evidence suggests that significant positive gains can be made, but are not limited to, such areas as enhanced school achievement, increased verbalization, overcoming behavior problems, more positive self-concept, improved peer relations, and more realistic goal setting.

2. No elementary guidance or counseling method or intervention seems superior to any other. Counseling interventions directed at bringing about specific behavior changes — verbalizing, for example — are more successful than general interventions based on discussions. The behavior modeling-social reinforcement group counseling approach has a better record of bringing about desired student changes.

3. Group guidance and elementary counseling approaches work effectively with students of differing abilities, ages, achievement, socioeconomic levels, sociometric status, sex, and race. Male students use counseling more than females.

4. The use of significant others such as teachers, parents, and peers can work to reinforce learning attitudes gained in counseling

and facilitate their transfer to broader personal and educational settings.

5. Adequately staffed and implemented elementary guidance programs can win the active support of parents and teachers. The effects are sufficiently visible and immediate to elicit support of elementary guidance over other specialized services.

PUPIL PERSONNEL STAFF RATIOS AND PUPIL OUTCOMES

The literature on pupil personnel services provides no definite statements on either optimum roles or optimum ratios for pupil personnel service specialists. Tindall (n.d., p. 227) suggests that the following staff ratios have earned professional consensus. These recommended ratios are based upon practice and observation and not upon empirical research and do not include important support personnel such as paraprofessionals, counselor aides, and other helping personnel who contribute a great deal to the overall impact of the program:

Pupil personnel staff administrator — 1
Elementary school counselor — 1:600
Secondary school counselor — 1:300
School psychologist — 1:2000
School social worker — 1:2000
School Nurse — 1:2000

Staffing programs rather than schools is a new trend; the type of program determines the number of specialists needed to offer a quality and comprehensive service.

SMALL AND RURAL SCHOOL GUIDANCE

Rural guidance personnel acknowledge that when it comes to implementing effective school guidance programs, small schools have some inherent disadvantages in comparison with their more affluent peers in urban areas. The new emphasis is to try to turn the disadvantages into advantages. Largeness is a mixed blessing, and large schools must grapple with problems that do not concern smaller schools.

Less than half of small schools have the services of a counselor at all. Therefore, new initiatives in small-school guidance stress the importance of involving the full staff in the guidance program, building upon the natural inclination in small schools for everyone to pitch in and help where help is needed. A program developed by Drier (Drier and Altshuld 1978) and his associates has already demonstrated its utility in numerous small-school settings.

CONCLUSION

Pupil personnel services programs make a difference. Students profit from them, as do schools, parents, and the community. And their impact has the potential to increase. Students will need guidance and support even more in the uncertain times ahead. Only diligent attention to the quality of functioning will ensure that pupil personnel services programs remain a vital force. A full commitment to pupil personnel programs as necessary services, combined with a critical attitude that considers their adequacy for each local situation, is a stance that will serve as well.

REFERENCES

Barclay, James R. "Descriptive, Theoretical, and Behavioral Characteristics of Subdoctoral School Psychologists." *American Psychologist* 26 (March 1971): 257–80.

Bardon, Jack I. "The State of the Art (and Science) of School Psychology." *American Psychologist* 31 (November 1976): 785–91.

Crown, M. L. "A Comparison of Three Group Counseling Techniques with Sixth Graders." *Elementary School Guidance and Counseling* 6 (1971): 37–42.

Drier, Harry N., and Altschuld, James W. "Guidance and Counseling Today and Tomorrow: Our Nation's Rural and Small Schools." In *New Imperatives for Guidance*, edited by Garry R. Walz and Libby Benjamin. Ann Arbor, Mich.: ERIC Counseling and Personnel Services Clearinghouse, 1978.

Fairchild, Thomas N. "School Psychological Services: An Empirical Comparison of Two Models." *Psychology in the Schools* 13 (April 1976): 156–62.

Gilmore, George E. "Models for School Psychology: Dimensions, Barriers, and Implications." *Journal of School Psychology* 12 (Summer 1974): 95–101.

Gilmore, George E., and Chandy, J. M. "Educators Describe the School Psychologist." *Psychology in the Schools* 10 (October 1973): 397–403.

Hinds, William C., and Roehlke, Helen J. "A Learning Theory Approach to Group Counseling with Elementary School Children." *Journal of Counseling Psychology* 17 (January 1970): 49–55.

Kaplan, Marvin S.; Chrin, Michael; and Clancy, Barbara. "Priority Roles for School Psychologists as Seen by Superintendents." *Journal of School Psychology* 15 (Spring 1977): 75–80.

Kelly, Eugene W., Jr., and Matthews, D. B. "Group Counseling with Discipline — Problem Children at Elementary School Level." *School Counselor* 18 (March 1971): 273–78.

Keogh, Barbara K.; Kukic, S. J.; Becker, L. D.; McLoughlin, R. J.; and Kukic, M. B. "School Psychologists' Services in Special Education Programs." *Journal of School Psychology* 13 (Summer 1975): 142–48.

Kranzler, Gerald D.; Mayer, George R.; Dyer, Calvin O.; and Munger, Paul F. "Counseling with Elementary School Children: An Experimental Study." *Personnel and Guidance Journal* 44 (May 1966): 944–49.

Lesiak, Walter J., and Lounsbury, Esther. "Views of School Psychological Services: A Comparative Study." *Psychology in the Schools* 14 (April 1977): 185–88.

Manley, T. Roger, and Manley, E. T. "A Comparison of the Personal Values and Operative Goals of School Psychologists and School Superintendents." *Journal of School Psychology* 16 (Summer 1978): 99–109.

Mayer, G. Roy; Kranzler, Gerald D.; and Matthes, William A. "Elementary School Counseling and Peer Relations." *Personnel and Guidance Journal* 46 (December 1967): 360–65.

Moulin, Eugene K. "The Effects of Client-Centered Group Counseling Using Play Media on the Intelligence, Achievement, and Psycholinguistic Abilities of Underachieving Primary School Children." *Elementary School Guidance and Counseling* 5 (December 1970): 85–89.

Peck, Hugh I., and Jackson, Billie P. "Do We Make a Difference: A State Evaluation." *Elementary School Guidance and Counseling* 10 (March 1976): 171–76.

Sandoval, Jonathan, and Lambert, N. M. "Instruments for Evaluating School Psychologists' Functioning and Service." *Psychology in the Schools* 14 (April 1977): 172–79.

Styles, William A. "Teachers' Perceptions of the School Psychologist's Role." *Journal of School Psychology* 3 (Summer 1965): 23–27.

Tindall, J. "The Guidance Program and Pupil Personnel Services." In American Personnel and Guidance Association, *The Status of Guidance and Counseling in the Nation's Schools*. Washington, D.C.: American Personnel and Guidance Association, n.d.

Tosi, Donald J., Upshaw, K.; Lande, A.; and Waldron, M. A. "Group Counseling with Nonverbalizing Elementary Students." *Journal of Counseling Psychology* 18 (September 1971): 437–40.

Warner, Richard W.; Niland, T. M.; and Maynard, P. E. "Model-Reinforcement Group Counseling with Elementary School Children." *Elementary School Guidance and Counseling* 5 (May 1971): 248–55.

Discussion

Edwin L. Herr

Walz is quite correct that there is essentially no research on the total effects of pupil personnel services. Most of the research focuses on particular specialists working directly with students rather than with each other; some studies involve teachers and counselors working together or independently toward mutual goals. Such information is frequently reported in evaluation studies of career education or in studies of deliberate psychological education. There are studies that focus on the work of school psychologists with mentally retarded, emotionally disturbed, or gifted children. There are also studies of school nurses or other school health personnel with regard to their involvement in health education or in helping unmarried pregnant girls. I am not aware of research on the efforts of school social workers or attendance personnel in relation to truancy, contacts with foster home placements, or other matters of child-family welfare, although there may be studies in those areas.

The point remains, as Walz has suggested, that most of the available research concerns the effectiveness of school counselors, followed by that pertinent to school psychologists. Almost nothing is addressed to the interactive effects or comparative effects of the pupil personnel services staff working in concert to solve specific student problems.

Given the caveats just expressed, however, the existing research base has some useful implications for planning programs of pupil personnel services and for preparing practitioners. One frequently has to extrapolate from research on the behavior of school counselors to that of other specialists in pupil personnel work, but as long as one is conscious of the limits on such extrapolation the available research data can be useful. I suggest here some dimensions that I think are pertinent. Although the findings cited come from syntheses of specific research studies during the past two years, only the references to the syntheses are cited; the individual research studies are cited in each synthesis.

THE CHARACTERISTICS OF EFFECTIVE COUNSELORS

Research on which behaviors characterize effective counselors has grown during the past fifteen years. Some but not all of this research has been focused upon counselors in school settings. In general, the research suggests the following:

1. There are therapeutic and nontherapeutic counselors. Both can be identified and trained (unless personality defects preclude) to provide the conditions that produce constructive behavioral and personality change.
2. Regardless of the different theoretical positions that guide the specific techniques used by particular counselors, those counselors considered therapeutic in their interactions with those they counsel share many common characteristics.
3. Experienced counselors, regardless of the theoretical position they were trained in or embraced as neophytes, are more alike than different in their provision of certain interpersonal conditions.
4. Whether conceived as wholly sufficient in their own right, or as minimum essentials to effective counselor-counselee interactions, interpersonal skills basic to therapeutic counselors include accurate empathic understanding, communication of respect, warmth, sincerity, and specific expression.

CHARACTERISTICS OF COUNSELOR EDUCATION PROGRAMS

1. Some counselor education programs are effective and produce growth; others fail. The differences seem to lie with the characteristics (for example, experience, national involvement, and training) and the systematic training in therapeutic skills provided to students.
2. Any type of supervised counseling practicum increases counselor effectiveness on such variables as empathy, reflective listening, and sincerity.

3. Counselors in practicum acquire more skills when the focus is on how they can respond to, rather than how they feel about, the counselee. For such purposes, behavioral approaches, rather than relationship approaches, to practicum supervision are most effective.
4. As the counseling process is dissected into its specific elements (for example, attending behavior, opening an interview) and counselor-candidates are trained systematically to perform them through microcounseling and similar processes, counseling skills are improved.
5. Systematic training of counselor-candidates in process variables, such as empathy and warmth, yields higher levels of such behavior than occurs when there is no such systematic training.
6. The provision of feedback about their performance to counselor-candidates via video- or audiotape is an important stimulus to a critical analysis of relationships and interaction.

COUNSELOR EFFECTS UPON STUDENT ACHIEVEMENT

1. In general, significant differences in academic achievement and in realistic choice of courses of study are found in favor of groups exposed to guidance and counseling as compared with those without such exposure.
2. Elementary school children who have been taught techniques for changing behavior by the elementary school counselor make greater academic gains in school attendance, school achievement, and social behavior than children in the control group.
3. Counseled students in the elementary school make better grades, and their parents report improved attitudes toward school over a three-year period.
4. The importance of desiring what one has chosen, rather than being at the mercy of others without any personal investment in the choice, is a factor in academic success in college; such behavior is aided by guidance.
5. Either group or individual counseling over time helps students whose ability is adequate or better to improve their

scholastic performance if they voluntarily participate in the counseling. Better results are likely if guidance focuses on the causes of underachievement and the steps to change them rather than a general approach.

6. Counselor teams who work closely with teachers, principals, and parents in dealing with emotional or social problems that are interfering with the child's use of his or her intellectual potential are helpful in increasing general levels of academic achievement.

7. Guidance and counseling processes integrated with remedial instruction in mathematics and reading have been found to increase academic achievement significantly.

COUNSELOR EFFECTS UPON STUDENT SELF-CONCEPT AND MENTAL HEALTH

1. Students exposed to guidance tend to organize their concepts about themselves in a more coherent way and to reconcile their differences between ideal and real self-concepts more effectively than other persons.

2. Middle school students who receive guidance designed to improve their interpersonal skills improve their general behavior and interpersonal relationships.

3. Elementary school children given relationship enhancement training by a counselor improve more on empathic acceptance and relationship skills than do children not so trained.

4. Planned guidance activities raise the awareness and the self-concept of sixth-grade children independently of sex, intelligence quotient, or school achievement.

5. Elementary school counselors' consultations with parents positively affect the motivation, self-esteem, and anxiety scores of black elementary school students.

6. Elementary school counselors' consultations with teachers on esprit and intimacy result in gains in self-perceptions and peer acceptance for their students.

7. Parent training groups provided by elementary school counselors improve communication skills in parent-child relationships.

8. Students who have been helped by counselors to evaluate their problems, to analyze their components, and to master them one at a time gain self-confidence.
9. Minority students who are assisted in deciding about vocational objectives typically have more positive self-concepts and higher goals than those who do not have such assistance.
10. The degree of self-esteem possessed by students corresponds to the appropriateness of vocational choice and to high school achievement.
11. A rise in the self-esteem of students exposed to guidance and other counseling is related to reduction in dropout rates, reductions in daily absence, and improvement in conduct and social adjustment.

COUNSELOR EFFECTS UPON STUDENT DECISION MAKING ON CAREER DEVELOPMENT

1. Guidance helps students become competent decision makers, select high school courses, and make high school plans more congruent with their abilities compared to students not exposed to such counsel.
2. Guidance can help students define or commit themselves to educational and occupational actions on the basis of personal values.
3. Decision-making processes can be taught to junior high and senior high school students within a guidance and counseling setting using a variety of modeling techniques, sequential learning exercises, and activities.
4. Directed learning by students of decision-making processes is more effective than nondirected practice. Such directed learning aids students in the transfer of decision-making skills to real-life circumstances outside of guidance and counseling settings.
5. Students counseled in middle school subsequently make more realistic choices in choosing high school courses and seeking part-time work, according to adult jury ratings.
6. Through group problem-solving methods, students can be helped to understand the relationship between educational and vocational development, to clarify goals, and to acquire

skill in identifying and using information for their decision-making needs.

7. Male and female students with identifiable educational goals — reasons related to why they do what they do — consistently are better prepared for college than students who have no such reasons for what they are doing.

CAREER PLANNING

1. Students exposed to systematically planned career guidance classes make greater gains on self-knowledge and its relation to occupations and engage in a greater number of career planning activities than do students who have not participated in such classes, which cover job satisfaction, career planning, values clarification, and other topics.

2. Junior high school students who are provided with guidance programs that are specifically designed to increase knowledge and explore nontraditional jobs do gain compared with control groups.

3. Student users of computer-based career guidance systems make larger gains on such characteristics as degree of planning, knowledge and use of resources for career exploration, awareness of career options and the costs or risks associated with them than the gains made by nonusers.

4. Both individual and group counseling that involves specific training in self-assessment, gathering pertinent career information, and planning skills can enhance student career planning.

5. If students learn about themselves before they are exposed to occupational information, or if they can request such information when they are ready, their career planning is significantly facilitated.

CAREER DEVELOPMENT/CAREER EDUCATION

1. Senior high school girls exposed to guidance programs that emphasize career awareness make significant improvement

in overall career awareness and in factual knowledge of the occupational status of women.

2. Short-term counseling (three sessions) with high school students facilitates the career maturity of these students with regard to such emphases as orientation to decision making, planning, and independence of choice.

3. Guidance films affect high school students' attitudes positively, motivate them to seek additional information, and help them make career choices. These outcomes are strengthened when such films are used as part of a planned guidance program.

4. High school students exposed to model-reinforcement and reinforcement counseling seek external information more intensely than students not so exposed.

5. The use of simulated occupational experience within guidance and counseling programs has positive effects on the occupational knowledge of secondary school students.

6. On criterion measures of self-concept, of academic achievement, and of school attendance, students exposed to career education do as well as or, in most studies, better than comparison students in traditional classes.

ADDITIONAL QUESTIONS

In addition to the types of research findings just reported, several other questions might be asked. Some have been researched; some have not.

What are the effects of the ratio of school counselors or school psychologists to students? So far as I know, and as Walz has indicated, no comparative studies of the differences in the ratios of school counselors or school psychologists to students have been attempted. No empirical base says that the effects upon school achievement of school counselors in the ratio of 250 to 1 will be greater than if the ratio is 400 to 1 or some other increment. Nor are there data suggesting that mentally retarded or gifted students will be better served if school psychologists are in the ratio of 1 to 1,000 students, rather than 1 to 5,000. However, logic suggests that the prevailing national average of 1 counselor per 411 students is too high if each student is expected to receive significant individual attention either for remediation or for personal development. Some data suggest that secondary school students now average sixteen minutes per year with a school counselor (at schools that have counselors); other data report a total of 7 hours of guidance and counseling, compared to 1,200 hours of instruction, during the six years of junior and senior high school (Ginzberg 1971).

In the face of evidence in the previous section that school counselors can make a difference in the school achievement, self-concept, and mental health of students or in the student's decision making and career planning, planners must ask whether ratios of 400:1 or 500:1 are likely to permit school counselors to be effective with all students if that is intended. If not, which children should have access to the resources that are available? Or, can sufficient numbers of school counselors be trained and employed to increase the ratio of counselors to students to levels that are likely to provide more time for counselor-student interaction? Then more students could gain the types of outcomes that school counselors in some schools now produce.

In the absence of specific data about the comparative effects on student behavior of different counselor-student ratios, but in the full awareness that school district reports indicate that such ratios are generally high, many school counselors and, indeed, preparatory institutions are emphasizing school counselor consultation with teachers or parents, rather than directly with pupils. Such schemes allow school counselors to address specific ways to handle student problems; the problems are actually handled by others. Such schemes also allow school counselors to assist teachers or parents in the creation of learning or living environments that are likely to reduce the incidence of student problems. From such a perspective, planners may decide to assign school counselors in proportion to teachers, classrooms, or families, rather than in proportion to students. When making such assignments, however, one must assume that the school counselor will not be working directly with a large number of students. If a counselor does handle many students in addition to counseling parents and teachers, the problem of the school counselor's load is compounded, not divided. In order to assign school counselors to a specific number of classrooms or teachers or families, it is necessary to be clear about how and on what bases they will be evaluated, whose behavior they are expected to affect, and to what ends. Obviously, these criteria will be different from a model in which the school counselor's primary purpose is direct one-to-one contact with students.

Another question which needs to be answered is, under current school counselor-student ratios, how much time should counselors spend on paper work and other routine clerical procedures (for example, writing recommendations, completing reports, maintaining permanent records)? Obviously, the answers would vary from school to school, but, if counselors are spending large amounts of time in such efforts, one alternative would be to provide better clerical support so that school counselors can be free to do what they are trained to do. Such an approach would be more cost-effective than hiring additional school counselors and then assigning them clerical responsibilities that limit their direct contact with students.

Similar questions are pertinent to school psychologists. With regard to ratios and role expectations, are school psychologists used best in consulting with teachers on behalf of special education or learning disabled children? Or should they work primarily with the parents of these children? Should they concentrate on individual intelligence testing as a way of screening students in or out of special education? Should they conduct behavior modification with individual children? One activity does not preclude others, but the expectations associated with each emphasis need to be carefully considered within the context of psychologist-student ratios and in designing performance-based criteria for such personnel.

The background of school counselors and school psychologists has been more visibly addressed in the literature than the background of other members of the pupil personnel services staff. Although much of the discussion is theoretical or rhetorical, there is also research on the issue, particularly regarding school counselors.

For example, since 1967 Pennsylvania has certified school counselors who have neither teaching experience nor teacher training, but who have successfully completed approved programs of counselor education. Baker (1974) and Baker and Herr (1976) have examined school administrators' perceptions of such counselors and their general ability to function within the schools. In terms of job performance, principals could not distinguish between school counselors who were trained as teachers and those who were not. Both types of school counselors were accepted by teachers and were able to work effectively with parents. (The school counselors without teacher training who were included in these surveys had been exposed to extended guidance internships in schools, and they were highly selected on other criteria that distinguish effective school counselors.)

Whether or not school counselors need to be originally trained as teachers or have experience as teachers seems to be well resolved by the existing research: under current conditions and in the schools used as sample sites, school counselors without teacher training or classroom experience have performed well. Even so, the preparation of school counselors' certification standards, and performance criteria influence school counselors' ability to teach or to work more directly with teachers in various collaborations. Of particular significance are the expectations in Public Law 94–142 that school counselors will work closely with teachers and parents in formulating individual educational prescriptions for special education students. In addition, school counselor involvement in career education or deliberate psychological education is making it increasingly necessary for school counselors to teach knowledge or skills that involve a wide range of topics: decision making, occupational opportunities, assertive behavior, self-assessment, job search, interpersonal relationships, and job interviewing. In some cases, the required teaching is done by the school counselor alone in group guidance units or courses, and in other instances it is done directly within the curricula in collaboration with a specific teacher. In either case, the school counselor must be able to organize and present content material effectively, or understand classroom procedures and subject content thoroughly. Such skills and understandings do not necessarily require all of the preparation or experience reflected in teacher training programs, or in actual service as a classroom teacher, but provisions do need to be made for staff development and for performance criteria that reflect the importance of these emerging school counselor roles.

REFERENCES

Baker, Stanley B. "Supervising Principals' Ratings of Their Secondary School Counselors." *Pennsylvania Personnel and Guidance Journal* 5 (1974): 32–34.

Baker, Stanley B., and Herr, Edwin L. "Can We Bury the Myth? Teaching Experience for the School Counselor." *NASSP Bulletin* 60 (November 1976): 114–19.

Ginzberg, Eli. *Career Guidance: Who Needs It, Who Provides It, Who Can Improve It.* New York: McGraw-Hill, 1971.

Herr, Edwin L. "Research in Guidance." In *New Imperatives for Guidance,* edited by Garry E. Walz and Libby Benjamin. Ann Arbor, Mich.: ERIC Counseling and Personnel Services Clearinghouse, 1978.

Herr, Edwin L. *Guidance and Counseling in the Schools: Perspectives on the Past, Present, and Future.* Washington, D.C.: American Personnel and Guidance Association, 1979.

5

Students

MARTIN L. MAEHR
AND ANN C. WILLIG

Aside from death and taxes, there seem to be few things more certain than the criticism of our social institutions, including the public schools. Writing in the April 1, 1979, edition of the *New York Times*, English psychologist Kathryn Tidrick expresses this opinion:

Why do intelligent and competent Americans who have spent many years in a series of reputable educational institutions often appear to English people to be fundamentally uneducated? I think it's because they work too hard. From an early age they have spent so much time writing term papers, studying for tests and pursuing independent research projects that they have never had a moment to themselves. As a result (I must say this even if it sounds insufferable), they lack that sense of measure, that instinct for what is of value in the life of the mind, that only comes with years of productive idleness. I mean by "productive idleness" time spent in undirected reading, uninterpreted thinking, and aimless talk. It is in these idle hours that an intelligent person becomes an educated person.

Tidrick goes on to lament the fact that the overburdening of children with homework is often "taken as proof of the school's

The authors are indebted to John Nicholls and Jane Maehr for helpful suggestions and to Joyce Fitch for bibliographic assistance.

essential seriousness." In dismay, she observes that all the waking hours of her own daughter are programmed by school assignments, leaving her no time "to educate herself." And she worries about the long-range effects: "What kind of person will her daughter grow up to be if all her waking hours are programmed for her in this way?"

But not everyone agrees with Tidrick. In fact, a common and vociferously stated opinion in the United States today expresses just the opposite — that schools are not tough enough. They grant too much freedom to students and they are typically more play than work — such is the basic theme that winds its way through the arguments put forward in support of competency-based education and the "back-to-basics" movement. These differing points of view prompt attention to a number of controversial issues that are critical in the formulation of educational policy and practice — issues that need to be examined carefully in terms of the available evidence. This chapter is concerned directly with one of the issues that has, in part, evolved from such debate: to what degree should the student be expected to initiate and control the teaching-learning process?

The issue is not just one of freedom but an ultimate concern with the educational outcomes that result from different types of student and teacher roles. These outcomes are examined here as they relate to two interdependent facets of the issue: a consideration of how much initiative and responsibility one should or can expect from students and, conversely, how much control and direction should be exerted over students by teachers and the schools.

OUTCOMES OF VARYING DEGREES OF TEACHER CONTROL

The psychologist Kurt Lewin, perhaps more than any other person, formulated questions concerning teacher control in such a way that workable answers could be obtained. In a now classic study on the topic, Lewin, Lippitt, and White (1939) not only produced interesting findings but established certain principles for educational practice that have worn well with time. Although the original study is not the last word on the subject, the conclusions reached by the researchers are, in general outline, still relevant — as the review of the literature which follows indicates. Basically, the study was a straightforward comparison of three organizational climates on group morale, productivity, and general behavior. The groups were composed of ten-year-old boys who were members of after-school "hobby clubs." The experimental differences between the groups resided in the fact that the adult leader played one of three different roles: (a) an *autocrat* who controlled virtually every facet of the activity, (b) a *laissez-faire leader* who more or less let the children do as they pleased, and (c) a *democratic leader* who, while taking an active role in the group's activities, encouraged participation and decision making on the part of the children. Results indicated clearly that the worst climate from almost any of the three perspectives was the laissez-faire condition, as might be expected. More interesting was that both the authoritarian and the democratic groups were, for all practical purposes, equally productive in the presence of the leader. But perhaps the most intriguing result was the behavior of the children when the leader was absent. Focusing particularly on the authoritarian and democratic groups, the researchers found that children in the democratic group were little affected by the absence of the leader. They seemed to work in about the same manner whether or not he was present. In contrast, the behavior of the children in the autocratic group seemed to be dependent on the presence of the leader. When he was absent, productivity not only decreased significantly but the general decorum of the group was drastically affected. The authoritarian leader apparently did not allow or encourage the development of reasons in the students themselves for the task at hand. The development of self-control and independent purpose in the children was apparently sacrificed in maintaining a tight rein.

This study focuses attention on certain basic issues and a host of questions. The major question is essentially one of definition: what is the essence of these three leadership styles or social climates? Of what elements are they composed and what form do they take in classrooms? These questions, not readily answered, will be a continuing challenge for educational research for some time. The research to date, however, has indicated some components of classroom climates that may be important. One such component, which again reflects degrees of control over or by students, concerns the way in which evaluation is carried out: Who controls it and in what way is it done? And, more importantly, what are the outcomes of different evaluation strategies with their differing loci of control?

OUTCOMES OF DIFFERENT EVALUATION   STRATEGIES

The effects of evaluation practices on classroom achievement has been a subject of considerable research in recent times. One line of this research has focused particularly on the amount of control over the evaluation that is granted to the student. Illustrative here is a series of studies conducted by Maehr and his colleagues. In an initial study (Maehr and Stallings 1972), the format involved having samples of middle school students work on "easy" and "hard" problem-solving tasks under either an "external" or "internal" evaluation condition. In the latter condition, stress was placed on performing the task for its own sake, with minimal threat that a teacher or some significant other would ever see the results. Even though the students received information about the correctness or incorrectness of their responses, they were not given comparative information on the quality of their responses nor were they led to believe that the quality of their performance was to be known to others. Feedback was to serve whatever intrinsic reasons they had. In many ways, the task was structured like play rather than work and that is how it was described to the participants. The external evaluation condition took the form of a standard classroom test in which the external evaluation of students' performance was specifically stressed. The results were instructive and, to some degree, surprising. The performance level of students was not necessarily increased by the threat of external evaluation. Only in the case of boys who were identified as high in "achievement motivation" was there an indication that external evaluation enhanced performance. Following performance, students showed differing continuing interests in the tasks, depending on the condition in which they had participated. The internal condition encouraged a continued interest in returning to work on the hard tasks, especially for students high in achievement motivation.

In a series of studies that followed, these results were expanded and enhanced. Particularly noteworthy here was a study conducted by Salili and others (1976) in which the cross-cultural generalizability of the Maehr and Stallings findings was tested. The instigating question for this study was whether external evaluation is detrimental only to children in countries where they grow up in a democratic society, experience "progressive" education or are, perhaps, coddled. Searching for a society that presents a contrasting picture, where education occurs in a more strict, autocratic atmosphere and where children are accustomed to frequent evaluation, Salili and others decided to focus on Iran. Here they replicated the Maehr and Stallings study with Iranian school children and, surprisingly, they obtained essentially the same results as in the original study. Although immediate performance was seemingly unaffected by variation in evaluation conditions, continued interest or motivation for working on the tasks at a later time was significantly and negatively affected. These results were again replicated with samples of United States subjects (Kremer 1976). Moreover, a secondary analysis of the data obtained in Iran and the United States further stresses the essential similarity of the effects of external and internal evaluation, regardless of culture.

All in all, placing a person in a situation in which the external control of evaluation is emphasized can have important negative effects on the development of an appropriate orientation toward learning. The combination of this finding together with recent research on intrinsic motivation (for example, Lepper and Greene 1978) suggests that an emphasis on externally determined evaluation will likely reduce motivation, especially when a child already has an interest in the learning task. The implications of this are fairly self-evident. Many educators, parents, and administrators assume that children will work if and only if external evaluation (grades, teacher approval, parental reward) is present; even bribery is not unheard of. Perhaps performance in the classroom will be maintained or even facilitated to some degree by external evaluation. However, these studies raise questions: Will this maintenance or facilitation of classroom performance occur at the price of reducing continued interest in the task? Is external evaluation detrimental to the inclination to work on a task on one's own, outside the context of formal schooling? These questions cannot be answered without a simultaneous consideration of the converse: student control, choice, and initiative.

OUTCOMES OF STUDENT CHOICE AND INITIATIVE

The other side in the distinction of classroom climates has to do with the degree of participation that the student has in decisions concerning what is to happen in the course of schooling. A number of studies have examined the effects of varying degrees of student participation in essential classroom/educational decisions. Although the results are not as simple and straightforward as one might like, they are sufficient to stress that the degree of participation in decision making is a variable that can significantly affect educational outcomes. In particular, it may well have its most important positive effects on such goals as attitudes, motivation, and personal development. It may, however, prove problematic when considered from a more limited perspective.

Some of the studies in this line have focused narrowly on the role of student participation and choice as it affects immediate, short-term educational objectives. Although these studies do not yield unequivocal conclusions, they appear to indicate that a large degree of student choice or participation in scholastic decision making may limit (or at least not enhance) short-term gains in achievement. These limitations produced by increased student choice can be seen in recent comparisons of "direct" versus "informal" approaches to instruction. Thus, Rosenshine and Berliner (1978) call attention to what is coming to be recognized as a key fact of education, namely that achievement test scores are associated with the amount of time students spend on the relevant learning tasks. This conclusion may seem more than obvious to some, but its importance is only recognized when it is observed that democratic or informal classrooms may allow for more off-task behavior. Recall that in the Lewin, Lippitt, and White study increased student participation in the democratic classroom had its greatest impact on productivity and morale at a later time, when the children were on their own. Positive effects on immediate productivity did not exceed those in the autocratic children.

Controversy over the merits of "open" versus "traditional" classrooms has also produced evidence on this point. Horwitz (1979) reviewed a host of studies; 102 of these studies addressed, among other things, the outcome of academic achievement. Although the results were decidedly mixed, open education does not appear, overall, to be superior to traditional education in determining short-term academic achievement. On the other hand, it does not appear to be inferior.

But to return to an essential point: There are positive outcomes other than short-term achievement, such as the enhancement of motivation and a long-term interest in achievement. We have already referred to these in discussing both the Lewin, Lippitt, and White study and the studies dealing with the effects of external evaluation. Further evidence regarding these positive outcomes and the role of increased student participation in classroom decisions is found again in the literature on open versus traditional classrooms. Many of the studies reviewed by Horwitz compared open and traditional classrooms not only in terms of academic achievement but also in terms of self-concept, attitude toward school, creativity, independence and conformity, curiosity, anxiety and adjustment, locus of control, and cooperation. Although results in these studies varied, when they did show significant differences between the two approaches in any of these nonachievement categories, they most often favored open education. Results on the independence-conformity and cooperation dimensions clearly favored the open school. Less overwhelming, but still evident, were the findings on attitude toward school as well as creativity and curiosity — all of which tended to favor the open school. In short, it seems that the major problem with open schools — if indeed there is one — is that they cannot consistently demonstrate better performance on standardized achievement test scores than can traditional schools.

It is clear when we refer back to our initial question — which asks to what degree students should be expected to initiate and control the teaching-learning process — that the answer depends upon the ultimate outcomes desired by the educational policy makers. We favor such desirable long-term outcomes as positive attitudes toward learning and continuing motivation for achievement. We have already seen that these outcomes are most likely to be produced by educational procedures that encourage student participation in classroom decisions and academic evaluation.

Researchers cannot be content with such broad, generalized conclusions, however. The next step is to discover the mediating variables, or the means by which student participation has its effects. In this respect, many believe that enhancement of motivation occurs as a result of the effect that participation has on the student's perceptions.

STUDENT PERCEPTIONS AS A CRUCIAL INTERVENING VARIABLE

Recently, considerable theoretical and empirical effort has been devoted to explicating the role of students' perceptions of a situation in determining subsequent choices and behaviors. The basic hypothesis has been that motivation, and ultimately achievement, will be enhanced by procedures that imbue in the student a sense of control over an outcome. Evaluation practices affect such perceptions of personal control and therewith affect motivation. But the importance of perceptions of personal control or responsibility as a mediating variable has perhaps been demonstrated most dramatically in one of the more extensive field studies in education.

de Charms (1976) employed this hypothetical variable in a most creative way in a school setting. He tested the idea that perceptions of control increase motivation in the most difficult of school settings — an inner-city school. Basically, de Charms conducted an extensive and involved training course designed to teach teachers, and subsequently their students, the effects of feeling like a "pawn" as opposed to an "origin" of their own behavior. The training included suggestions on how educational practices could affect such perceptions. A primary feature of this program, which was designed to change pawn perceptions to origin perceptions, was not unlike the democratic climate described by Lewin and his colleagues. That is, stress was placed on participation, on giving students (as well as teachers) a degree of choice and freedom to decide what would happen in the classroom. The overall results of this program were encouraging. As students developed a greater sense of being an origin — as they perceived themselves to be initiators and controllers of their fate — not only their morale but also their classroom achievement improved.

Parallel to de Charms's work is a large and ever-growing body of literature that similarly stresses the role of perceptions of personal responsibility or control in the creation of effective classroom behavior. That literature grows out of two lines of work — experimental work with the phenomenon of "learned helplessness," and research associated more generally with "attribution theory."

The learned helplessness work began in the realm of animal psychology with investigations into the effects of uncontrollable aversive stimuli, usually electric shock. The basic paradigm was to compare post-shock anxiety levels and escape-learning speed in animals given a mechanism for escaping shock and animals without such a control. Animals that experience uncontrollable shock demonstrate higher levels of anxiety and take longer to learn to escape shock when it subsequently is controllable than do animals that cannot escape shock. This phenomenon has been found in fish, rats, cats, dogs, and a variety of other animals (Seligman, Maier, and Solomon 1969).

Similar paradigms have been used with human beings and some of these have focused on the effects of perceived rather than actual control. For example, Glass, Reim, and Singer (1971) asked college students to perform paper and pencil tasks while a loud, noxious noise interrupted them intermittently. Some of the students were provided with a button and told that they could terminate the noise at any time, although the experimenter would prefer that they did not. Although no subjects actually used the button control, those who had this possibility and perception of control showed a greater tolerance for frustration and did a better job on the paper and pencil tasks than did those students without a control button.

Dweck and her colleagues (Dweck 1977) brought the learned helplessness paradigm into the schoolroom. Using a paradigm that was, in many respects, similar to the animal experiments where uncontrollable aversive stimuli are followed by stimuli that suddenly are controllable, they demonstrated that certain children who were assigned insoluble problems from one of two experimenters were unable subsequently to solve even easy problems for the experimenter who had originally given the insoluble problems. Dweck's explanation was that the children, like the animals in the studies by Seligman, Maier, and Solomon, had also developed a sense of helplessness, which prevented them from demonstrating their potential.

Further investigations by Dweck and her colleagues sought to determine why some children succumb to learned helplessness and why others do not. At this point, the learned helplessness studies tie in with attribution theory; they focus on the causes the children used in explaining their successes and failures and how these related to performance. Dweck found that children who attributed their failures to a lack of ability (something over which they had little control), were more apt to fall apart in the face of failure than children who attributed their failures to a lack of effort (something over which they do have control). Thus, the perception of one's control (or lack of control) in a situation proves to be crucial to behavior that leads to positive and negative outcomes. But Dweck and her group did not stop with this finding. They went on to demonstrate that children can be trained to change lack-of-ability attributions to lack-of-effort attributions, with a subsequent improvement in problem-solving skills and persistence in the classroom. This work has been complemented by other investigators (Andrews and Debus 1978, Wang and Stiles 1976) who have also shown that children's perceptions of the amount of control over outcomes can be changed. Thus, perceptions of personal responsibility or control are not only critical for future achievement but they are also teachable. Researchers are now turning their attention to how classroom teachers, with the kinds of resources generally assigned to them, can in fact enhance those attributions that lead to optimum motivation.

FREEDOM IN LEARNING: AN IMPORTANT CAVEAT

Although the review of the literature thus far certainly suggests the desirability of essential student participation and control in the educational process, at least for long-term gains, one essential caution must be noted. Different individuals may function optimally with differing degrees of control. For example, open education may have different effects on different persons. To oversimplify: it may be good for some but bad for others. If this is indeed the case, it is not surprising that a large number of the studies yield conflicting results. That such mismatches between educational environments and dispositions of students are critical factors is a proposal that has been given consideration from a number of different perspectives. Perhaps few have pursued this issue with greater intensity, at least in regard to open education, than Hunt (1975). Basically, Hunt has shown how individuals at different developmental levels respond differently to variations in the amount of imposed structure or freedom in their environment. In short, some people need more structure than others, particularly if they are to behave efficiently in terms of achievement goals. This essential point is revealed in a study by Fyans and Maehr (1979). In this study, students who attributed successful achievement to their ability were, when given a choice, the ones who chose tasks that would further the development of their competence. Those who were less sure of their competence tended to avoid such tasks. This general finding is complementary to that obtained by Shiffler, Lynch-Sauer, and Nadelman (1977) on the relationship of self-concept and task orientations in informal classrooms. In the Fyans and Maehr study a generally positive concept of self was associated with on-task, achievement-related behavior. Obviously, the school cannot allow those who lack a sense of competence to avoid the kind of challenges that will develop their competence. If self-direction alone does not encourage the proper confrontation with experiences and tasks that encourage intellectual growth, teacher-directed action must intervene. Fyans and Maehr (1979) conclude:

The broader perspective that may be emerging in these studies is that the kind of freedom of choice that is granted in so-called "open" classrooms is warranted for certain kinds of students: those who have a sense of competence. These students can be trusted to do the kinds of things that will facilitate intellectual growth with minimum direction and control on the part of the teacher. Indeed, given such a positive orientation toward achievement it would be dangerous to risk ruining a good thing by exercising anything more than minimal control over their behavior. Quite clearly, for other children, such freedom may have distinctly negative effects. Specifically, those students who lack a sense of competence are not likely to attend to that which facilitates intellectual growth. These students can hardly be left to their own devices [p. 505].

The adherents to the open classroom may perhaps argue that informal education allows the teacher to structure different environments for different students. Perhaps this is true, at least in theory, but giving parents, students, and teachers more specific options in instructional style may be the more workable way in which to match appropriate environments with students. The as yet unpublished experience of Bodine and Hill (1977) attests to the feasibility of such matching.

But the open classroom is only an example of a larger set of

principles of concern here: the outcomes of participation, freedom, and control. What emerges in this discussion is a tacit acceptance of the notion that proper self-direction on the part of students
is possible. Where it does occur the benefits are real, particularly in
terms of long-term achievement and educational goals that extend
beyond the classroom. Of course, the degree of student participation cannot be the same for all students or the same in all situations.
Truly creative teaching may be a matter of transferring control to
the student at an appropriate time and under workable conditions.
We do not assume that, regardless of developmental level or situation, the child should be in control. But the transfer of control from
teacher to student is indeed a goal to strive for. If one is concerned
with affective as well as cognitive outcomes, the students should be
involved in educational decision making to the maximum degree
possible, given their developmental and personal orientations.
Certainly, if one expects the schools to create independent achievers, individuals who have a continuing interest in learning and who
can handle freedom, then a democratic school climate is not only a
right but a necessity.

CONCLUSION

This chapter began with a dilemma commonly faced by schools.
There are those, such as Kathryn Tidrick, who worry about the
schools expecting too much — to the exclusion of children's own
rights to self-development. In contrast, a casual reading of popular
magazines and an occasional journal may lead the unsuspecting
reader to believe that "permissiveness" is responsible not only for
juvenile delinquency but also for supposed poor school performance: The school should expect more from students by exercising
greater control over their behavior. Although the issues are broader than those customarily dealt with by empirical research, the
evidence available clearly speaks an important word in this regard.
If one is concerned with the development of the whole child and
with long-term outcomes and if one assumes that the school should
indeed be concerned with these matters as well, then student participation in decision making, as well as freedom and openness in
learning, are clearly desirable. One cannot deny that granting
students a larger role in determining their education may be

judged to be inefficient in one case or another. But, overall, the evidence does not argue that recent experimentation with freedom in education indicates a necessity to return to traditional education. Neither does the evidence suggest that we have arrived at any one perfect model for enhancing student growth through granting freedom in learning. Indeed, both freedom and control must exist side by side in the classroom. When they are creatively employed by teachers to match individual student potential and need, it is then that the school is likely to be both efficient and effective.

REFERENCES

Andrews, Gregory R., and Debus, Raymond L. "Persistence and the Causal Perception of Failure: Modifying Cognitive Attributions." *Journal of Educational Psychology* 70 (April 1978): 154–66.

Bodine, R. J., and Hill, K. T. "Towards Individualized Learning: Implementing Alternative Classrooms in Elementary Schools." Paper presented at the University of Illinois (Urbana-Champaign) Conference on Educational Alternatives, Oakbrook, Ill., December 3, 1977.

de Charms, Richard. *Enhancing Motivation: Change in the Classroom*. New York: Irvington, 1976.

Dweck, Carol S. "Learned Helplessness and Negative Evaluation." *Educator* 19 (1977): 44–49.

Fyans, Leslie J., Jr., and Maehr, Martin L. "Attributional Style, Task Selection, and Achievement." *Journal of Educational Psychology* 71 (August 1979): 499–507.

Glass, David C.; Reim, Bruce; and Singer, Jerome E. "Behavioral Consequences of Adaptation to Controllable and Uncontrollable Noise." *Journal of Experimental Social Psychology* 7 (March 1971): 244–57.

Horwitz, Robert A. "Psychological Effects of the Open-Classroom." *Review of Educational Research* 49 (Winter 1979): 71–86.

Hunt, David E. "Person-Environment Interaction: A Challenge Found Wanting Before It Was Tried." *Review of Educational Research* 45 (Spring 1975): 209–230.

Kremer, Barbara K. "Classroom Evaluation, Developmental Level, and Continuing Motivation." Doctoral dissertation, University of Illinois, Urbana-Champaign, 1976.

Lepper, Mark R., and Greene, David, eds. *The Hidden Costs of Reward: New Perspectives on the Psychology of Human Motivation*. Hillsdale, N.J.: Lawrence Erlbaum Associates, 1978.

Lewin, Kurt; Lippitt, Ronald; and White, Ralph K. "Patterns of Aggressive Behavior in Experimentally Created 'Social Climates'." *Journal of Social Psychology* 10 (May 1939): 271–99.

Maehr, Martin L., and Stallings, William M. "Freedom from External Evalua-
    tion." *Child Development* 43 (March 1972): 177–85.
Rosenshine, Barak V., and Berliner, David C. "Academic Engaged Time." *British
    Journal of Teacher Education* 4 (1978): 3–16.
Salili, Farideh; Sorenson, Richard L.; Maehr, Martin L.; and Fyans, Leslie J., Jr.
    "A Further Consideration of the Effects of Evaluation on Motivation." *Amer-
    ican Educational Research Journal* 13 (Spring 1976): 85–102.
Seligman, M. E. P.; Maier, S. F.; and Solomon, R. C. "Unpredictable and Uncon-
    trollable Aversive Events." In *Aversive Conditioning and Learning,* edited by F.
    Robert Brush. New York: Academic Press, 1969.
Shiffler, Nancy; Lynch-Sauer, Judith; and Nadelman, Lorraine. "Relationship
    Between Self-Concept and Classroom Behavior in Two Informal Elementary
    Classrooms." *Journal of Educational Psychology* 69 (August 1977): 349–59.
Tidrick, Kathryn. *New York Times,* 1 April 1979.
Wang, Margaret, and Stiles, Billie. "An Investigation of Children's Concept of
    Self-Responsibility for Their School Learning." *American Educational Research
    Journal* 13 (Summer 1976): 159–79.

Discussion

Julie Stulac

Maehr and Willig suggest that a debate centering on the "toughness" of American public schools is being waged. They present one
view that schools are too demanding and note the opposite opinion
that schools are hardly as demanding as they could be. The authors
focus on several areas of research: teacher leadership styles, evaluation procedures, student participation in educational decisions,
and classroom structure. They point to several divisions in educational thought contrasting toughness with permissiveness, affective curricula with cognitive, open schooling with traditional, and
intrinsic motivation with extrinsic, to name a few. What is notably
missing is a framework within which the considerable data they
present may be judged or given meaning. They seem to favor
Dewey and the progressive educationist philosophy. As with most

seminal perspectives, however, Dewey's philosophy has many interpretations. In sum, we are never clear about what point or points of view Maehr and Willig espouse.

More seriously, they neglect to address directly the presumed topic of their paper — student expectations. I am unable to extract a conception of expectation from their discussion. Lacking a theoretical stance, the concept remains undefined, and one struggles to make sense of the reported studies. I suspect that they are reluctant to prescribe to others. This attitude is laudable in some circumstances but is not a useful one when applied to intellectual argument and coherent policy formation. In the context of this book, a firm stance — any stance — could have provided a basis for lively debate. As it is, my critical task is reduced to interpretive nitpicking of the several isolated studies. Since this would not advance the course of either social science research or policy development, I shall briefly advance a conception of expectations by drawing on material in social science research.

If schools are to genuinely recognize children's rights, then teachers, administrators, specialists, and aides shall have to explicitly readjust many of their present assumptions about teaching and learning. One fundamental transformation will be in the area of expectations: what must be expected of children, of teachers, and of schools. Since there is a broad body of research in this area, I will turn now to a discussion of this research and relate it to children's rights.

EXPECTATIONS

There are few maxims as empirically supported as that of the self-fulfilling prophecy. It is generally held that people act most of the time in accordance with what they believe others expect of them and with what they expect of themselves. They "define" situations in certain ways, and the ways in which these situations are defined affect how they and others will behave. Thus, we need to attend to the matter of what we expect of children and what we lead them to expect of themselves. This is often difficult because there are powerful social beliefs that shape and constrain our expectations. For example, many Americans believe that blacks are generally less competent than whites, that women are generally less competent than men, and that the poor are less competent than the rich at those activities we value socially, including school and job performance. Over time, many blacks, women, and poor people come to believe that they are, indeed, less competent, and these beliefs are translated into behaviors that confirm their own and others' expectations.

Several research studies have demonstrated this phenomenon. Cohen (1972) brought together black and white junior high school boys who did not know one another but who came from the same social class. In groups of four consisting of two white and two black children, the whites were substantially more likely to be active and influential in the research tasks than were the black children. This was the case even though the task had no academic component and the research was conducted in both black and white communities. These findings can be explained in terms of the self-fulfilling prophecy: when nothing is known about another except some socially valued characteristic (in this case race) then general beliefs about that characteristic will become relevant in the situation even though that characteristic has no rational relationship to the task at hand. This phenomenon has been reproduced in studies of persons holding jobs of higher and lower status (Bloom 1972), mixed sex groups (Lockheed and Harris, 1977), and students of varying reading abilities (Stulac 1975, Morris 1971). There is little question that the beliefs of the larger society are translated into performance differences among people in small groups.

If differences in performance between blacks and whites, girls and boys, and good and average readers is a function of expectations and not inherent in one's race, gender, or facility to read, then it should be possible to alter performance levels by changing people's expectations for their own and others' performance. This is precisely what Cohen and her associates accomplished. They taught black students how to assemble a transistor radio and these students, in turn, taught white students this valued skill. Following this treatment the boys did the same task the earlier groups had done. The differences between white and black performance were markedly reduced, demonstrating the role that expectations play in determining task performance. Although Cohen's work did not settle the question of whether poor performance leads to low expectations or vice versa, it does demonstrate that low expectations among group members can be changed and that these changes will produce different patterns of performance.

Altering behavioral patterns in the research laboratory does not imply that it would be a simple matter to change a feature or two of schools and produce the same results. Schools are extraordinarily complex social settings in which changes are not easily made. This seemingly obvious point was not appreciated by many architects of desegregation plans who believed that a redistribution of white and black children across a set of schools would eradicate pernicious achievement differences between these two groups. There is great variability in school climate in both black and white schools, and the movement of black children from even relatively unsupportive black schools to desegregated schools that view them as incompetent is certainly no guarantee of an increase in the quality of education.

There are many reasons schools fail to teach children effectively. Some children from low income or minority neighborhoods enter school predisposed to failure because they have already learned that there is no way the larger society is going to allow them to succeed (Ogbu 1974). When rigidly applied, the widespread practice of "streaming" or "tracking" by ability effectively militates against success in school for those located in the lower ranks (Metz 1978). Individualized instruction — a practice many have hoped might help teachers meet the diverse needs of children — can also lead to failure in school. Observational studies reveal that the technical challenges to teachers attempting to individualize instruction can be so overwhelming that many resort to providing students (especially those that are "slower") with "busy work" (McDonald and Elias 1976, Cohen 1979). Excessive reliance on worksheets leads to student inattentiveness and, ultimately, poorer academic performance. This litany of negative or ambiguous findings can be extended indefinitely because we as researchers have not properly conceptualized educational problems in terms of the social systems each school embodies. It is not a practice per se that can be validated or not as effective, but that practice in relation to the many other features of the setting that contribute to the phenomenon of the school.

Thus, when research moves from the laboratory to the "real" world, these several features must be taken into account. In translating her research to ongoing classroom settings, therefore, Cohen instructed several principals and teachers about how they might restructure classroom practices to diminish the development of unjustifiable expectations (Cohen, Lockheed, and Lohman 1976).

Competent biracial teams of teachers and administrators helped develop and carry out a school curriculum emphasizing cooperative, small-group learning. Tasks were structured to explicitly require the participation of all members. As with most school tasks, the activities at this school incorporated a variety of skills. These skills were carefully enumerated and positive expectations about student participation were noted. The finds suggested that children are capable of (a) valuing a variety of conceptually separable skills and, (b) attributing competence on at least some of these valued skills to all members of a group. That is, the familiar linear "smartness-dumbness" dimension can be shattered. Students did not perceive themselves and all others as equally and highly competent at all things; instead, they developed perceptions of themselves as more competent at some things and less competent at others. The stigma of "dumb in school" that bedevils so many of our so-called slow learners or below-average students faded.

In a theoretically related program of research, Brophy and Good (1970) examined the relationship between teachers' expectations of student performance and student participation and achievement in the classroom. Four teachers were asked to rank the children in their classrooms according to achievement. In each class three boys and three girls high and low on the teachers' lists were selected for observation. Subsequent observations of the teachers and students revealed the following:

1. High-expectancy students raised their hands more frequently and initiated more interactions than did low-expectancy children.
2. The students with high ratings produced more correct and fewer incorrect responses than those with low ratings.
3. The highly rated students received more praise and less criticism than the lowly rated students.
4. Teachers demanded and reinforced high-quality performances from the students with high ratings more frequently and consistently than they did for the students with low ratings.

These data are persuasive. When teachers assume a single dimension of competence in classrooms and can easily rank their students along it (in this case, achievement), then they develop expectations consistent with the ranking, and these expectations are translated into differential behavior toward the various students. If teachers give more praise and demand more excellence from the students rated highly, then the students with lower ratings enjoy less freedom and exercise fewer rights. Some children are free to achieve at the expense of other children.

To remedy this inequitable situation, one cannot think simply in terms of the number of statements of praise allocated to students or the amount of support teachers give in support of excellence. As Cohen and her associates demonstrated and as court decisions and theorists insist, educators must change their assumptions. They must assume that all children can learn and all children are capable of participating in decisions about their education. Children are entitled to pursue their education in the least restrictive environment possible within the constraints of the school system, and this, minimally, implies freedom from generalized low expectations for their academic performance.

REFERENCES

Bloom, Joan R. R. "The Effect of a Status Set on Decision Making in Small Task-Oriented Groups." Doctoral dissertation, Stanford University, 1972.

Brophy, Jere E., and Good, Thomas L. "Teachers' Communication of Differential Expectations for Children's Classroom Performance: Some Behavioral Data." *Journal of Educational Psychology* 61 (October 1970): 365–74.

Cohen, Elizabeth G. "Interracial Interaction Disability." *Human Relations* 25 (February 1972): 9–24.

Cohen, Elizabeth G. "Designing and Treating the Desegregated School: Problems of Status, Power, and Conflict." In *Desegregation: Past, Present, and Future*, edited by Elliot Aronson. New York; Plenum, 1979.

Cohen, Elizabeth B.; Lockheed, Marlaine E.; and Lohman, Mark R. "The Center for Interracial Cooperation: A Field Experiment." *Sociology of Education* 49 (January 1976): 47–88.

Lockheed, Marlaine E., and Harris, A. "Modifying Status Orders in Mixed Sex Groups of Fourth and Fifth Grade Children: An Application of Expectation States Theory." Paper presented at the annual meeting of the American Sociological Association, Chicago, 1977.

McDonald, Frederick, and Elias, Patricia J. *The Effects of Teacher Performances on Pupil Learning.* Princeton, N.J.: Educational Testing Service, 1976.

Metz, Mary H. *Classrooms and Corridors: The Crisis of Authority in Desegregated Secondary Schools.* Berkeley: University of California Press, 1978.

Morris, R. "A Normative Intervention to Equalize Participation in Task-Oriented Groups." Doctoral dissertation, Stanford University, 1971.

Ogbu, John W. *The Next Generation.* New York: Academic Press, 1974.

Stulac, Julie. "The Self-Fulfilling Prophecy: Modifying the Effects of a Unidimensional Perception of Academic Competence in Task-Oriented Groups." Doctoral dissertation, Stanford University, 1975.

Part 2

EDUCATIONAL PROCESSES AND RESOURCES

6

Management Strategies

STEPHEN J. KNEZEVICH

Educational management, a term that is now synonymous with administration, is at least once removed from the classroom, where student achievement or learning performance is influenced directly. Managers, including those at supervisory levels, work with and through other professional personnel to influence learning and its outcomes in the classroom. Leadership, procurement, and allocation of resources, organization of the enterprise, decision-making styles, school climate, professional working relationships, and approaches to personnel evaluation, are parts of the many-faceted management process and strategies. This chapter explores the question of whether there is evidence garnered through carefully controlled research to document the impact of management on learning.

School administration, or management, can be defined "as a social process concerned with identifying, maintaining, controlling, and unifying formally and informally organized human and material energies within an integrated system designed to accomplish predetermined objectives" (Knezevich 1975). This definition suggests the complexity of management and its pervasive influence on the system for delivering educational services.

A more precise descriptive title for this chapter would be "A Review of Research and other Publications on Selected Educational Management Strategies and Their Implications for the Development of Public School Standards." The five major topics considered are: (a) management and effective utilization of professional human resources, (b) instructional program management, (c) school climate, communications, and conflict management, (d) planning dimensions of management, and (e) policy development. The *Encyclopedia of Educational Research* (4th ed.), *Review of Educational Research,* various publications of the *Educational Research Service, ERIC,* and *Dissertation Abstracts* provided my sources of information. The quantity of research in many areas is sizeable, even though quality may be lacking. Rather than overwhelm the reader with citations of thousands of individual research reports, I frequently refer to summaries of research, which contain individual pieces. One of the advantages of using research summaries is that conflicting findings of two or more researchers may be noted, preventing an overreliance on a single researcher with no confirmation of additional studies. Quoting a single source can lead to unverified generalizations, given the great variation in quality of research design, the limitations of data, or the inappropriate treatment of data.

MANAGEMENT AND EFFECTIVE USE OF PROFESSIONALS

Professional resources essential to education and students' achievement may be influenced, for better or for worse, by management strategies and administrative styles. Research as well as less rigorous studies on selected dimensions of two types of professional personnel — teachers and administrators — are reviewed here. The focus is on supervision and evaluation of teachers, on administrator behavior in teams, and on decision-making styles.

Teacher and Administrator Evaluation

Research on teacher evaluation, or determination of teacher effectiveness, is voluminous; the topic has been studied for more than fifty years. The quantity can be overwhelming, but there is no evidence of a lessening of enthusiasm to design and execute new studies. The search can begin with each of the four editions of the *Encyclopedia of Educational Research,* and one can add the *Handbook of Research on Teaching,* edited by Gage (1963). Anderson and Hunka (1963), Biddle and Ellena (1964), Ryans (1960), Bolton (1973), and Medley (1961) offer other summaries. If interest can be measured by the number of studies and summaries published, the level of interest in teacher evaluation or effectiveness is matched in few other areas of educational research.

Unfortunately, the large quantity has produced neither widespread satisfaction with results nor the application of such knowledge to the real world of personnel evaluation. On the contrary, the generalization is that whether it is a question of the quality of designs or the credibility of results, few accept or are influenced by the research. In reporting on the impediments to the study of teacher effectiveness, Berliner (1976) cited problems of instrumentation, methodology, and statistics. Clearly then, quantity notwithstanding, the major problems in designing and implementing evaluation systems have not been resolved. Practitioners are more active than ever in their search for better ways of approaching teacher evaluation, of increasing acceptance of evaluation procedures by teachers, and of utilizing the results of the time and efforts dedicated to the appraisal of personnel.

Teaching is a complex act with a number of interacting variables: abilities, interests, and motivations of the students or learners involved; complexity of the learning situation; resources available for stimulating learning; reinforcement — or lack of it — of learning in the school situation from the home and other environmental forces; competencies of the evaluators; and so on. The multiple variables as well as the instruments used for collecting, processing, and interpreting data make appraisal a challenge yet to be satisfied. Some researchers pursue the determination of teacher effectiveness as a means of improving teacher preparation programs and others to improve on-the-job performance, determination of merit, or other reasons related to the operation of school systems. The lack of adequate theories on the evaluation of teachers and of models for evaluation to undergird research efforts or actual appraisal of teachers have contributed significantly to the many shortcomings in this field.

Reports from the field of actual practice as well as from the researchers suggest that teachers neither look forward to nor do they enjoy appraisals of their performance by supervisors or administrators. The reaction of teachers is to debate and control teacher evaluation issues during negotiations. The Educational Research Service (1979) summarized the views of both management and teachers on negotiating teacher evaluation.

The evaluation of administrators is a much newer development. Serious attention started in the 1960s and developed rapidly in the 1970s. The deficiencies reported for teacher evaluation are amplified in attempts to appraise the various types of administration. Management by objectives was introduced in some local school systems as an approach to administrator evaluation.

The revision of public school standards for the evaluation of teachers and administrators cannot gain much from research. There is a body of literature that cannot be classed as research but can be viewed as the best thinking at this time. Based on reviews of the literature as well as on some special study in the appraisal of eductional personnel, I believe that standards should be formulated to (a) demand that there be some system of appraisal for all types of educational personnel on a regular, if not an annual, basis; (b) encourage individual school districts to develop an evaluation system, rather than attempt to impose a state evaluation system or appraisal form; (c) promote the use of evaluation results to diagnose teaching or management performance problems and relate such data to the development of programs aimed at improving performance, rather than simply labeling personnel; (d) recommend special training for all involved in personnel appraisal; and (e) encourage evaluation of and subsequent modifications to personnel appraisal systems on a periodic basis.

Supervision

Research on the use and impact of specialized personnel, such as supervisors, on teachers in general and on the classroom learning situation specifically is sparse; often it is based on the results of doctoral dissertations and is characterized by a case study orientation from which generalizations are difficult. Once again the complications in behavioral research and the lack of adequate conceptual frameworks to guide research on the impact of supervisors are evident. The assumptions that only a few variables are involved in supervision are suspect. The competencies of persons bearing the title of supervisor are not the same. The abilities or levels of experience of those being supervised are not precisely the same, the characteristics of pupils served vary, the interest or complexity of the subject matter being taught by those supervised differs, the learning resources available to those supervised may be great or small, the school climate is not constant, and the level of acceptance of supervisors by those being supervised varies. In short, situations confronting the supervisor are diverse and the purposes of supervision, such as introducing change or improving performance, are no less varied. The diversity of factors from one situation to another makes the transferability of research results difficult unless there are sophisticated designs, well-developed conceptual frameworks, and carefully delineated assumptions. In their analysis of supervisor effectiveness, Harris and Hartgraves (1972) cautioned that only tentative conclusions can be drawn from existing studies, but they suggested some guidelines to follow.

Modification of teacher behavior through supervision remains a challenge. The prevailing opinion is that supervisors make a difference, but there is no definitive research to support this. Supervision is a potentially profitable management strategy. The translation of that potential to reality depends on a number of complex and interacting variables within the supervisory situation.

Much the same can be said about itinerant and supplemental teachers who bring special talents or curricula to a school. Research does not provide answers about their most effective utilization, assignment, or scheduling. Much of education remains an art rather than a science. The problem of translating the potential in specialized teaching resources into reality is similar to that previously described for supervisors.

Management Teams

The administrative, or management, team is a relatively new concept that emerged in the literature in the 1960s. It is not a clearly defined term, and not everyone using it means the same thing. Some substitute *teaming* as a new term for the older concepts of democratic school administration, participative management,

decentralized decision making, or shared responsibility for decisions. The propensity of principals, or middle management, in
some parts of the nation to form collective units for bargaining
directly with school boards triggered new interest in the management team concept. Some implied that the sharing of decision-
making activity with each member of the team would reduce the
likelihood of the formation of principal unions. Others focused on
the advantages of delegating specific kinds of decisions to each
level of the administrative hierarchy.

There are no definitive research efforts on management
teaming; personal opinions and case studies of how a specific
school district approaches the issues dominate. The appeal is to an
authority in group dynamics, such as Lewin, or an authority in
business organizations (not educational organizations), such as
Herzberg, McGregor, Drucker, or Odiorne. What research there is
comes from fields outside education, with adaptations to education
liberally interpreted to support the author's orientation.

Most writers about educational administration over the past fifty
years have denounced the autocrat, whether benevolent or not.
The more recent publications by Erickson and Rose (1973), other
publications reviewed by the ERIC Clearinghouse on Educational
Management (1977), and additional articles on shared decision
making, confirm and concur with the generalization of fifty years
earlier that autocratic managers are not the best managers. The
new element in recent research is the increased emphasis on middle management's role in decision making in an age of negotiations.

The Educational Research Service (1975a) approached the
issues somewhat differently, choosing to examine what decisions
should be decentralized, particularly those that reach the
principal's level. Knezevich (1975) perceived the administrative
team in terms of differentiated staffing applied to management
(rather than teaching). Complexity and size stimulated thinking
about the team concept in terms of its functions, structure, and
personality. The management team can be viewed as a formally
constituted cooperative social system of diverse specialists with
unique organizational roles bound together by mutual goals and
working in unison under the direction of a leader. The age-old
concept of interchangeability of individual members of the ad-

ministrative hierarchy falls apart in this age of increasing specialization. Traditionally, administrative services were expanded by
employing experienced generalists. I see the management team as
follows:

Management Team = Diverse Specialized Talents + Differentiated Roles (functions) + Unified
Action through Mutual Agreement
on Goals + Leadership

The unique decision-making style — democratic, laissez faire, or
autocratic — of an administrative leader may be demonstrated in a
team or nonteam organizational pattern. Decision-making styles of
a manager at any level of the hierarchy will contribute more to the
school or district climate than to management teaming. No research base refutes or supports such generalizations.

Prevailing thinking among most writers, rather than definitive
research results, suggests that standards for public schools today
should reflect the greater complexity and size of local school
systems. One administrator can no longer operate a total school
system efficiently; few even try. A team of diverse specialists is
needed. The standards should define and call for the formation of
management teams. Superintendents; deputy, associate, and
assistant superintendents; supervisors; directors; principals; assistant or vice-principals; and administrative assistants should be
identified by public school standards as members of the management team for district administration. Such standards may influence who has what kinds of authority to negotiate directly and
formally with the school board to determine their economic welfare and decision-making authority. Standards may also recommend a decision-making style that utilizes the creative talents of the
team members in a variety of professional positions while recogniz-
ing that with such authority goes accountability.

INSTRUCTIONAL PROGRAM MANAGEMENT

Class size, school schedules, length of school year, grading versus nongrading, individualization versus group instruction, and
organization of the day's activities are all part of the many and
diverse management strategies that seek to enhance student
achievement. Organization of instruction or program manage-

ment is only one of many variables influencing learning. Such factors, again, represent potential. Whether or not a few teachers and administrators take advantage of such potential is another issue. Since Chapter Seven in this volume focuses on instructional strategies in general, only those factors that deal with management will be considered here.

Class Size

This section reviews the twin factors of size (of classes, schools, and districts) and time (in schedules and the school year). The question of how many pupils should be assigned to a single teacher continues to be hotly debated. In the substantial body of literature on the topic, including research, case studies of school systems, and professional opinions, there is no agreement on how small is small or how large is large. (Small, as defined in the literature, may be anything under forty pupils to the other extreme of fifteen or fewer.) The problem is compounded by the failure to distinguish between student-staff ratios and pupil-teacher ratios. Little wonder that confusion reigns as to whether pupils learn more in ill-defined "small" classes as opposed to "large" ones.

The Educational Research Service (1978) provides the most recent and comprehensive summary of research on class size. One conclusion is that no clearcut guidelines for an optimum class size across all grade levels are provided by research. Again, class size is only one of many variables in the complex phenomenon known as learning. The Educational Research Service "Selected Bibliography" contained 149 publications, not all of which could be called research. Not long after the Educational Research Service summary, Glass and Smith (1978) employed what they called "meta-analysis" and concluded that the smaller the class, the larger the gains in pupil achievement. And still the debate rages.

Economic reality facing public education may be more influential than research in determining class size. Teacher and public opinion rank next in influencing class size. Doubtless, the extremes of more than forty and fewer than ten pupils per teacher are not likely to become the standard as yet. Educational research tools at present are not sufficiently refined to differentiate pupil gains in classes with twenty-five pupils per teacher from those where there are twenty-six pupils.

Public school standards on class size cannot be determined with precision, given the present status of research in education. Such standards could be set with confidence if optimum size were ascertained for the interests and capabilities of each student, each teacher's style, or the nature of each subject. Benefits from reducing class size are unlikely if the teacher continues with the same instructional strategies used with larger groups and fails to introduce more individualized approaches. At best, public school standards may suggest ranges and the avoidance of excessively large classes (more than forty pupils) or unusually small classes (fewer than ten pupils) for pupils in the normal or higher ranges of intellectual ability.

Size of School Districts and Attendance Units

The search for an optimum school district size or individual school attendance size has been going on for almost a century. The single best size has eluded educators here as well. The Educational Research Service (1974) summarized 261 studies on size of attendance centers and of local school districts. There are now fewer local school districts in the United States than in previous years. Student enrollments in each district are greater now than in the 1930s, the declines of the 1970s notwithstanding.

The issue is not whether bigger is better but whether improvement in the quality of educational services delivered and more effective use of scarce resources for education is possible through economy of scale. There have been more studies on the ranges in ideal enrollment for senior high schools than for elementary and junior high, or middle, schools. Studies before 1950 recommended lower enrollment standards for high schools. During the first third of this century, few justified high school enrollments of less than 100, and most set minimums no lower than 200 to 300. After 1950, studies elevated minimums to the 300 to 500 range. The recommended optimums were from 1,500 to 2,000 pupils for senior high schools. The major factors considered in arriving at standards for optimum size for senior high schools were comprehensiveness of educational opportunities (curriculum offerings), ability to attract high-quality faculty, optimizing per pupil expenditures, effective use of special facilities, and achievement of graduates at the college or university level.

Recommended middle school ranges submitted by most who have studied the issue are between 500 to 1,500. I would opt for 750 to 1,000. Recommended size for elementary schools is often put in terms of enough pupils to warrant only one teacher per grade, with the optimum number of single-grade classrooms in a given building being not less than six and more often no less than twenty. This suggests the optimum enrollment range per building would be from 500 to 720, depending upon the pupil-teacher ratio. The minimum is seldom set below 300.

The question of when a school is too big has received less attention. In my opinion, this may begin when enrollments at the high school level exceed the 2,000 level and definitely after 3,000. At the junior high, or middle, school, too big begins around 1,500. For the elementary school the number should be kept below 1,200. These are only opinions and must be tempered by the types of pupil services, the community served, and the objectives. Obviously, isolation in sparsely populated rural areas will influence the standards to provide flexibility in coping with the given situation. Creation and operation of effective intermediate units that provide services to small attendance units could justify units with enrollments below minimums in standard or below what is suggested by other data, based on the assumption of completely self-sufficient school units.

The battles surrounding the reorganization of local school districts appear to be over. By the 1960s, we had moved into the final phase. Almost 90 percent of the districts that existed fifty years ago have disappeared. About 15,000 districts remain and are slowly being reduced to between 5,000 to 10,000. The Southeast leads the nation in most efficient district structure. Data in 1971–72 showed the Southeast with 10.2 percent of the nation's school districts and 22 percent of the pupils. In contrast, the Great Lakes and Plains states had 41.3 percent of the local school districts and 28.2 percent of the pupils. The Educational Research Service (1974) documented the research studies and other reports and concluded that the optimum local district size as measured by pupil enrollments (some used numbers of teachers) was a wide-ranging figure — not less than 10,000 to not more than 50,000. There have been a few dissenting voices, such as Sher and Tompkins (1977), who wrote of the "myths of economy, efficiency, and equality" in the reorganization of districts. Such views are not likely to trigger an increase in the number of school districts.

School Year

The extended school year, or "year-round school," as a management strategy has been studied and discussed for more than thirty years. The intensity and seriousness of discussions of changing the traditional school year of nine or ten months appear to wax and wane in seven- to ten-year cycles. A Department of Health, Education, and Welfare study of twenty-four year-round schools by Abt Associates (1976) reported favorably on the movement. There are now more attendance units than ever before that claim to operate all year. The estimates vary, with most of the publicity going to those schools that start the practice rather than to those that later abandon it. The Canadian Teachers' Federation (1978) produced a bibliography on school-year plans, which lists publications since 1967, including 239 books (mostly pamphlets of eight to fifty pages or special reports), 157 articles, and sixteen theses, of which eleven were master's theses. There were at least as many reports on year-round school operations published prior to 1967 as after. The lack of definitive research to support the various year-round school proposals as a way to increase pupil learning or reduce operating costs has not lessened the enthusiasm of its devotees at annual conventions. Administrators interested in or committed to year-round school operations testify with such comments as "teachers were more relaxed," "attendance is up with vandalism down," "juvenile delinquency is reduced," "curriculum reform is facilitated," "there are improved student-teacher relations," "there are fewer sick days for all," and "parents love it." These imply that the unique school calendar deserves the lion's share, if not all, of the credit for educational improvements. Claims of the committed are not adequate substitutes for disciplined research.

Public school standards may well allow for flexibility in arranging how the usually statutory determination of the minimum time frame for the school year is scheduled, but it would be questionable at this time to mandate the recommendations of more enthusiastic proponents of year-round schooling. An examination of year-round school plans shows that, contrary to what the term implies, few if any students attend school all-year-round or almost fifty-two weeks per year. It is the school or the educational program that is in operation for twelve months of the calendar year. Pupils attend school for shorter consecutive periods or cycles of less than the nine months; nine weeks of school may be followed by a planned vacation of three weeks. Regular attendance is interrupted by more frequent vacations, each one of which is briefer than the typical two- to three-month summer recess. Teachers may be employed for eleven or twelve months (most serve nine or ten months as in the traditional year) and school operation continues for that period. The total time a student devotes to formal learning activities is about the same in the year-round school as in the traditionally scheduled school year. It is the spacing of vacations and school attendance by students that are different.

Schedules

Enthusiasm for different and so-called "innovative" daily and weekly school schedules waned considerably during the 1970s. During the 1950s and 1960s the alleged contributions of these schedules were only a bit more modest than those claimed for the year-round school calendar. The research on daily and weekly schedules, quarter versus semester versus trimester plans, and other school time plans is sparse, without definitive results, and has had little lasting impact on practice. Most "studies" are descriptions of a particular time distribution plan being implemented in a school, personal observations of some professionals in one or more schools in one or more school districts involved in some type of schedule "innovation," or general observations of someone from outside the school implementing a new type of schedule. The Educational Research Service (1975b) reported on case histories of some school districts using a four-day rather than a five-day week, as well as those using half-day sessions, as responses to the concerns about energy conservation during 1972–74.

The Educational Research Service (1975b, p. 32) observed that "the research studies . . . provide evidence with which to argue either that decreased instructional time negatively affects achievement or that decreased instructional time has no effect on achievement (up to a certain point at least)." Bloom (1974) concluded that "we are convinced that it is not the sheer amount of time spent in learning (either in or out of school) that accounts for the level of learning" but that "each student should be allowed the time he needs to learn a subject." Specific studies to fuel the conflicting arguments between length of instructional time and student achievement can be found in Carroll (1963), Harris and Yinger (1977), Husén (1972), Jarvis (1962), Jenkins (1973), Schultz, Kropp, and Curtis (1958), and Wiley (1973).

Organizing the instructional program to increase educational achievement is the assumed or directly asserted goal of all managers. Research does not support nor does it repudiate the efforts made to date to reach this goal. The complexity of human learning defies the dedication of researchers focusing on one or a few variables such as the actual quantity of time devoted to learning something, frequency of scheduled learning activities during the day or week, the division of time spans into quarters, semesters, or trimesters for an academic year; or more frequently interrupted learning times with shorter and varied vacations from instruction (characteristic of the so-called year-round school calendar). Prevailing professional preference rather than research may determine what the school standards will be with respect to the amount, scheduling, or other distribution of time available to stimulate learning and produce the desired level of student achievement. It would not be prudent to use standards to curtail experimentation with various time or scheduling configurations for schools.

Self-Concept, "Open Classrooms," and Achievement

Some researchers suggest that focusing on the student's self-concept would be a more productive strategy for increasing achievement than various manipulations of time. After reviewing evaluation research on educational intervention programs which have focused on self-concept change, Scheirer and Kraut (1979, p. 140) concluded that "these evaluations of educational interventions have generally failed to find an association between self-concept change and academic achievement." They discussed the methodological and theoretical shortcomings in the many studies reviewed; some studies used large samples drawn from various parts of the nation. According to Scheirer and Kraut, the research evidence to date suggests caution among educators and theorists who have previously assumed that enhancing a person's self-concept leads to academic achievement.

The so-called open classroom has been assumed by some to be a place where children feel better about themselves. Horwitz (1979, p. 76) reported mixed results from the sixty-one studies reviewed, which showed that "fifteen favored open schools, two favored traditional schools, fifteen showed mixed results, and twenty-nine revealed no significant differences." Any management strategy calling for the revision of public school standards to encourage or limit use or implementation of open classrooms to improve a student's self-concept is thus questionable. That any type of intervention aimed at changing the learner's self-concept will result in increased achievement has yet to be demonstrated with existing research tools. The value of open classrooms remains an open question.

SCHOOL CLIMATE, COMMUNICATIONS, AND CONFLICT MANAGEMENT

Climate

Because Chapter Eleven in this volume covers school climate, my comments here reflect primarily a management point of view. The work of Halpin and Croft (1962) helped to alert school administrators to the existence of school climate, which was assumed to have some impact on morale and productivity. The research is sparse and related publications repetitive. The results or outcomes thus far tend to focus on a clearer definition of basic concepts, ways to measure climate, and means of categorizing the various types of climate assumed to exist. No definitive research exists on how specific management strategies can modify a school climate (in whatever direction) over time (ERIC Clearinghouse on Educational Management, 1978b). Some authors suggest that the impact of school principals on the climate of a particular school building is minimal. Other writers, although without research evidence, suggest that management styles are related to whether the so-called open or closed school climate prevails. Those who write about improving school climate (ERIC Clearinghouse on Educational Management 1977a) more often than not present a personal point of view that reflects experience or conviction, but is not based upon research. I feel that concepts such as school climate lack the definitive models and data needed to influence the development of specific management strategies or to determine the direction of public school standards. This deficiency may change in the years that follow.

Communications

Communication is much like the weather. Everybody talks about it but most seem to be helpless in doing something about it. Berelson and Steiner (1964) summarized significant communication studies outside the field of education. These studies suggest that (a) people seek out communications favorable to their own predispositions, (b) rumors spread in direct proportion to the audience's receptivity to them, (c) the perception and misinterpretation of the substance of a communication are similarly related to the congeniality of the communication to the individual's value system, (d) facts are less potent than emotional predispositions in interpreting the significance of sensitive communications, and (e) the higher the intelligence and educational level the greater the reliance on obtaining information from print media. Most of what is called information theory or the mathematical theory of communications has not been applied to the problems confronting educational management today. Lane, Corwin, and Monahan (1967) outlined the impact of psychological and social factors that compound the communications problems in educational organizations.

There are many publications in education that are rhetorical in nature and stress such obvious generalizations as communication is important and needs to be improved in every school system, poor communication can destroy large and complex organizations, and every manager should work hard to improve communication with students, faculty, other administrators, the school board, and the community. These statements are self-evident. The general recommendations that dominate the literature are based more on personal preferences than on data.

There is a substantial research void in the area of specific management strategies related to communications in educational organizations of varying complexities. The filling of this void is more likely to come from teaming specialists in communication theory with those in educational management. The substantive content of public school standards that focus on communication awaits more research.

Conflict Management

Although case studies on conflicts within specific school systems have been recorded in educational literature for more than a hundred years, the acceptance of the conflict as a common, or at least not unusual, occurrence is a relatively recent event. Prior to 1960, the existence of a conflict was often denied or referred to in hushed tones until the crisis could no longer be hidden. Organizational conflict has come "out of the closet" as far as school management is concerned.

The acceptance of the inevitability of conflict is a prior condition that established the need for developing conflict management skills. The ERIC Clearinghouse on Educational Management (1978a) observed that "surprisingly little research exists on conflict management" in education. Nebgen (1977-1978) summarized about a dozen different pieces classified as research on conflict management techniques and their consequences; most focused on organizational conflict outside education.

The literature on conflict in education generally covers case histories or descriptions of how and why conflicts occur. In the latter instance, the emphasis is on definitions and descriptions of conflict; sources of conflict such as communication breakdowns, interpersonal or personality disputes, differences on goals and priorities, heterogeneity within the community served, collective bargaining squabbles, integration and segregation of schools, structural differentiation or the creation of hierarchy of position; and varying interpretations of management strategies pursued to reduce conflict. Research on management strategies for coping with conflict in educational settings is sparse. Significant strides have been made in the past decade in accepting the inevitability of conflict in educational organizations. Given the multiplicity of educational goals, the diversity of clientele served, and the variety of internal and external forces, to mention only a few factors, conflict in education is more likely to increase rather than decrease in the years ahead. It will be some time before research yields useful strategies for the management of particular types of conflicts in education.

PLANNING

Prior to 1960, the word *planning*, as used in professional education circles, was preceded by qualifiers that suggested the context or substance of such activities. There was educational facilities planning (school plant); fiscal planning (budget preparation); instructional planning; school transportation planning; and schedule planning. Thus planning is not a new concept in education. Planners were persons in education with highly specialized orientations who usually worked independently in a specific dimension of the system. Planning departments were rare unless the focus was on some systemwide effort such as school plant or fiscal planning. The time and goal frames were of short range, seldom for anything more distant than the next fiscal year or for one particular unit such as a school plant. It sometimes took more than one year to complete a building, but the planning phase was seldom more than one year in length. Planning was a sporadic rather than a continuing activity.

There is a sizeable body of literature on each of these more traditional dimensions of planning for the educational enterprise, but it is beyond the scope of this chapter to report on each of these significant studies. To illustrate, architects, engineers, and school plant specialists generated research reports that led to the "golden years" in educational plant planning and construction following World War II.

During the 1960s another perception of planning in education emerged. Planning began to be conceptualized as a general activity, a continuing function that assumed a long-range time frame of several years. New planning techniques, such as the Program Evaluation and Review Technique (PERT) or the Critical Path Method (CPM) were applied to such large and complex educational projects as school plants. In the late 1960s, school districts began to purchase and use sophisticated electronic computers. New types of planning strategies found in the federal government such as Planning, Programming, Budgeting System (PPBS or Program Budgeting) began to be considered for adaptation by educational managers in the late 1960s. By the early 1970s, management by objectives (MBO), a planning and decision-making technology used in private corporations, found its way into the educational literature. The so-called Delphi Technique generated interest in extended educational planning called "futurism." In short, new techniques, strategies, and time frames were developed during the late 1960s and 1970s to enhance the planning capabilities of school districts and to enable educators to cope with uncertainties. (See American Association of School Administrators 1973, Hack 1971, Hartley 1968, Alioto and Jungherr 1971, Knezevich 1973.) Most of the publications focusing on some dimension of the new perceptions on planning were not research oriented; they were rather collections of "best thinking" and submitted adaptations to education of planning strategies and technology from other fields. They focused on rational approaches and on concepts of quantitative analysis in planning.

There remain differing interpretations of what PPBS, MBO, and educational futurism are. The PPBS lost much of its appeal by the mid-1970s. MBO likewise became mired down by the paperwork generated and time consumed by it. Both may well emerge again in the 1980s to profit from the mistakes of the 1960s and 1970s. Dror (1967), in his seminal work on the planning process, recommended that the time had come to move from the rhetoric or "ideological discourses on the desirability of planning to examination of the substantive problems associated with the planning process, such as its nature, the phases of planning, conditions for successful planning, planning techniques, and so forth" (p. 93). The field of education is only beginning to move in the direction recommended by Dror and has been doing so without the aid of significant research efforts to date.

Input-Output Analysis

The study of school productivity through an examination of input-output relationships, or cost-effectiveness analysis, increased significantly during the 1970s. It may provide some clues for planning the more effective utilization of increasingly scarce resources for education. The more global studies by Coleman (1966) and Jencks (1972) generated doubts or produced mixed findings on the correlation between student achievement and per-pupil expenditure. Summers and Wolfe (1975), focusing on Philadelphia schools, identified inputs that appeared to have some impact on student achievement (school size, class size, amount of teaching experience of teachers in the schools, and quality ratings of the undergraduate colleges and universities where the teachers were educated) and those that do not affect student learning gains (matching student and teacher by race, physical facilities, pre-school experiences, characteristics of principals, and so forth). Rossmiller and Geske (1976) reviewed the limited research on school productivity as well as some of the problems encountered in input-output analysis applied to education.

To summarize, educational planning, input-output analysis, and the application of general systems or quantitative analysis are only beginning to have an impact on management strategies in education. It is premature for public school standards to mandate specific applications or to go beyond the recommendation for the allocation of resources for the enhancement of long-term as well as short-term planning for the more effective allocation and utilization of educational resources.

POLICY DEVELOPMENT

The research in the general area of state and national educational policy development and management, or the politics of education, is minimal, has had little impact on the profession, has yet to influence programs for professional preparation significantly, and has not generated directions or specific management strategies to be pursued. This is not to suggest that this condition is desirable but only to note that a void exists. There is much confusion in this arena and it may take another decade for the dust to settle.

It may be difficult to focus public school standards, which are generated and monitored by a state agency, in the general area of state and national educational policy development and management. It is clear, however, that state educational policy decisions in legislation, court decisions, and regulations provide the basic guidelines from which state school standards are generated. There is a prodigious challenge in the preparation of school standards that satisfy the demands of current state legislation, that are consistent with the spirit and substance of court decisions, that stimulate local school districts to pursue excellence, that will not inhibit professional and lay leadership, that can encourage innovations, and that influence levels of student achievement in a positive way.

Although the quality of and interest in research in education have increased during the past decade, it is regrettable that research in management strategies has contributed so little to the revision of school standards.

REFERENCES

Abt Associates. *The Importance of Year-Round Schools.* Cambridge, Mass.: Abt Associates, 1976.

Alioto, Robert, and Jungherr, J. A. *Operational PPBS for Education: A Practical Approach to Effective Decision Making.* New York: Harper & Row, 1971.

American Association of School Administrators. *Management by Objectives and Results.* Arlington Va.: American Association of School Administrators, 1973.

Anderson, C. C., and Hunka, S. M. "Teacher Evaluation: Some Problems and a Proposal." *Harvard Educational Review* 33 (Winter 1963): 74–95.

Berelson, Bernard, and Steiner, Gary A. *Human Behavior.* New York: Harcourt, Brace and World, 1964.

Berliner, David E. "Impediments to the Study of Teacher Effectiveness." *Journal of Teacher Education* 27 (Spring 1976): 5–13.

Biddle, Bruce J., and Ellena, William J., eds. *Contemporary Research on Teacher Effectiveness.* New York: Holt, Rinehart and Winston, 1964.

Bloom, Benjamin S. "Time and Learning." *American Psychologist* 29 (September 1974): 682–88.

Bolton, Dale. L. "Personnel Evaluation Research and Implication." In *New Directions for Education* 1 (Spring 1973): 21–36.

Canadian Teachers' Federation. *School Year Plans.* Bibliographies in Education, no. 67. Ottawa, Canada: Canadian Teachers' Federation, November 1978.

Carroll, John B. "A Model for School Learning." *Teachers College Record* 64 (May 1963): 723–33.

Coleman, James S. *Equality of Educational Opportunity.* Washington, D.C.: U.S. Government Printing Office, 1966.

Dror, Yehezkel. "The Planning Process: A Facet Design." In *Planning, Programming, Budgeting: A Systems Approach to Management,* edited by F. J. Lyden and E. G. Miller, pp. 93–116. Chicago: Markham, 1967.

Educational Research Service. "Summary of Research on Size of Schools and School Districts." *Research Brief.* Arlington, Va.: Educational Research Service, 1974.

Educational Research Service. "Decentralized Decision-Making." *Information Aid.* Educational Research Service, 1975a.

Educational Research Service. "The Four-Day School Week." *ERS Report.* Arlington, Va.: Educational Research Service, 1975b.

Educational Research Service. "Class Size: A Summary of Research." *Research Brief.* Arlington, Va.: Educational Research Service, 1978.

Educational Research Service. Negotiation Aid for School Management. *Negotiating the Teacher Evaluation Issue*. Arlington, Va.: Educational Research Service, 1979.

ERIC Clearinghouse on Educational Management. "Improving School Climate." In *The Best of ERIC*, no. 32. Eugene: University of Oregon, December 1977.

ERIC Clearinghouse on Educational Management. "Managing Conflict." *Research Action Brief*, no. 3. Eugene: University of Oregon, 1978a.

ERIC Clearinghouse on Educational Management. "School Climate." *Research Action Brief*, no. 4. Eugene: University of Oregon, 1978b.

Erickson, Kenneth A., and Rose, Robert L. "Management Teams in Educational Administration: Ideal? Practical? Both?" *OSSC Bulletin* 17 (December 1973): 1–18.

Gage, N. L., ed. *Handbook of Research on Teaching*. Chicago: Rand McNally, 1963.

Glass, Gene V, and Smith, Mary Lee. *Meta-Analysis of Research on the Relationship of Class Size and Achievement*. Boulder: Laboratory of Educational Research, University of Colorado, 1978.

Hack, Walter G., and others. *Educational Futurism 1985*. Berkeley, Calif.: McCutchan, 1971.

Halpin, Andrew W., and Croft, Don B. *The Organizational Climate of Schools*. St. Louis, Mo.: Washington University, 1962.

Harris, Ben M., and Hartgraves, William R. "Supervisor Effectiveness? A Research Resume." *Educational Leadership* 30 (October 1972): 73–79.

Harris, T., and Yinger, Robert J. "Time." In *Current Directions in Research on Teaching*, Conference Series no. 1, pp. 7–24. East Lansing, Mich.: Institute for Research on Teaching, September 1977.

Hartley, Harry J. *Educational Planning, Programming, and Budgeting: A Systems Approach*. Englewood Cliffs, N.J.: Prentice-Hall, 1968.

Horwitz, Robert A. "Psychological Effects of the 'Open Classroom'." *Review of Educational Research* 49 (Winter 1979): 71–86.

Husén, Torsten. "Does More Time in School Make a Difference?" *Saturday Review* 55 (April 27, 1972): 32–35.

Jarvis, Oscar T. *Time Allotments and Pupil Achievement in the Intermediate Elementary Grades: A Texas Gulf Coast Study*. Houston, Tex.: Houston University, Bureau of Educational Research and Services, 1962.

Jencks, Christopher, and others. *Inequality: A Reassessment of the Effect of Family and School in America*. New York: Basic Books, 1972.

Jenkins, J. R. "The Four-Day School Week: Scheduling Effects." *Journal of Educational Research* 66 (July-August, 1973): 479–80.

Knezevich, Stephen J. *Program Budgeting (PPBS)*. Berkeley, Calif.: McCutchan, 1973.

Knezevich, Stephen J. *Administration of Public Education*. New York: Harper & Row, 1975.

Lane, Willard R.; Corwin, Ronald G.; and Monahan, William G. *Foundations of Educational Administration: A Behavioral Analysis*. New York: Macmillan, 1967.

Medley, Donald M. "Teacher Personality and Teacher-Pupil Rapport." *Journal of Teacher Education* 12 (June 1961): 152–56.

Nebgen, Mary K. "Conflict Management in Schools." *Administrator's Notebook* 26, no. 6 (1977-78): 1–4.

Rossmiller, Richard A., and Geske, T. G. "Toward More Effective Use of School Resources." *Journal of Educational Finance* 2 (Spring 1976): 484–502.

Ryans, David G. *Characteristics of Teachers: Their Description, Comparison, and Appraisal.* Washington, D.C.: American Council on Education, 1960.

Scheirer, Mary Ann, and Kraut, Robert E. "Increasing Educational Achievement Via Self-Concept Change." *Review of Educational Research* 49 (Winter 1979): 131–50.

Schultz, Raymond E.; Kropp, R. P.; and Curtis, H. A. "A Comparison of Half-Day and Regular Session Pupil Achievement in Elementary Schools." *Childhood Education* 34 (May 1958): 422g–422h.

Sher, Jonathan P., and Tompkins, R. E. "Economy, Efficiency, and Equality: The Myths of Rural School and District Consolidation." In *Hearings Before the Sub-Committee on Elementary, Secondary, and Vocational Education,* 95th Congress, May 10–11, 1977, pp. 67–97.

Summers, A. A., and Wolfe, B. L. "Which School Resources Help Learning? Efficiency and Equity in Philadelphia Public Schools." *Federal Reserve Bank of Philadelphia Business Review* (February 1975): 4–28.

Wiley, David E. *Another Hour, Another Day: Quantity of Schooling, A Potent Path for Policy.* Studies of the Educative Process, no. 3. Chicago: University of Chicago, July 1973.

Discussion

Roald F. Campbell

In many ways I approach the problem of management strategies much as Knezevich has approached it. Both of us have had professional experience in public schools. Both of us have also served as professors of educational administration and as deans of schools of education. We may differ somewhat in the way we conceive research. As I understand Knezevich, he is chiefly concerned here with research findings. I prefer to put research in a larger context to include the ideas or concepts behind the research as well as the methodologies employed in the research. To rely on research findings alone may mean that a good idea is abandoned too soon.

For instance, findings may be inconclusive for several reasons, such as poor operational definitions, inadequate samples, insensitive instruments, or even superficial interpretations. Ideally, the whole process of thinking that went into the research as well as the findings ought to be considered. This kind of understanding cannot be had from examining research summaries.

Knezevich begins by expressing doubt that research could "provide direct guidance" to the revision of state standards and, in large part, his doubts are confirmed. But to seek empirically derived relationships between management strategies and educational outcomes, much as we would like to have such evidence, may be asking for the impossible, at least for now. A plea for more research relating organizational variables to school effects has been made by Erickson (1979). Few studies have dealt with such relationships and future studies will find the terrain difficult. It is hard enough to find relationships between teaching strategies and educational outcomes because of the many other variables found in the teaching and learning process. To determine relationships between management strategies and educational outcomes is obviously still more difficult. All the variables found in teaching, in home background, in socioeconomic status, in students' abilities and attitudes, and more are involved. At present, there may be no way to hold all of these variables steady while we look at a simple relationship between an administrative strategy and pupil learning. We can make some reasonable assumptions about these relationships; empirical evidence, I suspect, is a long way off.

Lacking direct evidence for the support or nonsupport of most management strategies, we may have to settle for bits of evidence that inform practice, but, when taken alone, are an inadequate basis for changing practice. For instance, I think of the work of Bloom (1964) on the development of children in the early years. An implication of his findings would have us devote a much greater proportion of our resources to early childhood education. But this implication has to be balanced with a number of other factors in the real world. Whether in state standards or in the operations of a local district, judgments have to be made about implications of research, often incomplete and quite specific in nature, and other factors present in the situation. Even when we are fortunate enough to have research that informs us, such information alone may not be sufficient grounds for policy change. We must still make judgments about the meaning of the research; as the research evidence grows, one hopes the judgments will become more and more informed.

NATURE OF RESEARCH PRESENTED

Knezevich approached in workmanlike manner the difficult tasks of identifying the studies bearing upon his assignment and of making some appraisal of the import of their findings. I find no serious omissions, but I also find seven areas to which I would have given somewhat greater emphasis, and I note each of these here.

1. The work of David Wiley receives mention, but I think his own and related work on the relationship between time in school (days in the school year and length of the school day) and student achievement deserve more attention. Wiley approached the matter somewhat tangentially; he was testing the hunch that time or lack of time spent in school might help explain the decline in achievement test scores. Even so, time in school is a managerial strategy and germane to our task. Wiley found that the number of days pupils attend school per year varies widely among the states, from an average of 146 in one state to 170 in another. For our purpose, the following conclusion is most pertinent: "In terms of typical gains in achievement over a year's period, we concluded that in schools where students receive 24 percent more schooling, they will increase their average gain in reading comprehension by two thirds and their gains in mathematics and verbal skills by more than one third. These tremendous effects indicate that the amount of schooling a child receives is a highly relevant factor for his achievement" (Wiley and Harnischfeger 1974, p. 9). Wiley's findings are among the more important pieces of evidence that can be found in the area of management strategy.

2. Although the bulk of the studies on class size and student achievement are inconclusive, as Knezevich points out, the recent work by Glass and Smith (summarized in Cahen and Filby 1979) should, it seems to me, be given more prominence. Glass and Smith reanalyzed 77 studies of class size, a total of 725 comparisons of achievement in different class size. In 60 percent of the cases achievement was higher in the smaller classes. There was a dra-

matic difference in achievement in classes of fifteen students when compared to classes of forty. In addition to looking at class size, Glass and Smith also examined the research designs used in the studies. They found that poorly designed studies tended to find that class size made little difference. Many of the early studies employed poor research designs, a factor which may have contributed to the inconclusive results of those studies. Clearly, the work of Glass and Smith requires that we take a new look at class size as a management strategy.

3. In his consideration of input-output analysis, Knezevich makes no mention of the work of Alan Thomas. In my view, Thomas is one of the few who has thought seriously about "the productive school." His book (Thomas 1971) bearing that name is worth pursuing, and his work in Michigan (Thomas 1968) may, for the purposes of this project, be even more useful. For instance, in response to the frequent canard that expenditures per pupil per year make no difference, Thomas divided the Michigan school districts into those with high ($510 or more), medium ($440–509), and low (less than $440) expenditure per pupil. Examples from his findings for junior high schools follow: in high-expenditure districts, 72 percent of the schools had classes for the verbally talented compared to 30 percent in low-expenditure districts; in high-expenditure districts, 65 percent of the schools had classes for the quantitatively talented compared to 32 percent in low-expenditure districts. These figures suggest that the chances for student achievement were more than twice as great in high-expenditure districts than in low-expenditure districts.

4. Another body of work bearing upon management teams has been ignored by Knezevich. I refer to the efforts of the Research and Development Center at the University of Wisconsin having to do with individually guided education (IGE), particularly that part of it devoted to the administrative team set up at the school building level. Although some may see IGE as something of a missionary movement, it seems to me that Lipham and his colleagues have something worthwhile to say about administrative teams. In this instance, the team is at the building level and is composed of a few teachers, the unit leader (a new position), and the principal. A number of studies having to do with the behavior of the principal and the effectiveness of the instructional program have been con-

ducted. Lipham summarizes the results of these studies as follows: "Research conducted to date regarding the leadership of IGE principals was cited, revealing that a systematic, positive, and significant relationship exists between the instrumental, supportive, and participative leadership behavior of the principal and the effectiveness of the instructional program in the IGE school. From these studies it was suggested that the principal not only be knowledgeable about but also skilled in exercising differential leadership behavior if the instructional program of the school is to be improved" (Lipham and Fruth 1976, p. 86).

5. Student tutoring also is omitted in Knezevich's chapter. Although student tutoring — one student tutoring another — might be seen as an instructional strategy, it can also be conceived as an administrative strategy. Indeed, this strategy will not be used extensively unless the principal of the school is convinced that the procedure has potential and unless he supports that conviction with the necessary administrative arrangements and resources to make the program work. For a number of years, Arthur Elliott (1977) has been interested in the administrative aspects of student tutoring, and he summarized the state of the field in an article. For instance, he cited a dramatic example of results obtained in one Los Angeles school over a five-year period. In 1966–67, when the student tutoring program in reading was begun, 4 percent of the first graders achieved average scores (fourth stanine or above) on a standardized reading test. With tutoring, the next 13 percent of the first graders achieved average scores, and at the end of five years 71 percent of the first graders achieved average scores. Even more important, at the fifth-grade level for the last two years of the program 81 percent and 63 percent of the students, respectively, achieved scores of average or better. This and other research cited by Elliott suggest that more attention should be focused on student tutoring as a management strategy.

6. Knezevich cites the work of Bloom, but I think the reference and the quotation are presented out of context. Bloom's statement refers to his concern about mastery learning, and the quotation has more meaning in that context. The mastery learning proposition, for which there is some research evidence, gets no mention in the Knezevich paper even though its import as a management strategy seems clear. Bloom says his central thesis "is that variations in

learning and the level of learning of students are determined by the students' learning history and the quality of instruction they receive. Appropriate modifications related to the history of the learners and the quality of instruction can sharply reduce the variation of students and greatly increase their level of learning and their effectiveness in learning in terms of time and effort expended. Where conditions for learning in the home and school approach some ideal, we believe that individual differences in learning should approach a vanishing point" (Bloom 1976, p. 16).

Bloom cites a number of studies and concludes that research and practice in mastery learning have demonstrated that a large majority of students can learn selected subjects to as high a level as the most able students. He acknowledges that to achieve this end some extra expenditure of time and help have been provided. Although Bloom suggests that this line of research has only touched the surface, the implications for management strategy have already begun to emerge.

7. Finally, I find no consideration by Knezevich of what has come to be called the politics of education. Concerns in this field have some relevance for such topics as conflict management and policy development, which are both treated in Knezevich's chapter. Much of the research in the politics of education has been critically analyzed by Boyd (1976) and could provide some additional insight on our topic. For instance, one of his concluding statements follows:

I have argued that if schools are not merely the "mirror images" of the communities they serve, neither are they almost completely insulated bastions dominated by unresponsive and self-serving professional educators. Instead, I have proposed that while educators tend to dominate local educational policy making, they usually operate within significant, and generally neglected or underestimated, constraints imposed by the *local* community and school board — not to mention those imposed by state and national forces. These constraints (or, put another way, the influence of the community and the board) are likely to vary primarily with the type of school district and the type of policy issue that is faced. The local citizenry and the board will tend to have more influence in *external, redistributive,* and *strategic* policy decisions, and in *smaller* and more *homogeneous* communities where the professionals tend to anticipate or reflect (especially in middle- and upper-middle-class communities) community demands. The professionals, on the other hand, will tend to have more influence in *internal* and *routine* policy decisions, and in *larger* and more *heterogeneous* communities [Boyd 1976, pp. 572–73].

Management strategy surely involves some appreciation of who is ordinarily involved in what type of decision.

REFERENCES

Bloom, Benjamin S. *Stability and Change in Human Characteristics.* New York: Wiley, 1964.

Bloom, Benjamin S. *Human Characteristics and School Learning.* New York: McGraw-Hill, 1976.

Boyd, William L. "The Public, the Professionals, and Educational Policy Making: Who Governs?" *Teachers College Record* 77 (May 1976): 539–77.

Cahen, Leonard S., and Filby, Nikola N. "The Class Size Achievement Issue: New Evidence and a Research Plan." *Phi Delta Kappan* 60 (March 1979): 492–95, 538.

Elliott, Arthur H. "Turning It Around in Education with Student Tutoring." *Clearing House* 50 (March 1977): 285–90.

Erickson, Donald A. "Research in Educational Administration: The State of the Art." *Educational Researcher* 8 (March 1979): 9–14.

Lipham, James M., and Fruth, Marvin J. *The Principal and Individually Guided Education.* Reading, Mass.: Addison-Wesley, 1976.

Thomas, J. Alan. *School Finance and Educational Opportunity in Michigan.* Lansing: Michigan Department of Education, 1968.

Thomas, J. Alan. *The Productive School.* New York: Wiley, 1971.

Wiley, David E., and Harnischfeger, Annegret. "Explosion of a Myth: Quantity of Schooling and Exposure to Instruction, Major Educational Vehicles." *Educational Researcher* 3 (April 1974): 7–12.

7

Instructional Strategies

LOUIS RUBIN

Research on instructional strategies, of necessity, involves both teaching and learning. As a consequence, experimental studies have explored a broad variety of issues: the interrelationship between cognition and affect, the comparative effectiveness of different teaching procedures, the advantages and disadvantages of prestructured lessons, alternative approaches to learning reinforcement, and so on. Still, the questions surrounding ideal teaching practice are far more complex than one might expect.

In human affairs people often must act before they know enough to act wisely, and such appears to be the case with instructional strategies. The intent of this chapter, therefore, is to summarize the findings from recent research and to extract implications for teaching. These recommendations, however, are necessarily speculative since — although many clues are available — the data are far from conclusive. Some instructional tactics, to be sure, seem more efficient than others, but learning outcomes are influenced by an enormous array of variables.

Part of the difficulty, perhaps, is attributable to the confusion surrounding the term *strategy* itself. Frequently treated as synonymous with method, strategy should embody something more than mere technique. A teacher, for example, may use either a heuristic or didactic method. The classroom management, however, can be permissive or authoritarian, the instructional materials may require individual or group activity, disparate evaluation mechanisms can be deployed, and alternative processes can be used to correct learning errors. Strategy, therefore, implies a composite of instructional provisions that together constitute a particular approach to teaching.

It is tempting to assume that an ideal strategy will, in every instance, be best. This, unfortunately, is not the case. Although some methods are generally effective and others ineffective, much depends upon the specific circumstances. A student may be more responsive to one procedure than another, a teacher's affinity for a tactic may compensate for its limitations, or some special condition may make the learning environment atypical. Hence, in most instances instructional strategies are not good or bad in abstract: they are successful or unsuccessful in a given situation.

This is not to say, obviously, that the fundamental principles of teaching and learning can be violated with impunity. Medley's (1973) investigations, as a case in point, demonstrate that highly successful teachers — no matter what strategies they use — are likely to respect certain essential conditions. They engineer classroom environments that are organized, supportive, and orderly. They are adept at using time to maximum advantage and sustaining pupil involvement. Even when their students are busy at their desks, they pay exceedingly close attention to what happens. Kounin (1970) makes the same point when he observes that effective teachers are "with-it" rather than "out-of-it"; that is, they seem to have an almost intuitive sense of what is going on.

The research on attribution theory is also relevant in this regard. Although the concept of personal causation (individual responsibility for learning) is hardly new, it recently has taken on increasing significance. The studies of de Charms (1976) offer a useful illustration: through student training programs, he sought to convince learners that their behavior — and their learning success — was chiefly determined by their own actions rather than by some outside force. Positive results were obtained, particularly in arithmetic and language skills. The conclusions suggest, among other things, that it is a grave mistake to restrict accountability to teachers alone: students, too, must assume at least some responsibility for their own learning achievement.

There is, in this same connection, a renaissance of interest in the value of hard work. In short, when students attribute learning failure to some external factor, they are not likely to expend much effort and, as a result, further failure is probable. But when, in contrast, they view poor performance as the expected consequence of insufficient endeavor, the will to invest greater energy in learning may increase. Put simply, expecting more of students may, in itself, constitute a useful strategy for improving learning. In view of these generalizations, then, what can be said about the experimental evidence?

Most research on classroom instructional strategies has been conducted under the rubric of "research on teaching." As defined by Gage (1972), such investigations encompass research on teacher effects — the consequences of specific teacher behavior on student achievement (Brophy and Evertson 1974, for example), and teacher education — the comparative merits of different training methodologies. Since the early 1960s research on teaching has reflected an assumption that teacher background and other "presage" variables, such as student abilities, affect "process" variables (the instructional modes used by teachers) and thus influence student achievement and other "products" of instruction. In their review of research on teaching, Dunkin and Biddle (1974) categorized hundreds of studies according to the linkages investigated in the presage-process-product continuum, as well as studies dealing with "context" variables: grade level, subject matter, class size, and the like.

Most investigations have examined the relationship among two or three variables at play. A study of the influence of teacher questioning techniques on student achievement, for example, would represent an exploration of a simple process-product linkage. Only rarely, however, have studies sought to examine all of the variables simultaneously or to determine the relative importance of each in influencing student outcomes. Hence, questions regarding the combinations of variables having the greatest influence on learning remain largely unanswered.

Much of the research on teaching has proceeded according to what Rosenshine and Furst (1973) referred to as the "descriptive-correlational-experimental loop." Presage-process type studies, wherein teacher characteristics (attitudes toward teaching) were related to instructional strategies (using student ideas), developed a methodology for describing teaching quantitatively. Once measures of such variables became available, correlational studies assessing their interrelationship and their effect on student performance were initiated. More recently, however, experimental inquiries have attempted to isolate promising correlational findings and to determine causal relationships. Dunkin (1978) and others, for example, have described and analyzed three contrasting methods of research on teaching: descriptive, correlational, and experimental.

Such research is not without its critics. Heath and Neilson (1974) object to the studies on methodological grounds — lack of randomization in treatment groups, inappropriate statistical techniques, and an inadequate theory base. Many scholars, on the other hand, take philosophical issue with the basic rationale. In particular, they fault the research on teaching for its simplistic presumption that an instructional strategy can be universally effective for all students. Much of the research, critics also contend, has been directed at the wrong questions. It is not surprising, therefore, that the efforts have yielded "completely equivocal, nonsignificant, and insignificant findings" (Gage 1978, p. 26).

Cronbach and Snow (1977), concurring with the jaundiced view of the studies on record, believe that: (a) instructional strategies should be carefully defined according to specific teacher behavior and studied independently from other correlated factors; (b) they should be tested systematically so that the effects are measured over a substantial period of time; and (c) learner characteristics, such as general mental ability, home experiences, and school-related anxiety, should be measured and incorporated in conclusions regarding the processes through which learners react to teaching. Summed up, the criticism implies that future research on teaching should be based, foursquare, on a clear conceptual premise of large scale and verified through broad replication. It should, furthermore, seek to clarify some important unknowns. Why, for example, do some learners respond poorly to higher-order questions, and why do many low-achieving students have difficulty with indirect unstructured instruction?

It may be impossible to answer such questions through research constrained by traditional methodology. A groundswell of interest has developed around various forms of interpretive analysis. Eisner (1977), for example, has referred to a "qualitative approach," Cronbach (1975) speaks of a "thick description," and Cole and Scribner (1975) suggest "ecological" explorations. These and other naturalistic inquiries could increase our understanding of why particular strategies succeed or fail.

In a recent study of novice teachers being "inducted" into classroom life, Doyle (1979) used an assortment of observational data to define classroom situations to which teachers must adapt and to identify the adaptive strategies used by successful practitioners. The situations, or classroom "states of nature," to use Shavelson's phrase, were reminiscent of those described by Jackson (1968). The classrooms were characterized by diverse activity serving a variety of purposes ("multidimensionality"), by the simultaneous occurrence of different events ("simultaneity"), and by unplanned developments ("unpredictability"). (See also Kounin and Gump 1974.)

Successful teacher trainees — those able to cope with such situations — exhibited a number of consistent adaptive strategies. Doyle labeled these "chunking" (the ability to group discrete events into larger units), "differentiation"—Kounin's (1970) term (the ability to discriminate among units in terms of their immediate and long-range significance), "overlap" (the ability to deal with two or more events at once), "timing" (the ability to monitor and control the duration of events), and "rapid judgment" (the ability to interpret events with a minimum of delay). These, admittedly, are not strategies as much as skills, but they illustrate what can be learned through systematic observation and analysis.

What Stake (1972) has called "portrayal" permits researchers to interpret the events intervening between teacher actions, student performance, and learning outcomes. Similarly, it permits curriculum input, classroom environmental influences, and student thinking processes to be taken into consideration. Traditional research presumes influence flowing from teacher to student, rather than reciprocally. But students frequently influence teachers. One suspects, in fact, that adept teachers base their strategies to a considerable degree on the responses of their students.

Doyle has offered two alternatives of his own; one is called the "mediating-process" approach and the other a "classroom ecology" system. The mediating paradigm takes into account learner behavior as well as the cognitive functions affecting learning. These include, for example, such mediating processes as attending, translating, and segmenting. Since, Doyle contends, student responses of this kind are instrumental in learning, they should receive as much research attention as teaching techniques and instructional strategy.

His second set of propositions, dealing with classroom ecology, focuses on the interplay between classroom environment and student. Like most of the other research in this area (for example, Cohen, Intili, and Robbins 1979), the methodology is largely ethnographic in nature. Children respond to a variety of environmental cues. They react not only to the teacher, but to other students, textbooks, grades, and so on. Doyle conjectures that more research on the way students learn to use cues that affect achievement would be helpful in developing better instructional strategies.

Medley (1973), yet one more critic of classical research on teaching, reasons that we have been led astray by the false belief that teachers' effectiveness is a unidimensional trait. For Medley, a good teacher is one who can adapt teaching to the students, the learning objectives, and the particular situation. Thus teacher competence and instructional strategies are one: "the function of process-product research is no longer seen as that of finding out which competencies a teacher should learn to use and which he should ignore; the function of such research is to provide information which will help the teacher decide which competency is likely to be useful in a given instance" (p. 44).

To touch upon another aspect of the problem, considerable interest has recently arisen about the art and science of teaching. Few theorists doubt that efficient teaching is enhanced by respecting principles that increase predictability and control. At the same time, however, pedagogical artistry also involves an ability to put aside customary dictates when something more spontaneous or inventive helps students learn.

Artistry in teaching is perhaps most evident in moment-to-moment teacher decision making. The subtle judgments that one must make during instruction to sustain learning momentum require an almost intuitive sense of timing. Good decision making, in turn, depends upon an ability to test and verify hunches through a kind of instructional probing.

During lessons involving classroom discussion, for example, a teacher must assess student thinking and estimate the degree of understanding that has developed. With these assessments as a base, the teacher needs to predict what additional benefits might be gained from the discussion and to choose the particular instructional strategies that offer the greatest advantage. In this way lesson objectives are translated into specific teaching tactics. In spontaneous decision making, therefore, the teacher must be perceptive, astute, quick to decide, and adept at altering directions when the situation requires.

In my own experimental studies, for example, I have sought to explore the art of teaching. We have tended to assume that the right subject matter, taught in the proper way, will result in classrooms that are good for children. Experience, alas, has proved otherwise. Good teaching materials and efficient techniques are not enough. Why is it, for example, that two classrooms — in which the teachers use essentially the same instructional methods and texts — are nonetheless strikingly different? What accounts for the fact that some classrooms are exciting, and others dreary? Why do students look forward to one teacher with delight and anticipate another with either disdain, despair, or dread?

The difference apparently lies in the intangibles of artistry. These intangibles transcend charisma, although gifted teachers often are blessed with charismatic qualities. They go beyond style because great teachers neither function in exactly the same way nor embrace similar beliefs about the purposes of teaching. They have only minimal connection with intelligence since the brightest teachers are not always the best teachers. They involve commitment and a powerful desire to accomplish intent, but commitment, too, is only a partial condition for artistry; zealous and highly dedicated teachers frequently achieve only meager results. Nor is artistry entirely dependent upon humanistic impulses and personal warmth. Great teachers, upon occasion, are authoritarian in their approach to instruction. The qualities that undergird teaching virtuosity are intangible precisely because they are difficult to analyze and describe. Yet they exist.

Although the characteristics of artistic teaching are subtle and elusive, not easily dissected and defined, they nevertheless can be cultivated. That is, teachers can develop an intuitive "feel" for what is right and wrong in their work styles. Parallels exist in other forms of human endeavor. Good cooks, for example, season to taste. Their finely honed palates, however, have been acquired through many years of practice. Still, students of cuisine who aspire to excellence are somehow able to learn this sense of taste from an apprenticeship with a master chef. Similarly, we speak of the nose that has been developed by a wine connoisseur, the ear of a fine musician, the eye of a skillful graphic artist, and the hand of a great sculptor. Seemingly, then, teachers can cumulatively master the subtle nuances of their craft.

Virtuosity in teaching, one might say, lies in using a particular method with great panache and dexterity. A number of devices may be appropriate in a given situation, but the trick is to use whatever is selected artfully. Of course, the choice of a technique is significant. Apt selection, in many instances, is two-thirds of the pedagogical battle. But prudent choice depends, primarily, on two factors. First, the method must fit the subject matter and the learning objectives. If the goal, for example, is to teach some basic rules of spelling, memorization may have more to offer than a discussion of phonetics. Second, the method must be congruent with the teachers' natural style. Using simulation or role playing, for example, to illustrate political manipulation, may appeal to some teachers and not others.

The characteristics associated with artistry involve skill, originality, flair, dexterity, ingenuity, virtuosity, and similar qualities that, together, produce exceptional performance. One might also say that artistry consists of master craftsmanship through which tasks are conceived, planned, and executed with unusual imagination and brilliance. Or, to approach the phenomenon from still another perspective, one might argue that it arises out of the subtle discrimination and judgment that stem from unusual perception and taste. Regardless of the descriptive terms used, however, artistry implies human performance that is exceptional in its proficiency and cunning.

Applied to teaching, artistry involves selecting aims that are of highest worth, using imaginative and ingenious tactics to achieve these aims, and accomplishing the aims with consummate skill. From even this elementary analysis, it is plain that artistic performance necessitates commitment, knowledge, discernment, astuteness — and uncommon dedication. These, moreover, must be blended together into an integral force. Great skill wasted on trivial objectives, virtuous intentions pursued unimaginatively or without ingenuity, and well-conceived tactics that are poorly executed all defeat the cause.

Research is presently being carried on at the University of Michigan's Institute for Research on Teaching (Clark and Yinger 1979) and by Shavelson and his colleagues (Shavelson 1978, Borko and Shavelson 1978) at the University of California at Los Angeles to analyze effective decision-making procedures. Much remains to be learned about spur-of-the-moment judgment and about training teachers to exercise instructional choices that are perceptive and shrewd while also rapid.

Finally, there is a growing belief that the strategy popularly known as "direct instruction" is more effective than other alternatives in extending conventionally measured elementary grade achievement. Indeed, Rosenshine (1979) regards direct instruction as the dominant theme in the current "experimental" cycle of research on teaching. Somewhat related are strategies involving instructional time. Because active student involvement in a learning task is critical, direct instruction embodies teaching methods that maximize the extent to which students are engaged in academically related activities, or academic learning time (Berliner 1979).

Corno (1979) has noted that the early work of Carroll (1963) and Bloom (1974), as well as the later efforts of Harnischfeger and Wiley (1976) on time spent in instruction and opportunity to learn, all view student behavior as the mediating factor between instructional strategy and learner achievement. In short, what students do with time allocated for learning a subject makes the difference in their achievement.

From later research as well, it appears that the importance of concentrated effort and sustained engagement is crucial: they, more than anything else, determine the success of a strategy. Many studies, for instance, have demonstrated that achievement test scores, adjusted for initial ability levels of students, correlate positively with measures of time spent on activities. Fisher and others (1978), in an extension of previous research by McDonald and Elias, reported that the academic learning time (defined as the number of minutes engaged in content-relevant activities of an appropriate difficulty level), accounted for a significant portion of the residual achievement variance beyond that attributable to student ability in second- and fifth-grade classes. Similarly, a major finding of Brophy and Evertson (1974), investigating second- and third-grade classes, was that greater learning occurs in classes where teachers are "successful classroom managers," and "keep their students actively engaged in productive classroom work most of the time" (p. 52).

These large-scale correlational studies provide considerable empirical support for the linkage in academic subject areas between student involvement and achievement during the early grades. Further verification of the relationship can be found in a number of smaller studies (Dunkin 1978, Good and Beckerman 1978), in literature reviews (Bennett and others 1976), and meta-analyses (Peterson 1979). Strategically, therefore, the point of significance is that the amount of time students spend engaged in academic tasks — unlike native ability and other unalterable variables — is at least partly under the teacher's control. In Bloom's words: "Time-on-task is then one of the variables that accounts for learning differences between students, between classes, and even between nations. Time-on-task can be altered positively (or negatively) by the instructional process, and thus has direct consequences for the learning that will take place" (Bloom 1980, p. 383).

How can teachers increase student involvement in learning? Several studies, during the past half-dozen years, have examined the relationship between various methods of teaching and student academic engagement (Brophy and Evertson 1974, Fisher and others 1978, McDonald and Elias 1976, Soar 1973, Stallings and Kaskowitz 1974). Other research has explored the connections between teacher behavior and learner involvement (Bennett and others 1976; Filby and Marliave 1977, Solomon and Kendall 1976).

More recently, Berliner and Rosenshine integrated much of the research into a model of "direct instruction" (Rosenshine 1979, Berliner and Rosenshine 1977, Berliner 1979). Five sets of provisions, they suggest, serve to make a classroom "academically focused." The first set is largely procedural:

1. Class time is mainly devoted to academically oriented activities, such as reading and mathematics.
2. Students working on these activities are observed to be "actively engaged"; that is, their eyes are focused on teacher or text, as if either listening or reading attentively; if writing, they persist in that activity without interruption from unrelated influences; during discussions they answer questions and follow the flow of information as evidenced by turning their heads, nodding, and so on.
3. The amount of content covered during time allotted to academic activity is consistently high.
4. The goals of instruction are made clear to students in advance, either through spoken or written statements.

The second set of provisions centers around the format of discussion sessions. Emphasis is on "controlled practice":

1. Students respond to questions eliciting factual information. The questions should be simple enough to generate a large number of correct responses, but difficulty should increase as students become more adept.
2. Following student responses, the teacher provides a brief commentary, indicating the degree of correctness and — where appropriate — additional "clues."

The focus of the third set is "feedback":

1. In addition to commenting on the correctness of student responses, teachers should occasionally ask probing questions, particularly of the more academically oriented students.
2. Occasionally, mild criticism should follow an incorrect response, before redirecting the same question to another student.
3. With students who are less academically oriented, it is useful to provide hints and suggestions, as well as to rephrase the question frequently. The object is to encourage maximum

student involvement. Following learner response, the teacher provides feedback, praises the student where appropriate (praise should be used with reserve), and continues the discussion.

4. In one-on-one discussions, the recommended processes are much the same for the two kinds of students.

A fourth group of recommendations deals with the teacher's monitoring of seatwork:

1. The teacher circulates around the room, looking for students who appear to be having difficulty, and works individually with such students, often using the techniques just described.

2. The teacher also tries to detect disengagement and refocus attention as quickly as possible.

The fifth set of postulations pertains to "grouping" patterns:

1. Teacher-led groups of approximately eight students are considered ideal since maximum supervision occurs when the teacher can attend to all students.

The study is generally representative of ongoing research and current thought regarding teaching strategies. Carefully organized instruction and the prudent use of classroom time are advantageous. Skillful teacher questioning that helps to prompt student attention, highlight significant ideas, and probe learner understanding is also beneficial. Beyond these, adroit teacher commentary that guides student thinking, clarifies misunderstanding, and encourages further effort can make a considerable difference. And finally, effective pacing and other motivational devices can do much to increase student commitment. These conceptions, at first blush, may seem to be little more than common sense. Yet, common sense is not as common as we like to think — scientific investigation that verifies "rules of thumb" is not without virtue.

Aside from these somewhat basic principles, however, the scene is more ambiguous. When we deal with phenomena that are difficult to interpret accurately, miscalculations and judgmental errors come easily. Nonetheless, three general inferences seem reasonable. First, irrespective of which instructional strategies are advocated, teacher training is indispensable. Even a good device, deployed in the wrong ways, produces little gain. Furthermore, since it cannot be assumed that all teachers will be equally adept with every technique, practitioners must become familiar with the characteristics of a teaching procedure, the conditions under which it offers maximum utility, its comparative advantages and disadvantages in relation to other alternatives, its corresponding evaluation mechanisms, and so on.

Second, instructional management is as important as teaching strategy. Maximal student learning depends not merely upon method, but upon reinforcement, efficient use of resources, student incentive, and the careful sequencing of instructional objectives. Thus, it would be a grave mistake to mandate particular pedagogical procedures without, at the same time, specifying the corollary provisions that ensure learning achievement. Two teachers, using exactly the same materials and methods, often obtain different results because of variations in their classroom management.

Third, although there is substantial evidence that the spontaneous instructional decisions that teachers make in the course of their teaching — the endless adjustments to changing classroom nuances — heavily influence learning outcomes, relatively little is known about improving such decision-making skills. Accordingly, we would be well-advised to initiate experimental studies of the source of teachers' attitudes and tactical judgments, explore new in-service training systems that may be beneficial, and test these systems in a variety of contexts. If perceptual error and the misreading of classroom signs seriously diminishes the effectiveness of an instructional strategy, it is difficult to exaggerate the importance of the needed research.

Much would also be gained if subsequent investigations could attend to unfinished business. We have yet, for example, to integrate the discrete bodies of theory on teaching and learning, our conceptualizations of instructional strategy are still fragmented and piecemeal, and we remain confused regarding what teachers most need to know and do in order to function effectively. This confusion extends into other dark areas. What distinguishes the teaching of science from that of history? Do the high school senior and the first-grader learn in the same way? And what constitutes a reasonable balance between teaching specific subjects and general intellectual skills? Thus an ancient dictum holds true: although the past has not been entirely useless, it is but prologue to what lies ahead.

REFERENCES

Bennett, S. N.; Jordan, J.; Long, G.; and Wade, B. *Teaching Styles and Pupil Progress*. London: Open Books, 1976.

Berliner, David C. "Tempus Educare." In *Research on Teaching: Concepts, Findings, and Implications*, edited by Penelope L. Peterson and Herbert J. Walberg, pp. 120–35. Berkeley, Calif.: McCutchan, 1979.

Berliner, David C., and Rosenshine, Barak V. "The Acquisition of Knowledge in the Classroom." In *Schooling and the Acquisition of Knowledge*, edited by Richard C. Anderson, Rand J. Spiro, and William E. Montague, pp. 375–96. Hillsdale, N.J.: Lawrence Erlbaum Associates, 1977.

Bloom, Benjamin S. "Time and Learning." *American Psychologist* 29 (September 1974): 682–88.

Bloom, Benjamin S. "The New Direction in Educational Research: Alterable Variables." *Phi Delta Kappan* 61 (February 1980): 382–85.

Borko, Hilda, and Shavelson, Richard J. "Teachers' Sensitivity to the Reliability of Information in Making Causal Attributions in an Achievement Situation." *Journal of Educational Psychology* 70 (June 1978): 271–280.

Brophy, Jere E., and Evertson, Carolyn M. *Process-Product Correlations in the Texas Teacher Effectiveness Study: Final Report*. Austin: Research and Development Center for Teacher Education, University of Texas, 1974.

Carroll, John B. "A Model of School Learning." *Teachers College Record* 64 (May 1963): 723–33.

Clark, Christopher M., and Yinger, Robert J. "Teachers' Thinking." In *Research on Teaching*, edited by Penelope L. Peterson and Herbert J. Walberg, pp. 231–63. Berkeley, Calif.: McCutchan, 1979.

Cohen, Elizabeth G.; Intili, Jo-Ann K.; and Robbins, Susan H. "Task and Authority: A Sociological View of Classroom Management." In *Classroom Management*, Seventy-Eighth Yearbook of the National Society for the Study of Education, Part 2, pp. 116-43, edited by Daniel L. Duke. Chicago: University of Chicago Press, 1979.

Cole, Michael, and Scribner, Sylvia. "Theorizing About Socialization of Cognition." *Ethos* 3 (Summer 1975): 250–68.

Corno, Lyn. "Classroom Instruction and the Matter of Time." In *Classroom Management*, edited by Daniel L. Duke, pp. 245–80. Chicago: University of Chicago Press, 1979.

Cronbach, Lee J. "Beyond the Two Disciplines of Scientific Psychology." *American Psychologist* 30 (February 1975): 116–26.

Cronbach, Lee J., and Snow, Richard E. *Aptitudes and Instructional Methods: A Handbook for Research on Interactions*. New York: Irvington/Naiburg, 1977.

de Charms, Richard. *Enhancing Motivation: Change in the Classroom*. New York: Irvington, 1976.

Doyle, Walter. "Making Managerial Decisions in Classrooms." In *Classroom Management*, edited by Daniel L. Duke, pp. 42–74. Chicago: University of Chicago Press, 1979.

Dunkin, Michael J. "Student Characteristics, Classroom Processes, and Student Achievement." *Journal of Educational Psychology* 70 (December 1978): 998–1009.

Dunkin, Michael J., and Biddle, Bruce J. *The Study of Teaching.* New York: Holt, Rinehart and Winston, 1974.

Eisner, Elliot W. "On the Uses of Educational Connoisseurship and Criticism for Evaluating Classroom Life." *Teachers College Record* 78 (Fall 1977): 345–58.

Filby, Nikola N., and Marliave, Richard N. *Descriptions of Distributions of ALT within and across Classes during the A-B Period: Technical Note IV-Ia, Beginning Teacher Evaluation Study.* San Francisco: Far West Laboratory for Educational Research and Development, September 1977.

Fisher, Charles W.; Filby, Nikola N.; Marliave, Richard S.; Cahen, Leonard S.; Dishaw, Marilyn M.; Moore, Jeffry E.; and Berliner, David C. *Teacher Behaviors, Academic Learning Time, and Student Achievement: Final Report Phase III-B, Beginning Teacher Evaluation Study Report VI.* San Francisco: Far West Laboratory for Educational Research and Development, June 1978.

Gage, N. L. *Teacher Effectiveness and Teacher Education.* Palo Alto, Calif.: Pacific Books, 1972.

Gage, N. L. *The Scientific Basis for the Art of Teaching.* New York: Teachers College Press, 1978.

Good, Thomas L., and Beckerman, Terrill M. "Time on Task: A Naturalistic Study in Sixth-Grade Classrooms." *Elementary School Journal* 78 (January 1978): 192–201.

Harnischfeger, Annegret, and Wiley, David E. "The Teaching-Learning Process in Elementary Schools: A Synoptic View." *Curriculum Inquiry* 6 (Fall 1976): 5–43.

Heath, Robert W., and Nielson, Mark H. "The Research Basis for Performance-Based Teacher Education." *Review of Educational Research* 44 (Fall 1974): 463–84.

Jackson, Philip W. *Life in Classrooms.* New York: Holt, Rinehart and Winston, 1968.

Kounin, Jacob S. *Discipline and Group Management in Classrooms.* New York: Holt, Rinehart and Winston, 1970.

Kounin, Jacob S., and Gump, Paul V. "Signal Systems of Lesson Settings and Task-related Behavior of Preschool Children." *Journal of Educational Psychology* 66 (August 1974): 554–62.

McDonald, Frederick J., and Elias, Patricia. *The Effects of Teaching Performance on Pupil Learning, Beginning Teacher Evaluation Study: Phase II, Final Report. Vol. I.* Princeton, N.J.: Educational Testing Service, 1976.

Medley, Donald M. "Closing the Gap between Research in Teacher Effectiveness and the Teacher Education Curriculum." *Journal of Research and Development in Education* 7 (Fall 1973): 39–46.

Peterson, Penelope L. "Direct Instruction Reconsidered." In *Research on Teaching,* edited by Penelope L. Peterson and Herbert J. Walberg, pp. 57–69. Berkeley, Calif.: McCutchan, 1979.

Rosenshine, Barak. "Content, Time and Direct Instruction." In *Research on Teaching*, edited by Penelope L. Peterson and Herbert L. Walberg, pp. 28–56. Berkeley, Calif.: McCutchan, 1979.

Rosenshine, Barak, and Furst, Norma F. "The Use of Direct Observation to Study Teaching." In *Second Handbook of Research on Teaching*, edited by Robert M. W. Travers, pp. 122–83. Chicago: Rand McNally, 1973.

Shavelson, Richard J. "Teachers' Estimates of Student 'States of Mind' and Behavior." *Journal of Teacher Education* 29 (September-October 1978): 37–40.

Soar, Robert S. *Final Report, Follow Through Classroom Process Measurement and Pupil Growth (1970-1971)*. Gainesville: Institute for the Development of Human Resources, University of Florida, 1973.

Solomon, Daniel, and Kendall, Arthur J. *Individual Characteristics and Children's Performance in Varied Educational Settings*. Rockville, Md.: Montgomery County Public Schools, 1976.

Stake, Robert E. "An Approach to the Evaluation of Instructional Programs (Program Portrayal vs. Analysis)." Paper delivered at the annual meeting of the American Educational Research Association, Chicago, 1972.

Stallings, Jane A., and Kaskowitz, David H. *Follow Through Classroom Observation Evaluation, 1972-73*. Menlo Park, Calif.: Stanford Research Institute, 1974.

Discussion

Leon Lessinger

Louis Rubin is to be commended for making the best of a bad situation. It is apparent from his review of the research that he has discovered an emperor who is wearing no clothes. The task was clear: Rubin sought what research has to say about the influence of instructional strategies on students' achievement, performance, and self-concept in school. There was evidently so little research of value that Rubin chose the only alternative open to him: he redefined the topic to be research on teaching. This maneuver obviated the requirement for a distinction between strategy and tactics in teaching and learning.

The empirical research literature has little of use to offer the practitioner other than a minimal verification of long-held common knowledge about teaching strategies. To supplement this rather bleak report, I will report some of the significant work of my colleague, Albert Mayrhofer, as it relates to both strategy and tactics in teaching. Building on the work of behaviorists, comparative ethologists and learning theorists, Mayrhofer (1977) demonstrated approaches that directly relate to the topics of this chapter.

Mayrhofer defines *strategy* as the overall plan of resource allocation to reach a desired goal. *Tactics* are the actual deployment of the resources to reach an objective. These definitions give perspective on the research findings in teaching and learning. In this arena, strategy is the plan for artistic orchestration of sequences of tactics in goal seeking. A tactic is the actual artistic orchestration of the components required to achieve an objective. A strategy is an evolving, dynamic, responsive time sequence of tactics. From this perspective, ideas about learning and the learners themselves are resources.

Mayrhofer shows how six "laws of learning" — contiguity, association, practice, readiness, novelty, and chaining — can be applied synergistically to enhance retention and transfer of a concept or principle. The law of association relates time to learning: the closer the time between two events approaches zero, the more likely the organism is to link events. The law of contiguity relates distance to learning: the closer the distance between objects, the more likely an organism will link them. Since distance is the interval between places and time is the interval between events, it follows that distance is a subset of time. Indeed, places are long-term events. Such understanding facilitates the achievement of the second taxonomic level in the work of Bloom and others (1956). To achieve this level of understanding, the visual mode is preferred. This mode reduces the time between events to zero, whereas the auditory mode does not. After all, a concept is the idea inherent in a pattern of data or precepts. The visual mode displays that pattern most expeditiously. The common observations that "a picture is worth a thousand words" and "example is the best teacher" hit the mark.

Through similar reasoning, Mayrhofer shows how the laws of practice and primacy influence retention and how the law of novelty influences readiness. By the orchestration of all the laws through the use of at least three contexts plus the use of the law of chaining, impressive gains in learning and its transfer become possible.

It is unfortunate that Rubin did not include references to the careful study done by the "older" masters like Ebbinghouse, Thorndike, and Katona who laid a pattern of generalization so usefully employed by Mayrhofer. If we view Rubin's work from the standpoint of research findings about "good practice," we find some profitable areas he did not address. Some examples follow.

In July 1974, the U.S. Office of Education, under the guidance of Associate Commissioner Thomas Burns, established a way of sharing educational programs that work. This method was housed in the Division of Education Replication and was part of a national diffusion network. Almost 200 programs were made available to school systems. Since that time the replications have approached 7,000. The programs contain the components of tactics and involve some of the elements of teaching. It is helpful to the educator to study this kind of "research" to determine its local usefulness in the improvement of learning.

The topic of educational engineering is worth reviewing when considering instructional strategies. Smith's (1971) seminal work on the engineering of education and training systems deals with the organization of tactics in a way that might lead some to define it as a strategy.

What research says about the results of a lack of strategy is great indeed. Mayrhofer (1977) insists that to manage a process productively, in this case the learning process, one must know the process. Stones and Morris (1972) and Goodlad, Klein, and associates (1970) contend that there is little evidence that teachers know the process of learning. Gropper (1974) defined instructional strategy and synthesized experience into usable form.

In summary, Rubin has demonstrated that formal research has little to say about the topic that is useful to practitioners. Research viewed as the consensus of reasonable professionals, however, has much to say. Some of what it says is of great value, particularly if synthesized after diligent reflection.

REFERENCES

Bloom, Benjamin S., and others. *Taxonomy of Educational Objectives. Handbook I: Cognitive Domain.* New York: David McKay, 1956.

Goodlad, John I.; Klein, M. Frances; and Associates. *Looking Behind the Classroom Door.* Worthington, Ohio: Charles A. Jones, 1970.

Gropper, George L. *Instructional Strategies.* Englewood Cliffs, N.J.: Educational Technology Publications, 1974.

Mayrhofer, Albert V. "A Conceptual Model of a Systematic Intervention to Improve Learning Productivity." Doctoral dissertation, University of Alabama, 1977.

Smith, Robert G., Jr. *The Engineering of Educational and Training Systems.* Lexington, Mass.: Heath, 1971.

Stones, E. and Morris, S. *Teaching Practice: Problems and Perspectives.* London: Methuen, 1972.

8

Educational Media

GENE L. WILKINSON

The field of educational media is eclectic, reflecting the diversity of background and interests of the individuals who work in the field and the trends exhibited in its growth. Professionals in the field share a common interest in the tools of teaching and learning and a common concern with the role and function of technology in education. With such diversity, however, definition of the field is vital.

The Commission on Instructional Technology (Tickton 1970–1971) noted two ways of defining instructional technology. One definition, "the media born of the communication revolution which can be used for instructional purposes alongside the teacher, textbook, and blackboard," is traditional (p. 21). It implies a concern with machines and materials — the objects, such as television, films, overhead projectors, and computers — that are part of educational media. Because such an approach is expected by those outside of the field, it will be followed here. However, such a definition is too narrow. The Commission's second definition states that instructional technology is "a systematic way of designing, carrying out, and evaluating the total process of learning and teaching in terms of specific objectives, based on research in human learning and communication, and employing a combination of human and nonhuman resources to bring about more effective instruction" (p. 21).

The growing acceptance of this second definition is one of the factors that led to the initiation of the work of the AECT Task Force on Definition and Terminology (Association for Educational Communications and Technology 1977). The definition developed by the Task Force is based on a number of assumptions concerning technology in education (Morris 1963); it states that: "*Educational technology* is a complex, integrated process involving people, procedures, ideas, devices, and organization for analyzing problems, and devising, implementing, evaluating, and managing solutions to those problems involved in all aspects of human learning. In educational technology, the solutions to problems take the form of all the *learning resources* that are designed and/or selected as messages, people, materials, devices, techniques, and settings. The processes for analyzing problems, and devising, implementing and evaluating solutions are identified by the *educational development functions* of research-theory, design, production, evaluation-selection, logistics, and utilization. The processes of directing and coordinating one or more of these functions are identified by the *educational management functions* of organization management and personnel management" (1977, p. 59). The term *educational media* is primarily concerned with just two aspects of the total domain of educational technology — materials and devices. Schools are concerned with materials and devices, but they are also concerned with the people who provide and operate them; the design, production, logistics, and utilization of them; their organization and management; and how they interact with learners. The focus is, or should be, on process.

Technology as process is reflected in the current research literature and is reflected in this review. A number of areas suggested by a broad definition of technology have been excluded. For example, literature dealing with instructional design and development, except as it applies specifically to the design of media materials, will be excluded. As Diamond (1978) points out, the theories and models in this area have not been field tested, research studies are scarce, and the existing reports are often incomplete and misleading.

Two major areas are considered — research on educational media and research on school media centers. The concern of this chapter is with the tools of instruction and how they should be organized for the most effective use within the public schools. Educational media refers here to those devices and materials, other than textbooks, that can be used to convey information in a teaching and learning situation. Media center refers to the organizational unit that provides educational media and media services within the school.

RESEARCH ON EDUCATIONAL MEDIA

Anyone seeking to do a comprehensive survey of the research dealing with educational media is faced with a frustrating task. From one point of view, the field of educational media is one of the newest and most comprehensively documented aspects of education. It reached maturity, along with the methodology of educational research and evaluation, during World War II and the recent expansion of graduate training programs. From another point of view, educational media is as old as the first primitive who scratched a crude drawing in the dust — an area rich in advocacy but poor in evidence.

Experiments dealing with the instructional use of media began near the end of World War I and grew with the development of commercial films and radio. One of the first conceptually sound studies of the use of motion pictures in a public school setting was conducted at the University of Chicago (Freeman 1924). The Chicago film studies could have provided a solid foundation for media research; however, they were neglected in favor of a more limited experimental design that still persists today — the comparative media study. Following the lead of Eastman Kodak Company (Wood and Freeman 1929) and Yale University (Knowlton and Tilton 1929), investigators compared the effectiveness of one medium to another medium and to conventional instruction. Such comparison studies found contradictory or nonsignificant results. Weber (1930) pointed out that further comparative studies were not needed and that other questions should be examined. However, there was no major shift in media research until the end of World War II.

Major military studies on the use of film in training during and after World War II (Hovland and others 1949, Carpenter and Greenhill 1956), the exploration of television as a training tool by the Navy and Pennsylvania State University, and the stimulation for research and innovation of the National Defense Education Act of 1958 led to expansion and intensification of media research during the 1950s and 1960s. At the same time, there was continuing dissatisfaction with the designs being employed in media research and with the questions being examined. Knowlton (1964) pointed out that much of the research on media was based on false assumptions — that assuming the key variable to be the means of information transmission rather than some aspect of the message, content, or the learner would lead to false or contradictory conclusions.

A new direction for media research, which focused primarily on the "attributes" of media rather than the media themselves, was needed. As stated by Levie and Dickie (1973), media attributes are: "properties of stimulus materials which are manifest in the physical parameters of media. The attributes of a medium, then, are the capabilities of that medium — to show objects in motion, objects in color, objects in three dimensions; to provide printed words, spoken words, simultaneous visual and auditory stimuli; to allow for overt learner responses or random access to information" (p. 860). Research of media attributes, as summarized by Lumsdaine (1963), Briggs (1968), and Levie and Dickie, however, continued to show the conflicting results characteristic of comparative media studies. Levie and Dickie suggest that:

Early research dealing with media attributes sought main effects — spoken versus printed words, color versus black and white, overt versus covert responding, and so forth. Invariably the emerging generalization has been that no single level of the independent variable is consistently superior and that often the variable is, in fact, inoperative. The question then turns to the more complex problem of discovering the conditions under which different levels will facilitate learning for what kinds of learners in what kinds of tasks? The shift of focus from main effects to interactions is typically accompanied by a shift in focus from the physical parameters of stimulus attributes to concern with inferences about the internal human processes that may be aroused or facilitated by media attributes [1973, p. 877].

A number of designs for generating and testing hypotheses concerning the interaction of media attributes and learner aptitudes have been suggested (Snow and Salomon 1968, Snow 1970, Clark 1975) and much work has been conducted in the area (Cronbach and Snow 1977), but problems still persist. As Salomon and Clark (1977) point out, such research falls short of accomplishing the objective of improving educational practice.

It is by *necessity* highly analytic and detached, and thus it is — by its very nature — unrepresentative of the real world of education.
    One of the major purposes of media research is to deepen the understanding of what functions media attributes can accomplish for different learners and different tasks. It must emphasize, first and foremost, *internal validity*. If the researcher wishes to ascribe a particular effect or function to a particular attribute, neatness of experimental comparison is necessarily called for. This calls for carefully arranged experiments in which *only* the desired variables are allowed to vary according to the researcher's rationale. However, when such is carefully done according to the canons of methodology, something of utmost importance is lost — namely, representativeness, or external validity [p. 106].

Possible solutions to these design problems have been suggested (Salomon and Clark 1977, Clark 1978) and should lead to more useful research in future years.
    On a pessimistic note, Clark (1978) observes that "the systematic, carefully planned and conducted media research project has been a rare event" (p. 99). If one looks quickly at the past sixty years of media research, there is much to support Clark's view; however, there is also much that can be learned from a selective look at the literature on media effectiveness.

COMPARATIVE MEDIA STUDIES

As each new medium — films, radio, television, programmed instruction, computers — has been introduced into the classroom, the natural question is can students learn from this medium, and if so, can they learn better from it than from some other medium? As a result, the most common type of media research has been the study that compares a specific medium of instruction against one or more other media — most often conventional instruction.
    A problem with research that examines the effectiveness of instructional media is that the results are not consistent. At one

point there is significant evidence for the use of media, then for conventional instruction, but most often there is no significant difference. Hartley (1966) examined 112 studies that compared programmed instruction with conventional instruction and found that 41 showed programmed instruction significantly superior, 6 showed programmed instruction significantly worse, and 37 showed no significant difference.

Part of this problem can be explained by inadequate research design. When Hartley applied minimal acceptance criteria to the studies, he was left with only 8 acceptable studies. Stickell (1963) identified 250 studies that compared television to conventional instruction. To determine if the research could be interpreted, he applied the following criteria: (a) experimental and control groups of at least twenty-five subjects, (b) which had been randomly assigned from the same population, (c) were taught by the same instructor, (d) measured by a testing instrument judged to be reliable and valid, and (e) evaluated by acceptable statistical procedures. After using these criteria, he was left with only ten studies that met the full standards and twenty-three studies that were acceptable but had minor problems.

Moldstad (1974) agrees that a number of problems exist with media research — the need for better designs, more insightful questions, more adequate sampling, and better integration of technology into instructional programs. But he notes that "many educational decisions must be made by administrators and school board members on information that might be considered somewhat incomplete by educational researchers" (p. 404). Generalizing from a number of studies, he concluded that "when instructional technology is carefully selected and used, (a) "significantly greater learning often results when media are integrated into the traditional instructional program; (b) equal amounts of learning are often accomplished in significantly less time using instructional technology; (c) multimedia instructional programs based upon a 'systems approach' frequently facilitate student learning more effectively than traditional instruction; (d) multimedia and/or audiotutorial instructional programs are usually preferred by students when compared with traditional instruction" (p. 390). Schramm (1973) reviewed the media research to examine Gagné's (1967) contention that "the required conditions of learning can be put into effect . . . by each medium" (p. 28). Schramm concluded: "Motivated students learn from any medium if it is competently used and adapted to their needs. Within its physical limits, any medium can perform any educational task. Whether a student learns more from one medium than from another is at least as likely to depend on *how* the medium is used as on *what* medium is used" (p. iv). These conclusions can be supported by an examination of a few media research studies which do show a significant difference.

Research on Motion Pictures

A number of investigators have examined the effectiveness of motion pictures (Hoban and Van Ormer 1950, May and Lumsdaine 1958). One of the earliest studies at the University of Chicago produced conclusions that still warrant attention:

1. The relative effectiveness of verbal instruction as contrasted with the various forms of concrete or realistic material in visual media depends on the nature of the instruction to be given and the character of the learner's previous experience with objective materials.
2. The comparison of the film with other visual media (slides, stereographs, still pictures) as a means of instruction when the medium variable is motion (for example, a film showing the motion of a steamboat was compared with a still picture of the same object) indicates that the film is superior within a restricted range and type of content, but that outside of this range the other media are as effective or more effective.
3. The peculiar value of a film lies not in its generally stimulating effect, but in its ability to furnish a particular type of experience.
4. It is inefficient to put into films actions which can be demonstrated readily by the teacher.
5. In teaching science and how to do or make something, demonstration is superior to the film.
6. Films should be so designed as to furnish to the teacher otherwise inaccessible raw material for instruction but should leave the organization of the complete teaching unit largely to the teacher.
7. The teacher has been found superior to all visual media in gaining and sustaining attention.
8. Each of the so-called conventional forms of instruction which employ visual media has some advantage and some disadvantage, and there are circumstances under which each is the best form to use [Saettler 1968, p. 116].

In a study that shows the advantages of films in aiding students to apply conceptual understanding to new problems, Rulon (1933) used specially designed films in a comparison of text-plus-film to text-only instruction in science. On factual items, the text-plus-film group scored 14.8 percent better on the initial test and 33.4 percent better on a recall test. On items measuring application, the experimental group scored 24.1 percent and 41 percent better than the text-only group.

Nelson (1952) experimented with the use of films to teach a specific unit on sulfur. Two sections were taught with a combination of lecture and discussion plus film. Eight sections were taught with lecture and discussion only. On the comprehensive examination at the end of the unit, the discussion plus film groups performed significantly better than the control groups. The experimental groups also did significantly better on a retention test five weeks after the unit.

In a study focused on tenth-grade history, Wendt and Butts (1960) assigned 315 students from seven schools to one of two different treatments. The control was a traditional two-semester course. The experimental treatment consisted of a one-semester course plus fifty-four carefully selected history films. The experimental group learned 86 percent as much history as the control group in half the time. In another study that examined learning efficiency from films, Stein (1958) found that students who had access to film loops learned to type significantly faster than students who did not have access to film loops.

In summarizing the results of film research for the Navy, Carpenter and Greenhill (1956) reached the following conclusions: (a) well-produced films, either used singly or in a series, can be employed as the sole means of teaching some types of performance skills and conveying some kinds of factual data, (b) tests given after viewing will increase learning when students have been told what to look for in the film and that a test on the film content would be given, (c) students will learn more if they are given study guides for each film used, (d) notetaking by students during the showing of a film should be discouraged because it distracts from the film itself, (e) successive showings of a given film can increase learning, (f) short films can be spliced end-to-end in a loop and are beneficial in practice and drill situations, (g) students can watch motion pictures for one hour without reduction in training effectiveness, (h) the effectiveness of film learning should be evaluated by tests,

(i) after a film has been shown, its major points should be summarized and discussed to prevent students from forming misconceptions, and (j) follow-up activities should be encouraged so that generalizations carry over.

Research on Television

Almstead and Graf (1960) reported on tenth-grade students taught geometry solely by television and fourth- and sixth-grade students taught reading by television with access to a unit that talked back when needed. Of the tenth graders, 85 percent passed the New York Regents Exam and 30 percent had scores over 90. This record compared favorably with regular classroom students. The fourth- and sixth-graders gained an average of ten months on a standardized test in nine months of study.

The Anaheim City School District (1963) has reported a series of studies dealing with 1,157 fifth graders over a nine-month period and 1,016 fourth graders over a twenty-six month period. They found that: (a) on forty-eight comparisons of pre- and post-television achievement on basic skills, thirty-two comparisons favored the television groups, no comparisons favored the non-television groups, and the television groups showed an overall advantage of four months over other groups; (b) of twenty-three comparisons between television plus regular instruction and regular instruction in normal classrooms, eleven favored television enriched, at the .05 level of confidence, while none favored regular instruction; and (c) on fourteen comparisons of large groups (seventy-six students) plus television with small groups (twenty-five or less) without television, seven favored television in large classrooms and two favored small classes.

One of the first school systems to integrate television fully into the total instructional program was Hagerstown, Maryland. Wade (1967) summarized the significant gains from the experience: (1) in grades three through six, rural students, who were averaging half a grade below the national norm in arithmetic before receiving instruction on television, all came to exceed the norm: grades three and four after one year, the others after two years. Pupils in grade five gained an average of 1.9 years in knowledge of arithmetic concepts in one year. (2) In junior-high general mathematics, the average achievement level of urban students rose in four years of television from the 31st to the 84th percentile on mathematics concepts and from the 33rd to the 68th percentile on problem solving. Rural students rose from the 14th to the 38th percentile on the same test of concepts but made very slight overall gains in problem solving. (3) In tenth-grade mathematics, urban schools rose from the 34th percentile before television to the 51st percentile after television. (4) Analysis of sixth-grade science achievement showed that students in classes where television was used improved more than conventionally taught students at all ability levels. (5) In both urban and rural Hagerstown schools, grade eight general science achievement on standardized tests was two years higher after several years of television than it had been before television was introduced. (6) When television was introduced as an additional resource in the teaching of U.S. history in rural Hagerstown schools, the percentile ranks on national norms increased from 28 prior to television, to 45 the first year, 46 the second, and 50 during the third year.

Questions can be raised about the results of the Hagerstown experiments. Were the reported results due to the effects of television or were they due to the systematic curriculum and instructional design and development required by the integration of television into the system? One example of systematic design and development of instructional television is "Sesame Street." Ball and Bogatz (1970) have reported the results of learning measures from "Sesame Street" based on a large sample of young children in four U.S. geographical areas. They found that the more that children watched the program, the more they learned of what it was designed to teach.

Chu and Schramm (1967) make the following observation concerning the results of research on instructional television: "There can no longer be any doubt that children and adults learn a great amount from instructional television, just as they do from any other experience that can be made to seem relevant to them — experiences as different as watching someone rotate a hula hoop or reading the encyclopedia. The effectiveness of television has now been demonstrated in well over 100 experiments, and several hundred separate comparisons, performed in many parts of the world, in developing as well as industrialized countries, at every level from preschool through adult education, and with a great variety of subject matter and method" (p. 1).

Research on Still Pictures

Numerous research studies have examined the effectiveness of still pictures in instruction, in both their projected (slides, filmstrips, transparencies) and nonprojected (photographs, study prints, charts) forms. Kelly (1961), for example, reported on the use of filmstrips to teach first-grade reading. He found that the experimental group did significantly better than the control group in word recognition, at the .01 level of confidence, and in sentence reading, at the .05 level of confidence.

In a comparison of lecture and discussion against lecture and discussion plus 200 transparencies that covered identical content in a college course on engineering descriptive geometry, Chance (1960) found: (1) the groups having the added use of transparencies did significantly better on the mean final examination and on final course grades, at the .05 level of confidence; (2) the three instructors unanimously agreed on the desirability of using transparencies in their teaching; (3) the use of transparencies resulted in an average saving of fifteen minutes per class period; and (4) students reported overwhelming preference for instruction using transparencies.

Brown, Lewis, and Harcleroad (1977) have stated that the research findings on the value of still pictures suggest the following implications for teaching:

Pictures stimulate student interest.

Properly selected and adapted, pictures help readers to understand and remember the content of accompanying verbal materials.

Simple line drawings can often be more effective as information transmitters than either shaded drawings or real life photographs; full realism pictures that flood the viewer with too much visual information are less good as learning stimuli than simplified pictures or drawings.

Color in still pictures usually poses a problem. Although colored pictures appear to interest students more than black-and-white ones, they may not always be the best choice for teaching or learning. One study suggests that if color is used, it should be realistic — not just color for its own sake. If only one color is to be added to an otherwise black-and-white picture, the teaching value may be reduced. But if what is to be taught actually involves color concepts, pictures in realistic color are preferred.

When attempting to teach concepts involving motion, a single still picture (including those in filmstrips) is likely to be considerably less effective than motion picture footage of the same action. Yet a sequence of still pictures, such as might be shot with an automatic 35mm still camera, might reduce flooding brought about by the too-fast flow of live action portrayed in some motion pictures and thus improve the viewer's grasp of concepts involved.

Verbal and/or symbolic cueing of still pictures through use of arrows or other marks can clarify — or possibly change — the message intended to be communicated by them [pp. 178–179].

Research on Audio Materials

Few current studies are concerned with audio instructional media. As Allen (1974) states, "Less is known about techniques for designing audio recordings to enhance learning than the other media. . . . This fact is disturbing, especially because of the recent phenomenal growth of recorded instructional materials offerings, as evidenced by widespread use of audio cassettes both as self-instructional materials and as sound accompaniments for film-strips or printed materials" (p. 86).

Much of the existing audio research dates back to the early days of instructional radio (Woelfel and Tyler 1945). Although most studies show no significant difference (for example, Gibson 1960), foreign language instruction has shown significance. Lorge (1963), reporting on a comprehensive, two-year study that involved ten schools and seventeen French classes in New York City, found that, if language laboratories were used at least twice a week for a minimum of twenty minutes: (1) ninth graders using the language laboratory were significantly superior to nonlaboratory students in speech fluency, (2) tenth-grade laboratory groups were significantly superior in both speech fluency and intonation, and (3) eleventh-grade laboratory students were significantly superior on speech comprehension.

Research on Programmed and Computer-Assisted Instruction

Goldbeck and others (1962) examined 150 high school government students who were in six different sections. One group learned from programmed texts, a second from regular classroom instruction, and a third from a combination of regular and programmed instruction. The third group performed significantly better than the other two. Fincher and Fillmer (1965) taught addition and subtraction of fractions to 309 fifth-grade arithmetic students. Those students who learned from programmed text-books were superior to students who were taught by lecture and discussion at the .05 level of confidence.

The efficiency of programmed instruction was demonstrated by Price (1963) in an experiment with thirty-six mentally retarded students. The students, whose IQ ranged from 42 to 66, were taught the 12-factor table in addition and subtraction by means of two different programs and by conventional instruction. Although there was no significant difference on the posttest, the convention-al group took 130 class periods to cover the material while the programmed groups averaged 86 periods.

In a study of computer-assisted instruction (CAI) conducted by Atkinson (1968), first-grade students were tutored in reading for twenty minutes on a computer terminal. On nine of ten compari-sons, on standardized posttests, the experimental groups were significantly better than the control groups. Suppes and Morning-star (1972) have reported a number of studies on the effectiveness of computer-assisted instruction. In one study, a large sample of first- through sixth-grade students in Mississippi were given ten minutes of arithmetic drill per day on a terminal. On seven of seven comparisons, the experimental group was significantly favored over the control group. In another study, dealing with Russian language students, they demonstrated the effect of CAI on student attitude. The control group received five hours of instruction in written and spoken Russian per week. The experimental group received the same amount of instruction by means of a CAI termi-nal. Both groups made use of language laboratories and home-work. Of the CAI students, 73 percent finished the full, year-long course while only 32 percent of the control students lasted the entire year.

In summarizing the findings of three different surveys of pro-grammed instruction research, Moldstad (1974), states that research on programmed instruction confirms "(a) that students can learn effectively, often more effectively from all types of programmed materials, whether in the form of linear or branching programs, and from programs on machines or programs in texts, than from more conventional instructional stimuli and (b) that frequently students learn equal amounts in far less time" (p. 396).

Research on Multimedia Instruction

Romano (1955) examined the effect of various projected media on learning of fifth-, sixth-, and seventh-grade science vocabulary. The control group received conventional instruction, including the use of blackboards, charts, models, flat pictures, and field trips. The experimental group received the same instruction plus motion pictures, filmstrips, 2 x 2 and 3¼ x 4 slides, and opaque projection. The instruction consisted of six units dealing with aspects of science. Control and experimental conditions were rotated from unit to unit. Measures were 50-item vocabulary tests for each unit, based on textbooks; the tests were given at the end of each unit and as a retention test after six months. Romano found that (1) all experimental groups showed larger gains, from 26.2 percent to 63.9 percent, in all units; (2) only two experimental groups, as compared to all of the control groups, showed a decrease in vocabulary on the retention test; and (3) both teachers and students expressed the opinion that motion pictures and projected still pictures enhanced learning.

Edwards, Williams, and Roderick (1968) have explored the use of multimedia in beginning typing and business machine operation courses. The control group received traditional instruction while the experimental group was taught in an open laboratory consisting of programmed materials, printed instruction sheets, continuous film loops, tape and slide sets, and drill tapes. The experimental group learned significantly more, at the .05 level of confidence, according to the end-of-term exams, and students preferred the experimental approach.

Schramm (1973) examined the literature dealing with the effect on instruction of adding one or more audiovisual or programmed medium and found that "such research as there is on this question almost invariably indicates that the addition of one or more supplementary or complementary channel of instruction makes a difference" (p. 67). This conclusion contradicts the findings of Travers (1967, Travers and others 1966) that there is little or no advantage to redundant materials in two channels, audio and visual, over a single channel presentation. The assumptions and procedures of Travers, however, have been criticized on a number of different grounds (Severin 1967, Conway 1967).

RESIDUE OF COMPARATIVE MEDIA STUDIES

Two characteristics are evident from a review of comparative media research: the number of studies that have deficiencies in their experimental designs and the number of nonsignificant differences that have been found.

The problems of media research design have been discussed by a number of reviewers (Lumsdaine 1963, Salomon and Clark 1977). For example, Greenhill (1967) suggested that "the most common of these problems has been the use of nonrandom groups and the confounding (uncontrolled mixing) of variables. In addition, some studies used very short tests, and some studies provided no evidence of test reliability. This situation makes interpretation of results difficult indeed" (p. 16). Regarding the lack of significance, Greenhill suggests that the result may be due to (1) measuring instruments that are not able to detect differences that may exist, (2) the use of predominantly verbal tests with visual media, (3) comparisons of complexes of variables that tend to cancel each other, (4) concern with single variables that are not sufficiently potent, or (5) the "law of compensatory effort."

Another cause of difficulties can be traced to problems of definition, as suggested by Levie and Dickie (1973):

Consider the question, "Are motion pictures more effective than textbooks?" One matter that must be considered before the question can be approached is, "What is a motion picture?" Clearly the things called "motion pictures" are not all of one sort. They may or may not employ high-speed or time-lapse photography or they may not depict motion at all. Motion pictures are usually regarded as being fixed-pace and fixed-sequence presentations, but even these characteristics are only artifacts of traditional utilizations and standard projection equipment. Thus, for research purposes, the concept "motion picture" is far too inexact to be useful as an experimental construct [p. 860].

Such imprecise definition of terms often leads to imprecise or contradictory results. Others, such as Knowlton (1964), Mielke (1968), and Salomon and Clark (1977), have suggested that the problem is not one of definition but that the original question was invalid, leading automatically to uninterpretable results, if results were obtained at all. In comparative media studies, only the medium chosen for instruction was allowed to vary. In such studies, "when only the least significant aspects of instruction are allowed to vary, nothing of interest could, and did, result" (Salomon and Clark 1977, p. 102).

Some authors have suggested that the finding of no significant difference is not necessarily a problem. Greenhill (1967) points out that "there is a practical value in such results in that consistent findings of nonsignificant differences in learning from different instructional methods give educational administrators some confidence that several alternative methods of instruction are available for use, and allows them to choose which one should be used in a specific situation on the basis of considerations other than relative instructional merits" (p. 4). One of the other considerations is economics. A number of authors (Scanlon and Weinberger 1973; Jamison, Klees, and Wells 1978) use the findings of no significant difference to suggest that technology might be a means of improving the productivity of education. Studies that have explored this question include one by Carter and Walker (1969), which predicted and compared the cost of the widespread adoption of instructional television (ITV) and CAI by public schools, and a General Learning Corporation (1968) study, which sought to compare a number of different media strategies under different conditions. The major problems with such economic comparisons of media systems is the same problem of definition found in traditional comparative media studies (Wilkinson 1973, 1976).

RESEARCH ON MEDIA ATTRIBUTES

The inadequacies of comparative media studies have led to a new approach to media research. Levie and Dickie (1973) suggest that "understanding media may be furthered by (a) specifying media in terms of attributes, (b) defining these attributes in terms which relate to the ways in which information is processed internally, and (c) discovering relationships between these attributes and other important instructional variables" (p. 877). Much of the research on attributes is tentative, primarily of interest to other researchers or materials designers, and will not be extensively reviewed in this chapter. Those who wish to explore this area are referred to the reviews by Lumsdaine (1963), Levie and Dickie (1973), and Fleming and Levie (1978). A few points, however, should be raised.

Schramm (1973) has stated that "there is almost a complete lack of studies intended to ascertain *under what conditions* and *for what purposes* one medium may be superior to another" (p. 62). One approach to this problem was proposed by Allen (1967), who attempted to define the appropriateness of various instructional media to different types of learning tasks.

Another aspect of the interaction problem is individual student differences. The effects of such individual differences are most often felt through teaching strategy, rather than the medium that conveys that strategy. For example, studies indicate that students with a low IQ will learn more effectively from programmed instruction if the program requires an active response from the learner (McNeil 1962); that students with high anxiety learn significantly better when given immediate feedback on the correctness of their responses (Campeau 1965); and that, although high-ability students learn equally well on two different versions of a multimedia presentation, low-ability students perform significantly better when given a presentation based on their specific abilities (Monahan 1966).

The identification of interactions between student, task, and media attributes is characteristic of some of the earliest and some of the best research on educational media. The new interest in this type of research will restrict the sort of generalizations that can be drawn from the research (Salomon and Clark 1977). Instead of continuing to search for the "best" medium, researchers will need to focus on more limited generalizations of the type formulated by Allen (1975) as a result of his extensive study of the research literature on media and intellectual abilities. Interaction studies also call for large numbers of subjects and task levels for generalizations of any kind to be developed (Salomon and Clark 1977).

Another common problem is that too often researchers fail to consider the importance of their findings to subsequent practice. For example, in a study of different types of programmed instructional materials, Sego (1974) found a significant aptitude-treatment interaction between students' level of cognitive style and types of materials. However, analysis of the interaction indicated that only 2 percent of the population would benefit from the use of different forms. His conclusions suggested potentially significant and useful theoretical relationships, but indicated that any immediate improvement in learning from the development and use of different forms of similar materials could not be justified economically.

RESEARCH ON SCHOOL MEDIA CENTERS

The concern in schools is not just with the direct effects of media, but also with how they can best be organized for effective use. A review of the research on the organization, services, and management of school media centers is complicated by the recent development of the unified media program, which combines all print and nonprint media within a single operational unit (American Association of School Librarians 1975). Previously, nonprint materials were under audiovisual programs, which were separate from the school library. Thus, these two areas represent two different strains that have not yet been fully integrated in the research literature.

Other educational research areas also need to be integrated with media center research. As Gaver (1969) points out:

The research that is focused on the school environment frequently has as much, if not more, significance for school libraries as the research focused on school libraries *per se*. Some examples from the past few years would certainly include the following: John Flanagan's [1962] identification, in his five-year study "Project Talent," of the quantitative provision for high school libraries as one of five determinants of a quality education for American youth; Merle E. Landerholm's [1960] analysis of the characteristics of quality education, in which he found the highest correlation between a quality criterion and the provision of specialists per thousand students to be with the provision of the school librarian, while guidance specialists ranked fourth and reading specialists sixth; and the Harvard study of Reading in the Elementary School [Austin and Morrison 1963], which analyzed the teaching of reading in more than 1,000 elementary schools in the United States and cited high among its forty-five recommendations a centralized library with a full-time teacher-librarian and provisions meeting with the ALA standards [p. 764].

Nelson Associates (1967), in their report to the National Advisory Commission on Libraries, identified the lack of research as one of the ten major problems facing school libraries. To determine the research needed by school librarians, Woodworth (1967) conducted a survey of school library leaders and found that the items of greatest concern were the contributions of the library to teaching and learning, teacher education and the library, attitudes of the school staff, evaluation of libraries, personnel studies, and the education of school librarians.

In addition to the need for specific studies, there is general dissatisfaction with the limited nature of the research that has been conducted. In reviewing the research on school media programs, Lowrie (1968) pointed out that "these studies are almost without question designed to show growth patterns or trends or to present the current status in a specific locale" (p. 52). More recently, Stroud (1979) points out that "There remains an ongoing need for research studies that assess the learning that takes place, that attempt not only to identify services patrons view as desirable but to assess the outcomes or the benefits of those services, that measure the impact of the media center program on the students, the teachers, the community, and the curriculum. Studies are needed to identify those practices or activities that alter behavior patterns, that have the most influence, and that are the most effective" [p. 278]. In spite of these difficulties, however, some studies can give direction to the planning of school media programs.

Descriptive Research on School Media Centers

A number of studies attempt to provide a foundation for evaluation and comparison of school media programs. Although many of these have been at the individual state or local level (for example, Loertscher and Land's [1975] survey of media services in Indiana elementary schools), a few studies, such as the AASL survey of outstanding media centers (Lohrer 1970), have had national impact on the development of both media program standards and guidelines for the training of media specialists.

An extensive review of the research literature on questions dealing with school media centers will not be presented here. Lowrie (1968) summarizes the research conducted prior to 1967 as follows:

Almost all the studies draw the following conclusions and thus fundamentally substantiate facts known: (a) collections assembled or selected by persons not qualified in book selection are inadequate; (b) better direction by local, regional and state consultants or supervisors is needed; (c) educational institutions should make a greater effort to coordinate the efforts of teachers and administrators and to improve their understanding of their role in relationship to the school library and utilization of its materials; (d) national standards now play a significant role in the development of criteria for most status studies; (e) in-service training programs for teachers should be developed in some form in all libraries or materials centers, since the role of the classroom teacher is crucial in promoting and expanding library services; and (f) lack of adequate personnel and insufficient funds are continuing hindrances to developing services [p. 60].

The general conclusions reached by Lowrie were also found by Aaron (1972a, 1972b) in her review of the literature from 1967 to 1971. She added that the concept of the instructional media center is increasingly accepted by educators in general and that federal funds are having a great impact on school libraries. The conclusions of Lowrie and Aaron are also endorsed by Barron (1977), who extended the research review to 1972-76.

Experimental Research on School Media Centers

The primary area of concern identified by Woodworth (1967) was for research that established the contributions of the library to the school program — the area with the fewest studies in the literature. In her review of the school librarianship research from World War II to the mid-1960s, Lowrie (1968) found only one doctoral study, out of fifty, that could be classified as a controlled research study. Only six of the over 100 studies cited by Barron (1977) attempted to measure the influence of the school media program on any other aspect of the school's program or on student achievement.

A few studies, however, do show an effect. Jensen (1970) found that media centers could influence teaching practice by supplying resources and services that helped to meet the individual needs of students. Yarling (1969) found that establishment of a centralized library led to significant student improvement in reading expression and library skills as compared to students in a control school. Greve (1974) used the Iowa Test of Educational Development and an index of library service levels to determine if there were relationships between the academic achievement of high school seniors and the library services offered in their schools. Based on a sample of 232 high schools in Iowa, he found a direct, positive correlation between the two variables.

In a study cited for its direct influence and as a pattern for further research, Gaver (1963) found that on most measures of effectiveness, such as amount of reading or quality of collections — including educational gain between the fourth and sixth grades, the elementary school library was favored over other provisions for providing materials to students and teachers. She concluded that "definite advantages accrue in schools that have school libraries manned by professional library staff" (p. 127).

In one of the few controlled experiments reported, Barrilleaux (1965) compared the effects of instruction employing different combinations of library resources and textbooks on aspects of science achievement by eighth- and ninth-grade students. Fifty-six eighth-grade students were divided into two groups that were matched in reference to mental ability and attitudes toward science. A single instructor, working from a prepared content outline, served both groups. The control group was issued a textbook while the experimental group employed a variety of different reading and reference materials. Both groups were encouraged to use additional library materials. The study was continued for a second year with forty-two of the subjects who were enrolled in the ninth grade. Measures employed were the Iowa Test of Educational Development (ITED), the Sequential Tests of Educational Progress (STEP), the Watson-Glaser Critical Thinking Appraisal, and the Test on Understanding Science, as well as evaluation of writing on science problems and observational measures of use of the library. The findings of the study were:

1. Science achievement: as measured on Test 2 and Test 6 of the ITED, there was on the average no difference between the groups. Within the experimental (nontext) group, however, students with high ability (on Test 2) and students with average ability (on Test 6) achieved significantly higher mean scores than the control group after two years. On the STEP test, the experimental group was statistically superior in overall effectiveness to the control group.

2. Critical thinking: as measured on the Watson-Glaser test, the experimental group showed superior achievement but not at a significant level.

3. Science attitudes: the experimental group achieved significantly higher scores than the control group.

4. Writing in science: evaluation of writing on science problems during the second year of the study showed that the experimental group had significantly higher mean scores than the control group. Analysis of interactions revealed that average ability students profited more from the experimental approach.

5. Library utilization: the experimental group scored significantly higher than the control group on such measures of library use as total number of library visits, time devoted to science-related library activities, and time devoted to all library activities. They also averaged higher on frequency of students pursuing unassigned material in areas of related interest, selecting elective reading, locating and using materials, and checking out materials.

The limited number of controlled research studies that focus on the total effect of the media program is not surprising. Media programs are multifaceted, interacting entities that have an impact on and are in turn affected by all other aspects of the school program. In situations of this type, it is possible that the only effective research strategies might be surveys and questionnaires with, at best, correlational measures.

Research on Media Personnel

The growing interest in the application of educational media and technology to all aspects of education during the twenty years following World War II led to an awareness of the need to analyze the functions of professionals who were developing training programs and designing guidelines for certification. The period from 1961 to 1971 saw at least eighteen major studies of manpower needs in the area of media (Brown 1971).

Of the media manpower studies, three are of primary significance — both because of the importance of the sponsoring agencies and because of their subsequent influence on the certification guidelines of such professional organizations as the American Association of School Librarians (AASL) (1976) and the Association for Educational Communications and Technology (AECT) (Galey and Grady 1977). The three projects were the Jobs in

Instructional Media Study (JIMS), conducted by AECT (Wallington and others 1969); the Media Guidelines Project (Hamreus 1970), conducted for the U.S. Office of Education; and the School Library Manpower Project (Case and Lowrey 1973), conducted by AASL. Each of these projects commonly sought (a) to objectively catalog specific tasks that are, or should be, performed by educational media personnel, (b) to analyze the nature of these tasks, (c) to classify them by the appropriate level of personnel — such as professional or clerical — for performing the task, (d) to group tasks into job clusters, and (e) to recommend training levels for each job cluster.

A few research studies have been conducted to determine if the presence of such trained personnel has any effect on the school media program and on students. A study by McCusker (1963) determined that elementary schools without school libraries with professionally trained personnel lack collections that are adequate to meet the needs of either the instructional program or the students. Attempting to determine the effect of having a full-time elementary school librarian, Wright and Grossman (1977) found that students in such schools showed increases in basic skills, library skills, and achievement over students in schools without full-time librarians. Hodson (1978) found that educationally disadvantaged students expressed negative feelings about the part-time status of librarians, highlighting a need for full-time professionals in schools with disadvantaged students.

Guidelines for Media Programs

One outgrowth of the descriptive and manpower studies has been the development of joint standards for school media programs by AASL and AECT (1975). Work on standards for school media was begun independently by the two associations. The original AASL standards were based on expert judgment, survey data, and questionnaires sent to schools that had been identified as having superior library facilities. The associations came together to work on joint standards, which were initially published in 1969 and then expanded and revised in 1975. These standards have had a major effect on school media programs. However, the national standards set goals to be strived for rather than minimal criteria for all programs. As a result, a number of states have developed their own standards, often based on the joint AASL and AECT recommendations.

The realization that effective local media programs must be planned to meet the needs of a specific location and curriculum and must be evaluated in terms of local goals and objectives has led to the development of a number of planning and evaluation tools (Daniel 1976). Three of the most useful of these tools have been devised by the Association for Educational Communications and Technology (1976), Liesener (1976), and Loertscher and Stroud (1976). The widespread use of such strategies would go a long way toward improving the quality of local school media programs and toward the generation of a systematic data base of information on school media programs.

CONCLUSIONS FROM MEDIA RESEARCH

A blanket indictment of the research on educational media is tempting. Countless studies have conducted exhaustive examinations of the wrong questions. Others have concentrated too much on status to the neglect of effect. Little research seeks to directly relate the existence of media centers to the academic achievement of students. Given the multifaceted nature of media and media centers and the difficulty of doing research on operating organizations, the lack of such research is not surprising.

In spite of the problems with existing research and the great number of studies which remain to be conducted, several general conclusions concerning media in public schools can be drawn from the research literature. There is evidence to support the following propositions:

1. When they are carefully selected or produced — taking into account both media attributes and student characteristics — and systematically integrated into the instructional program, educational media, including textbooks, have a significant impact on student achievement.

2. Media are more effectively and efficiently used when teachers have received specific training in the utilization of media.

3. Media are more effectively and efficiently used when the school provides an integrated media center based on national guidelines.
4. Media centers will have a greater impact when they are staffed by full-time, trained media specialists and when collections and services are based on and integrated into the instructional program of the local school.

Media, the tools of teaching and learning, must be available when, where, and in the quantity necessary to meet the needs of the teachers and students who use them. If the laborer is not provided with the tools necessary to do his job, he cannot be held accountable if the job is not completed properly.

REFERENCES

Aaron, Shirley L. "A Review of Selected Research Studies in School Librarianship, 1967-1971: Part 1." *School Libraries* 21 (Summer 1972a): 29–46.

Aaron, Shirley L. "A Review of Selected Research Studies in School Librarianship, 1967-1971: Part 2." *School Media Quarterly* 1 (Fall 1972b): 41–48.

Allen, William H. "Media Stimulus and Types of Learning." *Audiovisual Instruction* 12 (January 1967): 27–31.

Allen, William H. "Research on Instructional Media Design." In *Educational Media Yearbook 1974*, edited by J. W. Brown. New York: Bowker, 1974.

Allen, William H. "Intellectual Abilities and Instructional Media Deisgn." *AV Communication Review* 23 (Summer 1975): 139–70.

Almstead, Francis E., and Graf, Raymond W. "Talkback: The Missing Ingredient." *Audiovisual Instruction* 5 (April 1960): 110–12.

American Association of School Librarians, Certification of Media Specialists Committee. *Certification Model for Professional School Media Personnel.* Chicago: American Library Association, 1976

American Association of School Librarians and Association for Educational Communications and Technology. *Media Programs: District and School.* Chicago: American Library Association; Washington, D.C.: Association for Educational Communications and Technology, 1975.

Anaheim City School District. *Summary of Instructional Television Evaluation.* Anaheim, Calif.: Anaheim City School District, 1963.

Association for Educational Communications and Technology. *Evaluating Media Programs: District and School.* Washington, D.C.: Association for Educational Communications and Technology, 1976.

Association for Educational Communications and Technology, Task Force on Definition and Terminology. *Educational Technology: Definition and Glossary of Terms.* Vol. 1. Washington, D.C.: Association for Educational Communications and Technology, 1977.

Atkinson, Richard C. "Computerized Instruction and the Learning Process." *American Psychologist* 23 (April 1968): 225–39.

Austin, Mary C., and Morrison, Coleman. *The First R: The Harvard Report on Reading in Elementary Schools.* New York: Macmillan, 1963.

Ball, Samuel, and Bogatz, Gerry Ann. *The First Year of "Sesame Street": An Evaluation.* Princeton, N.J.: Educational Testing Service, 1970.

Barrilleaux, Louis E. "An Experimental Investigation of the Effects of Multiple Library Sources as Compared to the Use of a Basic Textbook on Student Achievement and Learning Activity in Junior High School Science." Doctoral dissertation, University of Iowa, 1965.

Barron, Daniel D. "A Review of Selected Research in School Librarianship: 1972-1976." *School Media Quarterly* 5 (Summer 1977): 271–89.

Briggs, Leslie J. "Learner Variables and Educational Media." *Review of Educational Research* 38 (April 1968): 160–76.

Brown, James W. "Recent Manpower Studies: Some Implications for AECT." *Media Manpower Supplement, No. 2.* Washington, D.C.: Media Manpower, March 1971.

Brown, James W.; Lewis, Richard B.; and Harcleroad, Fred F. *AV Instruction: Technology Media and Methods.* 5th ed. New York: McGraw-Hill, 1977.

Campeau, Peggie L. *Level of Anxiety and Presence or Absence of Feedback in Programmed Instruction.* Palo Alto, Calif.: American Institutes for Research, 1965.

Carpenter, C. R. and Greenhill, L. P. *Instructional Film Reports.* Vol. 2, Technical Report 269-7-61. Port Washington, N.Y.: Special Devices Center, U.S. Navy, 1956.

Carter, C. N. and Walker, M. J. "Costs of Instructional TV and Computer-assisted Instruction in Public Schools." In *The Schools and the Challenge of Innovation,* Committee for Economic Development. New York: McGraw-Hill, 1969.

Case, R. N. and Lowrey, A. M. *Behavioral Requirements Analysis Checklist.* Chicago: American Library Association, 1973.

Chance, C. W. *Experimentation in the Adaption of the Overhead Projector Utilizing 200 Transparencies and 800 Overlays in Teaching Engineering Descriptive Geometry Curricula.* Project 243. Washington, D.C.: U.S. Office of Education, 1960.

Chu, Godwin C., and Schramm, Wilbur. *Learning from Television: What the Research Says.* Stanford, Calif.: Institute for Communication Research, 1967.

Clark, Richard E. "Constructing a Taxonomy of Media Attributes for Research Purposes." *AV Communication Review* 23 (Summer 1975): 197–215.

Clark, Richard E. "Five Promising Directions for Media Research." In *Educational Media Yearbook 1978,* edited by J. W. Brown. New York: Bowker, 1978.

Conway, Jerome K. "Multiple-Sensory Modality Communications and the Problem of Sign Types." *AV Communication Review* 15 (Winter 1967): 371-83.

Cronbach, Lee J., and Snow, Richard E. *Aptitudes and Instructional Methods.* New York: Irvington, 1977.

Daniel, E. H. "Performance Measures for School Librarians: Complexities and Potential." In *Advances in Librarianship,* Vol. 6, edited by M. J. Voight. New York: Academic Press, 1976.

Diamond, R. M. "Research, Theory, and Instructional Development: A View from the Trenches." *Journal of Instructional Development* 1 (Spring 1978): 2–5.

Edwards, R. K.; Williams, M. L.; and Roderick, W. W. *An Experimental Pilot Study to Explore the Use of an Audio-Visual Tutorial Laboratory in the Secretarial Offerings at the Community College Level in Michigan.* Lansing, Mich.: Lansing Community College, 1968.

Fincher, Glen E., and Fillmer, H. T. "Programmed Instruction in Elementary Arithmetic." *Arithmetic Teacher* 12 (January 1965): 19–23.

Flanagan, John C., and others. *The Talents of American Youth.* Boston: Houghton Mifflin, 1962.

Fleming, Malcolm L., and Levie, W. Howard. *Instructional Message Design: Principles from the Behavioral Sciences.* Englewood Cliffs, N.J.: Educational Technology Publications, 1978.

Freeman, Frank N. *Visual Education.* Chicago: University of Chicago Press, 1924.

Gagné, Robert M. *The Conditions of Learning.* New York: Holt, Rinehart and Winston, 1967.

Galey, M. and Grady, W. F. *Guidelines for Certification of Media Specialists.* Washington, D.C.: Association for Educational Communications and Technology, 1977.

Gaver, Mary V. *Effectiveness of Centralized Library Service in Elementary Schools.* 2nd ed. New Brunswick, N.J.: Rutgers University Press, 1963.

Gaver, Mary V. "Is Anyone Listening? Significant Research Studies for Practicing Librarians." *Wilson Library Bulletin* 43 (April 1969): 764–72.

General Learning Corporation. *Cost Study of Educational Media Systems and Their Equipment Components.* Washington, D.C.: Department of Health, Education, and Welfare, 1968.

Gibson, R. E. "Final Report on the Westside High School Teaching-by-Tape Project." *Bulletin of the National Association of Secondary-School Principals* 44 (January 1960): 56–62.

Goldbeck, Robert A.; Shearer, J. W.; Campeau, Peggie L.; and Willis, M. B. *Integrating Programmed Instruction with Conventional Classroom Teaching.* Palo Alto, Calif.: American Institutes for Research, 1962.

Greenhill, L. P. "Review of Trends in Research on Instructional Television and Film." In *Research in Instructional Television and Film,* edited by J. C. Reid and D. W. McLennan. Washington, D.C.: U.S. Office of Education, 1967.

Greve, Clyde L. "The Relationship of the Availability of Libraries to the Academic Achievement of Iowa School Seniors." Doctoral dissertation, University of Denver, 1974.

Hamreus, D. G., ed. *Media Guidelines: Development and Validation of Criteria for Evaluating Media Training.* Monmouth: Division of Teaching Research, Oregon State System for Higher Education, 1970.

Hartley, James. "Research Report." *NEW Education* 2 (January 1966): 29–30.

Hoban, Charles F., and Van Ormer, E. B. *Instructional Film Research, 1918-1950.* Technical Report No. SDC 269-7-19. Port Washington, N.Y.: U.S. Naval Training Device Center, 1950.

Hodson, Yvonne D. "Values and Functions of the School Media Center as Perceived by Fourth and Sixth Graders and Their Teachers in Compared School Settings." Doctoral dissertation, State University of New York, Buffalo, 1978.

Hovland, C. I., Lumsdaine, A. A., and Sheffield, F. D. *Experiments on Mass Communication.* Princeton, N.J.: Princeton University Press, 1949.

Jamison, D. T.; Klees, S. J.; and Wells, S. J. *The Costs of Educational Media: Guidelines for Planning and Evaluation.* Beverly Hills, Calif.: Sage Publications, 1978.

Jensen, Louis R. "Educational Services Provided by Media Centers in Selected Elementary Schools." Doctoral dissertation, University of Nebraska, 1970.

Kelly, T. D. "Utilization of Filmstrips as an Aid in Teaching Beginning Reading." Doctoral dissertation, Indiana University, 1961.

Knowlton, D. C., and Tilton, J. W. *Motion Pictures in History Teaching.* New Haven, Conn.: Yale University Press, 1929.

Knowlton, J. Q. "A Conceptual Scheme for the Audiovisual Field." *Bulletin of the School of Education, Indiana University* 40 (May 1964): 1–44.

Landerholm, Merle E. "A Study of Selected Elementary, Secondary, and School District Professional Staff Deployment Patterns." Doctoral dissertation, Teachers College, Columbia University, 1960.

Levie, W. Howard, and Dickie, Kenneth E. "The Analysis and Application of Media." In *Second Handbook of Research on Teaching,* edited by Robert M. W. Travers, pp. 858–82. Chicago: Rand McNally, 1973.

Liesener, J. W. *A Systematic Process for Planning Media Programs.* Chicago: American Library Association, 1976.

Loertscher, David V., and Land, Phyllis. "An Empirical Study of Media Services in Indiana Elementary Schools." *School Media Quarterly* 4 (Fall 1975): 8–18.

Loertscher, David V., and Stroud, J. G. *Purdue Self-Evaluation System (PSES) for School Media Centers.* Idaho Falls, Idaho: Hi Willow, 1976.

Lohrer, Alice. *The Identification and Role of School Libraries That Function as Instructional Materials Centers and Implications for Library Education in the United States.* Urbana: Graduate School of Library Science, University of Illinois, 1970.

Lorge, S. W. *The Relative Effectiveness of Four Types of Language Laboratory Experiences.* New York State Research Project A-61/62. New York: New York City Board of Education, 1963.

Lowrie, J. E. "A Review of Research in School Librarianship." In *Research Methods in Librarianship: Measurement and Evaluation,* Monograph no. 8, edited by Herbert Goldhor. Urbana: Graduate School of Library Science, University of Illinois, 1968.

Lumsdaine, A. A. "Instruments and Media of Instruction." In *Handbook of Research in Teaching,* edited by N. L. Gage. Chicago: Rand McNally, 1963.

McCusker, Mary G. "The Accessibility of Books in Elementary Schools without Libraries." Doctoral dissertation, Columbia University, 1963.

McNeil, John D. "Programmed Instruction as a Research Tool in Reading: An Annotated Case." *Journal of Programmed Instruction* 1, no. 1 (1962): 37–42.

May, M. A., and Lumsdaine, A. A. *Learning from Films.* New Haven, Conn.: Yale University Press, 1958.

Mielke, Keith W. "Asking the Right ETV Questions." *Educational Broadcasting Review* 2 (December 1968): 54–61.

Moldstad, John A. "Selective Review of Research Studies Showing Media Effectiveness: A Primer for Media Directors." *AV Communication Review* 22 (Winter 1974): 387–407.

Monahan, P. E., and others. *Multimedia Instructional Programs in Mathematics – Demonstrations and Experimentation.* Whitewater: Wisconsin Heights School System, 1966.

Morris, Barry, ed. "The Function of Media in the Public Schools." *Audiovisual Instruction* 8 (January 1963): 9–14.

Nelson Associates. *School Libraries in the United States: A Report Prepared for the National Advisory Commission on Libraries.* Project no. BR-7-0961. Washington, D.C.: U.S. Office of Education, 1967.

Nelson, Courtenay M. "Effectiveness of Sound Motion Pictures in Teaching a Unit on Sulphur in High School Chemistry." *School Science and Mathematics* 52 (January 1952): 8–10.

Price, J. E. "Automated Teaching Programs with Mentally Retarded Students." *American Journal of Mental Deficiency* 68 (July 1963): 69–72.

Romano, Louis. "The Role of Sixteen Millimeter Motion Pictures and Projected Still Pictures in Science Unit Vocabulary Learnings at Grades Five, Six, and Seven." Doctoral dissertation, University of Wisconsin, 1955.

Rulon, Philip J. *The Sound Motion Picture in Science Teaching.* Cambridge, Mass.: Harvard University Press, 1933.

Saettler, Paul. "Design and Selection Factors." *Review of Educational Research* 38 (April 1968): 115–28.

Salomon, Gavriel, and Clark, Richard E. "Reexamining the Methodology of Research on Media and Technology in Education." *Review of Educational Research* 47 (Winter 1977): 99–120.

Scanlon, R. G. and Weinberger, J. A., eds. *Improving Productivity of School Systems through Educational Technology: Final Report of Symposium.* Philadelphia: Research for Better Schools, 1973.

Schramm, Wilbur. *Big Media, Little Media: A Report to the Agency for International Development.* Stanford, Calif.: Institute for Communication Research, Stanford University, 1973.

Sego, Lewis P. I. "The Interactive Effect of Inductive and Deductive Sequences and Cognitive Styles on the Acquisition of a Higher Order Concept in English Literature." Doctoral dissertation, Indiana University, 1974.

Severin, Werner. "The Effectiveness of Relevant Pictures in Multiple-Channel Communications." *AV Communication Review* 15 (Winter 1967): 386–401.

Snow, Richard E. "Research on Media and Attributes." *Viewpoints, Bulletin of the School of Education, Indiana University* 46 (1970) 63–89.

Snow, Richard E., and Salomon, Gavriel. "Aptitudes and Instructional Media." *AV Communication Review* 16 (Winter 1968): 341–57.

Stein, Sarah C. "An Experimental Study of the Use of Motion Picture Film Loops in the Instruction of Beginning Typewriting." Doctoral dissertation, University of Southern California, 1958.

Stickell, David W. "A Critical Review of the Methodology and Results of Research Comparing Televised and Face-to-Face Instruction." Doctoral dissertation, Pennsylvania State University, 1963.

Stroud, Janet G. "Current Research." *School Media Quarterly* 7 (Summer 1979): 277–79.

Suppes, Patrick, and Morningstar, Mona. *Computer-Assisted Instruction at Stanford, 1966-69: Data, Models, and Evaluation of the Arithmetic Program.* New York: Academic Press, 1972.

Tickton, S. G., ed. *To Improve Learning: An Evaluation of Instructional Technology.* 2 vols. New York: Bowker, 1970-1971.

Travers, Robert M. W. *Research and Theory Related to Audiovisual Information Transmission.* Washington, D.C.: U.S. Office of Education, 1967.

Travers, Robert M. W., and others. *Studies Related to the Design of Audiovisual Teaching Materials.* Washington, D.C.: U.S. Office of Education, 1966.

Wade, S. *Hagerstown: A Pioneer in Closed-Circuit Televised Instruction. New Educational Media in Action: Case Studies for Planners—1.* Paris: UNESCO and International Institute for Educational Planning. 1967.

Wallington, C. J.; Hyer, A. L.; Bernotavicz, F. D.; Hale, P.; and Silber, K. *Jobs in Instructional Media Study (JIMS): Interim Report.* Washington, D.C.: U.S. Office of Education, 1969.

Weber, J. J. *Visual Aids in Education.* Valparaiso, Ind.: Valparaiso University, 1930.

Wendt, P. R. and Butts, G. K. *A Report of an Experiment in the Acceleration of Teaching Tenth-Grade World History with the Help of an Integrated Series of Films.* Carbondale, Ill.: General Publications, 1960.

Wight, Lillian, and Grossman, A. *Maximum Utilization of School Library Resources.* Ed. 154–781. Edmonton, Alberta: Edmonton Public Schools, 1977.

Wilkinson, Gene L. "Cost Evaluation of Instructional Strategies." *AV Communication Review* 21 (Spring 1973): 11–30.

Wilkinson, Gene L. "Economic Evaluation of CAI in Special Education." *Proceedings of the Society for Applied Learning Technology* 5 (1976): 82–88.

Woelfel, Norman, and Tyler, I. Keith. *Radio and the School.* Tarrytown-on-Hudson, N.Y.: World Book, 1945.

Wood, Ben D., and Freeman, Frank N. *Motion Pictures in the Classroom.* Boston: Houghton Mifflin, 1929.

Woodworth, M. L. *The Identification and Examination of Areas of Needed Research in School Librarianship: Final report.* Madison: University of Wisconsin Library School, 1967.

Yarling, James R. "Children's Understandings and Use of Selected Library-Related Skills in Two Elementary Schools, One with and One without a Centralized Library." Doctoral dissertation, Ball State University, 1969.

Discussion

Lewis Miller

In this discussion I consider the situation of the school board officer who has responsibility for making policy decisions entailing the expenditure of public monies. Among the multitude of proposals to be considered will be those concerning expenditures for media of instruction, expenditures that must be weighed against the great variety of other difficult and often expensive proposals that constantly face school boards. What, then, are the kinds of questions that would be asked, and what are some of the considerations that should be raised and criteria to be employed before making such decisions?

In his *Big Media, Little Media*, Schramm (1967) asks, "How do educators and planners, schools and governments, go about choosing media of instruction?" In his response he writes, "There is no cookbook of recipes for media selection that can be applied automatically in every educational system. It is necessary to carefully consider local needs, situations, and resources, and then interpret such guidelines as exist" (p. 263). Although it is not a "recipe" book in any usual sense, this book by Schramm is the most useful volume I have seen on this subject. The first advice I would offer to school board decision makers who must wrestle with this question is to obtain a copy. In view of my regard for Schramm's text, I am pleased and confident, in this instance, to be a broker, and I shall rely on his work to a considerable extent.

Beginning with a working definition for "media of instruction," as we should begin, Schramm reminds us that "so far as we know, there has always been instructional technology." Whether it is a finger or a stick for making marks on sand, or pictographs on rock faces, or the medium of print, or electronic media, the tools that teachers have used over the years "are simply information-carrying technologies that *can* be used for instruction," and "the media of instruction, consequently, are extensions of the teacher." The teacher, then, is and will probably remain the focal point for the selection and use of a medium of instruction. Thus, school board officers need a well-researched survey on the needs and interests of teachers in their jurisdiction.

If available media of instruction were simply books and chalkboards, the task of the school board officer would, of course, be relatively much simpler, but media have proliferated exponentially in this century. The array of media now being sought by teachers includes the print media, radio, film, filmstrips, overhead projectors, slide projectors, audio cassettes, television, video cassettes, the "electronic blackboard" linked by telephone lines, teletext, and so on. And more recently the array has been complicated by the inclusion of the wondrous computer, with its own assortment of possible uses ranging from a highly centralized network for computer-assisted instruction (with students individually linked to an expensive computer) to the decentralized uses of microcomputers by each of a number of students in a classroom. (The Children's Television Workshop, for example, has developed a "program analyzer" consisting of a system with individual wireless hand-held units; each unit is able to record and store in its memory over 500 responses, which may then be read out by a relatively inexpensive suitcase-size microcomputer.) No wonder the minds of contemporary school board administrators may be boggled by the complexity of proposals for new media placed before them by the more adventuresome teachers.

With this complexity there are obvious cautions to observe. We should be reminded, however, that throughout recorded history, beginning with Socrates' distrust of the written word, conservative people have been cautious about new media. Socrates felt that print could not adequately serve as a medium for philosophy (for philosophy, at least, I believe he was right). Even before Gutenberg, influential members of the religious and political establishments in Europe worried about what could be taught through the circulation of hand-written texts. With Gutenberg there was fear and panic in some circles of the establishment. What damage might be wrought if the Holy Bible got into the wrong hands?

Those of us who have dedicated our lives to some of the new media are sensitive to some of the cautions we hear today, and we see similarities in these cautions with those raised in earlier days. Often couched in statements that include such phrases as "back to the basics," and "in these times of financial constraints," we hear the question, "Why spend scarce money on these new electronic gadgets when the teacher, book, and chalkboard can do the job better?" Thus I feel compelled to try to allay some of these alarms.

In *Big Media, Little Media,* Schramm (1967) responds to three questions, Can the media teach? Can they teach as well as a teacher? Is one medium any more effective than others? His response follows: "From the experimental studies we have plentiful evidence that people learn from the media, but very little evidence as to which medium, in a given situation, can bring about *most* learning" (p. 43).

It is impossible here to explore the complexities of selecting and using the enormous variety of possible educational applications of a vast array of media. In his text of almost three hundred pages, in which he surveys applications and costs of the most obvious of the "big" and "little" media, Schramm makes no claims for having found definitive answers. His survey of a number of case studies from various parts of the world, however, does provide useful data for review by the school board decision maker.

So, too, in considering costs of specific media, I would highly recommend *The Costs of Educational Media: Guidelines for Planning and Evaluation* (Jamison, Klees, and Wells 1978). Its authors are quick to point out that there are no definitive answers, no algorithms, that will provide ready conclusions for the decision maker. The decision maker must, then, appreciate that he or she is often in the unenviable position of having to make value judgments that are tinged with a host of factors that go beyond educational objectives, which are difficult enough to set down. And in making value judgments, one goes beyond certainty and logic. As John Stuart Mill so aptly put it, "Questions of ultimate ends are not amenable to direct proof."

Although it seems impossible to arrive at definitive answers in the tasks of selecting specific media for specific situations, it is possible to adopt a more systematic approach than is often the case. A variety of approaches may be used; even though the planning and evaluation systems most in vogue at any particular time are always being amended and modified, a particular agency or jurisdiction should opt for a planning and evaluation system in its selection and utilization of media. Such a system may, of course, be used for most of its other tasks as well.

Whatever planning and evaluation system might be adopted in the selection of media for educational purposes, there are three broad areas or "vectors," as Schramm (1967) terms them, that must be considered. These are the "task vector," the "media vector," and the "cost vector." As Schramm puts it, "At whatever level the decision is made it is necessary to specify the task to be done, and to estimate the probable effectiveness of different media for doing them and the probable cost of using those different media for the objectives named. Thus the decision requires information from three different sources — pedagogy, economics, and media research and experience" (p. 264). Underlining, again, that this is by no means a simple task, Schramm proceeds to provide a helpful analysis of each of the three vectors. His analysis of costs and media is perhaps nowadays especially helpful in this period of financial constraints. In making cost-effectiveness comparisons of different media, we tend often to ignore hidden costs, making comparisons at the point of utilization, or receiving end, of the media being compared. Thus, for example, the costs of books and print materials to a jurisdiction most often ignore the total costs to the society of the publications industry that produced the materials.

This point is also touched on by Jamison and others (1976). They suggest, for example, that as we are increasingly undertaking cost analyses of various educational projects, "it is worthwhile to examine the costs (and benefits) of undertaking evaluations, and, in particular, cost evaluations." They then provide the following comparison of cost analyses: "The total cost of the research and writing of this book was, we would estimate, on the order of $125,000, plus or minus 30 percent. A comprehensive cost analysis of a complete range of technological options for educational reform in a country or region could cost $50,000 to $150,000, though such valuable information could be produced by a $5,000 to $10,000 consulting effort properly done" (p. 20). Such costs, along with other hidden costs, should also be borne in mind by the school board administrator who must weigh the alternatives presented at budget time. A budget of from $50,000 to $150,000, for example, could provide a needy school board with a significant quantity of overhead projectors and videotape playback machines as well as the rights to educational films and videotapes. And yet, without such cost analysis and without evaluations of our projects, we are left in uncertainty. Of course, the decisions are seldom either-or decisions. Compromises must be made, and the dilemmas are seldom easy.

There is no end to the tasks confronted so briefly here, just as there is no end to the tasks confronted in reviewing standards for public schools. I hope that Schramm is proven to be right in the conclusion of his book when he writes, "It seems to us that research and experimentation is going to emphasize in greater degree the *content* of instructional media." Such an emphasis, he suggests, with a concern for more clearly identifying the needs and interests of teachers, for appreciating our objectives, and then of ascertaining the most effective use of media for specific purposes, would probably make a considerable difference in the amounts of money we spend on the "big media" as well as the "little media" and on the effectiveness of both.

REFERENCES

Jamison, Dean T., and others. *Cost Analysis for Educational Planning and Evaluation: Methodology and Application to Instructional Technology.* Princeton, N.J.: Educational Testing Service, 1976.

Jamison, Dean T.; Klees, Steven J.; Wells, Stuart J. *The Costs of Educational Media: Guidelines for Planning and Evaluation.* Beverly Hills, Calif.: Sage Publications, 1978.

Schramm, Wilbur. *Big Media, Little Media.* Beverly Hills, Calif.: Sage Publications, 1967.

9

Extracurricular Activities

LUTHER B. OTTO

What are the effects of participation in high school extracurricular activities on students? Are there long-term effects? Are extracurricular activities vital components of a total educational experience, or are they a drain and diversion of school resources? This chapter reviews the research that addresses these questions.

We observe three caveats. First, we differentiate between "evidence" and "suggestive findings." By *evidence* we typically mean results based on representative samples that apply multivariate statistical analyses and introduce appropriate control variables. Results based on less rigorous studies are labelled *suggestive findings*. Second, most of the research has studied males only; findings that apply to females are noted. Similarly, most of the studies apply to whites only; findings that apply to blacks or other minorities are noted. Third, participation in extracurricular activities may refer to the *amount* of participation or to participation in specific *kinds* of extracurricular activities. We consider the literature on both.

We review the research on participation in extracurricular activities as it relates to (a) academic performance, (b) aspirations and other attitudes, (c) later life achievements, and (d) other outcomes. In the discussion and conclusions we review why and how the effects of extracurricular activities occur, note the limitations of our knowledge, and consider the implications of our findings for school policy.

ACADEMIC PERFORMANCE

Two student cultures receive most attention in the research literature. One emphasizes scholarship, the other peer acceptance. Coleman (1959, 1961, 1965) argues that the adolescent society is characterized by irresponsibility, hedonism, and a nonchalance in scholastic matters that is antithetical to educational goals. Affirmation of one value system means a negation of the other. Others, however, indicate a positive relationship between participation in extracurricular activities and students' educational aspirations (Spady 1970, Otto and Alwin 1977). Whether the student cultures are viewed as compatible or competitive — more specifically, whether participation in extracurricular activities is believed to help or hurt academic performance — one thing is certain: the subject is controversial.

There is no evidence — only anecdotes and testimonials — that the amount of participation in extracurricular activities affects academic performance, whether favorably or unfavorably. But much attention has been given to the effects of participation in athletics. The most thorough research is reported by Hanks and Eckland (1976), who examine the relationship of participation in athletics on the grades of a national sample of 2,077 juniors and seniors. The study takes into account students' earlier grades as sophomores, their course of study, academic ability, family socioeconomic status, educational expectations, and the influence of teachers and peers. Hanks and Eckland (1976, p. 292) find no relationship and conclude that "athletics appears neither to depress nor to especially enhance . . . academic performance." Independent studies by Rehberg and Schafer (1968), Spreitzer and Pugh (1973), Lueptow and Kayser (1973), and Hauser and Lueptow (1978) confirm these results.

Yet, much popular literature and some limited research report slightly higher grade point averages for athletes than for nonathletes. Why? Because participation in athletics helps students get higher marks? No evidence supports that claim. But there is evidence that higher grades are associated with the characteristics of students who go into athletics (Lueptow and Kayser 1973, Hauser and Lueptow 1978, Hanks and Eckland 1976). Similarly, high school eligibility requirements based on grade point averages prohibit those with low marks from participating (Otto 1975). Finally, athletes may disproportionately enroll in "easier" courses or be graded more leniently, as some have alleged, but that issue has not been researched. In summary, the evidence is that participation in athletics neither helps nor hurts student grades. If athletes get better grades, it is probably for other reasons than their participation in sports.

Research by Schafer and Armer (1968) supports this conclusion. They present evidence that participation in athletics has a stronger relationship with grade point average among working class youth not enrolled in precollege curricula. They also report that participation in major sports and higher levels of participation are associated with higher grade point averages. The evidence is not strong. Nonetheless, the findings suggest that the relationship between participation in extracurricular activities and academic performance may vary by characteristics of the student, the sport, and the extent of involvement.

ASPIRATIONS AND OTHER ATTITUDES

The literature on adolescent peer cultures recognizes the influence of high school peer groups in shaping the educational plans of students. We ask two questions. First, does the amount of participation in extracurricular activities affect students' educational aspirations? Second, does participation in particular forms of extracurricular activities affect educational aspirations?

Two studies indicate that the amount of participation is positively related to students' aspirations. Spady (1970) studied 297 male seniors in two West Coast high schools and presented suggestive findings that participation in more than one extracurricular activity (service-leadership activities and athletic activities) has a stronger relationship with educational aspirations than does participation in either one separately; he also found that participation in single activities is a stronger predictor of aspirations than is nonparticipation. Similarly, Snyder and Spreitzer (1977) studied 603 female athletes in Ohio. They took into account the levels of education of the students' parents, the students' grade point averages, parents' and teachers' educational encouragement, and the educational expectations of the students' peers. Their evidence supports the findings for males: participation in both athletic and music programs was associated with the highest levels of educational aspirations, participation in only one activity had a weaker association, and nonparticipation showed the weakest association. Moreover, the relationship is strongest for students with below average grades. The findings indicate a positive association between amount of participation in extracurricular activities and level of educational aspirations.

Research on particular forms of extracurricular activities, notably athletics, is more plentiful. An early study by Rehberg and Schafer (1968) of 785 seniors in six high schools in Pennsylvania provides evidence of a positive relationship between participation in athletics and college plans. This study considered a number of other variables, for example, parental socioeconomic status, students' academic performance, and parents' educational encouragement. The evidence is that the positive relationship between participation in athletics and college plans is not due to the characteristics of students who participate in athletics, and the authors conclude that athletics does have a salutary effect on educational aspirations. The evidence is compelling. It is supported by numerous independent studies including Schafer and Rehberg (1970), Spady (1970, 1971), Rehberg (1969), Otto and Alwin (1977), and Picou (1978).

Hartzell and Picou (1979) studied a random cluster sample of 1,344 white and 434 black female high school seniors from Louisiana. Their suggestive findings apply to both white and black female athletes; those who participated in interscholastic sports had higher educational aspirations than their nonparticipating peers. When the level of interscholastic athletic achievement was differentiated between "participants" and "achievers" (as indicated by "all state" or "all conference" recognition), the effect on plans to obtain an advanced degree became even more pronounced. In another study Picou (1978) presents suggestive findings that a positive association exists between participation in athletics and educational aspirations among black males.

Finally, Spady (1971) studied five categories of participation and suggested that service-leadership has a large positive effect and varsity sports has a small positive effect on educational aspirations. Otto (1977) examined seven categories of participation and reports that only academic performance is related to educational aspirations. The samples for both studies are extremely limited, however, and the findings are tenuous.

Schwartz (1973) approached the relationship between extracurricular activities and attitude change from the perspective of task experience theory. She found that participants in the play production of *The King and I* experienced greater positive attitude changes on eight attitude dimensions than did participants in speech and debate or nonparticipants. Details of the study (sample size, age, gender, control variables, duration of effect) are lacking. Nonetheless, the suggestive findings support the general evidence for a relationship between participation in specific forms of extracurricular activities and adolescent aspirations.

In summary, there is evidence that the extent of participation in selected extracurricular activities is positively associated with the level of educational aspirations. There are suggestive findings that the relationship holds for males and females, blacks and whites.

LATER LIFE ACHIEVEMENTS

In his *Adolescent Society,* Coleman (1961) argued poignantly that the climate of values in high schools had the effect of recruiting people with mediocre abilities into important social positions rather than attracting those with high levels of ability. Does the amount of participation in extracurricular activities affect later life achievements?

Otto conducted a series of studies on the achievement process of 442 young men from Lenawee County, Michigan, high schools from age seventeen to thirty-two (Otto and Featherman 1975, Otto 1975, 1976a, 1976b, 1977). The analyses took into account numerous predictors of achievements including fathers' occupational prestige, levels of parental education, measured intelligence, academic performance, and educational and occupational aspirations. The studies controlled on an important psychological variable, adolescent personal adjustment. Otto examined in considerable detail the relationship between the amount of participation in extracurricular activities and educational, occupational, and income achievements fifteen years after high school. The research not only provides evidence that the extent of participation has a salutary effect on achievements, but also that extent of participation is the only variable in a rather complex set that had a consistent positive effect on all three socioeconomic achievements: education, occupation, and income. Hanks and Eckland (1978) provide independent supporting evidence and conclude that "schooling . . . may actually have a number of significant outcomes that have tended to go unnoticed and may be just as important as the learning that takes place in the classroom" (p. 489).

But what about participation in particular forms of extracurricular activities? For example, does participation in athletics have a positive effect on later life achievements? The title of Spady's (1970) article, "Lament for the Letterman," is telling. Studying the effects of participation in five areas — service-leadership, varsity sports, social activities, performing arts, and nonparticipation — Spady laments that although athletic participation increases levels of educational aspirations, it does not give participants the necessary skills to fulfill those aspirations. Spady's (1971) findings suggest that the most positive effects on educational attainment are associated with participation in service-leadership activities. Participation in varsity sports has a small effect. Participation in performing arts and social activities together with nonparticipation has a negative effect on educational achievements.

Hanks and Eckland (1976, 1978) took more variables into account in their thirteen-year post-high school study of a national sample. They present evidence that participation in athletics is unrelated, either positively or negatively, to educational achievements thirteen years later. Using the same data analyzed in Otto's earlier studies, Otto and Alwin (1977) conducted a thorough investigation of the effects of athletic participation on educational, occupational, and income achievements fifteen years after high school. They provide evidence for a small positive effect of participation in athletics on educational, occupational, and income achievements.

Finally, using a more restricted subsample for a special purpose analysis, Otto (1977) provides suggestive findings that participation in athletics has a positive effect on educational achievement but not on occupational achievement; participation in the performing arts has a positive effect on occupational achievements but not on educational achievements; service-leadership activities and vocational (academic) programs have no effect on either form of achievement; vocational farm programs negatively affect later occupational prestige; and participation in leisure and recreational activities has a positive association with educational and occupational achievements fifteen years after high school.

In summary, studies of the effect of extracurricular activities on later life achievements are limited in quantity and quality and the evidence is equivocal. The two strongest studies present conflicting evidence, but they are consistent, however, in that neither provides evidence that participation in athletics has a negative effect on early career achievements.

OTHER OUTCOMES

What else does participation in extracurricular activities affect? A recurring maxim in the theoretical literature is that an individual's personal integration is related to social integration. Using the data described above, Otto and Featherman (1975) examined adolescent personal adjustment and the social and psychological causes of self-estrangement and powerlessness among males fifteen years after high school (see also Otto 1976a). Their findings present limited evidence that level of participation in extracurricular activities is related to higher levels of adolescent personal adjustment. The evidence is much stronger concerning later outcomes. The extent to which an adolescent participated in high school extracurricular activities positively affects a variety of later life outcomes beyond educational, occupational, and income achievements at age thirty-two. The extent of adolescent participation affected adult socializing patterns, social integration, sense of self-estrangement, and powerlessness. The relationships tend to be modest. Nonetheless, they are positive and persist for as long as fifteen years after high school. Participation in high school extracurricular activities has a positive effect on more adult outcomes than does any other single variable in the analysis.

Hanks and Eckland (1976, 1978) provide supporting evidence with regard to adult social participation and alienation. They report positive short-run effects of participation in extracurricular activities and "even stronger long-run effects of adolescent social participation on membership in adult voluntary associations and indirectly on political behavior" (1978, p. 489).

Attention has also been given to assessing whether participation in athletics acts as a deterrent to delinquency. Schafer (1969) studied official records of delinquency and took into account individuals' academic performance and fathers' occupational prestige. The findings do not suggest a relationship between participation in athletics and reported delinquency. Landers and Landers (1978) studied the same relationship and report that nonparticipation is associated with reported juvenile offenses. However, Peek and others (1979) have severely criticized the latter study and argue that it is seriously flawed. Participation in extracurricular activities is associated with a number of favorable outcomes, but the notion that participation in athletics acts as a deterrent to delinquency is suspect.

DISCUSSION AND CONCLUSIONS

The evidence is that participation in extracurricular activities contributes to a number of important and desirable social and behavioral outcomes measured as late as fifteen years after high school. Though the magnitude of the effect is modest, the breadth of effect on later life outcomes is remarkable. No consistent evidence indicates that participation in high school extracurricular activities has negative effects on the variables measured.

Participation produces positive results. But why and how? Several explanations have been offered. One is that useful content is learned — "attitudes," "capacities," (Spady 1971) or "interpersonal skills" (Otto 1976b, p. 231). A second is that participation gives a young person visibility and important future "contacts" (Otto 1976b) — not what you know but who you know. A third explanation is that participation in extracurricular activities, especially athletics, elevates a student's peer status, which (in ways unspecified) transfers the effect of athletics to educational aspirations (Spady 1970, 1971, Spreitzer and Pugh 1973). A fourth explanation is that some individuals are born achievers (Spady 1971, Otto 1977). In high school they achieve in extracurricular activities. In later life they achieve in terms of education, occupation, and income. None of these explanations, however, has been supported by research (Otto and Featherman 1975, Otto 1977, Otto and Alwin 1977). Yet another explanation, a social psychological one (Otto and Haller 1979), does have support in the research literature. The explanation is that students assess their achievement potential, set their own goals, and significant others provide encouragement to them on the basis of the youth's past performance in extracurricular activities as well as performance in the formal academic curriculum. However, the fact that a relationship between extracurricular activities and achievements exists even after the level of students' aspirations has been taken into account suggests that participation does more than raise students' aspirations. Some form of learning also takes place that has payoffs in later life, but the content of that learning has not been established.

The results of participation are favorable, perhaps because unfavorable outcomes have not been studied as much. Are there no undesirable outcomes, psychological or structural? Are there no "battered child athletes," no unsavory features of the "jock subculture"? There is substantial anecdotal evidence for athletes being charged with drug, sexual, or other abuses. Is this because societal stars make newspaper headlines? Or is the incidence of abuse higher among athletes? The literature is conspicuously silent about the costs of participation in extracurricular activities.

Other questions remind us of the limitations of our present knowledge. Are the benefits most pronounced if participation occurs early or late in high school years? Do the benefits occur primarily in individual or team activities? Same-sex or coeducational activities? High or low supervision programs? Do activities that closely parallel the structure of the curriculum have stronger effects than less compatible programs? Does group size make a difference? We know little about what features of extracurricular activities are associated with positive outcomes.

Title IX has given impetus to assuring nondiscrimination based on race and sex. But there are other barriers to participation. As Otto (1975) has cautioned: "High school policies which deny participation in extracurricular activities to those who have not achieved a minimal grade point average may be penalizing those very students who can least afford it — students from relatively deprived backgrounds who, even without further penalty, are socially handicapped and destined for limited educational attainments" (p. 172). But educational systems can do more than remove barriers that unwittingly withhold students from growth. There must also be a conscious effort to exploit the benefits of known positive experiences. Extracurricular activities are extra not because they exist outside of the formal learning process and curriculum, but because they provide an additional learning experience through which schools can and do affect early career achievements.

REFERENCES

Coleman, James S. "Academic Achievement and the Structure of Competition." *Harvard Educational Review* 29 (Fall 1959): 330–51.

Coleman, James S. *The Adolescent Society.* Glencoe, Ill.: Free Press, 1961.

Coleman, James S. *Adolescence and the Schools.* New York: Basic Books, 1965.

Hanks, Michael P., and Eckland, Bruce K. "Athletics and Social Participation in the Educational Attainment Process." *Sociology of Education* 40 (October 1976): 271–94.

Hanks, Michael P., and Eckland, Bruce K. "Adult Voluntary Associations in Adolescent Socialization." *Sociological Quarterly* 19 (Summer 1978): 481–90.

Hartzell, M. J., and Picou, J. Steven. "Success in Interscholastic Sports and the College Plans of Women Athletes." *Tahper Journal* (Spring 1979): 12–13.

Hauser, William J., and Lueptow, Lloyd B. "Participation in Athletics and Academic Achievement: A Replication and Extension." *Sociological Quarterly* 19 (Spring 1978): 304–9.

Landers, Daniel M., and Landers, Donna M. "Socialization via Interscholastic Athletics: Its Effects on Delinquency." *Sociology of Education* 51 (October 1978): 299–303.

Lueptow, Lloyd B., and Kayser, Brian D. "Athletic Involvement, Academic Achievement, and Aspirations." *Sociological Focus* 7 (Winter 1973): 24–36.

Otto, Luther B. "Extracurricular Activities in the Educational Attainment Process." *Rural Sociology* 40 (Summer 1975): 162–76.

Otto, Luther B. "Social Integration and the Status-Attainment Process." *Journal of Sociology* 81 (May 1976a): 1360–83.

Otto, Luther B. "Extracurricular Activities and Aspirations in the Status Attainment Process." *Rural Sociology* 41 (Summer 1976b): 217–33.

Otto, Luther B. "Girl Friends as Significant-Others: Their Influence on Young Men's Career Aspirations and Achievements." *Sociometry* 40 (September 1977): 287–93.

Otto, Luther B., and Alwin, D. F. "Athletics, Aspirations, and Attainments." *Sociology of Education* 50 (April 1977): 102–13.

Otto, Luther B., and Featherman, David L. "Social Structural and Psychological Antecedents of Self-Estrangement and Powerlessness." *American Sociological Review* 40 (December 1975): 701–19.

Otto, Luther B., and Haller, Archibald O. "Evidence for a Social Psychological View of the Status Attainment Process: Four Studies Compared." *Social Forces* 57 (March 1979): 887–914.

Peek, Charles W.; Picou, J. Steven; Alston, Jon P.; and Curry, Evans W. "Interscholastic Athletics and Delinquent Behavior: Appraisal or Applause?" *Sociology of Education* 52 (October 1979): 238–43.

Picou, J. Steven. "Race, Athletic Achievement, and Educational Aspirations." *Sociological Quarterly* 19 (Summer 1978): 429–38.

Rehberg, Richard A. "Behavioral and Attitudinal Consequences of High School Interscholastic Sports: A Speculative Consideration." *Adolescence* 4 (Spring 1969): 69–88.

Rehberg, Richard A., and Schafer, Walter E. "Participation in Interscholastic Athletics and College Expectations." *American Journal of Sociology* 73 (May 1968): 732–40.

Schafer, Walter E. "Some Social Sources and Consequences of Interscholastic Athletics: The Case of Participation and Delinquency." *International Review of Sport Sociology* 4 (1969): 63–81.

Schafer, Walter E., and Armer, J. Michael "Athletes Are Not Inferior Students." *Transaction* 6 (November 1968): 21–26, 61–62.

Schafer, Walter E., and Rehberg, Richard A. "Athletic Participation, College Aspirations, and College Encouragement." *Pacific Sociological Review* 13 (Summer 1970): 182–86.

Schwartz, Henrietta. "Open Curtain — Open Mind." *Administrator's Notebook* 21 (1973): 1–4.

Snyder, Eldon E., and Spreitzer, Elmer. "Participation in Sports as Related to Educational Expectations among High School Girls." *Sociology of Education* 50 (Winter 1977): 47–55.

Spady, William G. "Lament for the Letterman: Effects of Peer Status and Extracurricular Activities on Goals and Achievement." *American Journal of Sociology* 70 (January 1970): 680–702.

Spady, William G. "Status, Achievement, and Motivation in the American High School." *School Review* 79 (May 1971): 379–403.

Spreitzer, Elmer, and Pugh, Meredith. "Interscholastic Athletics and Educational Expectations." *Sociology of Education* 46 (Spring 1973): 171–82.

Discussion

William H. Schubert
and Herbert J. Walberg

The research that Otto cites and the arguments he advances illuminate a much neglected domain of educational research. He is to be commended for his own research, which contributes substantially to the emergent body of literature on extracurricular activities. Otto's portrayal of research clearly reveals the ways in which participation in such activities is associated with academic performance, aspirations, and achievement relative to income, education, occupation, and other social and behavioral outcomes. Otto balances this presentation with perceptive caveats about limitations of the current state of research and by noting that the research reviewed reflects benefits more than costs of extracurricular participation. That research on this topic should be studied by educational policy makers is an inescapable conclusion. Indeed, those who create, implement, and evaluate school policy should encourage increased research on the impact of extracurricular policies and practices.

Note that Otto referred to Dewey's emphasis on providing real life experiences in schools as a principal influence on the creation of extracurricular activities. Dewey (1916) regarded education as a lifelong process of reconstructing experience in an effort to enhance meaning and direction in subsequent experience. Although Dewey is cited more than any other author in curriculum literature, less than 1 percent of the books produced on curriculum in the twentieth century deal substantially with extracurricular activities (Schubert 1980). This paucity of attention given to extracurricular activities by those who write about curricula attests to a lack of integrated study of the fundamental curriculum question: What excellences or dispositions do we wish to foster in young persons as we teach them the knowledge, skills, and values accumulated by humanity?

This question may be approached through another image. Think of students as personal theory builders. Through their experiences they continuously evolve conceptions of the world and how it works. It is, indeed, unlikely that they process experience in two separate categories: curricular and extracurricular. Thus, those who plan curricular experiences cannot defensibly neglect the powerful extracurricular dimension, for all of the experiences of schooling contribute to students' images of the world and its operation. The curricular and extracurricular must be regarded as a unified force that implements the policy dispositions designed to benefit student lives. As Whitehead (1929) contends, "You may not divide the seamless coat of learning" (p. 11). Thus, we argue that the concept of extracurricular should be extended beyond the school's auspices to nonschool educative experiences as well.

The study of life consequences of schooling is considered by Broudy (1970) and Walker (1976) as a major need in today's curriculum research. Otto offers promising research on life consequences of extracurricular participation. Those interested in curricula express a concern with both hidden and overt aspects of school experiences that offers hope that curricular policy makers will use research on extracurricular activities in their deliberations.

Progress toward this hope, however, would be a necessary but insufficient contribution to a Deweyan conception of educational policy. Such a conception must not only simulate society within school, it must embrace societal sources of student education as well. Bremer (1979) argues that the community itself must be seen as a curricular enterprise, while Cortez (1979) notes countercurricular forces in the social lives of students outside of school. Cremin (1976), Martin (1980), and Fantini (1980) call for educational systems that orchestrate the numerous agencies and situations that have an impact on education, not schools alone. Although these sources lend authoritarian, diverse, and well argued support to the idea that nonschool educational experiences are a worthy domain for curriculum inquiry, they do not provide empirically verified support.

According to Tyler (1977), the impacts of such agencies and situations are worthy subjects for curriculum research. It was Tyler

(1949) who synthesized the conceptual lenses that have oriented curriculum study around four principal topics for the past thirty years: purposes, learning experiences, organization, and evaluation.

Schubert (1981) begins with the premise that curriculum research should enable curriculum policy makers to formulate and implement dispositions that add meaning and direction to student lives; he promotes a broadened use of Tyler's topics. Curriculum research must reveal knowledge about sources of student perspectives. Principal sources include homes, families, jobs, media, peers, avocations, and nonschool organizations. Schubert reviews research on these areas and relates it to curriculum. Moreover, he suggests that each of these sources of student education embodies an informal curriculum that can be described relative to the Tylerian (1949) model, as well as other analytic curricular frameworks. Clearly, empirically substantiated research such as that provided by Otto on extracurricular activities would contribute to the study of nonschool curricula as a vast expansion of the notion of extracurricular.

The causal connections among extracurricular activities and educational goals may be uncertain, but rough, though straightforward, estimates of children's annual time budgets (see Table 9-1) serve as a useful quantitative framework to reveal the immense educative potential of extramural, extracurricular, or nonschool activities. The perhaps typical six intramural classroom hours of school days compare unfavorably with the average of seven hours per day in which the television is on in American households — nearly constantly during afternoon, dinner, and evening hours in over 35 percent of a recent sample of households (Roberts and Bachen 1981).

Classroom time consumes only about half the child's potentially educative hours on school days and less than a quarter of all such hours during the year. These hours for comparison are equivalent in time to twenty-seven full-time, forty-hour weeks or roughly a half year of an adult's work.

Subtracting time attributable to tardiness, absence, leaving early, interruptions, and inattentiveness in recent samples of high school classes leaves as little as a quarter but on average perhaps half of this time, 540 hours of thirteen and a half full-time weeks of

Table 9-1.

Rough Estimates of Hours of Potential
Educative Activity for Elementary School Children

	Curricular	Extra-curricular	Totals
School Days			
Days per year	180	180	
Hours per school day	6	6[a]	
Subtotal/hours per year	1,080	1,080	2,160
Other Days			
Days per year	—	185	
Hours per day	—	12[b]	
Subtotal/hours per year	0	2,220	2,220
	1,080	3,300	4,380

[a]Calculated as twenty-four hours per day minus six hours for school, ten hours for sleep, and two hours for meals and other maintenance activities.
[b]Calculated as twenty-four hours per day minus twelve hours for sleep, meals, and other maintenance activities.

intramural hours (Walberg and Frederick in press). Of course, some of the knowledge presented during these remaining hours the student already knows, and some the student is as yet incapable of learning. Perhaps half of the time is suitable to the typical student, leaving 270 hours or nearly seven full-time weeks, which amounts to 25 percent of the intramural hours or 12.5 percent of the potentially educative time on school days or 6.18 percent of such time during the calendar year (see Table 9-1).

Readers may wish to apply alternative estimates and assumptions to this formulation. The estimates, although rough, give some upper bounds to the effects of curricular activities that the schools presently provide and help to explain why their effects seem small, since the range from lowest to highest curricular quality or quantity or their product may be slight compared to the range of extracurricular or nonschool figures.

Arguments for the unrecognized value of the student's time and the need for budgeting it productively and wisely may be made on humanistic or economic grounds (Walberg 1981). Doubling and even redoubling productive educational time and its efficiency may raise the fulfillment of human potential through education. Educational productivity is needed for later adult accomplishments and for curricular and extracurricular activities. An hour a day of concentrated instruction, effort, and practice may be enough to achieve a degree of comparative excellence (say, the 99th percentile in norms of unselective national samples of comparable age peers) in either mathematics, foreign language, chess, ballet, many sports, or comparable pursuits. World-class performance or one's best in such endeavors may require four to ten hours a day over periods of from one to twenty years (Walberg 1981). More explicit pricing and valuing of such goals and more complete data on the means to attain them are likely to help educators, parents, and students make more informed decisions concerning time allocations among curricular, extracurricular, and nonschool educative activities.

If those who determine school policy genuinely wish to have a beneficial impact on the outlook of children and youth, they must adopt an ecological perspective that acknowledges the importance and interdependence of school and nonschool curricula and time on the lives of students. Research that provides a knowledge base for this kind of policy deliberation is embryonic, but its worth to educational productivity is obvious. To integrate extant research on curricular and extracurricular outcomes could be an invaluable initial step toward this end. The end-in-view, to use a productive Deweyan phrase, should be no less than a conception of curriculum policy that embraces not only curricular and extracurricular dimensions of schooling, but the implicit curricula in student lives outside of school as well.

REFERENCES

Bremer, John. *Education and Community.* Sheparton, Australia: Waterwheel Press, 1979.

Broudy, Harry S. "Components and Constraints of Curriculum Research." *Curriculum Theory Network* 5 (Spring 1970): 16–31.

Cortez, Carlos E. "The Societal Curriculum and the School Curriculum: Allies or Antagonists?" *Educational Leadership* 36 (April 1979): 475–79.

Cremin, Lawrence. *Public Education.* New York: Basic Books, 1976.

Dewey, John. *Democracy and Education.* New York: Macmillan, 1916.

Fantini, Mario. "The Expanding Domain of Curriculum Inquiry." Paper presented at the meeting of the American Educational Research Association, Boston, April 1980.

Martin, John H. "Reconsidering the Goals of High School Education." *Educational Leadership* 37 (January 1980): 278–82.

Roberts, Donald F., and Bachen, Christine M. "Mass Communication Effects." *Annual Review of Psychology* 32 (1981): 307–356.

Schubert, William H. *Curriculum Books: The First Eighty Years.* Lanham, Md.: University Press of America, 1980.

Schubert, William H. "Knowledge about Out-of-School Curriculum." *Educational Forum* 45 (January 1981): 185–98.

Tyler, Ralph W. *Basic Principles of Curriculum and Instruction.* Chicago: University of Chicago Press, 1949.

Tyler, Ralph W. "Desirable Content for a Curriculum Syllabus Today." In *Curriculum Theory,* edited by Alex Molnar and John A. Zahorik. Washington, D.C.: Association for Supervision and Curriculum Development, 1977.

Walberg, Herbert J. "A Psychological Theory of Educational Productivity." In *Psychology and Education: The State of the Union,* edited by Frank H. Farley and Neal Gordon, pp. 81–108. Berkeley, Calif.: McCutchan, 1981.

Walberg, Herbert, and Frederick, Wayne. "Instructional Time and Learning." In *Encyclopedia of Educational Research,* edited by Harold Mitzel. Washington, D.C.: American Educational Research Association, in press.

Walker, Decker F. "Toward Comprehension of Curricular Realities." In *Review of Research in Education,* vol. 4, edited by Lee S. Shulman, pp. 268–308. Itasca, Ill.: F. E. Peacock, 1976.

Whitehead, Alfred N. *The Aims of Education and Other Essays.* New York: Macmillan, 1929.

Part 3 —————

EDUCATIONAL CONTEXTS

10

Facilities

C. W. McGUFFEY

Educational facilities have undergone significant changes from the period when the typical schoolhouse in the United States was a rural one-room school building. The forerunner of the modern school plant was the building constructed for the graded elementary school of the mid-nineteenth century. This new architectural type was designed to meet the needs of the first fully graded, public elementary school in the United States — the Quincy Grammar School constructed in Boston in 1848. As the schoolhouse changed from its early ancestor to the modern air-conditioned, adequately lit, carpeted, multistory building of the present, research played a minor and insignificant role in shaping the school building until the 1930s.

Although human beings have been investigating the nature of their surroundings since the dawn of history, the use of research as a tool for the improvement of educational buildings is of recent origin. Clearly, as Rummel (1964) pointed out, other approaches to the solution of problems preceded the research approach. The greatest impact of research on educational building has occurred since the 1930s and began with the studies of school ventilation and lighting. The approaches to these areas were piecemeal at first, but became more comprehensive as heated debates developed over contradictory findings resulting from incremental studies. Research groups were formed by such organizations as the Illuminating Engineering Society and by foundations to promote and support more comprehensive approaches to research about educational buildings. More recently the American Institute of Architects and the Council of Educational Facility Planners, International, have formed research organizations. The lack of a single, coordinated research organization with concern for the impact of the total physical environment on education and on the learner in educational settings may continue to hamper more comprehensive approaches to research on educational facilities. The "coordinated classroom" concept originated by Harmon (1950) is an idealized construct that is yet to be realized.

PURPOSE AND SCOPE

The research that deals with facilities and pupil achievement, performance, and self-concept is reviewed in this chapter. More specifically, the chapter reports the research findings on the impact of the physical environment, building configuration, and programmatic variables on educational outcomes. Additionally, conclusions supported by the weight of evidence are presented.

The selection of the research to be reviewed was based on broad guidelines. Studies were included that used methods indicating that they were survey, descriptive, ex post facto, quasi-experimental or experimental types, or variations of such types. Studies that could be classified as either basic or applied research, including both laboratory and field-based research, were also included. The selection of specific variables for consideration imposed further limitations on the scope of the review. Physical environment variables were limited to school building age, thermal factors, visibility (seeing factors), hearing factors, and color and interior painting. Building configuration variables were limited to open space, amount of space, windowless facilities, and underground facilities. Site size, building utilization, building maintenance, special instructional facilities, support facilities, and school plant size were the selected programmatic variables. Another significant limitation was the availability of research, which has been extremely limited in certain selected programmatic areas.

THE IMPACT OF SELECTED PHYSICAL ENVIRONMENT VARIABLES

The research literature summarized in this section relates to specific factors for which there is an organized body of literature. The types of research range from surveys and opinion polls to formally organized experimental projects. The type of research, a brief summary of the procedures used, and the pertinent findings and conclusions of the authors are reported here.

School Building Age

The age of a school building has been used as a surrogate factor to study the composite impact of school plant variables on pupil achievement at elementary, middle, and secondary school levels. McGuffey and Brown (1978) explained:

Research and development in industry have made modern school buildings a more effective educational resource. Climate control and carpeting in schools are developments of the last two decades. Fluorescent lighting and the research related to vision and glare control are likewise of recent origin. Consequently, one would expect to find a better quality physical environment in newer school buildings than in older ones.

School buildings deteriorate with age due to use, weather, and lack of proper maintenance. They become obsolete primarily because of design characteristics and because of the failure of owners to make adaptations as technology and education change. . . . Therefore, one can readily associate building condition and obsolescence with school building age [pp. 6–7].

A number of input-output studies were reviewed that considered school building age as one of a larger number of educational resource variables having a potential impact on pupil achievement. These studies utilized stepwise multiple regression as the basic statistical procedure for the analysis of data on the age of buildings and on students' achievement.

Using the school as the unit of analysis, Thomas (1962) considered thirty-two independent variables including school building age in relation to eighteen dependent variables used as measures of pupil achievement. The study included 206 schools. Stepwise multiple regression was run for each of the eighteen dependent variables. All thirty-two independent variables were entered into the equation on each run. A school building's age was consistently positive and significantly related to each of the eighteen achievement variables.

Burkhead, Fox, and Holland (1967) studied a sample of thirty-nine Chicago schools, twenty-two Atlanta schools, and 177 large schools in other major cities from Project Talent. The school was used as the unit of analysis. The age of school buildings and twenty-six other independent variables were regressed against fourteen dependent variables, six of which were measures of achievement. Building age was significant in reading score regression, but was not significant on the school median verbal score for tenth graders.

In a study utilizing a sample of 597 white and 458 black sixth-grade students, Michelson (1970) used data from an unknown number of schools in a large city in the east of the United States. Thirty-three independent variables, including school building age, were considered in relation to five student achievement variables. The sample was stratified by race; seven regressions were run for whites and five for blacks. The age of school buildings was significantly negative in the single equation model for blacks on verbal scores, but was not significant for whites or blacks in the simultaneous equation models.

A report by Guthrie and others (1971) dealt with the research on a number of educational issues, including the relationship between school resources and student achievement. The sample included 5,284 sixth-grade students attending eighty-nine elementary schools in Michigan. Guthrie and his associates calculated 360 rank order coefficients utilizing three dependent variables, twelve independent variables — including building age — and ten deciles determined from socioeconomic status ranks. The dependent variables were the scores on reading, mathematics, and verbal tests. Each independent variable was tested thirty times in relationship with dependent variables with no control for the influence of other independent variables. School building age was significant in twenty-two of the thirty times it was tested.

McGuffey and Brown (1978) studied the interrelationships of the age of classroom units (ACU), socioeconomic status (SES) variables, and student achievement variables, as represented by the scores on the subtests of the Iowa Test of Basic Skills (ITBS) for fourth and eighth grades, and the Test of Academic Progress for the eleventh grade. The relationship between fourteen independent and fifteen dependent variables was analyzed through the use of data from 188 school districts in Georgia using stepwise multiple regression. The unit of analysis was the school district, which ranged in size from 343 pupils to 80,571 pupils. Regression equations including only significant SES variables.for each of the 15 dependent variables were constructed to form the basis for the value added by significant ACU variables. In eleven out of the twelve tests at the fourth-grade level, ACU variables were significant, either positive or negative. At the eighth-grade level, ACU variables were significantly negative in only one of seven tests. Finally, ACU variables were significant, either positive or negative, in nine of eleven tests at the eleventh-grade level. The range of variance (R^2) explained by school building age was .5 percent to 2.6 percent in fourth grade, 0 to 2.6 percent in eighth grade, and 1.4 percent to 3.3 percent in eleventh grade. Total variance accounted for by SES and ACU variables was less than 60 percent for fourth grade, approximately 20 percent for eighth grade, and less than 16 percent for eleventh grade. The results showed a differential effect, both for content and grade level, when the variances of both SES and ACU variables were combined.

In a follow-up of the McGuffey and Brown study, Plumley (1978) investigated the relationship of school building age and the achievement of fourth-grade pupils in a random sample of elementary schools using the individual school as the unit of analysis. Seven dependent variables representing the scores of the six subtests and the composite score on the ITBS were utilized. The seven independent variables were measures of socioeconomic status; race; modernized, partially modernized, or nonmodernized buildings; date of building construction; and date of modernization. Stepwise multiple regression analysis was used. Nonmodernized buildings accounted for 3.3 percent to 6.4 percent of the variance on three of the five subtests, and 5.3 percent on the composite score of the ITBS. The findings of the study indicated that the older the school buildings, without the elements of modernization, the lower the composite, vocabulary, reading, language, work study, and mathematics scores on the ITBS (p. 103). The correlations were significant at the .05 level.

Chan (1979) conducted a second follow-up of the McGuffey and Brown study in which he investigated the relationship of school building age and academic achievement of eighth-grade pupils in a random sample of schools in Georgia. The unit of analysis was the individual school. The dependent variables were the composite score and the subtest score on the vocabulary, reading, language, work study, and mathematics sections of the ITBS. The independent variables were SES; modernized, partially modernized, and nonmodernized school buildings; and age of school buildings. The hierarchical inclusion method of multiple regression and the analysis of covariance with socioeconomic status as covariate were used. Multiple regression was employed to analyze the relationship between dependent and independent variables and to determine the amount of variance in achievement due to the age of school buildings. Analysis of covariance was used to compare achievement among pupils housed in modernized, partially modernized, and nonmodernized school buildings when SES was used as a covariate.

The findings of the study by Chan (1979) indicated a statistically significant relationship at the .05 level between school building age and academic achievement as measured by the composite, vocabulary, and mathematics scores of the ITBS. The amount of variance was .982 percent for composite scores, 1.919 percent for vocabulary scores, and 1.127 percent for mathematics scores after SES was taken into account (pp. 80–81). The results yielded by the analysis of covariance with SES as a covariate indicated that the achievement scores of pupils assigned to modernized school buildings were consistently higher than scores of pupils assigned to nonmodernized school buildings; however, significant differences were found at the .01 and .05 levels, respectively, for vocabulary and language scores (pp. 65–66).

Thermal Factors

A number of studies were reviewed in which the research analyzed the various thermal factors and their relationships that have some impact on human comfort and efficiency and on academic achievement.

Herrington (1952), an environmental physiologist, argued that the central problem of air-conditioning and heating is the control of human heat loss. He stressed the fact that thermal optima are sensitive to age, sex, activity, clothing and, in some instances, the need for a relaxing or stimulating effect. The body reacts to extremes of heat and cold. If the body receives too much heat, the individual collapses on the floor involuntarily as the temperature center overrides positive control. At the other extreme, exposure to severe cold results in shivering, then the temperature center overrides the conscious desire of posture control and contracts all body muscles. The individual becomes locked in a folded position, knees against the chest and arms rigid, which conserves heat. In between these two extremes is an area referred to as the "comfort zone." The comfort zone is an approximate, not an absolute, quantity. Some of the factors basic to achieving thermal comfort are: air temperature, radiant temperature, air movement, and humidity.

Herrington (1952) also explained the differences of sex, age, and the sedentary level of work. A kindergarten child has a heat loss requirement 150 percent of that of a sedentary teacher in her sixties. Temperature differences usually amount to about five degrees. A similar difference exists between men and women. The natural metabolic difference is approximately 10°. Thermostats controlled by women usually average 3–4° higher than those controlled by men. According to Herrington, the effect of temperature and humidity on human activity is deep-seated in a psychophysiological sense, and human tolerance for deviations from optimal conditions should not lead us to discard the gains in efficiency and reductions in climate-induced fatigue (p. 371).

Several studies have attempted to establish optimum thermal conditions. Herrington cited Vernon, Bedford, and Warner (1927), Osborne and Vernon (1922), and Mackworth (1946), who presented evidence of the effects of a nonoptimal thermal environment on the accident rate of three classes of workers. The findings of these studies indicated that as temperatures varied both below and above the optimum, accident rates increased two- to threefold.

Increases noted at below optimal levels affected dexterity primarily while higher than optimal temperatures decreased general alertness and increased physiological stress. These studies and other available evidence (McConnell and Yaglou 1926, Winslow and Herrington 1949, Karpovich 1959) indicated that temperatures above 80° tend to produce harmful physiological effects that decrease work efficiency and output. The findings of these and other studies support the long-held thermal theory of ventilation, which states that poor ventilation interferes with heat loss from body surfaces produced from the effects of temperature, humidity, and air movement.

The New York Commission on Ventilation conducted major investigations into physiological and psychological reactions to various atmospheric conditions by school children in classroom settings and in "experimental chambers" at City College in New York (New York Commission on Ventilation 1931). These investigations were conducted between 1913 and 1917 under the direction of G. T. Palmer and between 1926 and 1929 under T. J. Duffield, and their contributions are numerous. Some of the findings pertinent to this review follow:

1. The study of the effects of air flow and room temperature upon respiratory illness in schools showed no significant differences between 69°F and 74.5°F and an air flow of 28.6 cubic feet per minute and 13.9 cubic feet per minute (p. 37).

2. Experimental results confirmed earlier investigations that excessively high temperatures produce harmful physiological effects and that an effective temperature of 67–73°F is desirable (pp. 41–42).

3. The study of the effect of overheating on the performance of physical work showed that 15 percent less work was performed at 75°F than at 68°F with 50 percent relative humidity and no air movement; while at 86°F with 80 percent humidity, the decrease was 28 percent as compared to that performed at 68°F (pp. 45–46).

In conclusion, the commission recommended that schools maintain room temperatures between 68 and 70°F with sufficient air movement to eliminate objectionable odors and avoid excessive drafts. Overheating must be avoided to maintain physical comfort and resistance against disease.

A number of studies have dealt with the effects of temperature control on achievement and performance. The types of studies vary; some lack internal validity while others suffer from problems of sampling and statistical measurement.

Mayo (1955) studied two matched groups of U.S. Navy trainees. The study used 808 subjects who were being taught electrical theory. One group was taught in an air-conditioned building while the other was taught in a building ventilated with exhaust fans. Median effective temperatures in the air-conditioned building were 71.3°F in the morning with little ventilation during the day. The median temperature in the non-air-conditioned building was 86.3°F in the morning and 92.5°F in the afternoon.

Course content and exams were the same for all subjects. The investigation covered the first month of an eight-month course. Measures of performance were taken following the first eighty hours of instruction and the second eighty hours. Although 79 percent of the subjects in the non-air-conditioned building felt that their performance had been adversely affected, no significant difference was found between the performance of the two groups. The study failed to reveal data on air movement in the air-conditioned building.

Nolan (1960) made a comparative study of military students' grades earned in a winter month and in a summer month. The hypothesis advanced was that academic learning is affected by temperature conditions. Students involved in the experiment were selected on a random basis from two separate courses of instruction taught during a winter and a summer month and were divided into three similar groups for a summer and winter month based on general aptitude and education criteria. All students received identical instruction and efforts were made to control learning factors. Mean grades for each unit in each course were used for comparison among the groups and between summer and winter months. In all groups, students earned higher grades during the winter months. Significant differences were found for four out of six groups, and Nolan concluded that high temperatures have an adverse effect on academic learning.

Peccolo (1962) conducted an experiment to determine the difference in learning between a group of students in an "ideal" thermal environment and a control group in a "regular" classroom's thermal environment. Forty-four pairs of fourth-grade students matched on the basis of achievement, intelligence, age, weight, height, and occupation of parents were used. The study was carried out in a two-room school in classrooms that were identical except for ceiling height. Learning was measured by the number of correct responses to a repeated series of ten paper and pencil tasks. Five tasks involved reasoning activities, four dealt with routine clerical activities, and one with new concepts. The experiment was duplicated with a second set of fourth-grade children occupying opposite rooms to balance the difference in ceiling heights of the two classrooms. Analysis of variance was used to summarize the data. A three-factor design was used to determine the change in performance of the two groups in the experimental situation. A two-factor design (treatment × levels) was used to analyze the performance of the two groups on the last trial. The significance level of the F-test was set at .05. Peccolo concluded that significantly higher gains were made by pupils in the experimental group on all reasoning and some clerical tasks, differences in the scores of the experimental and control groups on the new concepts task was not significant. The interaction between trials and levels and treatment results favored the experimental group in the ideal thermal environment on all of the tasks, although the experimental effect varied on some tasks from level to level.

Stuart and Curtis (1964) investigated the effects of alternative thermal environments on school plant operating costs and the comfort, achievement, conduct, and health of pupils in one climate-controlled school and two non-climate-controlled schools over two academic years and two summer terms. The schools differed in respects other than their thermal environments.

In this experimental design, the analyses of summer school data showed that of the nine comparisons the first summer, the mean gains of the experimental school exceeded those of the control school in all comparisons. Of the sixteen comparisons of the second summer, the mean gains of the experimental school equaled those of the control school.

The analyses of the academic year data revealed that the mean gains of the experimental school exceeded the first control school on twenty-six of forty-two measures the first academic year and on thirty-five of forty-two measures the second academic year. The comparisons between the experimental and second control schools indicated that the mean scores of the two schools were equal for the first year but the experimental school mean gains exceeded those of the control school on thirty-four of the forty-two measures during the second academic year. Prior records of the second control school indicated that in previous years the pupils of the second control school had been superior in achievement to the pupils of the experimental school. The analyses showed that of the six sets of comparisons — four regular academic terms and two summer terms — the experimental schools' gains were superior in four comparisons, equal in two, and inferior in none. According to Stuart and Curtis: "The record may be interpreted as indicating that the gain in achievement of the students in Oak Grove (experimental school) was superior to that of the students in the non-climate-controlled schools over the period in this study" (p. 221).

McCardle (1966) followed up the Peccolo experiment to determine the effect of alternate thermal conditions on learning and to see whether the thermal environment had an effect on time placement of subjects. A two-classroom building with thermal control capabilities was used. Recommended standards for a good thermal environment were created in a model room while thermal conditions similar to those in a regular classroom with no thermal control were created in a marginal room. Sixth-grade pupils were matched as pairs based on ITBS scores, intelligence quotient (IQ), and sex; forty matched pairs were selected. Pupils were matched further in pairs of high ability (IQ of 110 or better) and low ability (IQ of less than 110). Attempts were made to control instruction and teacher variables. Three learning tasks — a routine task, a role task, and a conceptual task — were included in the study. A Type VI (Lindquist) design was used to analyze routine tasks while a Type III (Lindquist) design was used to determine role and conceptual tasks. The significance level established was .05. The pupils in the model room showed a greater number of correct responses and required less time to complete the program materials tasks than pupils in the marginal room. Six of the fifteen main effects analyzed were significant.

Harner (1974) reviewed the research relating to the optimal temperature levels for the performance of certain academic skills.

He reported that reading and mathematical skills were adversely affected by temperatures above 74°F. Reading speed and comprehension were most affected by temperature. A significant reduction in reading speed and comprehension occurred between 73.4°F and 80.6°F. Between 68 and 73.4°F was the ideal temperature range for reading. Harner also found that achievement in mathematical operations such as multiplication, addition, and factoring have been shown to be significantly reduced by air temperatures above 77°F. He reported that mathematical operations are performed best at temperatures between 68 and 74°F.

In summary, the overwhelming weight of the evidence from the research reviewed here supports the hypothesis that the thermal environment affects academic achievement at various grade levels within the school.

Visual Factors

Seeing has been the subject of intense research since the work of Luckiesh and Moss (1937), which created controversy in the field of illumination engineering for years. The basic question is how much light is needed for seeing? According to Bitterman (1948) the major problem was one of developing techniques for the evaluation of lighting standards.

Tinker (1939) summarized experimental results on color, light intensity, and light distribution with major emphasis on intensity standards. Tinker's recommendations were based on the kind of investigations he thought were essential. His conclusions represented the critical illumination level beyond which no increase in efficiency of performance was found. The following levels are from Tinker's list:

	Footcandles
1. Reading (speed) 10-point type	3
2. Reading (fatigue) 10-point type	3
3. Reading	4
4. Reading performance in school	4–6
5. Reading achievement in school	4–6
6. Computing arithmetic problems	less than 9.6 recommended

Tinker recommended that minimum intensity at desk-top level be no less than ten footcandles for schoolrooms.

Luckiesh and Moss (1940) conducted a series of tests over a three-year period using matched experimental and control groups in the fifth and sixth grades. Matching was based on performance on the New Stanford Achievement Test, the Otis Self-Administering Test of Mental Ability, chronological age, and evaluation of home conditions. Physical conditions of the classrooms were typical of schools in the 1940s. The experimental classrooms were electrically lighted with six opaque luminaires with 300- and 500-watt lamps while the control classrooms were lighted with four prismatic glass luminaires with 150-watt lamps. Over three years the light level intensities for outer, center, and inside rows of classroom fixtures averaged 47, 27, and 26 footcandles, respectively, for the experimental room while for the control room the average was 47, 17, and 11 footcandles, respectively, for each row. The results indicated a statistically significant increase in the scores of pupils in the experimental classrooms over those in the control classrooms.

Tinker (1948) used experimental and control groups to study the combined effects of marginal seeing conditions on reading perception rate. The control group was adapted to an illumination level of twenty-five footcandles, then tested for reading two prepared forms written in 10-point roman type. The experimental group was initially adapted to twenty-five footcandles. Later, the experimental group was adapted to three footcandles, then tested similarly except under three footcandles using the same copy written in 8-point italic type. The results showed a 10.4 percent reduction in reading speed, which was statistically significant at the .01 level. Combined conditions of illumination level and size and form of type that were individually marginal decreased reading perception rate.

Tinker (1959) investigated the effects of illumination intensity on seeing efficiency with differences in brightness contrast between print and paper. Test materials were printed on paper with different reflectances so that brightness contrasts varied. Illumination levels used were 5, 25, 50, 100, 200, and 400 footcandles. Speed of reading and print visibility were measured under each treatment condition. The results showed that increased illumination levels above five footcandles had an insignificant effect on reading speed when brightness contrasts between print and page were large. However, at intermediate contrast ranges, the speed of reading increased between five and twenty-five footcandles. With poorer contrasts, lighting levels had to be increased between 50 and 100 footcandles to obtain a significant increase in the speed of reading. At twenty-five footcandles the contrast between print and page makes a difference in reading speed; if contrast is inadequate, extreme increases in the level of lighting are unlikely to help.

Cooper (1958) reported on the culmination of an eight-year study at the University of Michigan's Vision Research Laboratories. A new system was developed at the laboratory for scientifically determining the amount of light required to perform any practical seeing task comfortably and efficiently. The system was based on the postulate that "an identical amount of light is required to perform any visual task of total equal difficulty" (p. 15). This new system was hailed as "one of the most dramatic and significant developments that had occurred in the lighting industry since Edison's invention of the electric lamp seventy-nine years ago" (p. 16).

Classroom tests were conducted by Chorlton and Davidson (1959) of glare conditions at various locations in the room under various levels of illumination. The visual tasks were reading no. 2 pencil leading on ruled matte paper and reading print on various stock papers. The samples used were tasks taken from elementary schools. The tasks were performed under different types of illumination systems, including general diffused, direct, and luminous indirect systems.

Measurements were taken under each illumination system and at various lighting levels. The threshold of visibility was determined for an observer at a desk for a glare condition, then a no-glare condition. The lighting levels were then raised to a glare, and the threshold of visibility was again determined and expressed as a percentage loss or gain from no glare.

There was a decreasing loss of contrast for the general diffused and direct lighting systems at higher footcandle levels, while for the luminous indirect system the loss did not change at higher footcandle levels. According to the researchers, the significant factors that affect loss of contrast in a school situation are visual task, type of lighting system, and lighting levels.

Blackwell (1959) studied the relation between contrast required for detection and illumination quantity for simple disc targets, which varied both in size and length of exposure. The data used in the original study involved only a single class of discs of four minutes and exposure duration of one-fifth of a second. Contrast sensitivity increased progressively as luminance increased. Blackwell also reported footcandle levels for a variety of tasks similar to those performed in schools. These data are presented in Table 10-1.

Table 10-1

Task	Footcandles
1. Reading while writing: sample of ink writing, one sixth-grade pupil	1.38
2. Reading while writing: sample of #2 pencil writing; 12 sixth-grade pupils with poorest writing in a class of 31	63.0
3. Reading: 8-point bodoni type	1.87
4. Reading: 6-point text type	2.98
5. Reading: 8-point text type	1.13
6. Reading: 10-point text type	0.94
7. Reading: 12-point text type	.60
8. Reading: typed original, good ribbon	.97
9. Reading: Thermofax copy, poor quality	589

The recommended lighting specification system for current use (1959) was based on a level of visual capacity of five assimilations per second (APS) and a field factor of fifteen for all visual tasks. This research established the basis for determing how much light is needed for various seeing tasks. The Illuminating Engineering Society adopted the specification system.

Blackwell (1963) reported on the results of his eight-year study at the Vision Research Laboratory, as well as subsequent laboratory studies of the effect of light on sight. He observed that the eyeball is not damaged structurally by bad lighting, either insufficient quantity or poor quality. Blackwell goes on to point out, however, that the effectiveness of information collection is reduced in bad light. Seeing in bad light can lead to the development of ineffective programming of the information collection process which may become habitual. Bad lighting can also lead to discomfort. Poor visibility leads to poor eye adjustment which leads to discomfort. Blackwell's (1959) studies determined the degree to which different seeing tasks required different lighting levels for equal visibility. His methodology was further strengthened and made more comprehensive and applicable to the range of conditions found in the field through subsequent investigations.

Blackwell and Blackman (1968) reviewed the most recent studies in the refinement of the method used for determining the quantity of illumination for various types of tasks. The concern of this research effort was to determine whether the standard visual performance curve produced in earlier studies could be used to predict visual performance when the targets differ in shape and size from the four-minute disc. The results showed that the standard curve can predict the effects of the quantity of illumination on the visual performance of many tasks. The results further showed that visual acuity is often a special form of contrast sensitivity. Contrast sensitivity appears to be a logical criterion for evaluating the effects of luminance on visual performance. Finally, the study confirmed that increasing light intensity has a beneficial effect upon visual performance up to an extremely high saturation point.

Sampson (1970) made a series of measurements of contrast rendition of pencil handwriting under a wide variety of classroom lighting systems to determine the selection of lighting systems for classrooms. Eighteen projects were included in the study, which used the Visual Task Photometer and the Spectra Spot Brightness Meter for field readings. Illumination levels were recorded for thirteen locations in the normal classroom seating area and two or more other readings on chalk and tack boards. To show the quality of shadow and form rendition for each lighting system, geometric forms were photographed on a desk in the center of the room.

As part of his conclusions, Sampson (1970, pp. 90–91) stated the following general principles:

1. The eye is most efficient for close visual work when the illumination level is adequate and the task is slightly brighter than the surrounds.

2. Large dark areas in an environment should not be less than one-third the brightness of the task.

3. Adaptation is equally affected by either dark or bright areas.

4. Where no close visual work is being done, environment brightness is unimportant; however, where visual accuracy is required, the brightness of the surrounds becomes more critical as the need for accuracy becomes more important.

5. Side-wall reflectances, including cabinets and tack boards, should be from 40 percent to 60 percent, and, if possible, 80 percent at locations above the top line of the chalk board.

6. The ceiling should be as nearly white as possible and at least as bright as the side walls.

7. Direct sunlight should not be allowed to come into the classroom, and windows in the side walls should be shielded to control the brightness to a maximum of 300 footlamberts.

8. Ceiling-mounted luminaires and the ceiling should be approximately equal in brightness.

9. Light sources of large area and low brightness are more effective than small sources of high brightness.

Color and Interior Painting

Several studies were reviewed that deal with color in the classroom and its impact on pupil performance. Although inconclusive, these studies provide support for the hypothesis that color selection for classroom interiors has an impact on academic achievement and pupil performance.

Lewinski (1938) studied the affective responses of twenty-four male and twenty-five female students at Iowa State University. Subjects were seated in a windowless experimental room with walls painted a flat white. The room was illuminated by two floodlights with six colored filters: red, yellow, purple, orange, blue, and green. Each colored illuminant was presented to each subject three times. After each stimulation the subject reacted to three scales: pleasant-unpleasant, stimulating-depressing, cold-hot. The conclusions drawn by Lewinski follow:

1. Blue and green were judged pleasant.
2. Orange and yellow were unpleasant.
3. Red, yellow and orange were judged stimulating colors.
4. Purple was the most depressing illuminant.
5. Blue and green were judged cold and cool colors.
6. Yellow, orange, and red were given "warm" and "hot" responses.
[pp. 155–160].

Rice (1953) reported the results of two experimental studies, one in West Lafayette, Indiana, conducted by the Department of Occupational Psychology at Purdue University, and the other in Baltimore, Maryland, conducted by Johns Hopkins University's Institute for Cooperative Research. Although no data were presented, according to Rice the Purdue University study showed that children in the experimental group had better physical growth, less visual disability, and fewer personality handicaps than those in the control group. The results of the Baltimore study conducted by Johns Hopkins were reported more completely. Three schools similar in size and age, pupil-teacher ratio, and socioeconomic status were selected. The cooperation of the administrators was obtained, but teachers and pupils were unaware of the study.

All three school plants needed painting. During the first year, neither school was painted. One was left unpainted during the experimental year. The second was painted in the conventional colors — green walls and white ceilings — while the third school plant (experimental) was painted according to the principles of color dynamics, following a paint manufacturer's specifications, which involved the use of bright, warm, or cool colors.

Comparisons in achievement and certain performance traits were made for children in kindergarten, first and second grades, and third through sixth grades in the three schools. Seven performance traits were analyzed for grades three through six. Four performance traits were examined in grades one and two. In the kindergarten, selected behavior and performance traits were studied. Pupil report cards and teacher rating scales were used as measures for achievement and for behavior and performance traits. Attendance records were also examined.

The results showed that for the two years of the study, kindergarten children from the experimental school made a 33.9 percent improvement in satisfactory behavior and performance traits. Differences for children in grades one and two were small in favor of the conventionally painted school. Children in grades three through six in the experimental school made an 8.9 percent improvement in the seven performance traits, while those in the conventional school improved 0.5 percent, and those in the unpainted school declined by 2.7 percent. Absences in the experimental school declined by 12.7 percent. Absences increased by 7.6 percent and 3.7 percent, respectively, in the conventional and unpainted schools.

Rudner (1962) studied the relationship between color and pupil achievement in six elementary classrooms and eight secondary classrooms. Classrooms were painted at midyear. Data on achievement were collected before and after the classrooms were painted. Statistical analysis revealed that in only one of the fourteen classrooms was color a significant factor in pupil achievement, within the hues, values, and intensities of colors used in the study.

Ketcham (1964) reported a study similar to the one reported by Rice (1953). Three schools that needed painting were selected for the experiment. One school was left unpainted; the second was painted with light buff walls and white ceilings. The third school, the experimental one, was painted according to the principles of color dynamics: the corridor walls were painted yellow, north-facing classrooms were painted pale rose, and the classrooms facing south were painted in shades of blue and green.

The study involved a two-year comparison of social, health and safety, and work habits and achievements in social studies, science, language arts, arithmetic, art, and music. The pupils in the experimental school showed the greatest improvement in each of the areas, while pupils in the unpainted school showed the least improvement (Ketcham 1964).

Experimental studies ("Blue Is Beautiful," 1973) conducted by Henner Ertel and his associates at Munich's Gesellschaft für Rationelle Psychologie showed that the proper selection of colors could raise the intelligence quotients of children. A random sample of 473 children played in rooms that were painted in "beautiful" colors such as light blue, yellow, yellow-green, or orange; their IQ's went up by as much as twelve points. Children who played in "ugly" rooms painted white, black, or brown averaged a drop in IQ of fourteen points. Researchers found that the beautiful colors stimulated activity and alertness while the ugly colors made children duller.

The study was extended to evaluate two groups in nine color-coordinated rooms. A separate control group played in a conventional room. After six months, the experimental group gained an average of fifteen IQ points more than the control group; the control group had begun the experiment with slightly higher IQ scores. After eighteen months, the experimental group was twenty-four points ahead.

The research team also measured the percentage improvement in social behavior between the experimental and control groups. In the experimental group, friendly words and smiles increased 53 percent and negative reactions such as irritability and hostility decreased 12 percent.

The available evidence strongly supports the hypothesis that the color used in school buildings has an impact on pupil achievement and performance.

Hearing

The studies included here are those reporting the impact of noise on achievement in the performance of simple and complex mental tasks, and the effects on performance of certain acoustical properties of buildings. A study involving the use of carpeting, usually associated with noise control, has been included here.

Morgan (1917) studied the effects of sound distractions on memory. The material to be memorized was included in a list of ten three-letter words; each word was paired with one of the numbers from zero to nine. Each experimental session consisted of continuous runs of four ten-word lists. For some subjects, the first and third lists were accompanied by noise, and for other subjects the alternate runs were noisy. Results were measured by the number of correct responses from the possible thirty in the first keying response on a mechanical device. Two days later the subjects were given a test for recall, recognition, and retention. The effect of the noise upon the immediate learning stage was questionable: some scores were better, some were worse than for the quiet period. Over the two runs in noise subjects tended to adapt to the distraction, but students worked with greater speed during noise. Scores for recall, recognition, and retention tests showed that associations formed during noisy conditions were more superficial than in conditions of quiet. Morgan concluded that noise distraction interfered with the learning of simple associations and that subjects were tenser while learning in noise.

Laird (1930) cited the results of thirty experiments dealing with the effects of auditory stimuli on humans. One experiment dealing with the accuracy in immediate memory for nonsense syllables showed that short-term memory increased 15 percent while delayed memory increased 8 percent if a complex noise was reduced from fifty to forty decibels.

In another experiment, 300 college students were divided into two groups for testing. The control group took the test twice in relative quiet while the experimental group took the test in relative quiet the first time, then repeated it in extremely noisy conditions. The experimental group had an improvement of 6.4 percent while the control group had an improvement of 10.1 percent. In still another experiment, the reduction of a complex noise from fifty decibels to forty resulted in an increase in excess of 30 percent in the mental multiplication of three-digit numbers by three-digit numbers.

Hall (1952) studied the effects of background music on the reading comprehension of 278 eighth- and ninth-grade pupils during their regularly scheduled study halls. Reading comprehension was measured by the use of Forms A and B of the Nelson Silent Reading Test, Vocabulary and Paragraph, Grades 3–9. The control group took both forms without background music; the experimental group took one form with background music and the other form without. The music program and volume were controlled according to standards used for industrial background music. Approximately 58 percent of the pupils showed an increase in scores on tests administered with background music. Mean gain was 2.5 percent, and boys had larger mean gains with background music than girls. The greatest improvement was by ninth-grade pupils in the lowest quartile on IQ tests. The majority of the students — 83 percent — desired music as a permanent feature of the study hall (pp. 451–458).

The effects of acoustical conditioning of classrooms on the efficiency of verbal communications were investigated by Dixon (1953). He used noises such as those generated by passing trains, heavy automotive traffic from a six-lane highway, planes on an approach pattern of a military air field, and children on playgrounds. These noises were recorded for control purposes. The experimental classroom, constructed in 1952, was located in a school plant with an environment free of exterior noises. The classroom design provided for adequate sound conditioning as recommended by acoustical engineers. The various exterior noises were recorded so that they could be controlled. Articulation testing lists were prepared to ensure control. Dixon employed nonsense syllabi lists to control learning material. Syllables were selected in groups of three; each was included in a different list, which in turn was used in a different acoustical environment. The three different acoustical environments were the same except that each had a different absorption coefficient. They listened to the lists of nonsense syllables from a recorded magnetic tape. The two groups of subjects were twenty-seven fifth-grade pupils with normal hearing and thirteen pupils with hearing deficiencies.

The hypothesis tested was that an acoustically conditioned classroom increased the efficiency of verbal instruction when in competition with high intensity noises. The "t" test for small un-correlated samples was used to analyze the data. Dixon found a great magnitude of acoustical improvement from condition to condition. The experiment demonstrated that children with both normal and deficient hearing can participate with greater efficiency in acoustically treated classrooms.

Fitzroy and Reid (1963) conducted a study to determine the minimum acoustical separation necessary to permit a group of pupils or an individual teacher to work effectively. Field tests were made with measurements of noise reduction between rooms. Calibrated tape recordings were taken of sound levels with classes in session and with classes present but silent; some measurements were made in unoccupied classrooms. Thirty-seven schools, located throughout the United States, were visited and analyzed; both elementary and secondary schools were included. Questionnaires were completed by teachers, pupils, and the principal in each school, and approximately half of the teachers in each school responded to an opinion poll regarding the acoustical environments of their classrooms. Measurement data were translated into noise reduction measures, speech interference level, and articulation indexes.

Based on the analysis of measurement data, survey data, and the teacher opinion poll, Fitzroy and Reid found that school buildings would be completely acceptable for teaching and learning if built with noise reductions between classroom areas of eighteen to twenty decibels, with classrooms near optimum reverberation periods and articulation indexes of 0.01 or less.

Conrad and Gibbins (1963) studied the effects of carpeting on the sonic environment, and the extent to which carpeting affects students' behavior and learning. Their project was designed to measure pupils' achievement, personal and social characteristics, and behavior; attitudes of pupils, teachers, and parents; and the sonic environment. Six pairs of classrooms, one pair for each of grades one through six, were randomly selected for study in six different schools. Approximately 360 pupils were involved in the study. A smaller number of students were included in the analysis of achievement and personality. Pupil observations and sound measurements were made on a random basis. The "t" test analyzed the data, and a confidence level of .05 determined statistical significance.

As a group, pupils in the primary grades in the carpeted classrooms showed a mean yearly growth of statistical significance. In grades four through six, the mean yearly growth was greater for pupils in the carpeted classrooms, with the exception of sixth grade, but the difference was not significant. The results of the personality tests showed statistical significance at the .05 level for pupils in grades four and five. There were greater mean changes in personality adjustment of pupils in the carpeted rooms for both primary and intermediate grade groups and for all grades; however, the differences were not significant. Although twenty-four different types of pupil and teacher behavior were observed, the research failed to find measurable differences in behavior due to carpeted or uncarpeted floors.

In regard to the quality of the sonic environment, reverberation time was measured before and after the installation of carpet in the classroom. A significant difference (p = .01) was found between sound pressure levels of the carpeted and uncarpeted rooms; the difference favored the carpeted rooms. Generally, high and low frequency sound levels were lessened in carpeted rooms, but speech frequencies were not similarly reduced. The researchers concluded that carpeting has a positive effect on the learning environment.

THE IMPACT OF SELECTED BUILDING CONFIGURATION VARIABLES

Numerous factors relating to building configuration — height, shape, interior space organization, and arrangement — have been examined by researchers and reported in the research literature. The review of available research included studies of space, windowless facilities, and underground schools.

Amount of Space

Concepts regarding the amount of space required for educational programs have changed substantially over the years of public education in the United States. Unfortunately, the approach used to solve the problem of space requirements has been that of trial and error and speculation and argumentation, rather than research. Little research has dealt with the relationship between space and academic achievement, performance, and self-concept.

Hall (1966) discussed how people's behavior is influenced by their perceptions of space. Territoriality, defined as behavior by which an organism lays claim to an area and defends it against members of its own species, involves places in which things are done — learning, playing, hiding. Spacing is one of the key features of territoriality. Hall referred to spacing mechanisms in people as being reflected in what Hediger identified as personal distance, defined as a series of irregularly shaped bubbles that serve to maintain proper spacing among individuals. Personal distance and social distance can be observed in the interaction between people of the same species. Personal distance, the normal spacing that noncontact animals maintain between themselves and others, varies from 2½ to 4 feet. Social distance is not rigidly fixed but is determined in part by the situation and may vary from four to twelve feet. Hall's research points to the need for organizing the classroom environment by using the appropriate personal and social distance as the basis for the physical separation of pupils. Crowding relates to the concepts of territoriality and dominance and, according to Hall, disrupts social functions and leads to disorganization. Antisocial behavior increases in crowded conditions. The effects of crowding can be counteracted by providing the right kind of space.

Desor (1969) studied the phenomenon of crowding under a set of model conditions. Two potential theories were considered: (1) being crowded means receiving stimulation in excess of some tolerable level from conspecifics and (2) being crowded means not having sufficient space that is around one's body and unoccupied by conspecifics. The theory that crowding is excessive interpersonal perception was tested. Scaled-down models of rooms and small people-like figures were constructed. Ten male and ten female graduate students were used as subjects and directed to place the imaginary people in the model rooms according to situations presented. The results of the series of experiments rejected the theory that crowding is a lack of space, in favor of the thesis that crowding occurs when a person sees himself surrounded by too many other people (Desor 1969).

Just what constitutes crowding in educational buildings has not been clearly established. Cramer (1976) examined the relationship between space density, pupils' attitudes toward their school buildings, and incidents of pupils' disruptive behavior. Three school buildings of different ages and conditions were used. One school building was old, dilapidated, and had not been modernized; another was old but had just undergone major renovation; the third was relatively new. Space density was computed by calculating an index of students per square foot. The old, nonmodernized building had more space per pupil than did the renovated or new buildings, yet pupils' attitude scores were significantly lower for the old, nonmodernized building where the number of disruptive incidents was higher. Cramer (1976) concluded that the quality of space may be more important than the amount of space.

Ertel ("Blue is Beautiful," 1973) studied the impact that the size of a room had on child development. Children tested by psychologists of Munich's Gesellschaft für Rationelle Psychologie preferred play areas that were much larger than had been hypothetically expected. Minimum play space requirements were established, as a result of their study, at 3.6 square yards for children under two years of age, and 24 square yards for children aged seven to nine. In smaller spaces, children's mental performance and behavior deteriorated. Ertel also explored the impact of ceiling height and found that a seven-foot height was preferred.

Open Space

Open space schools, one of the innovations of the 1960s, have no interior partitions; some schools characterized as modified open space have multiple instructional areas consisting of two or more classrooms without interior partitions. The term is not always clearly used, and there is some tendency to confuse open space schools with open education, although the terms are not synonymous.

Rather than attempt to report on all of the extensive research on open space schools, some selected research articles and reports on pupil achievement, performance, and self-concept are reviewed.

Johnson (1970) compared pupil achievement in an open space elementary school to achievement in a traditional elementary school. He used a sample of eighty-eight pupils with eight equal-sized samples of third- and fifth-grade boys and girls randomly drawn from both schools. Achievement was measured with the

Iowa Test of Basic Skills on which students from both schools scored above average. The differences between schools were not significant.

Kennedy (1971) compared the effects on elementary pupils' cognitive gains between an open space school and a traditional school. Pupils from comparable socioeconomic backgrounds in grades two through five from both schools constituted the sample. The SRA achievement test battery was administered to the total sample while the Otis-Lennon Mental Ability Test and reading tests were administered to a random sample of pupils. Evidence was inconclusive as to the superiority of the open space or traditional school for cognitive gain over the one-year period of study.

In a longitudinal study lasting four years, Killough (1971) analyzed the effects that ungraded elementary programs in an open space school had on the cognitive achievement of pupils. His experimental group was composed of 150 pupils in grades one through five in an ungraded open space school. The control group was 150 pupils in the same grades randomly selected from four traditional elementary schools without ungraded programs. SRA achievement tests and several mental ability tests were used. After two years, pupils in the open space school had statistically significant achievement gains in most cognitive areas over the pupils in the traditional schools.

McRae (1970) studied the effects of open space on reading achievement at the secondary school level. He hypothesized that pupils entering secondary school from classes in open space elementary schools would not do as well on standardized reading tests as pupils from traditional schools. The Gates-McGinnitie Reading Test was given twice, one year apart. The sample consisted of thirty-four pupils from open space classes and thirty-four randomly selected pupils from traditional classes. Open space pupils performed at lower levels than pupils taught in traditional classes; however, after one year the open space pupils tended to catch up.

Teachers in two elementary schools — one open and one traditional — were surveyed by Brunetti (1971). He asked the teachers to rate a sample of their pupils on nine learning traits, five academic traits, and four social-emotional traits. The schools, in the same district, served similar pupil populations and used the same curriculum materials. The rating instrument was administered in February and again in June. Children in the open space school were rated lower in February and higher in June. Their growth was significantly greater in social-emotional learning traits — peer relations, adult relations, independence, and personal decision making.

Sackett (1971) studied the self-concept and achievement of sixth-grade pupils in an open space school, a self-contained school, and a departmentalized school all in the same school district. The Coopersmith Self-Esteem Inventory, the Lorge-Thorndike Intelligence Test, and the Iowa Test of Basic Skills (ITBS) were administered to the pupils in the sample, and data were tested for statistical significance. The self-concept mean score for sixth graders in open space schools was lower than for pupils in the other schools. The mean scores on the ITBS for open space pupils was significantly lower than in the other two schools.

Using a sample of 461 pupils from a single school, Warner (1970) studied pupil performances in open space and self-contained classrooms. The SRA Achievement Series, Form C, was administered to second-grade pupils, and the ITBS was administered to third- and fourth-grade pupils. The results showed that differences were not statistically significant for scores of pupils in second and third grades. Fourth-grade pupils in self-contained classrooms showed superior achievement in arithmetic scores. The researcher concluded that both facilities were about the same.

Musemeche and Adams (1974) investigated the social and emotional impact of an open space elementary school and traditional schools on the noncognitive performance of a sample of 208 elementary pupils. Sixty-four pupils (experimental group) were from an open space elementary school while 144 pupils (control group) were from traditional elementary schools. The students were compared on the basis of teacher responses to an instrument containing factors associated with the social and emotional maturity of pupils. Composite mean scores for both the emotional and social aspects were statistically significant at the .01 level in favor of the pupils from the open space schools.

Lovin (1972) investigated the relationship of pupils' attitudes about the school's physical environment and their perceptions of themselves as learners. The sample population consisted of 520 pupils in grades four through seven from two small elementary schools, with 374 pupils in the control group and the remainder in the experimental group. Pupils were administered both the Waetjen Self-Concept as a Learner Scale and McGuffey's Our School Building Attitude Inventory as pretests and as posttests. All pupils were members of the same elementary school at the time of the pretest; however, 165 subjects (experimental group) were transferred to a new, modified open space facility soon after the pretest. The study type was a nonequivalent control group design of a quasi-experimental nature. Group means were calculated and hypotheses were tested through analysis of covariance and Duncan's multiple range test of differences. The findings showed that the pupils in the control group from the traditional school had significantly higher mean differences in self-concept.

This review failed to reveal that either the open space school or the traditional school is superior in regard to pupil achievement. The limited research dealing with self-concept revealed that a pupil's self-concept fares better in the traditional school. Social and emotional factors appeared to be superior in the open space environment. Clearly, additional investigation is needed to either validate or reject the inconclusive findings of existing research on pupil achievement and performance in the open space school.

Windowless Facilities

In the early 1960s, national attention was directed to the subject of windows in schools. Since windows were an operational nuisance, a continuing maintenance expense, a source of glare, and a source of heat loss in the winter and gain in the summer, some people began to wonder if they could be eliminated.

The School Environments Research Project was begun in 1959 to investigate the educational significance of environmental conditions for different students. One of their immediate concerns was what occurs when young children are taught in windowless classrooms. This investigation was a test of the proposed SERP method of environmental evaluation (Larson 1965). A case study was planned to study the behavioral reactions of both teachers and pupils. Two schools that were similar in shape and size and had virtually the same neighborhood surroundings were selected. The procedures involved an analysis of three distinct stages: (1) observations during a full school year with existing fenestrated classrooms, (2) observations during a full school year after the windows had been removed; and (3) observations during at least one half-year after the windows in the test unit were replaced.

One objective of the case study was to determine if there were differences in the achievement of pupils in two different environments. One environmental variable, windows, was manipulated in one school; the other elementary school was used as a control. Pupils were grouped into three categories of high, average, and low ability. The subjects involved in the study were reading, spelling, writing, arithmetic, and art. The Iowa Test of Basic Skills and the Gates Reading Tests were used to measure achievement. No pattern of class behavior indicated that a view of the outdoors was essential to the learning process. Also, no consistent pattern of pupil performance was detected that could be attributed to the absence of an outside view. Classroom windows were found to have little, if any, effect on a child's ability to learn.

Underground Facilities

The use of school buildings as fallout shelters in case of nuclear attack was encouraged as a part of national defense policy in the 1960s. To study one of the questions raised in the public debates, the Department of Defense provided funds to build an underground school building and to research the question of what measurable, harmful effects to children can be attributed to attending an underground school. The major hypothesis tested was that no significant differences in educational outcomes occurred among pupils in conventional schools, in windowless schools, and in underground schools (Cooper and Ivey 1964). Four Artesia, New Mexico, schools were used in the research. Stanford Achievement Tests were administered in the fall to grades four, five, and six as an annual routine and were repeated in May. In the noncognitive area, Sarason's Test Anxiety Scale for Children and General Anxiety Scale for Children were administered in the spring. The teachers were given Taylor's Personality Scale of Manifest Anxiety and other scales for measuring attitudes. Pupils were also given the Morse Classroom Behavior Questionnaire to measure their attitudes toward learning and their perceptions of themselves in school. Average daily attendance records provided data on the absentee rate.

Data on achievement were collected four times during the two years of the study. The research question on achievement was: Did pupils in an underground experimental school achieve at a rate comparable to that of pupils in the other schools? Regression analysis was applied to the data, and gain scores were computed for each teacher, variable, and year. The five subtests of the Stanford Achievement Battery — paragraph meaning, word meaning, spelling, arithmetic reasoning, and arithmetic computation — were analyzed and showed that variations in gain scores between schools were fluctuations due to chance. The pupils in the experimental school achieved at rates comparable to their peers in other schools.

THE INTERACTIONS OF SELECTED PROGRAMMATIC AND PHYSICAL ENVIRONMENT VARIABLES

The school building is a teaching and learning resource composed of physical space, objects, furniture, and their arrangement. It is order and disorder, light, color, heat, ventilation, and sound forming a complex, intangible presence to its occupants. It bombards pupils with physical and emotional stimuli. It communicates a message of what is expected to happen in that particular place. The school building helps structure the formal and informal relationships between teacher and learner and between learner and learner. It is the shelter — the life support system — that defines the learner's physical existence for a period of time.

Getzels (1975) discussed the classroom as representing not only conceptions of space for learning but also conceptions of the learner. According to Getzels, "Classrooms teach lessons of their own; they tell the child who he is supposed to be and how he is supposed to learn" (p. 12). He adds: "One classroom tells the child he is an empty organism operating through rewards and punishments at the command of the teacher; a second classroom tells him he is an active organism learning through the solution of problems that satisfy his needs; a third classroom tells the child he is a social organism learning through interactions with others; the fourth classroom tells him he is a stimulus-seeking organism learning because he intrinsically has to" (p. 12).

Although the interaction of programmatic and physical environment variables is assumed to influence educational outcomes, little research reflects such interactions. The major areas of the limited research here are those where, in the judgment of the author, a potential impact exists: site size, building utilization, building maintenance, support facilities, special instructional facilities, and school plant size.

Site Size

Only two research studies were located that examined school site size either in interaction with a program variable or in relationship to pupil achievement, performance, or self-concept. Numerous publications relate the accumulation of conventional wisdom and experience in regard to the purposes, functions, and characteristics of a good school site (Castaldi 1977, Connecticut State Department of Education 1960, Council of Educational Facility Planners 1976, Taylor 1958).

Using data from the Equality of Educational Opportunity Survey, Michelson (1970) studied the relationship of thirty-three independent variables to five measures of pupil achievement. Size of school site, one of the independent variables, was positive and significant in Reading 3, Mathematics 1, and Mathematics 2 on the single equation model for whites. This study was discussed in relation to school building age earlier in this chapter.

Guthrie and others (1971), in a study reviewed earlier, used size of school site as one of fourteen independent variables to determine the relationship with three measures of pupil achievement. Of thirty tests run on the independent variable, school site size was significant and positive five times. This result compares with two positive and significant runs for teacher experience.

Building Utilization

Building utilization has long been an economic factor in the operation of school programs, but few studies of the input-output type have included building utilization in some form as an independent variable.

Using the school as the unit of analysis, Katzman (1968) studied fifty-six Boston Schools, using six dependent variables and ten independent variables. Stepwise multiple regression was run for each dependent variable. Utilization failed to show a significant relationship to any of the dependent variables.

Fox (1969) studied the relationship of nine independent variables and two dependent variables. An index of building utilization was one of the nine independent variables. One dependent variable was a measure of achievement, the other was holding power. Two simultaneous equations, one for each dependent variable, were derived using a two-stage least squares analysis. Under the theory that schools trade off between the two outputs, each independent variable enters the other dependent variable's equation as an independent variable. Index of building utilization was not significant and was deleted from the remainder of the calculation.

Building Maintenance

School buildings deteriorate with age. Since a building's age is a factor in building deterioration, the condition of older buildings depends to a large extent on the adequacy of maintenance and operations. In studies of achievement using school buildings' age as an independent variable, it has consistently been a significant factor. Deterioration and obsolescence due to aging can usually be slowed or remedied by proper maintenance procedures. Cramer (1976) examined the attitudes and behavior differences of students in an old, dilapidated, and poorly maintained building in comparison to students in new and in old but newly modernized school buildings. The pupils in the dilapidated school had a higher major disruptive incidence ratio and significantly worse attitudes than the pupils in the modernized building — a finding that has implications for both maintenance and modernization programs.

Maintenance activities involve color selection and choice of proper reflectance values in paint for classroom walls and ceilings, correct choice of lighting fixtures and levels in relighting programs, and proper temperature levels in heating and cooling maintenance and modernization. Maintenance is important because physical environment variables have an impact on cognitive and noncognitive outcomes, and improper maintenance can negate the positive effects of physical planning.

Support Facilities

Support facilities are those specialized spaces, such as the auditorium, cafeteria, gymnasium, and library or instructional resource center, that serve the school program through the accommodation of support services. A number of the input-output studies that have already been reviewed used variables such as the presence of a cafeteria, auditorium, and gymnasium, or the total number of books, or books per student, in the school library. The use of these variables indicated the presence of certain support facilities.

Mollenkopf and Melville (1956) used the number of school facilities (auditorium and gymnasium) as one of twenty-seven independent variables analyzed in a correlation study of achievement measured by test scores. The variable on number of facilities failed to correlate significantly with any achievement measures.

In a study of black and white sixth-grade pupils in an eastern city, Michelson (1970) used the presence of an auditorium, gymnasium, or cafeteria as an independent variable in a school achievement study. That variable was significant and positive in five of seven single regression equations for whites, including one verbal, two reading, and two mathematics equations. The variable (auditorium, gymnasium, or cafeteria) failed to show significance for either blacks or the two simultaneous equation models.

No studies were located that used the library as a variable in a study of school achievement, although factors were used that indicated the presence of a library. The number of books in the library was used by Thomas (1962) and Michelson (1970) as an independent variable in studies of school achievement. Thomas found the number of library books consistently significant and positive in relation to achievement measures. Michelson found the number of library books significant and positive for whites in one verbal single equation model, one mathematics single equation model, and one simultaneous verbal equation and for blacks in one verbal single equation.

Library volumes per student was used as an independent variable by Coleman and others (1966), Burkhead, Fox, and Holland (1967), Levin (1970), Guthrie and others (1971), and Smith (1972) in their studies of school achievement and attitude. Coleman found library volumes significant and positive — a finding supported by Smith. Burkhead, Fox, and Holland failed to find library volumes per student significant in achievement, but found the variable significant in relation to percentage of graduates who went on to college. Guthrie and others found volumes per student significant and positive in fourteen of thirty regression runs. Levin, on the other hand, found the variable significant and positive only in relation to students' attitudes.

Special Instructional Facilities

The role that special instructional facilities play in achievement is a relatively unexplored area in the research on educational buildings. Historically, as new subjects were introduced into the curriculum, people assumed that a special space was needed to serve that subject. The literature is replete with argument and discussion regarding the nature and characteristics of special instructional spaces for kindergarten, primary, middle, secondary, and handicap programs. Documents such as the *Guide for Planning Educational Facilities* (Council of Educational Facility Planners (1976), *Planning Facilities for Athletics, Physical Education, and Recreation* (Athletic Institute 1974), and others have provided information to architects and school district planning committees to serve as guidelines in planning and modernizing educational facilities and in evaluating existing facilities.

Coleman and others (1966) and Smith (1972) studied the impact of science laboratory facilities (as an independent variable) on verbal achievement. Science laboratory facilities were used in conjunction with other facility and curriculum variables in a multiple regression analysis. The unique contribution of facilities and curriculum variables in the Coleman study exceeded 3 percent. For southern Negroes, these variables added about 8 percent. Smith supported Coleman's findings. Laboratories, according to Coleman, have a consistent relationship of moderate size to achievement.

Size of Schools

School size is clearly a function of the capacity of a school building in that the number of seats and instructional spaces are in direct proportion to the amount of square feet available in the school building. The size of the building can limit or extend the school's enrollment, thus, school size is often considered an educational facilities factor. Additionally, the curriculum's scope reflects the number and type of spaces provided for instructional purposes, which in turn reflect the space available in the building.

Research studies have shown a positive relationship between school size and the number of courses offered (George Peabody College 1965, 1966, Jackson 1966, Morris 1964, Woodham 1951). Similarly, research has shown that the amount of space available for special instructional facilities increased with school size (Koelsche and Solberg 1959; Weaver 1962).

Program quality is also related to school size. Pearce (1972) examined the relationship between an elementary school's size and program quality in 587 public elementary schools in Georgia. Pearce hypothesized that the frequency of occurrence of quality indicators would differ significantly in relation to the school's size. The number and percentage of responses by size category were reported and chi square values computed for each category. The school enrollment ranging from 300 to 399 possessed twenty-nine of thirty-three discriminating indicators. Schools of less than 300 were at a considerable disadvantage in the frequency of the presence of program quality indicators.

Pethel (1978) investigated the relationship between high school size and program quality in all high schools in Georgia that contain grades nine through twelve. Eighty-four program quality indicators were confirmed by a jury of professors of secondary education, standards coordinators from eight southeastern states, and the current officers of the Georgia Association of Secondary School Principals. Significant discriminatory values for eighteen of the eighty-four jury-selected items and significant differences between the means of the five group sizes were found. The difference existed between the three smaller groups and the two larger groups. Between 1,313 and 1,976 pupils was determined as the optimum size range to achieve program quality.

Is school size the primary factor in determining program quality regardless of cost? Lott (1968) studied Texas high schools and concluded that the size of a school was a primary factor regardless of expenditures. Hamilton and Rowe (1962) reviewed the work of a number of researchers dealing with school size and concluded that higher academic achievement is most likely to occur in larger schools.

Gray (1961) studied the relationship between size and a number of qualitative and quantitative factors in forty secondary schools in Iowa. Mean gain scores between grades ten and twelve on the composite score of the Iowa Test of Educational Development measured achievement. Correlations were not found significant at the .05 level.

In a study of the impact of several school-related variables, Coleman and others (1966) found that "one variable that explains a relatively large amount of variance at grades nine to twelve . . . is school size" (p. 313). Coleman adds, "Most of its (school size) apparent effect vanishes if various facilities and curricular differences are controlled. That is, the higher achievement in larger schools is largely accounted for by the additional facilities they include" (p. 313). No doubt school size and facilities variables are highly correlated but Coleman does not indicate this.

Perl (1973) studied the relationship between student scores on tests of academic ability and various measures of achievement. The data were from Project Talent, and a sample of 3,600 student responses was used. When students' and classmates' family background were controlled, school enrollment (size variable) was significantly related to achievement measures.

Hall (1956) researched the relationship between size and selected student characteristics, including the results of certain test scores from English, social studies, science, and mathematics. Findings showed a strong tendency for average test scores to increase as school size increased. The correlation between size of school and achievement, with socioeconomic status of family held constant, was .60.

Street, Powell, and Hamblen (1962) studied the relationship of student scores on the Stanford Achievement Test to school size. After statistically controlling socioeconomic status and IQ differences, they showed that students in high schools with more than 300 students tended to outperform students in schools with fewer than 300 students in the same school districts. Sher and Tompkins (1976) criticized the research on school size: "Many of the studies (reviewed) compared achievement scores of children in small schools with (achievement of) children in large schools. However, only a handful of studies controlled for variables such as socioeconomic status or IQ that also affect achievement" (p. 18).

SYNTHESIS OF RESEARCH FINDINGS

The available research is a mixed bag of study types and methodologies presenting diverse problems of sampling, measurement, and statistical analysis. The reader should be aware of the danger inherent in synthesizing such research results and in generalizing from the findings of individual studies.

The alternatives for presenting the findings are limited to (1) eliminating judgmental conclusions and numerically tallying the findings of significance or (2) drawing conclusions based on the reviewer's judgment while attempting to control recognized bias. The counting approach places all studies, regardless of design, on an equal basis when some should obviously be given more weight than others. On the other hand, a synthesis by the reviewer must of necessity require a systematic and scientific evaluation of the studies reviewed. This is an extremely difficult and time consuming methodological process, and the problem of reviewer bias must also be considered. This chapter used a combination of the counting approach and the reviewer's judgment based on the consistency of findings. The judgments of the reviewer are based largely on impressions received while reviewing the research reports. One must always keep in mind that because of the nature of research in education, it rarely, if ever, proves anything. Studies producing similar results give added support to our confidence about other results.

Conclusions Supported by the Weight of the Evidence Drawn from the Studies

Based on the findings of the research studies reviewed, the following conclusions are presented according to the factors already identified.

Building Age. Seven studies were reviewed in which building age was one of several independent variables analyzed to determine effects on school achievement. In all studies, building age was significant, although not in all regression runs. Some variations existed with regard to impact on grade level or specific subject matter achievement scores. However, it is reasonable to conclude that building age has a statistically significant impact on school achievement.

Thermal factors. The thermal environment controls human heat loss and optimizes conditions so that learning can occur most effectively. Nine studies were reviewed and eight of the nine found that thermal factors had a significant impact on school achievement and performance. Some studies that were reviewed had sampling limitations, and generalizability beyond the population used in the study is questionable. However, the consistent recurrence of similar findings strongly suggests that thermal variables have an impact on student achievement and human performance.

Seeing factors. Laboratory studies, sponsored by the Illuminating Engineering Society and conducted by Blackwell over an eight-year period with substantial follow-up, demonstrated clearly the impact of visibility factors in schools on students' ability to see and to assimilate information. Of the ten studies reviewed (including Blackwell's), all demonstrated significant effects of visibility on visual performance.

Color and Interior Painting. Five studies were reviewed relating color to pupil achievement and performance. The studies were limited in their sampling, and generalizability is questionable. However, four of the five studies found that color had an impact on achievement or performance. In the fifth study, statistical significance was found in only one of fourteen classrooms. The findings are mixed; however, the evidence suggests that color has an impact on pupil performance in classrooms.

Hearing Factors. The review of seven studies that dealt with hearing factors and their impact on pupil achievement and performance all indicated a significant impact. One showed, however, that desirable sound improved conditions, while the other six demonstrated that unwanted sound (noise) interfered with verbal communication and adversely affected pupil performance. Although the generalizability of the individual studies is questionable, there is little doubt that noise can create sufficient interference with verbal instruction to hinder learning.

Amount of Space. Only two studies were reviewed that related to pupil performance. The findings were mixed. More study is needed, particularly on the question of crowding.

Open Space. In these nine studies of open space and achievement, performance, and self-concept, the studies on self-concept significantly favored traditional schools, while those on achievement indicated a mixed set of results. Findings dealing with noncognitive variables other than self-concept indicated that open space had a significantly favorable impact. More study is needed.

Windowless Facilities. Only one study was reviewed in which both cognitive and noncognitive variables were analyzed in relation to the presence or absence of windows. Findings showed that classroom windows have little, if any, effect on a child's academic performance.

Underground Facilities. The findings of the one study reviewed showed no differences in pupil achievement, anxiety, or attitude between above-ground schools — with or without windows — and an underground school.

Site Size. Of the three studies examined that considered the impact of the size of a school site on achievement, performance, and self-concept, two showed a significant relationship in a small number of regression runs. The third, a descriptive type, discussed the need for site acreage from a programmatic perspective.

Building Utilization. No relationship was found between a building's utilization and pupils' achievement in the two studies considered.

Building Maintenance. One study was reviewed which examined attitude and behavior differences between students in an old, dilapidated, and poorly maintained building, a relatively new building, and a newly modernized building. The results were significant in favor of the newly modernized building.

Support Facilities. Several studies were located that used support facilities as independent variables in an analysis of school achievement. Two studies used the existence of the cafeteria, gymnasium, and auditorium as the independent variable. One found no relationship, while the other had a mixed result. Seven studies used library volumes and volumes per student as independent variables. One had mixed findings, three found significant positive results, three found no significant differences in achievement, and one found positive results on attitude.

Special Instructional Facilities. Two studies were found that dealt with science facilities. Both found a significant positive relationship between the presence of science laboratories and achievement.

Size of Schools. Sixteen studies were reviewed dealing with school size. Five studies showed a positive relationship between size and program offerings. Two studies revealed that the amount of space available for special instructional facilities increased with school size. Three studies found size a significant factor in program quality, while one did not. Four studies showed that school size was a positive significant factor in pupil achievement, while one did not. One review of the literature criticized the research on school size as being fraught with measurement and control problems.

School facilities affect pupil achievement. The variance that can be accounted for is small. However, when the total amount of variance accounted for by all school-related variables is similarly small, the impact of facilities takes on considerable importance. Continuing research may well demonstrate an even greater amount of variance attributable to facilities variables — particularly as measures are refined and more research is conducted on the interaction and cumulative effects of facilities variables. Two conclusions are warranted: (1) obsolete and inadequate school facilities detract from the learning process; modern, controlled physical environments enhance it and (2) facilities may have a differential impact on the performance of pupils in different grades and for different subjects.

REFERENCES

Athletic Institute and American Association for Health, Physical Education, and Recreation. *Planning Facilities for Athletics, Physical Education, and Recreation.* Washington, D.C.: American Association for Health, Physical Education, and Recreation, 1974.

Bitterman, M.E. *Lighting and Visual Efficiency: The Present Status of Research.* London: Illuminating Engineering Society, 1948.

Blackwell, H. R. "A Specification of Interior Illumination Levels." *Illuminating Engineering* 54 (1959): 334.

Blackwell, H. R. "A General Quantitative Method for Evaluating the Visual Significance of Reflected Glare, Utilizing Visual Performance Data." *Illuminating Engineering* 58 (1963): 61.

Blackwell, H. R., and Blackman, O. M. "The Effect of Illumination Quality upon the Performance of Different Visual Tasks." *Illuminating Engineering* 63 (1968): 143–52.

"Blue Is Beautiful." *Time,* 17 September 1973, p. 66.

Brunetti, Frank A., Jr. *Open Space: A Status Report.* Stanford, Calif.: Stanford University, August, 1971.

Burkhead, Jesse; Fox, Thomas; and Holland, John W. *Input and Output in Large-City High Schools.* Syracuse, N.Y.: Syracuse University Press, 1967.

Castaldi, Basil. *Educational Facilities: Planning, Remodeling, and Management.* Boston: Allyn & Bacon, 1977.

Chan, Tak Cheung. "The Impact of School Building Age on the Achievement of Eighth-Grade Pupils from the Public Schools in the State of Georgia." Doctoral dissertation, University of Georgia, 1979.

Chorlton, J. M., and Davidson, H. F. "The Effect of Specular Reflection on Visibility: Part II — Field Measurement of Loss of Contrast." *Illuminating Engineering* 54 (1959): 482–88.

Coleman, James S., and others. *Equality of Educational Opportunity.* Washington, D.C.: U.S. Government Printing Office, 1966.

Connecticut State Department of Education. *School Sites: Selection and Acquisition.* Hartford, Conn.: State Department of Education, 1960.

Conrad, M. J., and Gibbins, N. L. *Carpeting and Learning.* Columbus, Ohio: Bureau of Education Research and Service, 1963.

Cooper, B. D. "The Blackwell Report." *Better Light Better Sight News,* 1958, pp. 14–16.

Cooper, J. G., and Ivey, C. H. *A Comparative Study of the Educational Environment and the Educational Outcomes in an Underground School, a Windowless School, and Conventional Schools.* Santa Fe: New Mexico State Department of Education, 1964.

Council of Educational Facility Planners. *Guide for Planning Educational Facilities.* Columbus, Ohio: Council of Educational Facility Planners, 1976.

Cramer, Robert J. "Some Effects of School Building Renovation on Pupil Attitudes and Behavior in Selected Junior High Schools." Doctoral dissertation, University of Georgia, 1976.

Desor, Jeannette Ann. "The Psychology of Crowding: An Experimental Investigation." Doctoral dissertation, Cornell University, 1969.

Dixon, Martin T. "Comparing Acoustical Control and the Efficiency of Verbal Communication." Doctoral dissertation, Stanford University, 1953.

Fitzroy, D., and Reid, J. L. *Acoustical Environment of School Buildings.* New York: Educational Facilities Laboratories, 1963.

Fox, Thomas G. "School System Resource Use in Production of Interdependent Educational Outputs." Paper presented at the Joint National Meeting of American Astronautical Society and Operations Research Society, Denver, Colo., 1969.

George Peabody College for Teachers. *Organization of School Systems in Georgia.* Nashville, Tenn.: George Peabody College for Teachers, 1965.

George Peabody College for Teachers. *High Schools in the South: A Fact Book.* Nashville, Tenn.: George Peabody College for Teachers, 1966.

Getzels, Jacob W. "Images of the Classroom and Visions of the Learner." In *Learning Environments,* edited by T. G. David and Benjamin D. Wright. Chicago: University of Chicago Press, 1975.

Gray, Stuart C. "A Study of the Relationship between Size and a Number of Qualitative and Quantitative Factors of Education in Four Sizes of Secondary Schools in Iowa." Doctoral dissertation, State University of Iowa, 1961.

Guthrie, James W.; Kleindorfer, G. B.; Levin, H. M.; and Stout, R. T. *Schools and Inequality.* Cambridge, Mass.: M.I.T. Press, 1971.

Hall, Edward T. *The Hidden Dimension.* New York: Doubleday, 1966.

Hall, Jody C. "The Effect of Background Music on the Reading Comprehension of Two Hundred Seventy-Eight Eighth- and Ninth-Grade Students." *Journal of Educational Research* 45 (February 1952): 451–58.

Hall, Morrill M. "A Study of Some of the Relationships between Size of School and Selected Characteristics of Students, Teachers, and Principals." Doctoral dissertation, Florida State University, 1956.

Hamilton, DeForest, and Rowe, Robert N. "Academic Achievement of Students in Reorganized and Non-Reorganized Districts." *Phi Delta Kappan* 43 (June 1962): 401-4.

Harmon, D. B. *The Coordinated Classroom.* Grand Rapids, Mich.: American Seating, 1950.

Harner, David P. "Effects of Thermal Environment on Learning Skills." *CEFP Journal* 12 (April 1974): 4–8.

Herrington, Lovic P. "Effect of Thermal Environment on Human Action." *American School and University* 24 (1952): 367–76.

Jackson, J. L. *School Size and Program Quality in Southern High Schools.* Nashville, Tenn.: George Peabody College for Teachers, 1966.

Johnson, C. E. *A Comparative Study of Student Achievement and Student Participation Pattern in the Howard County Model Elementary School.* Clarksville, Md.: Howard County Board of Education, 1970.

Karpovich, Peter V. "Physical Work in Relation to External Temperature." In Peter Karpovich, *Physiology of Muscular Activity.* Philadelphia: W. B. Saunders, 1959.

Katzman, Martin T. "Distribution and Production in a Big City Elementary School System." *Yale Economic Essays* 8 (Spring 1968): 201-56.

Kennedy, V. J. "Comparison of the Effects of Open Area Versus Closed Area Schools on the Cognitive Gains of Students." *Educators Report and Fact Sheet,* February 1971, 1–4.

Ketcham, Howard. "These Colors Fit Your School Decor." *Nation's Schools* 74 (November 1964): 61.

Killough, C. K. *An Analysis of Longitudinal Effects That a Nongraded Elementary Program, Conducted in an Open Space School Had on the Cognitive Achievement of Pupils.* Houston, Tex.: Bureau of Educational Research and Service, College of Education, University of Houston, 1971.

Koelsche, Charles L., and Solberg, Archie N. *Facilities and Equipment Available for Teaching Science in Public High Schools, 1958—1959.* Toledo, Ohio: University of Toledo, 1959.

Laird, D. A. "The Effects of Noise: A Summary of Experimental Literature." *Journal of the Acoustical Society of America* 1 (1930): 256–61.

Larson, C. Theodore. *The Effects of Windowless Classrooms on Elementary School Children.* Ann Arbor: Architectural Research Laboratory, University of Michigan, 1965.

Levin, Henry M. "A New Model of School Effectiveness." In *Do Teachers Make a Difference? A Report on Recent Research on Pupil Achievement*, pp. 55–75. U.S. Office of Education Report, OE-58042. Washington, D.C.: U.S. Government Printing Office, 1970.

Lewinski, Robert J. "An Investigation of Individual Responses to Chromatic Illumination." *Journal of Psychology* 6 (July 1938): 155–60.

Lott, Thomas L. "A Study of the Interrelationship among Size, Expenditure Level, and Quality in Selected Texas High Schools." Doctoral dissertation, University of Southern Mississippi, 1968.

Lovin, Joseph C., Jr. "The Effect of the School's Physical Environment on the Self-Concepts of Elementary School Students." Doctoral dissertation, University of Georgia, 1972.

Luckiesh, Matthew, and Moss, Frank K. *The Science of Seeing.* New York: Van Nostrand, 1937.

Luckiesh, Matthew, and Moss, Frank K. "Effects of Classroom Lighting upon Educational Progress and Visual Welfare of School Children." *Illuminating Engineering* 35 (1940): 915–38.

McCardle, Robert W. "Thermal Environment and Learning." Doctoral dissertation, University of Iowa, 1966.

McConnell, W. J. and Yaglou, C. P. "Work Tests in Atmosphere in Still and Moving Air." *Transactions of the American Society of Heating and Ventilating Engineers* 32 (1926): 239–48.

McGuffey, Carroll W., and Brown, Carvin L. "The Impact of School Building Age on School Achievement in Georgia." *CEFP Journal* 16 (1978): 6–9.

Mackworth, N. H. "Effects of Heat on Wireless Operators." Cited in *American School and University* 24 (1952–53): 368.

McRae, B. C. *The Effect of Open Area Instruction on Reading Achievement.* Vancouver, British Columbia: Board of School Trustees, Department of Research and Special Services, 1970.

Mayo, George D. "Effect of Temperature upon Technical Training." *Journal of Applied Psychology* 39 (August 1955): 244–49.

Michelson, Stephan. "The Association of Teacher Resourceness with Children's Characteristics." In *Do Teachers Make a Difference? A Report on Recent Research on Pupil Achievement*, pp. 120–68. U.S. Office of Education Report, OE-58042. Washington, D.C.: U.S. Government Printing Office, 1970.

Mollenkopf, William G., and Melville, S. D. *A Study of Secondary School Characteristics as Related to Test Scores.* Princeton, N.J.: Educational Testing Service, 1956.

Morgan, John J. B. "The Effect of Sound Distractions upon Memory." *American Journal of Psychology* 28 (April 1917): 191–208.

Morris, H. J. "Relationship of School Size to Per Pupil Expenditures in Secondary Schools of Nine Southern States." Doctoral dissertation, George Peabody College for Teachers, 1964.

Musemeche, Richard A. and Adams, Sam. "Open Space Schools and the Non-cognitive Domain." *CEFP Journal* 12 (October 1974): 4-6.

New York Commission on Ventilation. *School Ventilation and Practices.* New York: Teachers College, Columbia University, 1931.

Nolan, James A. "Influence of Classroom Temperature on Academic Learning." *Automated Teaching Bulletin* 1 (Summer 1960): 12–20.

Osborne, E. E., and Vernon, H. M. "Two Contributions to the Study of Accident Causation." Cited in *American School and University* 24 (1952–53): 368.

Pearce, Clyde C., "An Investigation into the Relationship of School Size and Program Quality of Public Elementary Schools in Georgia." Doctoral dissertation, University of Georgia, 1972.

Perl, Lewis J. "Family Background, Secondary School Expenditure, and Student Ability." *Journal of Human Resources* 8 (Spring 1973): 156–80.

Peccolo, Charles M. "The Effect of Thermal Environment on Learning." Doctoral dissertation, University of Iowa, 1962.

Pethel, Glenn E. "An Investigation of the Relationship of School Size and Program Quality in the Public High Schools of Georgia." Doctoral dissertation, University of Georgia, 1978.

Plumley, J. P., Jr. "The Impact of School Building Age on the Academic Achievement of Pupils from Selected Schools in the State of Georgia." Doctoral dissertation, University of Georgia, 1978.

Rice, Arthur H. "What Research Knows about Color in the Classroom." *Nation's Schools* 52 (November 1953): i–viii.

Rudner, Morris J. "A Study of the Effect of Classroom Color on Student Achievement." Doctoral dissertation, New York University, 1962.

Rummel, J. Francis. *An Introduction to Research Procedures in Education.* New York: Harper & Row, 1964.

Sackett, John W. "A Comparison of Self-Concept and Achievement of Sixth-Grade Students in an Open Space School, Self-Contained School, and Departmentalized School." Doctoral dissertation, University of Iowa, 1971.

Sampson, F. K. *Contrast Rendition in School Lighting.* New York: Educational Facilities Laboratories, 1970.

Sher, Jonathan P., and Tompkins, Rachel B. *Economy, Efficiency, and Equality: The Myths of Rural School and District Consolidation.* Washington, D. C.: National Institute of Education, 1976.

Smith, M. S. "Equality of Educational Opportunity: The Basic Findings Reconsidered." In *On Equality of Educational Opportunity*, edited by Frederick Mosteller and Daniel P. Moynihan. New York: Vintage Books, 1972.

Street, Paul; Powell, James H.; and Hamblen, John W. "Achievement of Students and Size of School." *Journal of Educational Research* 55 (March 1962): 261–66.

Stuart, Fred, and Curtis, H. A. *Climate Controlled and Non-Climate Controlled Schools.* Clearwater, Fla.: Pinellas County Board of Public Instruction, 1964.

Taylor, J. L. *School Sites: Selection, Development, and Utilization.* Washington, D.C.: U.S. Government Printing Office, 1958.

Thomas, James Alan. "Efficiency in Education: A Study of the Relationship between Selected Inputs and Mean Test Scores in a Sample of Senior High Schools." Doctoral dissertation, Stanford University, 1962.

Tinker, Miles A. "The Effect of Illumination Intensities upon Speed of Perception and upon Fatigue in Reading." *Journal of Educational Psychology* 30 (November 1939): 561–71.

Tinker, Miles A. "Cumulative Effect of Marginal Conditions upon Rate of Perception in Reading." *Journal of Applied Psychology* 32 (October 1948): 537–40.

Tinker, Miles A. "Brightness, Contrast, Illumination Intensity, and Visual Efficiency." *American Journal of Optics* 35 (1959): 221–36.

Vernon, H. M.; Bedford, T.; and Warner, A. G. "The Relation of Atmospheric Conditions to the Working Capacity and Accident Rate of Miners." Cited in *American School and University* 24 (1952–53): 368.

Warner, Jack B. "A Comparison of Students' and Teachers' Performances in an Open Area Facility and in Self-Contained Classrooms." Doctoral dissertation, University of Houston, 1970.

Weaver, C. H. "An Investigation of the Influence of Size on the Quality of the High School." Doctoral dissertation, University of North Carolina, 1961. *Dissertation Abstracts* 23 (1962): 516–17.

Winslow, C. E. A. and Herrington, L. P. *Temperature and Human Life.* Princeton, N.J.: Princeton University Press, 1949, 211–221.

Woodham, William J., Jr. "The Relationship between the Size of Secondary Schools, the Pupil Cost, and the Breadth of Educational Opportunity." Doctoral dissertation, University of Florida, 1951.

Discussion

O. K. O'Fallon and L. Douglas Young

The educational facility of today has evolved from a place to house students while they learn to a vital tool of the instructional process. Such evolution must of necessity recognize the relationship of facilities to pupils' achievement, performance, and self-concept. The challenge of new teaching methods and instructional media has been met by improved architectural and engineering concepts to provide a learning environment that influences pupils' achievement.

As practiced by the School Planning Laboratories at the University of Tennessee and similar public and private agencies, school planning has become a type of practical research. Such planning has regularly involved those who use school buildings — pupils and teachers. Their knowledge of what is needed to enhance learning and teaching has enabled them to request spaces and physical environments that incorporate the best that has come out of engineering, architectural, industrial, and educational research. As a result, schools have become more comfortable, attractive, and useful.

McGuffey's review of the research concerning the relationship between physical environment and achievement, performance, and the self-concept of pupils supports the importance of the educational facility to the teaching and learning process. His review strongly suggests that the facility does indeed help learning and should therefore incorporate the environmental considerations that have been verified by research.

The purpose of this discussion is to support the findings reported by McGuffey and to supplement them where possible with additional research and by experience with the planning process.

ADDITIONAL STUDIES

Thermal Factors. Mincy (1961) designed a study to analyze and appraise conditions relating to thermal environment in classrooms in selected schools. He found that more classrooms failed to meet the criterion of mean radiant temperature than any other thermal criterion. More adequate ventilation was needed in fourteen of the twenty-seven classrooms. Air movement within the selected classrooms ranged from no perceptible movement to 100 feet per minute. In a review of the research on the thermal environment and its effect on man, Ackerman (1965) recognized the factors that relate the comfort of an individual to his thermal environment.

Seeing Factors. In a review of the research relating to luminous environment and its effects on man, Boyd (1965) reinforced and verified the importance of the elements of visibility identified by McGuffey. Like McGuffey, Boyd indicated a need for further research that would relate the requirements of the visual environment to the process of learning. Much of the research reviewed, however, points to the need for the use of standards concerned with the quantity of light needed at task level, reflectance ratios, quality of light, the influence of glare on seeing, and proper use of daylight. Acuff (1962) analyzed and appraised the visual environment in classrooms of selected schools. He found a range of 9 to 359 footcandles of light in these classrooms. Seventy percent had a window brightness exceeding the brightness ratio for the classroom, and only 7 percent of the classrooms had surface reflectances meeting the established criterion. He concluded that school personnel seemed generally unaware of the visual needs of pupils and exhibited limited knowledge about ways to better control the visual environment.

Color and Interior Painting. McGuffey's conclusion that color has an impact on pupils' performance is obliquely supported by two doctoral dissertations undertaken at the University of Tennessee. Johnson (1962) identified guidelines for color choices in various schoolhouse areas. She concluded that the prime factor in color choice should be the provision of a learning environment that enhances the mental, physical, and emotional well-being of those occupying the facility and that school color selection should suit a particular school. Ritchie (1977) investigated color preferences of pupils at secondary, elementary, and primary levels. His primary finding was that the students preferred blue and liked red, yellow, black, green, white, blue-green, and violet. The same pupils gave low ratings to gray, yellow-orange, and blue-violet.

Hearing Factors. Barnett and Erickson's (1965) review of research supports McGuffey's conclusion that noise can interfere with verbal instruction. They concluded that, for conventional school buildings, background noise should be limited to levels consistent with good speech communication; the basic noise-control demands are put on the building. But when speech communication is not desired, manipulation of the acoustical environment to moderately higher levels should prove beneficial.

Womack (1962) established criteria relating to background noise, reverberation time, and noise reduction of classroom walls and applied them to three classrooms in each of nine schools. Analysis of his observations and instrument measurements produced findings that support conclusions congruent with those from previous reviews. Etheridge (1972) limited his investigation to floor covering and sound reverberations. His data supported the generalizations that the acoustical qualities of asphalt and vinyl asbestos tile do not differ, that cork tile is more sound absorbent than other tiles and approached carpet in the ability to absorb sound, and that wool carpet absorbed sound best.

SUPPORT AND REINFORCEMENT FROM FACILITY PLANNING AND USE

The emergence of innovative teaching methods has necessitated broader utilization of facilities by requiring variable spaces, cooperative teaching, and extensive use of technical aids to learning, all of which are hampered by the design factors of the older buildings. There is greater emphasis on the development of general concepts and on the use of information and skills, rather than on the acquisition of facts. Greater participation of pupils in planning learning activities is also evident. Creativity is receiving more attention than conformity. Teachers are placing less dependence on textbooks and are creatively combining other resources for students to use in various learning units. Community resources, both material and personal, are being considered for the enrichment of learning.

The function of exploration is now receiving new emphasis. As a result of a better understanding of the needs of students, educators are concerned with providing a more relaxed atmosphere for growth and maturation. More importance is being given to aesthetic conditions in design and to space for social contacts, group activities, and independent study.

Thermal Factors. Because thermal factors affect pupils' achievement, performance, and self-concept, more attention is being given to how school buildings create an environment for teaching and for learning. Every day the creation of a suitable and an adequate environment becomes more important to the comfort, health, and productivity of students and to the efficiency of the school staff.

Contrary to what one would expect, the primary thermal problem in school classrooms is one of cooling, not heating. Solar heat through glass, varying occupancy loads, and a fluctuating outside temperature often create overheated classrooms. A lack of proper control of the thermal environment results in inefficient work patterns and discipline problems.

Seeing and Color Factors. Many activities in school require concentrated perception, that is, focusing the eyes upon a visual task as opposed to casual viewing. Reliable research indicates that critical seeing requires vast expenditures of physical energy. A poor visual environment, if not harmful to the eyes, may cause undue strain and tension in seeing, thereby causing fatigue and irritation, which create behavior problems. Therefore, if a proper learning environment is to be established, a pleasing visual environment is crucial. A large percentage of all learning is acquired by vision, so proper lighting and balanced lighting are essential. The assumption that more light, either natural or artificial, will automatically improve vision is false; added intensity may create a harmful brightness or glare. Proper levels of illumination with controlled brightness differences are necessary.

Both quality and quantity of light must be considered to secure balanced lighting. Light quality depends on the location and intensity of the source and the surrounding environment. Natural and artificial lighting may be utilized, although natural light is extremely difficult to control. Artificial lighting should be adequate to meet the minimum levels of illumination required for any particular area. Geographical location, nearby structures, outside details, orientation, size and shape of rooms, interior architectural problems, types of lighting fixtures, temperature of lamps, age of occupants, and the room's function are other considerations in choosing colors.

The colors used on walls, ceilings, and floors have a tremendous effect on the total environment, including lighting. Dark colors reflect light poorly; consequently, if there are too many dark objects, much of the light will be absorbed, and those dark colors can produce a feeling of gloom. Color causes certain emotional reactions and may create illusions of coolness, warmth, dimension, and distance. The psychological and physiological welfare of the student is greatly improved by the correct use of color within the school.

Hearing. Uncontrolled and unabated sounds in schools with little or no acoustical treatment can be serious barriers to learning. The interference with proper communication in the classroom is only part of the sound control problem. Noise significantly affects the mental and emotional health of teachers and pupils alike. Noise may be annoying or distracting; it may cause fear or anxiety; it may lead to irritation, frustration, and fatigue. The educational opportunities lost when sound control is ignored may be reflected by distraction from work, restlessness, lack of a reasonable climate for study, apparent disorder, and poor behavior patterns.

Many instructional activities involve oral communication between teacher and pupil and among pupils. The increased use of projected and recorded materials involves critical listening. The problem of acoustical control is essentially that of the prevention of sound transmission from one area of a building to another and providing acoustical comfort for those within a given area. Some instructional units, by the very nature of the activities taking place, produce sound of high intensity. These areas are usually isolated into separate clusters so that the sound produced is not transmitted to other instructional areas. Only rarely is it advisable to group areas of high sound level with those requiring a minimum of distracting sound.

A school by nature produces noise and by necessity requires quiet. These factors impose requirements on arrangement of spaces, noise prevention by sound insulation, and sound suppression and reverberation control through acoustical treatment.

CONCLUSION

If the educational program is adequately defined, the activities required to implement the program are identified, and the desired physical environment specified, the building's design — both internally and externally — could be determined by the architect. The school building should be designed as defined by the users. Because change is inevitable, the school should also be adaptable to new pupil demands and program developments.

Although most people recognize the interactions of selected programmatic influences and physical environment factors with educational outcomes, little research supports this view. The school itself defines a climate in which learning is encouraged or discouraged, is enhanced or inhibited, and is made comfortable or uncomfortable. The variables that interact to influence educational outcomes in addition to light, color, heat, ventilation, and sound include: the site on which buildings are located; building accessibility; utilization, maintenance, energy use; support facilities; areas for special instruction; and the size of the school plant. Based on research alone and recognition of the voids in the research, McGuffey's conclusions that obsolete and inadequate school facilities detract from the learning process, that modern, physical environments enhance pupil performance, and that facilities may have a differential impact on students' performances seem warranted.

REFERENCES

Acuff, William Turner. "A Study of the Visual Environment in Selected Classrooms." Doctoral dissertation, University of Tennessee, 1962.

Ackerman, Joseph R. "The Thermally Related Environment and Its Effects on Man." In *Environmental Evaluations*, series 2, pp. 73–100. Ann Arbor: University of Michigan, 1965.

Barnett, Norman, and Erickson, Bruce E. "The Sonic Environment and Its Effect on Man." In *Environmental Evaluations*, series 2, pp. 133–56. Ann Arbor: University of Michigan, 1965.

Boyd, Robert A. "The Luminous Environment and Its Effect on Man." In *Environmental Evaluations*, series 2, pp. 101–32. Ann Arbor: University of Michigan, 1965.

Etheridge, Raymond M. "A Study of Factors Involved in Determining Acoustical Differences between Resilient Floor Coverings and Carpet." Doctoral dissertation, University of Tennessee, 1972.

Johnson, Bettye U. "A Study of Color in the Classroom Environment." Doctoral dissertation, University of Tennessee, 1962.

Mincy, Homer F. "A Study of Factors Involved in Establishing a Satisfactory Thermal Environment in the Classroom." Doctoral dissertation, University of Tennessee, 1961.

Ritchie, Jack C. "An Investigation Concerning Color Preferences of Selected Primary, Elementary, and Secondary Students for a Rural and Urban Area." Doctoral dissertation, University of Tennessee, 1977.

Womack, Darwin W. "A Study of Factors Involved in Establishing a Satisfactory Acoustical Environment in the Classroom." Doctoral dissertation, University of Tennessee, 1962.

11

Educational Climates

HERBERT J. WALBERG

Education is the development of special and general abilities of the mind, particularly knowledge and modes of thought and feeling associated with culture. Definitions of climate refer to the typical weather conditions of a region throughout the year averaged over a series of years. Thus, a preliminary definition of educational climates is the general qualities of educative contexts that influence the development of the mind. Such a definition, however, is too broad for our present purposes, because it includes instructional and management strategies, teaching personnel, and extracurricular activities, as well as instructional media, community, and family. These topics are addressed in other chapters; a more restrictive definition for this chapter is necessary.

Student learning is affected by psychological climate, through the process of perception by students and also by other significant persons involved in education, such as teachers, parents, and administrators. Thus, this review emphasizes students' and others' perceptions of the following climates: classroom, school, open, teaching, and home.

Recent educational research on student perceptions comes under the heading of climate, morale, or social environment. These terms emphasize that the psychological perception of the composite qualities of classes and other groups rather than their so-called objective characteristics, such as group size and counts of individual or collective behavior, determines the climate of classrooms.

A few classroom examples may help to illustrate the importance of student perception in research on climate. Research in laboratories indicates that rewards, praise, or positive reinforcements raise the probability of occurrence of the positively reinforced behavior. Increased praise and other rewards, however, do not consistently enhance learning in natural settings of learning. Why not? First, the learner may become satiated by too many reinforcements. Second, some teachers may be too liberal in allocating praise for small accomplishments, and such reinforcement is discounted by the learners. A mild "okay" or a wink once a month from a strict teacher can be far more reinforcing than dozens of "great"s, "good"s, and "fine"s from teachers who gush. Third, reinforcements need to be suited to the efforts of the learner and what may be easy for one student may be difficult for another student who might be far more deserving of praise. Fourth, in natural settings of learnings, particularly among adolescent students, praise by a teacher may constitute negative reinforcement because the student may be teased for being the teacher's pet. Thus, although objective indexes of teacher and student behavior in classroom settings certainly have their place in research, they do not tell the whole story in regard to complex, weighted, subjective judgments made by students and others who have an important influence on learning.

Ancient philosophers recognized the need for a balanced understanding of human beings in terms of the head, the heart, and the hand, or, in modern psychological terminology, cognition, affect, and volition. But it has often been said that psychology lost its soul a long time ago, destroyed its mind at the turn of the present century, and is now having trouble with behavior. Moreover, although psychologists have made valiant efforts to apply laboratory findings to natural settings of human action, the results have often been discouraging. For example, the so-called behavioral and cognitive revolutions in psychology are not notable for producing higher levels of achievement in test performance and self-concept among students in ordinary classrooms in recent decades. What has been lacking in much psychological theory and research on school learning is the consideration of student perceptions of the social environment of their classes and the direct or indirect linkages of perceptions to measures of student outcome, such as standardized test performance, interest in the subject, self-concept as a learner, and student behaviors that are of interest to public policy makers, educational practitioners, parents, and students.

About a decade ago, however, research began on student perceptions of the social-psychological aspects of their science classes in U.S. high schools and then expanded to other subjects, grade levels, and countries. This research shows that student perceptions can be validly measured and that they serve as indexes, for classes or individual students, of the amount of cognitive, affective, and behavioral learning that takes place during the school year or during shorter periods of time.

This research was influenced by psychologists Kurt Lewin, Egon Brunswick, Sigmund Freud, and Henry Murray, but their writings did not focus sharply on educational settings nor did they report statistical evidence on the linkages between climate and educational outcomes. Numerous historical, theoretical, and methodological issues are not fully discussed here because they are not entirely relevant to the relationship between climate and learning outcomes. The following publications may aid interested readers in pursuing topics briefly considered here: Insel and Moos (1974) on psychological research in a variety of settings; Campbell (1970) and Marjoribanks (1974) for valuable but neglected collections of research on substantive learning environments carried out in Australia, Canada, England, and the United States; Kahn and Weiss (1973), Moos (1979), Randhawa and Fu (1973), Shulman and Tamir (1973), and Walberg (1971, 1974a, 1974b, 1974c, 1976) for substantive and methodological reviews; and Walberg (1974b, 1979) for source books on a variety of learning environment instruments, studies, and evaluations by a number of groups in several nations.

DEFINITIONS AND LIMITATIONS OF PRESENT RESEARCH

Many of the writings on climates are not useful for the present review. Some are purely theoretical or definitional without empirical evidence, others are purely anecdotal and, although the relations they hypothesize are plausible, they have not been subjected to scientific tests. Moreover, many of the writings on the five climates considered here fail to demonstrate the particular relationship of interest here between climate and educational outcomes.

Empirical investigators have defined climate operationally in a variety of ways in original studies, but the following working definitions will give the reader an idea of the general aspects of climate involved in the five settings treated in this review.

1. *Classroom climate:* the student perception of the social-psychological aspects of the classroom group that influence learning. Principal, teacher, parent, and observer perceptions of the classroom group are also of interest, but little relevant research is available on these role groups.
2. *School climate:* teacher or student perceptions of the school morale or social-psychological environment that affect learning.
3. *Open climate:* originally, joint teacher-student decision making with respect to the goals, means, and pace of learning, rather than control solely by the teacher or the student. Later, some people used the term to imply permissiveness in learning with little input from the teacher, and others used the term to imply large physical spaces in the school building for many students. Unless otherwise noted, the original meaning of open education is used in this review.
4. *Teaching climate:* the kind of climate (authoritarian or laissez-faire) that controls the learning process. As Baumrind (1971) and Brophy and Putnam (1979) note, the kind of climate often termed democratic is not really democratic at all in the sense of decisions being made by majority vote. Rather it is authoritative, in which the teacher has a position of authority and retains the ultimate decision-making power rather than acting in a dictatorial or permissive manner. Authoritative teachers, however, are good listeners and take care to see that

everyone is clear about the reasons for decisions. Authoritative climates of this nature in homes and classrooms are associated with greater development of autonomy, independence, and self-concept. (Specific teaching techniques and strategies and related topics are treated in other chapters.)

5. *Home climate:* the behaviors and processes on the part of parents to provide intellectual and emotional stimulation for their children's general development and school learning.

Classroom climates receive the greatest attention since more of the research in this area is highly controlled for alternative causes of educational outcomes. In addition, comprehensive research syntheses will be cited where possible, rather than selected narrative and subjective reviews that characterize much writing on education.

Classroom Climates. To estimate the sign and size of the correlations of student perceptions of social-psychological environments of their classes with learning outcomes and adjusted gains, Haertel, Walberg, and Haertel (1979) recently analyzed 734 correlations from a comprehensive, international collection of twelve studies of ten data sets on 823 classes in eight subject areas containing 17,805 students in four nations. Of thirty-six hypotheses theoretically derived in 1969, thirty-one were supported. Learning outcomes and gains, including student achievement, performance, and self-concept, were positively associated with perceived cohesiveness, satisfaction, task difficulty, formality, goal direction, democracy, and the material environment and negatively associated with friction, cliques, apathy, and disorganization.

Much of the research on student perceptions of their classes employed the Learning Environment Inventory (LEI) or the My Class Inventory (MCI). Table 11-1 shows sample items from the LEI, which is intended for students in junior and senior high schools. The LEI consists of 105 items, seven items per scale on each of fifteen scales. Students rate their classes on a four-point scale of "strongly agree," "agree," "disagree," and "strongly disagree" on each of the items. For example, on the cohesiveness scale, a student is asked to agree or disagree with such items as "All students know each other very well." The seven items on each scale are summed for analysis.

Table 11-1.

*Sample Items, Reliabilities, and Consistencies
of Fifteen Variables*

Variables	Sample item	Class reliability	Percent positive correlations with learning
Affect			
Cohesiveness	All students knew each other very well.	.84	86
Satisfaction	The students enjoy their class work.	.79	100
*Friction	Certain students are responsible for petty quarrels.	.80	0
*Apathy	Students don't care what the class does.	.77	14
*Cliqueness	Some students refuse to mix with rest of the class.	.74	8
Status			
Democracy	Students have about equal influence on the class.	.61	85
Competitiveness	There is much competition in the class.	.56	67
*Diversity	Interests vary greatly within the group.	.36	30
Favoritism	Certain students are favored more than the rest.	.65	10
Task			
Goal direction	Each student knows the goals of the course.	.73	73
Material environment	The room is bright and comfortable.	.79	86
Formality	The class has rules to guide its activities.	.87	65
Difficulty	Students find the work hard to do.	.81	87
Speed	The course material is covered quickly.	.76	54
*Disorganization	The class is disorganized and inefficient.	.87	6

Note: The learning criteria include cognitive, affective, and behavioral measures including higher mental processes and self-concept. The variables marked with an asterisk are usually negatively associated with learning.

The 105 items on the LEI can be administered in approximately twenty-five minutes and produce, in most cases, highly reliable estimates of the morale, climate, or learning environment of the class. To save students' time, some investigators have omitted some of the scales or reduced the number of items per scale from seven to thirteen without much sacrifice in reliability. The scales have been translated into several languages and used in a number of countries in Africa, Asia, Europe, and South America; occasionally they require some modification to make them suitable for the particular setting of the investigation.

The MCI is an adaption of the LEI for elementary school research. It consists of sixty items, nine items per scale on each of five scales. The vocabulary level of the items has been reduced, but occasionally it is necessary to read the items to some students and explain them to classes of poor readers. Working from these two standardized instruments, a number of investigators have modified the items and scales to suit them to their particular research interest and setting.

When the scales are weighted and added to form a composite index of the environment conducive to learning, the predictive validity of the scales increases substantially. Seven studies added sets of scales to weighted regression equations, which also included ability or pretest measures or both as controls. The average incremental variance accounted for in learning outcomes is 20 percent with a range from 1 percent to 54 percent. Thus regressions containing the control and perceptual variables account for large amounts and, in some cases, nearly all of the total variance in learning outcomes. These analyses show that the scale measures taken during the course of learning afford an accurate prediction of how much will be learned during the school year and serve as a useful index of the amount that the class is learning at any given time.

Because learning environment scales provide a predictively valid index of the amount of learning gains made during the academic year as indexed by standard tests, the scales can occasionally substitute for the standardized achievement tests themselves. Since the scales are closely linked to affective and behavioral outcomes as well, they are useful indexes in a variety of settings and subject matters. In addition, the scales are content free; that is, what social-psychological perceptions are conducive to learning in one set of circumstances are also conducive to learning in other circumstances.

Because different curricula, teachers, and forms of instruction emphasize different sets of goals and outcomes of learning, standardized tests are not always an accurate or fair assessment across learning settings; in these circumstances, the LEI scales form a useful index of curriculum, instructional, and other kinds of educational effects. Since the earlier research demonstrated the predictive validity of the instruments, recent research has employed the scales to provide statistically reliable sensitivity to educational treatments such as curriculum, teacher training, and instructional innovations, as well as to project efforts to increase student teamwork, cross-sex and cross-ethnic group cooperation, and similar properties. Other work reveals that student perceptions reflect and mediate teacher and student characteristics and that they provide diagnostically valuable profiles for class and individual morale or climate that can be used as guidelines for improvement.

In summary, scales measuring student perceptions of the social-psychological environment of learning provide useful independent, mediating, and dependent variables in educational investigations in natural settings. They complement and supplement current behavioral and cognitive variables that modern psychologists emphasize and reveal social realities in classes that are neglected in laboratory-derived research. Even if the purpose of research does not concern student perceptions themselves, the perceptions can be used as control variables so that subtle cognitive and behavioral effects may be detected in complex natural settings. Lastly, it is the student who is the client of the educational system and the person whom the system is attempting to influence. Surely these perceptions should be one basis of consideration and accountability in the evaluation of instruction, curriculum, and other aspects of the education program.

School Climate. Ellett and Walberg (1979) recently reviewed investigations of school climates. Although a great deal of administrative research on school climates has been carried out with such instruments as the Leader Behavior Description Questionnaire and the Organizational Climate Description Questionnaire, only two studies have shown linkages between the school climate or staff morale and student outcomes. Coughlan and Cooke (1974) administered the School Survey, a measure of the morale of the teaching staff, in schools that were making exceedingly high or exceedingly low gains among samples from a universe of approximately 400 public schools in Chicago. Their work shows that teachers in schools with the greatest achievement gains perceived their schools as being more educationally effective and saw themselves as having more constructive supervisory relations with the principal, closer community contact, and a greater voice in the educational program than did teachers in schools with the lowest achievement gains. Subsequent research in Georgia on this survey instrument demonstrated significant correlations of teacher perceptions of the staff morale with student-perceived school climate and student achievement when school attendance, socioeconomic status, and school size were statistically controlled.

Subsequent research (Ellett and Walberg 1979) being carried out at the University of Georgia on a large number of schools in that state shows that the principal appears to be the key figure in generating and reinforcing staff morale in the school, which in turn appears to influence the classroom climate, which in turn leads to greater gains in student achievement. The Georgia research suggests that the ebb and flow of causal functioning runs between principal and teacher and between teacher and student. Although there are exceptions, the teacher mediates between the principal and a student, and all three are influenced by factors external to the school environment. The general association of greater principal-student interaction with low student test performance and greater teacher alienation may be attributable to external forces, such as neighborhood family disruptions and associated school behavior problems that cause teacher alienation and require direct principal interventions. It may also stem from such internal problems as short circuiting the teachers, which leads to poor staff morale and ultimately to low test performance by students.

In psychological terms, the principal requires information to perceive or diagnose internal and external climates accurately; then the principal formulates intentions likely to improve the climate and behaves in a manner to communicate or accomplish these intentions. There is room for error and loss of information at the stages of perception, intention, and behavior; parallel processes in teacher and students can also be faulty. To gather adequate climate information, to reflect carefully enough to arrive at the best intentions, to determine optimal behaviors to accomplish such intentions, and to enact or communicate them with sufficient clarity may be costly in terms of human time and effort. Obviously, selective perception, attention, and behavior are required in the chain of events preceding the principal's impact on facets of staff morale, school climate, and student outcomes. The work at the University of Georgia is highly promising because it integrates the many aspects of climate that bear upon student achievement, such as principal competencies, staff morale, school and class climates, and measures of educational achievement and of self-concept.

Open Climates. Recently Horwitz (1979) and Peterson (1979) reviewed the literature on open climates of learning in contrast to traditional climates of learning. Open climates were generally referred to as "a style involving flexibility of space, student choice of activity, richness of learning materials, integration of curriculum area, and more individual or small-group than large-group instruction" (p. 72–73). This open classroom teaching style was compared to the climate of traditional teaching. Horwitz used a "box score" or voting method to synthesize the findings across the research studies. For each study he tallied whether the results favored open teaching, traditional teaching, or indicated no significant differences. From the same corpus of literature, Peterson calculated "effect sizes," which show the difference in the open and traditional climates in standard deviation units. Horwitz was able to tabulate the results of approximately 200 studies, but Peterson could calculate effect sizes for only 45 studies since many investigators presented insufficient information for such calculations.

Horwitz's tabulation of 102 studies of composite achievement on standardized tests shows that, on average, there are no consistent differences on achievement between open and traditional climates. Peterson reported a similar conclusion. The results of both reviews, however, indicate that students in open climates tend to be more creative than those in traditional climates. Creativity in the studies reviewed was typically assessed with paper and pencil tests, and answers were scored for fluency, flexibility, originality, and elaboration.

Horwitz and Peterson also reviewed affective outcomes of learning, including self-concept, attitudes toward school and teachers, curiosity, locus of control, anxiety, and independence as measured either by paper and pencil instruments or behavioral counts and ratings by trained observers. The reviews suggest that open climates surpass traditional ones in improving educational attitudes and in promoting student independence and curiosity. But there is little difference between the two types of climates in the development of self-concept, the locus of control, and anxiety.

Teaching Climates. As noted by Brophy and Putnam (1979), Baumrind (1971) provides a useful framework for looking at teaching climates as well as group leadership styles and parent behaviors. She classified leadership climates as authoritarian, authoritative, and permissive. These classifications are similar to those used in previous studies of group leadership begun by Lewin and others, except that the term *authoritative* is substituted for *democratic,* since most educational groups that are called democratic do not follow majority rule. Effective teaching climates are authoritative in the sense that the teacher or parent, as Brophy and Putnam note, "has a position of authority and responsibility, speaks as a mature and responsible adult, and retains ultimate decision-making power. Rather than act in authoritarian manner, however, authoritative leaders solicit input, seek consensus, and take care to see that everyone is clear about the rationale for decisions as well as the decisions themselves" (p. 194).

Baumrind showed that, compared to other children, the children of authoritative parents showed the most advanced levels of autonomy, independence, confidence, and self-concept. Brophy and Putnam cite evidence that authoritative teachers produce higher levels of achievement, self-concept, and other educational outcomes than do teachers who take complete responsibility for decision making, or delegate it completely to the child. As defined by Brophy and Putnam and implied by the earlier work by Lewin on group climate, and by Baumrind on parental climate, the authoritative teacher is similar to the operational definition by Walberg and Thomas (1972) of open education in that the teacher and student assume joint or contractual responsibility for decision making with respect to the goals of learning and the means and rate by which they are accomplished.

Home Climates. From a systematic search of educational, psychological, and sociological literature, Iverson and Walberg (1979) reviewed eighteen studies of 5,831 school-age children on the correlation of the home environment and learning in eight countries over a nineteen-year period. Correlations of intelligence, motivation, and achievement with indexes of parent stimulation of the student in the home are considerably higher than those with indexes of social-economic status. Specifically, the median of 92 simple correlations of home environment and learning was .37, with a range of 0.2 to .83, and the median of 62 multiple regression-weighted composites was .44, with a range of .23 to .81.

The work reviewed on home environment contrasts with sociological surveys that include social-economic measures such as parent education, income, and occupation and family constellation studies that analyze number, birth order, and spacing of children, all of which show weak relations to educational outcomes. Research on home environments investigates specific social-psychological ratings of behavior thought to be conducive to learning. Researchers, who began this tradition in Chicago, developed lists of parental behaviors and parent-child interactive behaviors that seem likely to foster intellectual and affective growth. These variables are specific and potentially changeable, and ratings of them are made by home interviewers who ask such questions as: "Do you read to the child," "To which museums have you taken the child," and "Who plans family vacations?" Sets of these questions produce information for rating variables in the home environment, such as academic guidance, achievement, activeness of the family, intellectuality of the home, work habits of the family, and language models — all of which are hypothesized and demonstrated to be important influences on achievement. The most recent research on home environment has focused on the presses for academic guidance, achievement both for the child and the parents, and activeness of the family, because these aspects of the home environment seem most readily influenced by intervention programs.

DISCUSSION AND CONCLUSIONS

Educational climates influence student achievement, performance, and self-concept, as well as other valuable educational outcomes. Climate measures are practical, inexpensive, and valid, and they predict learning gains more accurately than do so-called objective variables such as student social class, teacher behaviors and other characteristics, school and class size, and educational expenditures.

Constructive educational climates may be viewed as means to valuable educational ends or as worthy ends in their own right. Information on educational climates may be conveniently gathered and fed back to school staffs for the planning, execution, and evaluation of data-based educational improvement programs. Climate measures should be included along with standardized tests and other assessments in national, state, local, and school accountability, evaluation, and research efforts.

In summary, the research on climate leads to the following conclusions (although certain qualifications have been noted in the text and in the primary studies and reviews):

1. Classroom climate: student perceptions of high degrees of cohesiveness, satisfaction, task difficulty, formality, goal direction, democracy and material environment in their classroom group, and low degrees of friction, cliques, apathy, and disorganization are associated with larger amounts of learning and other constructive traits.

2. School climate: teacher perceptions of good staff morale or social-psychological climate of the school are associated with large amounts of student learning; specifically, teacher perceptions of an educational program that is effective, of constructive principal-teacher relations, of effective community-school interaction, and of a strong voice by teachers in the formulation and execution of the educational program are associated with student achievement.

3. Open climates: open climates, in contrast to traditional ones, do not deter learning or self-concept, but may promote more constructive educational attitudes, independence, and curiosity.

4. Teaching climate: authoritative rather than dictatorial or permissive climates seem most constructive in promoting gains in measurable learning and self-concept.

5. Home climate: the educational stimulation and social-psychological supportiveness of the student in the home by the parents are more closely linked to learning and self-concept development than are social class indexes and the number of children in the family.

REFERENCES

Baumrind, Diana. "Current Patterns of Parental Authority." *Developmental Psychology Monographs* 4 (1971): 1–103.

Brophy, Jere E., and Putnam, Joyce G. "Classroom Management in the Elementary Grades." In *Classroom Management,* Seventy-Eighth Yearbook of the National Society for the Study of Education, Part 2, edited by Daniel L. Duke, pp. 182–216. Chicago: University of Chicago Press, 1979.

Campbell, W. J., ed. *Scholars in Context: The Effects of Environments on Learning.* Sydney, Australia: Wiley, 1970.

Coughlan, Robert J., and Cooke, Robert A. "Teacher Morale." In *Evaluating Educational Performance: A Sourcebook of Instruments, Methods, and Examples,* edited by Herbert J. Walberg. Berkeley, Calif.: McCutchan, 1974.

Ellett, Chad D., and Walberg, Herbert J. "Principal Competency and School Climate." In *Educational Environments and Effects: Evaluation, Research, and Policy,* edited by Herbert J. Walberg. Berkeley, Calif.: McCutchan, 1979.

Haertel, Geneva D.; Walberg, Herbert J.; and Haertel, Edward H. "Social-Psychological Environments and Learning: A Quantitative Synthesis." Paper presented at the annual meeting of the American Educational Research Association, San Francisco, April 1979.

Horwitz, Robert A. "Effects of the 'Open Classroom'." In *Educational Environments and Effects: Evaluation, Research, and Policy,* edited by Herbert J. Walberg. Berkeley, Calif.: McCutchan, 1979.

Insel, Paul M., and Moos, Rudolf H. "Psychological Environments: Expanding the Scope of Human Ecology." *American Psychologist* 29 (March 1974): 179–88.

Iverson, Barbara K., and Walberg, Herbert J. "Home Environment and Learning: A Quantitative Synthesis." Paper presented at the annual meeting of the American Educational Research Association, San Francisco, 1979.

Kahn, S. B., and Weiss, Joel. "The Teaching of Affective Responses." In *Second Handbook of Research on Teaching,* edited by Robert M. W. Travers. Chicago: Rand McNally, 1973.

Marjoribanks, Kevin, ed. *Environments for Learning.* London: National Foundation for Educational Reseach, 1974.

Moos, Rudolf H. "Educational Climates." In *Educational Environments and Effects: Evaluation, Research, and Policy,* edited by Herbert J. Walberg. Berkeley, Calif.: McCutchan, 1979.

Peterson, Penelope L. "Direct Instruction Reconsidered." In *Research on Teaching: Concepts, Findings, and Implications,* edited by Penelope L. Peterson and Herbert J. Walberg. Berkeley, Calif.: McCutchan, 1979.

Randhawa, Bikkar S., and Fu, Lewis L. W. "Assessment and Effect of Some Classroom Environment Variables." *Review of Educational Research* 43 (Summer 1973): 303–21.

Shulman, Lee S., and Tamir, Pinchas. "Research on Teaching in the Natural Sciences." In *Second Handbook of Research on Teaching,* edited by Robert M. W. Travers. Chicago: Rand McNally, 1973.

Walberg, Herbert J. "Models for Optimizing and Individualizing School Learning." *Interchange* 2, no. 3 (1971): 15–27.

Walbert, Herbert J. "Educational Process Evaluation." In *Educational Evaluation: Analysis and Responsibility,* edited by Michael W. Apple, Michael J. Subkoviak, and Henry J. Lufler, Jr. Berkeley, Calif.: McCutchan, 1974a.

Walberg, Herbert J., ed. *Evaluating Educational Performance: A Sourcebook of Methods, Instruments, and Examples.* Berkeley, Calif.: McCutchan, 1974b.

Walberg, Herbert J. "Learning Models and Learning Environments." *Educational Psychologist* 11, no. 2 (1974c): 102–9.

Walberg, Herbert J. "Psychology of Learning Environments: Behavioral, Structural, or Perceptual?" In *Review of Research in Education,* vol. 4, edited by Lee S. Shulman, pp. 142–78. Itasca, Ill.: F. E. Peacock, 1976.

Walberg, Herbert J., ed. *Educational Environments and Effects: Evaluation, Research, and Policy.* Berkeley, Calif.: McCutchan, 1979.

Walberg, Herbert J., and Thomas, Susan C. "Open Education: An Operational Definition and Validation in Great Britain and United States." *American Educational Research Journal* 9 (Spring 1972): 197–208.

Discussion

Richard J. Riordan

Walberg had to make some sharp decisions in delimiting his chapter. He chose to be guided by what he knows best — social psychology, particularly as it relates to the perceptions of those most closely involved with the school learning process. In doing so he obviously risks short-changing many fine efforts that have been made to explore and research the impact of climate on learning outcomes. But he also zeros in on some of the most exciting and promising areas of educational research.

THE RESEARCH AS PRESENTED

The lack of agreement regarding what constitutes and contributes to school climate makes the task of definitively or exhaustively reviewing the research an unwieldy one. For example, Walberg's decision to include home climate as one of his five areas is logical if one thinks about the importance of the home with regard to learning. However, the immense body of research on family environment leaves that portion of his chapter a matter of lip service at best and a distraction at worst.

The other four divisions of climate could probably have been dealt with more understandably as two: classroom climate and school climate. The open climate category is mainly an issue in the classroom, as is the teaching climate. The school, insofar as it is an autonomous sociological unit, can be studied independently of both the system to which it belongs and the individual classrooms that reside in it. Many research studies and other data such as achievement scores are reported this way. Similarly and particularly in self-contained elementary schools, classroom climate can be largely a product of what takes place in any particular classroom. The case is not being made here for the lack of relationship between the two units but only for a more understandable division for reporting the research.

The Horwitz research that Walberg cites as part of the section on open versus traditional learning climates does not add much to our understanding of the issue — or at least it does not help us in finding a direction to take. Indeed, another review by Horwitz (1979), which was not cited by Walberg, draws the seemingly sterile conclusion that open classroom programs can be viable alternatives *if teachers and parents are interested in them.* With a fair abundance of research on the issue of open or closed classrooms, the amount of teacher and parental interest, which is so fundamental to school climate, may well be one of the most important barometers of productive classroom climates. The more that teachers are interested in their work, the better the students learn. Were I to look for more climate research to support this, the parental involvement efforts of Follow Through and the study of the teacher interest variable in Head Start programs would surely be productive leads. And, of course, all of the work on humanizing climates for learning, such as that done by Schmuck and Schmuck (1974), is pertinent.

In this connection, the deliberate attempt to involve peers in the learning process has an especially close connection with classroom climate research. The climate implication, or the principle involved, is the same as for the open classroom or parental involvement. That is, the more we induce a climate that resembles an active partnership in learning, the more likely it is that there will be positive outcomes. McGee, Kauffman, and Nussen (1977) have an excellent review of research done in climate intervention through involving the child as a change agent. Several of the research studies they cite show promise of helping us understand the way peer interventions with individual children may change the climate considerably. The use of outside consultants, such as psychologists or counselors, has been a frequent if disappointing topic for study. But the use of such an abundant natural resource as students in ways that have reciprocal benefit has great potential. Another review that bears more directly on learning outcomes is one by Devin-Sheehan, Feldman, and Allen (1976) on peer tutoring.

Brookover (Brookover and Erickson 1975) was one of the first to engage in large-scale sociological research regarding academic self-concept, or concept of self as a school achiever. He, among others, recognized that children with an adequate or better generalized self-concept may suffer severely from lack of faith in their abilities as school achievers. Likewise, the views of many students of themselves as students are far more favorable than their views of themselves and their competencies in other areas. Much of the research in this area has been broken down to show self-concept by subject matter, for example, concept of self as achiever in mathematics. Studies of the self-concept, differentiated by sex, in mathematics and English have invited large-scale curricular revisions to eliminate the stereotype that boys are good in mathematics and girls are good in English.

For our purposes here, however, one of the most relevant findings (Brookover and others 1978) dramatically underscores the importance of school climate. This random sample of Michigan elementary schools revealed that socioeconomic status, racial composition, and school climate were all correlated with academic achievement. The largest correlation with achievement, however, was the climate variable they called "student sense of academic futility." Their further analysis demonstrated that students' perceptions of the expectations and evaluations by teachers were clearly related to achievement. If the students felt that success was possible in school, they achieved better. This study made no claim to demonstrate how these climate characteristics develop in a school. However, in the face of consistently overwhelming evidence that socioeconomic status is the major factor in determining achievement outcomes and self-concept formation, it is refreshing and inspiring to see evidence that climate interventions may potentially compete with conditions that seem less susceptible to change.

SIGNIFICANT ISSUES IN THIS AREA

Instrumentation is a major methodological issue. What are we going to use to measure perceptions of school climate? I will avoid comparative examinations of the various climate instruments of the type Walberg uses, but I do not want to imply that there is solid agreement regarding what should be asked or what perceptions are important — both crucial issues in deciding what an "effective" climate is. There is, however, general agreement as to what sociometric variables or questions are important. One practical aspect of instrumentation is the extent to which the climate is surveyed. One question is how thorough the instrument will be, and another is how frequently it will be given. Both of these depend on what is to be accomplished, of course, but they have underlying time and cost considerations that strongly influence the decision. Time and expense are always issues when instrumentation is being considered, whether for research purposes or simply diagnostic purposes with an individual classroom or child. The ideal is to get the most and best data with the least expense, and this always results in trade-offs. This compromise has been the typical case in intelligence testing where the Wechsler Intelligence Scale for Children (WISC) is used when the group tests for a given child provide results that are suspect or need further detailing. Climate research is no different. The short, inexpensvie instruments, such as Walberg cites, have all the limitations inherent in a lack of thoroughness. Where broad indexes are desired and where large numbers are involved, we usually have accepted the compromises that are necessary because they satisfy time and expense constraints. At the exact intervention point, however, we are hesitant to act on such data because of the crucial necessity of being correct in our actions. An imprecise intervention may only make things worse.

Climate intervention is the most critical issue in this area. It simply does not matter much if we know everything about a school or classroom climate and then cannot or will not act on that information. Here Walberg's review is perhaps most deficient and perhaps with good reason. There is not a wealth of systematic research with regard to classroom climate intervention. And, further, Walberg's work and interest has been in tapping the more global indexes that can contribute to an academic understanding of learning environments.

One of the most complete systems for describing classroom climates is the Barclay Classroom Climate Inventory (Barclay 1974, 1978). This system has as a strength the fact that it pulls together three inputs instead of the usual one. It elicits sociometric evaluations from the child, the child's peers, and the teacher and puts them together to form a profile that is essentially a multitrait, multimethod factor analysis. It is computerized and creates factor statements and scores that detail the child in the classroom environment. Further, the report offers individualized prescriptions for children and can relate them to achievement results.

The importance of multiple perceptions in climate descriptions cannot be overemphasized. What the teacher perceives and what peers perceive about a particular child is crucial to both self-concept and achievement learning outcomes. Instruments such as Barclay's enrich the data base considerably and may be of increasing value to child behavior consultants or others who wish to study the classroom climate closely. If Walberg's contention that climate measures can often do the job of achievement measures is correct, the few extra dollars for a thorough instrument may well be worth the investment. He also suggests that in some instances climate measures can replace other group measures. Additionally, if there are chances that the data will be used by climate interventionists with individual children, much further expense may be saved from individual testing that could become unnecessary.

One of the most recent studies using Barclay's instrument (Barclay and Kaehle 1979) looked at the impact that mainstreamed mentally retarded students had on other students, the classroom climate, and themselves in 150 classrooms in Ohio. Although the argument for mainstreaming may no longer be that handicapped students will achieve better academically, it has been thought that they will at least develop better social skills and self-concepts. This study shows that they were thoroughly rejected by both peers and teachers; their dramatic impact on the classroom climate was the opposite of what mainstreaming was intended to do. The point here is not to suggest that the instrument is a flawless tool or to contend that this study settles the mainstreaming argument. What is important is that technology that taps the complexities of classroom climates is available and is being further developed. With massive climate interventions occurring on a regular basis because of broad social manipulations, such as Public Law 94-142, we need to make use of the most sensitive and complete instrumentation possible to formulate prevention strategies or diagnose climate disturbances. Instruments such as Barclay's are no more expensive (about one dollar per child) than many group achievement tests, and they produce a wealth of information.

What is needed in this whole field is more research regarding the application of a rapidly developing prevention technology, and more use of the data we gather and knowledge we have regarding classroom climates. That is, as we have come to know more about classroom climates, we are beginning to develop strategies for remediating the negative aspects of those climates. We are also beginning to be able to construct climates from scratch that will prevent negative conditions from developing. To oversimplify, we have found that there are temperament clusters in classrooms that are susceptible to a relatively limited number of different treatments — a promising finding in that climate control for effective learning may not be the impossible task as is so often thought. We may be able to mediate the classroom climate through preventive consultation. The school psychologist, school counselor, principal, or behavioral consultant, by whatever name, may be able to look at classroom data and assist the teacher with some simple strategies that will assure optimum outcomes for many in the class, particularly the less powerful.

CONCLUSION

The research Walberg reports regarding the roles of the principal and the teacher in school climates points up the way climate research has benefitted from the work done on the social psychology of groups. There are many similarities between ideal climates in the classroom and ideal school or other climates. To briefly encapsulate what both empirical and action research point to as ideal, I offer the following five conditions:

1. Communication is open and active, featuring dialogue rather than monologue.
2. High levels of attraction exist for the group as a whole and among its members.
3. Norms are supportive for getting work done, as well as for optimizing individual opportunities to be different.
4. Members share high amounts of potential and actual influence both with one another and with the leader.
5. The processes of working and developing together as a group are important in themselves and open to examination and change.

Lonsdale (1964) referred to school climate as a global index of task-achievement and need-satisfaction integration. In addition to the research reported by Walberg, definitions such as these have turned administrative researchers more in the direction of organizational development studies (for example, Mullen 1976). Consequently, such research has depended heavily on management theory and technology, other outgrowths of social psychology.

Walberg is certainly correct in concluding that educational climates have important influences on student achievement, performance, and self-concept as well as on other valuable educational outcomes. Similarly, as we are coming to understand such influences better, it seems crucial to include climate measures as part of the standard assessment package in all schools and systems. As in all efforts at accountability, climate monitoring and intervention plans will be fraught with potential pain. It can be threatening because to some extent we are after cause-effect data. Sometimes teachers and principals are the cause as well as the students. Such being the case, the change or increase of speed in this direction must begin with the solemn agreement that constructive learning is the aim and low-key expert assistance is available. Whatever tendencies we have to be punitive, righteous, or power bent certainly will be quickly seen and thwarted, and result in wasted, if not destructive, efforts. An accountability philosophy may seem like good business, but if it scares people to death we will only get a lot of strange passive-aggressive behavior that will defeat all requests for cooperation.

If many of the educational commentators are correct, constructive educational climates may be so vitally important that priorities should be drastically rearranged. What can need improvement more than school and classroom climates if Silberman (1970) was accurate in calling American classrooms basically "banal and joyless"? The research efforts in this area are becoming more sophisticated each year and give hope that equally sophisticated and effective climate intervention formulas are on the way.

REFERENCES

Barclay, James R. "Needs Assessment in the Elementary School." In *Evaluating Educational Performance: A Sourcebook of Methods, Instruments, and Examples,* edited by Herbert J. Walberg. Berkeley, Calif.: McCutchan, 1974.

Barclay, James R. *Classroom Climate Inventory – Manual.* Lexington, Mass.: Educational Skills Development, 1978.

Barclay, James R., and Kaehle, T. J. "Impact of Handicapped Students on Other Students in the Classroom." *Journal of Research and Development in Education* 12 (Summer 1979): 80–92.

Brookover, Wilbur B., and Erickson, Edsel L. *Sociology of Education.* Homewood, Ill.: Dorsey Press, 1975.

Brookover, Wilbur B., and others. "Elementary School Social Climate and School Achievement." *American Educational Research Journal* 15 (Spring 1978): 301–18.

Devin-Sheehan, Linda; Feldman, Robert S.; and Allen, Vernon L. "Research on Children Tutoring Children: A Critical Review." *Review of Educational Research* 46 (Summer 1976): 355–86.

Horwitz, Robert A. "Psychological Effects of the Open Classroom." *Review of Educational Research* 49 (Winter 1979): 71–86.

Lonsdale, Richard C. "Maintaining the Organization in Dynamic Equilibrium." In *Behavioral Science and Educational Administration,* Sixty-Third Yearbook of the National Society for the Study of Education, Part 2, edited by Daniel E. Griffiths. Chicago: University of Chicago Press, 1964.

McGee, Charles S.; Kauffman, James M.; and Nussen, Judith L. "Children as Therapeutic Change Agents: Reinforcement Intervention Paradigms." *Review of Educational Research* 47 (Summer 1977): 451–77.

Mullen, D. J. *A Diagnostic Study of the Human Organization in Schools*, Final Report, Project 3-0476. Washington, D.C.: National Institute of Education, 1976.

Schmuck, Richard A., and Schmuck, Patricia A. *A Humanistic Psychology of Education — Making the School Everybody's House*. Palo Alto, Calif.: National Press Books, 1974.

Silberman, Charles E. *Crisis in the Classroom: The Remaking of American Education*. New York: Random House, 1970.

12

Community

MARIO D. FANTINI

Citizen involvement, especially parental involvement, in the processes of education is deep-rooted in American history. Lay participation has been a matter of policy as well as practice in our public schools since their founding. Today, lay boards of education act as school trustees in local systems nationwide. Schools, in turn, have become extensions of the family home as teachers and administrative officials find themselves assuming parental tasks with accordant responsibility and, indeed, occasional strain.

That educational personnel are called upon to serve in loco parentis indicates the functional tie between institution and home. It suggests, too, the complex nature of that bond insofar as the concept, as explicitly stated, affirms a parental element within the educational process at the same time that it transfers parental authority to the schools. As a result, the in loco parentis association is, in some respects, one of opposition as well as identification —

Note: The author acknowledges, with gratitude, the contributions made to this work by Marcia S. Curtis and Vanessa Mas.

the more schools assume parental offices, the more parents become removed from direct involvement in the schools.

The double-bind of lay participation in education reflects the basic democratic principles out of which such participation originated. The abdication of immediate citizen involvement in the governance and business of public schools is as true to democratic theory as is the assertion of one's right to direct control. Parents have different participatory roles or functions in the schools, all of which fall under the broad description "parent participation." We may distinguish three general categories of parental involvement in the schools: parents as decision makers, directly involved in the governance and the policy-making decisions of the schools; parents as educational producers, actively involved in the labor of teaching, either inside or outside the school; and parents as clients, receiving more or less critically the educational services of the professional personnel in the schools. In a democracy we recognize the value of parent participation in matters of governance as a right. Even without evaluating the possible impact on student achievement, governance-related participation is an end in itself in a democratic society and must be valued as such. However, the other forms of parental involvement in the schools are clearly recognizable as means to an end — the end being an increase in student achievement. We must keep these distinctions in mind when we review the literature dealing with assessments of parent participation in the schools.

A REVIEW OF THE LITERATURE

Contemporary evidence tells us that public education is not only a professional business; it is the public's business, too. Therefore, we find the community quite naturally seeking to reestablish its rightful role in this process and to reevaluate educational procedures within the current climate of reform.

Historical evidence, furthermore, affirms that we cannot overlook the past. Nor can we afford to design future systems without building upon research already at hand. We can, however, set our perimeters to coincide with present needs and demands. To do so, we first must concentrate our study upon the efficacy of community participation as one means toward a subsequent educational end. This is not to deny the very valid consideration of community participation as an end in itself, to be guarded for itself. But as such, community involvement as a valued right and political act — whether direct or representational — requires no further justification. But as it affects student achievement (including reading, writing, and self-concepts), the phenomenon of parental participation does ask for continued exploration as well as delineation.

Such is the purpose of our survey: to suggest the impact community participation may have upon learning as it pertains not only to one's environment but also to one's place there. Further defining our examination of present research and practice, we have established, once again, a continuum of involvement, which places indirect representative types of citizen action at one end and direct classical types of democratic commitment at the other. We have also recognized an additional subdivision that sets intervention for school governance apart from parental intervention for immediate service to child development and to education. Of equal importance in themselves, these two diverse forms may have distinctly unequal bearing upon actual academic performance and individual achievement. The distinction, therefore, is significant and perhaps even crucial. As we review the literature on the relationship between citizen participation and school achievement, we will emphasize the role of parents as instructional complements to the school, although we will also survey the effects of lay governance on learning and self-concept.

The Coleman report (1966), one of the most comprehensive bodies of data collected during the 1960s, will serve as another foundation of research. We are working with a small and restricted body of literature. In fact, Filipczak, Lordeman, and Friedman (1977) concluded that while advantages to involvement are claimed to be numerous, the causal linkages between increase in involvement and the subsequent benefits are not often clearly stated, except possibly in a group of studies in the field of parent training. There is, in short, a serious lack of data on the effects of increased parental involvement in the schools, as Stearns and Peterson (1973) noted.

Stearns and Peterson, however, do verify our basic premise that the forms of parental participation must be distinguished. Regarding federal programs that require parent involvement (including

the Right to Read, Title I of the Elementary and Secondary Education Act, Follow Through, and the Bilingual/Bicultural Program),
they observed three manifestations of parental activity: parents as
tutors of preschool children and school-age children; parents as
paid school employees, and parents as administrative advisors and
decision makers. Stearns and Peterson (1973) further observed this
phenomenon: for parents as employees and parents as decision
makers, no direct evidence was found to confirm or reject the basic
hypothesis about impact on children, although there is evidence of
benefits to participating adults.

Liechty (1979) identified five types of educational participants
within a county school district: "inactives," "voters," "parents"
(those involved in a particular activity for self and family),
"citizens" (those engaged in elective activities and cooperative endeavors), and "activists" (those responsible for cooperative activities and dynamic endeavors). Participation, clearly, is not the same
across the board. This study substantiates the obvious expectation
that different groups within a given community will choose different types of participation in that community.

The Coleman report, based upon self-administered questionnaires distributed among school principals and teachers, has
spurred a limited number of subsequent surveys. One such reassessment of the Coleman data, carried out by Jencks (1972), concluded that PTA attendance does relate significantly to school
achievement. In reading and mathematics tests, children of parents belonging to local PTAs scored between two and four months
above those children whose parents did not regularly attend.

However, Madaus and others (1979) found evidence directly
contradicting the conclusions of the Coleman report. The results
of a long-term, large-scale longitudinal study of schools in Ireland
suggest that differences in school characteristics such as academic
atmosphere and activities significantly affect student achievement.
Furthermore, this study found individually designed tests to be
more accurate and sensitive indicators of school achievement than
the standardized tests, warning us against misinterpreting previous data based on these standardized test results. Although we
must allow for differences in the school systems in Ireland and the
United States, Madaus's study does allow us to define factors in the
schools that significantly influence student achievement, among

them a climate of high expectations and a commitment to high academic values in the schools.

During the 1960s, a number of parent-focused intervention programs brought community members into direct teaching relationships with preschool and school-age children. Like the Stearns-Peterson work, these programs indicate that such relationships typically show a greater impact upon actual achievement than do the more formal PTA-governance relationships, which mainly affect self-concept rather than learning. Watson (1977), for instance, evaluated an experimental school curriculum that focused on community involvement in Gainesville, Florida. Examining pre- and poststudy achievement scores on six sections of the Scholastic Achievement Test, Watson found generally higher scores among students actively involved in the community with a significant increase in language achievement. A study coordinated by Jackson for the Dade County Public Schools corroborated Watson's findings with evidence that for each 2.5 months of tutorial assistance provided by a community volunteer, reading and mathematics scores increased by 1.5 years, as measured by the Metropolitan Reading and Mathematics Tests.

Wagenaar (1977) conducted a similar study to investigate the relationship between school achievement and community support. Wagenaar's hypothesis was that schools experiencing high levels of community involvement have higher achievement levels than those experiencing low levels of involvement and support. Data were gathered from official documents made available by the school system, and questionnaires were sent to principals in a sample of 135 elementary schools. Findings indicated that several dimensions of community involvement and support have a moderate positive relationship with achievement in schools with both high and low socioeconomic status, but no relationship was found between achievement level and community participation in decision making.

Baker (1971) concluded that parent participation influences the learning environment, which is related to a significant degree to changes in learners. In an evaluation of a family school program conducted in the school district in University City, Missouri, Spencer (1979) reported data supporting the hypothesis that a significant relationship exists between family involvement and reading achievement. More specifically, Spencer's data revealed that students in grades eight and nine made greater gains in reading achievement than did students in grades three to six. In another study, Armor and associates (1976) reported on the role of parents in aiding schools to implement successful reading programs. Between 1972 and 1975, poor black and Mexican-American sixth-grade students in twenty elementary schools in Los Angeles showed significant increases in reading scores. In black neighborhoods the more vigorous the school efforts to involve parents in community and school decision making, the better sixth-grade students in those schools fared in reading attainment.

In a review of programs in which parents stay at home as volunteers, Maethner (n.d.) reported that educators in St. Paul, Minnesota, have developed an ongoing home-based program involving parents as tutors for their own children. Mothers, fathers, and grandparents of over 50 percent of the students in participating schools have been trained to assist their youngsters in mathematics as a supplement to the normal school curriculum. As a result, student achievement in this area has jumped significantly.

Berlin and Berlin (1973) confirmed Maethner's conclusions with findings pertinent to Head Start programs nationwide. They found that school programs of remediation showed no lasting effect, except for children whose mothers became directly involved in the classroom process. They also pointed out the functional relationship between improved school achievement and self-concept in children. To continue parental involvement in the education of children, the authors suggested that the schools embark on a parent-effectiveness training program that might enhance parents as educators of their children.

Finally, in the most systematic study yet of the educational consequences of parental involvement, Guttentag (1972) assessed the productivity of one experimental district in Harlem during the late 1960s. Did children in the experimental Intermediate School 201 (IS 201) learn any more than they had before community participation in the former organization? Guttentag referred to the results of the 1971 achievement testing and compared IS 201 scores with those of New York City as a whole during 1968–69. Children in IS 201, especially first and second graders, did well in the context of city-wide figures. Guttentag cited one IS 201 school that surpassed national norms in reading. Reading levels in IS 201 schools held up in 1968–69 at a time when city reading levels fell. Mean scores on achievement tests rose between 1969 and 1971 in the second through sixth grades. She concluded that achievement in the community-controlled schools apparently improved during their three years of existence. As far as self-concept is concerned, the IS 201 children seemed more optimistic about their own success, with an enhanced sense of control of fate, than was the case with comparison children. Both credit for success and blame for failure tended to be placed by children on teachers, parents, and schools rather than on themselves. Guttentag reported that they more often gave credit to teachers for their own good performance than did comparison children. This strong orientation toward significant others may well be related to external control attitudes thought to be central to feelings of fate-control and therefore to self-concept formation.

CONCLUSION

The review of the literature thus far leads to the following tentative conclusions. Of the two basic patterns of community participation, participation for school governance shows no significant impact on school achievement, except for the self-concept of the child whose parents participate in school governance. Such children exhibit an enhanced self-image, although the evidence is inconclusive.

On the other hand, the pattern of involvement that focuses directly upon the educational process, with the parent participating as an educator, does show a relationship to school achievement in reading and mathematics as well as self-concept. Thus to a certain degree, the different forms of parental participation are recognized in the existing body of literature, some of which acknowledges parental participation as an end in itself and a valuable activity regardless of its effect on students' academic achievement or on the development of self-concepts. However, when the results of parental participation in the schools are examined, the research suggests that only those forms of participation directly involved in instruction have a positive measurable impact on achievement and self-concepts in the schools. The result is a trend toward greater efforts in the training of parents as teachers and a continued rise in volunteer efforts in schools. The closer collaboration of the home and the school in the affairs of improving students' achievement is similarly gaining greater support.

In the aftermath of the reviews of federal intervention programs of the 1960s and 1970s, it is safe to conclude that the more the scholastic objectives are clarified, the more the participants are prepared to assume roles in the instructional process, and the more likely are measurable differences in academic performance. The more global forms of participation in the governance of schools are less likely to have consequences for the scholastic performance of students, with some noticeable exceptions. The trend toward increased participation, however, is continuing not only in the federal programs requiring increased parental participation, but also in states such as California and Florida, which have mandated participation at the individual school level. The formation of parent councils and district-wide advisory councils are in part a response to the call for increased accountability. Such councils, combined with increased parent-as-educator models of participation, are now being viewed as contributing maximally to increased performance on the part of students, as well as to a new responsiveness on the part of school officials to the aspirations of the community they serve.

REFERENCES

Armor, David, and others. *Analysis of the School Preferred Reading Program in Selected Los Angeles Minority Schools.* ED 130 243. Santa Monica, Calif.: RAND Corporation, 1976.

Baker, Wanda Harris. "Effects of Preschool Enrollment and Parent Participation on Academic Growth." Doctoral dissertation, University of Southern California, 1971.

Berlin, Roxie, and Berlin, Irving N. "School's Training of Parents To Be Effective Teachers." (1973). ED 099 110.

Coleman, James S., and others. *Equality of Educational Opportunity.* Washington, D.C.: U.S. Government Printing Office, 1966.

Filipczak, James; Lordeman, Anne; and Friedman, Robert M. "Parental Involvement in the Schools: Toward What End?" Paper presented at the annual meeting of the American Educational Research Association, New York City, April 1977.

Guttentag, Marcia. "Children in Harlem's Community Controlled Schools." *Journal of Social Issues* 28, no. 4 (1972): 1–20.

Jackson, Audrey, and others. *Plan, Polish, Promote, and Practice: A School Volunteer Program.* ED 091 396. Gainesville: Florida Educational Research and Development Council, 1974.

Jencks, Christopher S. "The Coleman Report and the Conventional Wisdom." In Frederick Mosteller and Daniel P. Moynihan, *On Equality of Educational Opportunity.* New York: Vintage Books, 1972.

Liechty, Thornton A. "Patterns of Citizen Participation in Education." Paper presented at the annual meeting of the American Educational Research Association, San Francisco, April 1979.

Madaus, George F., and others. "The Sensitivity of Measures of School Effectiveness." *Harvard Educational Review* 49 (May 1979): 207–230.

Maethner, Judith A. *Parents at Home: The New Volunteers.* Washington, D.C.: National School Volunteer Program, n.d.

Spencer, Thomas L. "An Evaluation of the Family School Program, 1977–1978." Paper presented at the Conference on Education, University City School District, University City, Mo., March 1979.

Stearns, M. S., and Peterson, S. N. *Parent Involvement in Compensatory Education Programs: Definitions and Findings.* Menlo Park, Calif.: Educational Policy Research Center, Stanford Research Institute, 1973.

Wagenaar, Theodore C. "School Achievement Level vis-à-vis Community Involvement and Support: An Empirical Assessment." Paper presented at the annual meeting of the American Sociological Association, Chicago, 1977.

Watson, K. J. *The Going Places Classroom: A Community Involvement Program of Action Learning for Elementary Students.* Research Monograph no. 23. Gainesville: University of Florida, 1977.

Discussion

Miriam Clasby and James Stanton

We are in strong agreement with Fantini's assertion that he is working with a restricted body of literature and that the cited research emphasizes the lack of data on the effects of increased parental involvement in the schools. In his paper "What Does Research Say about the Effects of Parent Involvement on Schooling?" the late Ira Gordon states: "The evaluation and research methodological problems inherent in evaluating and assessing whether parent involvement makes a difference [on educational achievement] are many and complex, especially if one attempts to assess the national efforts" (1978, p. 10). The complexities of the research task suggest the need for great caution in interpreting findings and lead us to take issue with Fantini because of (a) the incompleteness of the research findings and (b) the weakness of the analysis of the problems of governance-related participation.

INCOMPLETENESS OF RESEARCH FINDINGS

Fantini's survey of research findings raises two major concerns: critical background information is lacking for each of the studies, and findings are woven together without attention to the problems of comparability. As presented, the research simply does not provide an adequate basis for deriving implications. It is premature to draw firm conclusions without more information on each of the projects: their explicit goals, the background of their student and community and parent participants, the roles of professional educators and support staff, the substance of the project, the amount and frequency of parent and community involvement, the procedures for measuring outcomes, and the relationship of project activities to other home and school activities.

Similarly, although the findings are informative, the loose connections between the kinds of programs reported on and the contradictory nature of some of the findings make it difficult to define the links between parent and community participation and student achievement. We thus have few answers to such critical questions as:

1. Does who provides the increased instructional time make a difference in terms of gains in student achievement?
2. Is the parent's role in the school more effective than the parent's role in the home, or are both necessary to improve student achievement?
3. Which instructional strategies yield the best results for parents and students, enhancing the child's self-concept, teaching concepts and teaching skills? Must the strategies be individualized?

4. How is the role of the school maximized?
Without answers to these kinds of questions, policy options cannot
be clearly outlined.

PROBLEMS OF GOVERNANCE-RELATED
   PARTICIPATION

We feel that further elaboration is needed on Fantini's assertion
in his conclusion that participation for school governance shows no
significant impact upon school achievement, with the exception of
the self-concept of the child of individual governing parents.
There are sound explanations why research on school governance
produces such findings: this type of participation has not been
specifically designed to improve student performance, and, furthermore, such participation has been weakly implemented.

Because councils and advisory committees are the predominant
vehicle for citizen participation in educational decision making and
because most existing councils result from one of the many federal
mandates for councils, it is important to review regulations governing these programs. The specific mandated responsibilities for
parents focus on such tasks as deciding on eligibility of children
and participating in and approving proposals for refunding programs. Regulations historically have not prescribed any programmatic activity or process, any technical assistance, or any funding
whereby citizen participation in decision making could reasonably
be expected to have an impact on student achievement. Thus,
research looks for an outcome when the activity is not specifically
focused to achieve that outcome and when there are no programmatic and financial resources specifically directed to achieve
that goal. Evaluation of nonprograms is of limited usefulness.
Rather than assume that the absence of a demonstrated relationship between governance-related participation and student
outcomes means that there is no relationship, we must make clear
that, given common patterns of governance-related participation
and its research, we simply do not know the nature of the relationship.

Further, for a variety of reasons beyond the control of councils,
the vast amount of available evidence suggests that citizen participation in decision making is not showing a significant impact on

even their mandated responsibilities. In her report "Parent Involvement in Contemporary Education Programs," McLaughlin (n.d.) gives an indication of the problems in the 1960s and early 1970s. The report is based on a review of literature on university demonstration projects and some 500 Title I programs and general literature on compensatory education. Field trips were made to Connecticut, Tennessee, and California to look closely at "model" parent involvement projects. The report states: "By law, Title I programs are required to have a District Advisory Council (DAC) which includes parents and through which parents can make their feelings regarding resource allocation and program design known. We were unable to locate an evaluation which indicated a DAC functioned as intended by law. Where DAC membership and responsibilities are understood, parents are often prevented from assuming them" (p. 8). The author concludes: "The great majority of compensatory programs, especially Title I, subscribe to the first formulation of the parent role (parents as passive recipients of program services and efforts). . . . Most compensatory programs, by their very design, lock the parent into the role of recipient and preclude the involvement of parents at any significant level in program operation or in the process of education" (p. 9).

In a recent evaluation of parent involvement in compensatory education programs, Kaplan and Forgione (1978) draw on data from an investigation of Elementary and Secondary Educational Assistance Title I activities in eight state departments of education and thirty-two school districts. A major component of each of the forty case studies was the issue of parents' involvement. Parents, professional educators, and community representatives were interviewed at the school and district levels, and the issue of parental involvement in compensatory education programs was also examined in interviews with state and federal administrators of compensatory education. In describing the problems in parent participation, Kaplan and Forgione state: "Measured on a district-by-district basis, effective parent involvement would seem to be the exception rather than the rule. Problems of educator apathy and lack of commitment, limited PAC [Parents Advisory Council] role conceptions, inadequate communications and training activities, and problematic membership policies all contributed to this situation in most of the districts visited in the study" (p. 12).

The central point made in these and other studies examining

effectiveness of school councils (for example, Cunningham and others 1978, Stanton and Zerchykov 1979) is that, given the lack of direction and support, governance-related participation exists more in rhetoric than in practice. In the following section, alternate perspectives on parent involvement lead to different conclusions about the policy implications of research findings.

ALTERNATE PERSPECTIVES

Before outlining a conceptual framework, assessing research evidence, and interpreting research findings, it is important to emphasize that this discussion rests on the assumption that the individual school is the appropriate locus for most intense and productive school-community relationships. This assumption is reinforced by recent attention to school-site management (Cunningham and others 1978), and it carries a number of implications for decentralization of decision-making responsibilities to the school level. It is outside our scope here to address organizational issues inherent in a heightened emphasis on the individual school, but the trend has potential for strongly influencing the quality and style of community participation in schools.

We present four basic propositions about community participation in schools, which will be supported by research evidence:

1. Conceptual wholeness: it is helpful to examine programmatic goals and design in the context of a holistic view of community participation in schools.
2. System integration: to avoid "blaming the victim" — shunting the burden of instructional outcomes from the school to the parents and the community — it is essential to consider community participation in relationship to the total school operation.
3. Rules of evidence: to prevent the dangers of relying on inadequate information and building policies and practices on false certitude, it is essential to acknowledge the limitations of current measures of student outcomes and of survey and case study research on participation.
4. The state of the art: to avoid premature formulation of policies and practices for community participation, it is necessary to clarify long-range purposes and to develop policies and practices through a participatory planning process.

In general, propositions 1, 2, and 4 suggest guidelines for program development, while proposition 3 raises a caveat for research design. Here the first two propositions will be used to build a conceptual framework for the discussion.

Conceptual Wholeness

Relying on a concept of community participation that treats various modes as discrete entities militates against designing policies and practices that are interrelated and mutually reinforcing. Conversely, a holistic view of community participation provides a base for a "system" approach. The following figures suggest one way of conceptualizing school-community relationships as an interactive network:

1. As a public institution, the school is an entity with permeable boundaries, open to its "community," with both general and specific channels for communication exchange. (See Figure 12-1.)

2. Activities such as volunteer tutoring by parents and community members, parents hired as classroom aides, programs for parent education, home visits, and parent-teacher conferences can be categorized and "instruction-related." In addition to providing a range of additional resources for instruction, these activities also build communication channels among school personnel and community members. (See Figure 12-2.)

3. Other activities, such as special-purpose task forces, PTA, and parent advisory councils, can be categorized as governance or decision-making related, with communication exchanges between school and community. (See Figure 12-3.)

4. Some individuals may be members of several groups. Also, various instructional groups may be represented in decision-making groups. Maximizing these mutual relationships increases communication exchange both internally (within constituted groups) and externally (with the larger community). (See Figure 12-4.) This final diagram makes it easier to focus on two different types of structures (instruction-related and governance-related) and the communication exchange, which they depend upon and facilitate.

Figure 12-1.
The School Open to the Community

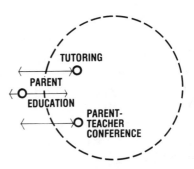

Figure 12-2.
Examples of Instruction-Related Involvement and Related Communication Channels

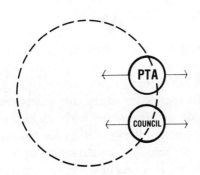

Figure 12-3.
Examples of Governance-Related Involvement and Related Communication Channels

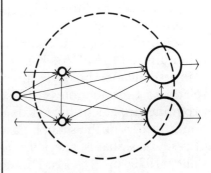

Figure 12-4.
Communication Channels: Instruction-Related and Governance-Related Involvement

Several different types of studies tentatively affirm the importance of a holistic approach and the central function of communication channels in that approach. The Home-School-Community Relationship Project at the Wisconsin Research and Development Center has attempted to focus on various approaches that are an integral part of any systematic approach to strengthening the relationship between the home and the school (Ingram 1979). In a case study conducted in an inner-city school serving minority students, sixty-four parents of students in grades four to six were interviewed to examine the relationships between effective school-community relations and student achievement. Activities involving school-community relations included extensive use of the telephone, volunteer services (and donations) by parents, and three advisory councils associated with federal programs.

Three different statistical procedures were used to analyze the data organized in the five variables of access, communication, involvement, participation, and (problem) resolution. Communication was the most important variable for an effective school-community relations program (explaining 49 percent of the variance). Although no single school-community relations activity showed a positive impact on student achievement, the data clearly indicated that resolution had a positive impact on student achievement: "Parents viewed themselves as playing a meaningful role in solving problems because staff members sought their opinions and often utilized them" (p. 12). After noting the importance of the principal's leadership style and of staff attitude toward community relations, Ingram notes: "Effective school-community relations programs appear to have little or no relationships with socioeconomic factors of the school, past program, [or] unusual allocation of resources, that is, specialization in media or public relationship skills" (1979, pp. 13–14). He urges consideration of using a wide variety of mechanisms that incorporate one-way and two-way communication.

Although two additional case studies are underway at Wisconsin, the body of evidence to date must be considered exploratory rather than definitive. A related study at the same Research and Development Center, however, reinforces the importance of a holistic approach that allows for differentiation of role — providing opportunities for parents and citizens to engage in a wide range of activities. The study draws on a conceptual framework originally developed by Verba and Nie (1972) for analyzing political participation. The findings highlight the broad base of participants (95 percent engaged in at least one educational activity). Nevertheless, different groups of participators specialized in selected kinds of educational activity.

Liechty (1979) interviewed 130 registered voters in a county school district and used factor analysis to identify five types of educational participators:

1. Inactives — 5 percent (less than Verba and Nie inactives).
2. Voters — 17 percent (same as Verba and Nie voters).
3. Parents — 24 percent (same as Verba and Nie "parochial" participants, engaging in particularized activity for self and family).
4. Citizens — 17 percent (less than Verba and Nie's "communalists," engaging in cooperative and elective activities).
5. Activists — 37 percent (much larger than Verba and Nie's activists, accounting for more than 50 percent of the total activists engaging in cooperative and dynamic activities). Nearly 40 percent of those interviewed engaged in one or more activities described as difficult (requiring most initiative).

These data are descriptive, but they suggest that participants are not homogeneous, and they support the expectation that different groups of people will opt for different modes of involvement.

One of the most compelling arguments for a system approach appears in *Men and Women of the Corporation*, a study in which Kanter (1977) identified structural constraints within an organization that produce both deviant and positive behaviors. Drawing on systematic interviews and survey data, she hypothesized that behaviors are influenced by (1) the structure of opportunity; (2) the structure of power; and (3) the relative numbers (tokenism). She concluded with recommendations for structural changes to increase opportunity, share power, and reduce tokenism. Because personnel were restricted in the ways they could use their talents and skills to make contributions, the organization lost valuable resources, and the frustrations produced alienated or hostile behaviors.

Both the methodology and the findings of the corporate-sector study hold important implications for education and the public service sector. They point to the importance of examining organizational arrangements and the ways in which they advance or obstruct progress toward goals by contracting or expanding the range of resources mobilized to achieving common goals. But a full system view places school-community relations within the context of the total school operation; this leads to the second proposition.

System Integration

For more than a decade, academic research has emphasized the statistical significance of nonschool variables on student performance (sex, race, father's education, and so forth), and some research issues related to this will be addressed in this section. One consequence of this emphasis, however, is a tendency to use family background as an explanation for underachievement by students. Given such a situation, school activities designed to engage parents in instructional activities or decision making run a substantial risk of deflecting responsibility from the schools and placing it on the individual and the family. In this context the growing body of literature on instructional effectiveness merits attention. Some of the research draws on preschool experience, and some specifically addresses the issue of school effectiveness for low-income and minority students.

The Consortium of Development Continuity conducted long-term follow-up studies of fourteen infant and preschool experiments (Lazar 1977). Careful and complex secondary analysis indicated that low-income children who had participated in preschool programs were far less likely to be assigned to special education programs or to be held back in grade than similar children who had not participated in such programs and that these positive effects continued through the critical years of primary school. To identify the programs that were most effective in improving school performance, researchers rated twenty-one programs on twenty-five variables such as goals, length and sequence of program, and staff training and ratios. All programs were equally effective in reducing the percentages of children retained a grade in school. Certain types of programs, however, were more effective than others in reducing the percentages of children placed in special education, and these programs had the following characteristics: high adult/ child ratio, goals to improve parent behavior, high parental involvement, visits by program staff to the child's home, program staff worked with children at an early age. Within the context of a structured educational program, parental involvement emerges as a significant variable.

In a review of the literature of effective schools, Edmonds (1979) gives special attention to a study by Brookover and Lezotte (1977), which used state-mandated criterion-referenced measures of student performance in basic skills to identify elementary schools characterized by consistent improvement or decline in pupil performance. In relating the findings of this study to his efforts to identify and analyze schools that are instructionally effective for poor children, Edmonds noted that "the overriding point here is that, in and of itself, pupil family background neither causes nor precludes elementary school instructional effectiveness" (p. 31). In summarizing the range of factors identified as contributing to school effectiveness, he points to four as consistently essential instructional determinants of pupil performance: leadership by the principal, especially in the area of instruction; high expectations for students; atmosphere conducive to learning; and emphasis on instruction with related assessment of progress.

These data on school effectiveness assume central importance in any discussion of the relationship between parent and citizen participation and student performance because they reinforce the responsibility and potential of the school for influencing student performance and they point out directions for accomplishing that task. At another level, the data suggest that, in the absence of such features as leadership, expectations, atmosphere and instructional emphasis within the school, activities designed to have an impact on student performance by increasing community participation are, at best, incomplete and, at worst, diversionary.

A more complete view of a school comunity partnership, then, calls for an integrated model, in which activities for community participation, whether instruction-related or governance-related, are set within a school context characterized by leadership, high expectations, atmosphere for learning, and instructional emphasis. Furthermore, various modes of participation are interrelated through formal and informal communication channels.

Relying on this conceptual framework, we now turn to the core question: To what extent, if any, does a program for community participation, as substantiated by research in the field, affect students' performance in schools or their self-concept? This formulation of the question assumes that the goal of community participation is the improvement of student performance. Accepting this assumption means that discussion will focus on issues related to student outcomes and ignore issues related to alternate goals for community participation (such as the political goals of strengthening the accountability of public institutions, providing opportunities for the exercise of citizenship or building community cohesiveness).

Rules of Evidence

Despite the apparent value of establishing a causal link between community participation and student performance, we take the position that the norm-referenced standardized instruments most commonly used for measuring student outcomes are inadequate, and, therefore, inappropriate, to use as criteria for making decisions about programs for community participation in schools. Furthermore, neither large-scale statistical studies nor narrowly focused case studies provide grounds for certitude to guide policy and practice.

The case against the use of available student outcome data rests primarily on the recent history of research on school inputs and outputs.

For more than a decade, the findings of the Equal Educational Opportunity Survey, known as the Coleman report (1966), have dominated social science research on schools. Coleman found that black students had access to educational resources nearly equal to those of white students, but that black student performance was substantially below white student performance (just as the poor performed below the affluent). The differences in performance seemed to be explained by family background: "Schools bring little influence to bear on a child's achievement that is independent of his background and general social context" (p. 325).

Reanalyses of the Coleman data (Jencks and others 1972) and other studies (for example, Mayeske and others 1972) have produced mixed results, some reaffirming the original conclusions, others challenging them. A recent report of a large-scale longitudinal study of schools in Ireland (Madaus and others 1979) directly contradicts the Coleman findings. Designed primarily to compare standardized nonreferenced tests and curriculum-oriented tests in terms of their sensitivity to instruction, this research provides strong evidence that differences in school characteristics do contribute to differences in achievement, and that tests geared to the curricula of the schools are more sensitive indicators of school performance than norm-referenced standardized tests. The authors warn against misreading their findings. Previous studies did not use the classroom as the unit of analysis, and differences between school systems in Ireland and in the United States may explain some of the differences in results. In general, however, the study shows clearly that school resources can contribute to student achievement. Predictors of achievement, for the most part, reflect the climate or activities of the school rather than static characteristics, such as size, physical amenities, and teacher qualifications. The most important factors affecting achievement are "the academic demands of courses, the students' concern for and commitment to academic values, the amount of time spent on study and homework, and, in general, the climate of high expectations on the part of students and their teachers" (Madaus and others 1979, p. 225).

This emphasis on the inadequacies of norm-referenced standardized tests for assessing the quality of instruction joins a growing chorus of critics. The *National Elementary Principal* (1975), for example, devoted a complete issue to problems related to standardized testing. More recently, Goodlad (1979), in previewing the results of an eight-year, multi-million dollar study of schooling in America, told school administrators: "Much of what is taken to be desirable today for schools will result in a decline in the quality of education provided there, even while test scores go up" (p. 337).

Although some progress has been made in the development of criterion-referenced and minimal competency tests that are sensitive to the curriculum and thus more attuned to differences in schools, academicians are still engaged in what Madaus and others (1979, p. 226) describe as "the search for suitable measures of school outcomes." Given the inadequacy of present testing technology, norm-referenced tests are inappropriate for judging the worth of policies for community participation.

Narrowly focused case studies present a different problem. On the one hand, they avoid the dangers of large-scale statistical studies which, by applying the rational model of the biological and natural sciences to the social sciences, result in "context stripping." Mishler (1979) argues that the search for lawful generalizations that are valid across contexts may well be a misdirected search, because investigators in the social and psychological sciences are learning that findings appear to be dependent on context. Case studies provide a more in-depth look at school operations; they tend to place behaviors in a meaningful context, illuminating complexities and variations. On the other hand, it is extraordinarily difficult to accumulate knowledge in a way that leads to generalizations because individual case studies lack both consistency in perspective and rigor in analysis.

The Ingram study (1979) cited earlier emphasized the importance of the leadership role of the principal in school-community relationships and concluded that effective school-community programs appear to have little or no relationship to socioeconomic factors, additional resources, or specialized skills. Another case study from the Wisconsin Research and Development Center, however, specifically focused on supports and constraints influencing school-community relations (Bartels 1979) and reached different conclusions. In the Bartels study, the first influential factor supporting the school-community relations program was the allocation of Elementary and Secondary Education Act (ESEA) Title I funds and special state funds both requiring home-school communications and parents' involvement in program planning. The decentralized program planning and the political leadership style of the principal were identified as the two chief factors contributing to success. Another external factor — a district desegregation plan — introduced a serious constraint by producing changes in the teaching staff which threatened to jeopardize both the individualized instructional program and the tradition of talking candidly to parents.

By using a different lens, by focusing on supports and constraints, Bartels arrived at conclusions in some ways similar and in some ways contradictory to the Ingram study. Both studies identify the role of the principal as pivotal, but Bartels's study found that external factors produced positive and negative impacts on school-community relations. Such small-scale, context-rich studies of single schools cannot produce any more certitude than statistical research based on standardized tests, but they can bring critical issues to the surface and provide a base of knowledge for further exploration.

Given the limitations of existing research, then, what grounds are appropriate for making decisions concerning community participation in schools? Drawing on trend data, on documentation of recent experiences, and on the previously described studies of school effectiveness, we can develop a position on community participation in schools that is grounded in logic.

The State of the Art

Since the middle of the 1960s, various federal and state initiatives have given new legitimacy to community participation in schools. Almost every piece of federal legislation since the Elementary and Secondary Education Act of 1965 has included provisions for participation by representatives of those being served. Both the federal Freedom of Information Act and the state "sunshine" laws have opened citizens' access to public decision making. Court decisions on student rights and on school desegregation have affirmed the role of citizens in public institutions.

At the same time, national opinion polls consistently confirm citizens' willingness to work more closely with schools. For example, in the eighth annual Gallup poll of public attitudes toward the public schools (Gallup 1976), 90 percent of those surveyed were willing to serve on citizen advisory committees (appointed by local school boards) to deal with school problems such as discipline, teacher evaluation, curriculum, textbook evaluation, athletic programs, and the like. Another 77 percent approved the idea of courses for parents to help them help their children in school.

This broad legitimation of, and general support for, public participation in schools represents a new direction. This direction, however, runs directly counter to a previous pattern of professional domination of schools (Zeigler 1974, *School District Governance* 1977). Both the newness of the phenomenon and the departure from past experience combine to produce an unsettling situation.

Using the twofold categorization of instruction-related and governance-related modes of participation, we can examine pertinent documentation of recent experiences for each mode. Although we have outlined our reservations about the use of standardized achievement tests, we accept the array of evidence which indicates that instruction-related participation improves student performance — the expected outcome, in light of the literature on school effectiveness. Any intervention designed to increase instructional emphasis, whether by parents or volunteer tutors, also points to characteristics of principals' leadership, high expectations for students, and an atmosphere conducive to learning — the characteristics of effective schools identified by Edmonds.

There are at least three ways to build an argument in support of governance-related community participation. First, such an intervention can be seen as an exercise of leadership to increase expectations, improve climate, and strengthen instructional emphasis, contributing to school effectiveness and thus, indirectly, to student achievement. Second, a system approach to school-community relations incorporates multiple modes of participation to improve school climate and to build a base of widespread understanding of, and support for, school operations. Finally, solid evidence substantiates the conventional wisdom that group decision making produces better decisions than individual decision making (*Participative Decision Making* 1977). For all of these reasons, community participation may contribute to school effectiveness and thus, indirectly, to student achievement.

In principle, then, both instruction-related and governance-related participation can be judged to be positive policies. The next question is, How should the interventions be made? Here, too, the instruction-related participation has clearer documentation. A wide array of demonstrably effective programs are available; for example, in *Educational Programs That Work,* the U.S. Office of Education (1978) has identified a variety of programs validated by research as successful; details on necessary administrative structure, training, and support services are available from each program.

Documentation on governance-related participation is much more problematic because models have been designed at both federal and state levels, but implementation has been extremely spotty. Despite increasingly specific regulations and legislation for ESEA Title I Advisory Councils — the largest federal initiative for parent participation — evidence is accumulating that many councils exist only as token or paper groups, if they exist at all. An evaluation of school councils in Florida, conducted four years after they were mandated by the state, estimated that fewer than 10 percent were functioning as deliberative groups (Cunningham and others 1978, p. 268). The analysis described a pattern of "devolution of responsibility." The legislation assigned responsibility to principals who were burdened with implementing a requirement without preparation and without incentives for compliance. Although in California and South Carolina, recent legislation that ties school councils to state funding patterns seems to offer promise of somewhat more positive results, the clear message emerging from recent state experience is that mandates alone produce minimal resslts (Davies and others 1978a).

The weak record of mandates for community participation in school governance signals a generalizable problem inherent in any intervention to increase the role of citizens in schools. This type of intervention is not simply an educational innovation, and it cannot be examined solely in terms of educational consequences. Interventions that bring parents and citizens to the schools have organizational as well as social and political consequences that must be considered in the development of policy. Instruction-related activities, for example, shift the roles and responsibilities of teachers, their relationships with students, and their interactions with other adults. Governance-related activities shift the roles and responsibilities of administrators, their relationships with staff and with the central office, and their interactions with the community. Whether these shifts are positive or negative in character, whether professionals are resistant or open, whether community members are compliant, contrary, sophisticated, naive — all depends on a wide range of variables that have not yet been adequately explicated. What is certain is that the consequences will vary according to specific circumstances. Furthermore, the shifts will jostle traditional social and political leadership roles and alignments within the community. Such changes take on added significance and complexity when they are related to efforts to improve equality of educational opportunity.

The organizational and community changes inherent in community participation need not be unanticipated consequences, but recent history indicates that they have not been adequately addressed in shaping school policies and practices. The formulation of any new policy for citizen participation in schools should take into account the failures and frustrations of previous efforts, as well as the tenuous state of the art, to design community participation programs to enhance student achievement.

CONCLUSION

Existing research offers, at best, a weak and frequently misleading base for guiding decisions about community participation in schools. Structured models for instruction-related participation do show evidence of having an impact on student achievement, but it is unclear how they fit into a comprehensive model for community participation. New models of governance-related participation have not been sufficiently implemented to yield impact data. Research both inside and outside the field of education supports the concept of a comprehensive program for instruction-related and governance-related community participation designed to have a direct and indirect impact on student achievement.

Moving beyond data on impact and drawing on analyses of citizen participation prepared for the Institute for Responsive Education (Davies and others 1978b, 1979, Stanton and Zerchykov 1979), we can formulate some guidelines for policy development for community participation:

1. The intent of the policy must be clearly identified, including goals, purposes, incentives, and implementation strategems with realistic time frames.
2. The policy should not be formulated without the participation of those constituencies directly affected by the policy — principals, teachers, parents, school board members, and superintendents.
3. The policy must have sufficient flexibility to accommodate local differences.
4. The policy must be accompanied by the technical assistance and resources necessary to support its implementation.
5. The policy should include a research component that will begin to build a data base appropriate to its goals and purposes.

Policy development is comprehensive, participatory, and long range; open to phased implementation, internally consistent with its goals; and indicative of the commitment of time and resources that it requires for success.

REFERENCES

Bartels, Lois I. "Supports and Constraints to School-Community Relations in an Urban, Inner-City School." Paper presented at the annual meeting of the American Educational Research Association, San Francisco, April 1979.

Brookover, Wilbur B., and Lezotte, Lawrence W. *Changes in School Characteristics Coincident with Changes in Student Achievement.* East Lansing: College of Urban Development, Michigan State University, and Michigan Department of Education, 1977.

Coleman, James S. *Equality of Educational Opportunity.* Washington, D.C.: U.S. Government Printing Office, 1966.

Cunningham, Luvern, and others. *Improving Education in Florida: A Reassessment.* Report prepared for the Select Joint Committee on Public Schools, Florida Legislature, 1978.

Davies, Don, and others. *Federal and State Impact on Citizen Participation in the Schools.* Boston: Institute for Responsive Education, 1978a.

Davies, Don; Clasby, M.; Powers, B.; and Zerchykov, R. *Patterns of Participation in Educational Decision Making.* Vol. 1: *Overview.* Boston: Institute for Responsive Education, 1978b.

Davies, Don, and others. *Patterns of Participation in Educational Decision Making,* Vol. 2: *Grassroots Perspectives.* Boston: Institute for Responsive Education, 1979.

Edmonds, Ronald R. "Some Schools Work and More Can." *Social Policy* 9 (March 1979): 28–32.

ERIC Clearinghouse on Educational Management. *Participative Decision-Making. Research Action Brief.* ED 136 356. Eugene, Ore.: ERIC Clearinghouse on Educational Management, July 1977.

ERIC Clearinghouse on Eductional Management. *School District Governance. How Democratic? Research Action Brief.* ED 144 169. Eugene, Ore.: ERIC Clearinghouse on Educational Management, August 1977.

Gallup, George H. "Eighth Annual Gallup Poll of the Public's Attitudes Toward the Public Schools." *Phi Delta Kappa* 57 (October 1976): 187–200.

Goodlad, John I. "Changes Lowered Educational Quality, Goodlad Says." *Education, U.S.A.,* July 9, 1979, p. 337.

Gordon, Ira J. "What Does Research Say about the Effects of Parent Involvement on Schooling?" Paper presented at the meeting of the Association for Supervision and Curriculum Development, San Francisco, March 1978.

Ingram, John E. "School-Community Relations and Student Achievement." Paper presented at the annual meeting of the American Educational Research Association, San Francisco, April 1979.

Jencks, Christopher; Kellaghan, Thomas; Rakow, Ernest A.; and King, Denis J. *Inequality: A Reassessment of the Effects of Family and Schooling in America.* New York: Basic Books, 1972.

Kanter, Rozabeth M. *Men and Women of the Corporation.* New York: Basic Books, 1977.

Kaplan, Bernard A., and Forgione, Pascal D. "Parent Involvement in Compensatory Education Programs: Problems and Potential Strategies across Thirty-Two School Districts." Paper presented at the annual meeting of the American Educational Research Association, Toronto, Canada, March 1978.

Lazar, I.; Hubell, V. R.; Murray, H.; Rosche, M.; and Royce, J. *Summary Report: The Persistence of Preschool Effects. A Long-Term Follow-up of Fourteen Infant and Preschool Experiments.* DHEW Publications no. (OHDS) 78–30129. Washington, D.C.: U.S. Government Printing Office, 1977.

Leichty, Thornton A. "Patterns of Citizen Participation in Education." Paper presented at the annual meeting of the American Educational Research Association, San Francisco, April 1979.

McLaughlin, Milbrey. *Parent Education in Compensatory Education, Report No. 6* Boston: Center for Educational Policy Research, Harvard University, n.d.

Madaus, George F., and others. "The Sensitivity of Measures of School Effectiveness." *Harvard Educational Review* 49 (May 1979): 207–30.

Mayeske, George W., and others. *A Study of Our Nation's Schools.* DHEW Publication no. (OE) 72–142. Washington, D.C.: U.S. Department of Health, Education, and Welfare, 1972.

Mishler, Elliot G. "Meaning in Context: Is There Any Other Kind?" *Harvard Educational Review* 49 (February 1979): 1–49.

"Scoring of Children: Standardized Testing in America. A Symposium." *National Elementary Principal* 54 (July 1975): 1–109.

Stanton, James, and Zerchykov, R. *Overcoming the Barriers to School Council Effectiveness.* Boston: Institute for Responsive Education, 1979.

U.S. Office of Education. *Educational Programs That Work.* ED 163 664. San Francisco: Far West Laboratory for Educational Research and Development, 1978.

Verba, Sidney, and Nie, Norman H. *Participation in America: Political Democracy and Social Equality.* New York: Harper & Row, 1972.

Zeigler, L. Harmon; Jennings, M. Kent; and Peak. G. W. *Governing American Schools: Political Interaction in Local School Districts.* North Scituate, Mass: Duxbury Press, 1974.

The Georgia State Department Project on Public School Standards

BERNARD A. KAPLAN AND RONALD LUCKIE

This appendix explains the rationale, background, and processes of the Georgia State Department Project on Public School Standards, which generated the present book. Other states, local school districts, or other scholarly and citizen groups may wish to replicate the procedures, extend them, or bring them up-to-date in the future. The two of us, as Consultant to the project and Assistant Superintendent in the Division of Planning, Research, and Evaluation, respectively, helped in formulating the project and recorded the facts and our impression of them during its several phases.

RATIONALE AND BACKGROUND

State school standards were first required for Georgia's public schools in 1964 when the legislature enacted the Minimum Found-

Note: We thank Charles McDaniel, State Superintendent of Schools in Georgia, for his courage to use research findings in policy decisions; H. Titus Singletary, Associate Superintendent, for his leadership and direction; the staff of the Division of Planning, Research, and Evaluation for work beyond the call of duty; and the staff of the Georgia Educational Television Network for outstanding production of the television programs.

ation Program, which required the Georgia State Board of Education to develop and apply standards to each public school in the state. In 1966, the statewide standards were pilot-tested in all schools. During this pilot period, the standards were revised and improved, data were collected on them, and methods of applying the standards were established.

The standards specified the minimum number of library books per child that a school must provide, the minimum educational level of teachers, the minimum number of courses that a school must offer students, and so forth. The standards also dealt with the opportunities and services provided by the school system, including such criteria as the number of supervisory staff available in each area of the curriculum, the presence of written school board policy, and the qualifications of personnel.

The application of these standards became the primary mission of the State Department of Education; the department staff was divided into teams that visited all schools to monitor their application. The standards and monitoring appear to have improved the educational opportunity for students.

In 1974, however, the legislature enacted a new school finance law and required the State Board of Education to establish performance-based criteria with which to evaluate the instructional program of each public school. The State Department and State Board of Education determined that standards or criteria that increase the likelihood of producing positive student performance and self-concept should be encouraged. The concern for positive self-concept of students recognized that certain practices may enhance student academic achievement but could harm the student's personality. Given these two considerations — student achievement and student self-concept, the board was faced with determining appropriate practice within the considerations' constraints. The research literature on student achievement and self-concept was reviewed to determine good practice.

The State Department of Education staff in the Division of Planning, Research, and Evaluation was called upon to address this issue. The staff recognized that few, if any, research findings on educational methodology were so clear-cut that an opponent of the practice could declare the evidence faulty or questionable. The staff also recognized that a great deal of conflicting evidence on any issue or practice exists in the research literature and that this is one reason so little educational research is put into practice. Therefore, the question of evidence became a paramount issue.

The staff was aware that jury trials had been conducted for evaluation purposes, but never for establishing broad policy decisions. However, it became more and more appealing as a method for dealing with conflicting evidence on educational research findings. A plan for placing varying educational practices on trial was developed. Evidence from educational research was argued before a judge and jury. The State Board put practices on trial — not research, not particular standards or criteria, but educational practices or methods that had been researched.

The plan called for standards and criteria to be developed around practices which research evidence supported to the extent that a judge and jury would declare them favorable if the evidence so indicated. This trial system was followed thoroughly.

THE PROCESS

Once the State Department decided to draw on the research findings as a prime basis for determining the content of the revised school standards, an approach for accomplishing this was designed and implemented. Twelve areas for consideration were included:

1. Instructional
2. Administrative and supervisory personnel
3. Guidance and Pupil Support Service Staff
4. Instructional strategies
5. Management strategies
6. Facilities
7. School climate
8. Extracurricular activities
9. Instructional media
10. Community and family
11. Student expectations, rights and privileges
12. School lunch and transportation services

One key area — the curriculum — was intentionally omitted because it was seen to be the primary concern of local districts. The last area, school lunch and transportation services, was dropped because of the difficulty of identifying qualified experts (from a research standpoint) in the time available.

For each of these areas, an eminent educator-researcher was commissioned to prepare an in-depth review of the research evidence to ascertain the extent to which a given practice, approach, or provision affects students' performance in schools or their self-concepts. Writers of the research papers were to be concerned with what empirical research of the past ten years has a direct impact or substantial influence on student performance and self-concept.

Once the reports were prepared, another set of authorities were invited to review them and to prepare written critiques. This latter group of reviewers were requested to consider whether any significant research findings may have been overlooked or slighted, and further, whether there were significant differences with respect to interpretations to offer.

The State Department of Education developed a roster of names of potential writers and reviewers for the respective content areas. In addition, it prepared sets of questions relating to practice and provisions, again pertaining to each area, for the reviewers to answer in the course of their respective assignments. Such questions were designed to help to focus the research review when the research was extensive and the field broad. In the area of management strategy, for example, one question was: "Does the research indicate whether it makes any difference, in terms of student performance or self-concept, how schools are administered or staffed for this purpose?" The writers could expand or depart from these lists of suggested questions if they chose.

A timetable was developed, a budget approved, and a consultant was assigned to the project in the area of research, planning, and evaluation. He contacted the various writers to commission the papers and coordinate the form, format, and scheduling of the preliminary drafts.

Once the eleven papers reviewing the research in the field were obtained, they were shared with those individuals who had agreed to critique them, adding eleven written commentaries. These twenty-two papers were then edited, retyped, and duplicated. Simultaneously, each set of papers was reviewed and summarized by an independent researcher to identify major findings as well as the arguments for and against specific approaches.

The next phase was to ensure a sound review and airing of interpretations; key groups in Georgia were involved: the State Board of Education, State Department of Education staff, local school administrators and staff, professional organizations in the state, students, parents, business personnel, and legislators. In order to accomplish such a review and sounding of interpretations, a trial-by-jury process was developed. Each author and each critiquer appeared in Atlanta before a select jury, consisting of representatives invited from the aforementioned constituencies. The two authors were instructed that they would have this opportunity to summarize their major findings and conclusions and to defend them or expand on them through cross-examination. Someone familiar with courtroom practice was chosen to preside as judge and the cross-examination was placed in the hands of selected Georgia educators drawn from the State Department, colleges and universities, and local school districts. Because these proceedings were videotaped, a mock courtroom set was developed in one of the state's educational television studios. All of the jury proceedings were consolidated into one-hour programs for presentation to the general public via the state's educational television network.

Once the presentation had been made and the cross-examinations conducted, the jury was empowered to raise additional questions. After the summations, the jury retired to make its recommendations. (Prior to the "trials," copies of the various papers had been shared with the jurors.) These recommendations were announced and became the basis, along with the twenty-two commissioned papers, for the Department's next steps in the process of revising the school standards.

All the materials prepared, including the respective jury findings, decisions, and recommendations, were turned over to the Bureau of Research, Planning, and Evaluation, which summarized them and submitted its report to the Department of Education's Office of Public School Standards for further development, hearings, and submission to the State Board of Education for final adoption.

Index

Academic atmosphere. *See* Climate, classroom; Climate, educational; Instructional environment

Academic failure, and self-concept, of student, 68, 70

Academic learning time (ALT), 73–78, 169–70; achievement and, 169–70; and attitude, of student, 77–78; reading instruction and, 75–77; research on, 75–78; teaching practices and, 78. *See also* Time, instructional

Academic performance, extracurricular activities and, 217–19, 225–29. *See also* Achievement; Performance; Productivity

Accountability, of teachers, 163

Achievement, as affected by: academic learning time, 169–70,

175; acoustical conditioning, 257–58; administrative behavior, 34, 45; athletics, participation in, 218–19; behavior, of teachers, 61–62, 164, 290; building age, 239–42, 274; building maintenance, 268; career guidance, 105; climate, of classroom, 289–91; color, of classroom, 253–55, 274, 285–86; communication, of teachers, 63–64; community, 215–20, 297, 328–32; content coverage, 81–82; crowding, 260–61, 275; counselors, 6, 101–02, 106; direct instruction, 55, 79, 169; evaluation, 114–15; expectations, 125–29; extracurricular activities, 218–19, 221–23, 225, 228; facilities, 232–74, 282–85; feedback, of teachers, 59–61, 80,

347

171; governance, of education, 323–25, 336–39; home environment, 300; individual instruction, 65–66, 80–81; instructional environment, 316, 336; instructional television, 189–91; light levels, 248–53; management, of classroom, 64–66; management, educational, 133, 143–45, 173; mastery learning, 159; media centers, 201; media personnel, 203; motion pictures, 187–89; multimedia instruction, 199; noise, 256, 274, 286; open vs. traditional schools, 116–17, 261; parents, 220, 316–20, 328; parent-teacher associations (PTA), 316; praise, 58–59, 290; questioning, by teachers, 56–58, 79–80, 163; resources, 137, 240; site size, 267; still pictures, 191–92; teaching, 49–70, 220, 299; thermal factors, 243–48, 274, 284; time, engaged in learning, 50–53; underground facilities, 265–66, 274; windowless classrooms, 265, 274. *See also* Performance; Productivity

Achievement, predictors of, 221–22

Achievement, standards for improving, 342

Administration, of education: decision-making structures and, 14; empirical findings and, 14; management and, 154

Administrative theories, improved practices and, 35

Administrators: behavior of, 14–19, 34; community and, 4, 7, 18, 323–28; curriculum development, role in, 128; decision making of, 23–28; as engineers of education, 44–45; evaluation of, 136; evaluation, view of, 115; as leaders, 28–33; and learning productivity, influence on, 4, 34; management by objectives and, 136; management teams of, 137–39; psychological climate and, 289; research on, 17–19, 34–35; roles of, 15–19, 309; social systems theory and, 15–17; training of, 35

Adolescents: achievements of, 222–23, 225; aspirations of, 219–21, 228; characteristics of, 218; later-life achievements and, 222–23, 225; peer groups and, 219–220, 225; and social participation, effects of, 244

Age of classroom units (ACU), 241

American Association of School Librarians, 199, 202–04

American Institute of Architects, 238

Anxiety, of students, teaching techniques and, 164

Aspirations: of adolescents, 219–21, 228; extracurricular activities and, 217–21, 228; of minorities, 220–21

Association for Educational Communications and Technology (AECT), Task Force on Definition and Technology, 189, 202–04

Athletics, student involvement in: achievement and, 218–19; delinquency and, 224

Attendance units, management of, 141–43

Attendance: teaching and, 52–54; year-round schooling and, 143–44

Attitude, of students: academic learning time and, 77–78; change in, 221; and extracurricular activities, effects on, 218, 224; management strategies and, 55

Attitude, toward environment: behavior and, 261; and self-perception, of students, 203–04

Audio materials, as instructional media, 192

Autocratic decision making, 139

Axiomatic organizational theory, 19–20

Back-to-basics movement, 112

Basic skills acquisition: criterion-referenced measure of, 331–33; direct instruction and, 55; teaching and, 52

Behavior, of administrators, 13–19, 34

Behavior: psychological study of, 290; social, 15–17

Behavior, of students: and building, effects of, 260–68, 274; and climate, of classroom, 64; communication and, 64; and counseling, effects of, 94–95; family and, 297; and leadership styles, effects of, 113; mediating process approach and, 166; and noise, effects of, 259; observation of, 73; and parents, influence of, 291; perceptions and, 118–20; and personal space, effects of, 260–61; public policy and, 291; and questioning, of teachers, 56–58; socioeconomic status and, 54; and teaching, effectiveness of, 49, 52–54, 62–67; and teaching, influence of, 299

Behavior, supervisory: achievement and, 34; learning productivity and, 3; student outcomes and, 15–19

Behavior, of teachers: achievement and, 61–62, 164, 290; controlling, 61–62, 161–62; impact on student, 15, 49–70, 137, 259; as instructional strategy, 161–62

Behavioral outcomes, classroom climate and, 295–97

Behavioral science, research on administration and, 34

Bilingual/bicultural programs, 316

Building age: achievement and, 273–74; input-output analysis and, 239. See also Facilities; Instructional environment

Buildings, school. See Facilities; Instructional environment

Career achievement, extracurricular activities and, 223, 225

Career guidance, 99, 103–05; and achievement, effects on, 105; counseling and, 99, 103–04; planning and, 103–04

Case studies: of parental involvement, 328; as a research methodology, 40; of school operations, 334

Child development, 155; classroom size and, 261

Children's rights, 125.

Citizen advisory committees, 335

Citizen participation: and achievement, effects on, 315–20, 329–332; in decision making, 323; education and, 313, 320. See also Community

Classroom ecology, environment and, 166

Classroom, as a learning environment, defined, 226

Classroom management. See Instructional strategies; Management

Classroom, organization of space in, 260

Classroom, size of: and

achievement, effects on, 156–57;
child development and, 261; as
management strategy, 140–41;
156–57; mental performance
and, 261

Classroom, structure of, open vs.
traditional, 81, 120–24, 292,
298–99, 301 *See also* Open
classrooms; Open climate

Climate, classroom: concept of,
292–96, 301; curriculum and,
296; ethnography and, 168; open
vs. traditional, 304; organization
of, 260; and parents and
teachers, interest of, 304, 305;
peer involvement and, 305;
Public Law 94–142 and, 308. *See
also* Climate, educational;
Instructional environment

Climate, educational: administrative
research and, 296; definition of,
289; home as, 293, 300–02;
learning outcomes and, 4, 8;
management of, 133, 137,
146–47; measurement of,
306–07; open, 292, 298-99, 301;
research on, 292–99; schools and,
292, 299, 301; teachers, 292,
296–98, 304–06; *See also* Climate,
classroom; Instructional
environment

Cognitive development, task
structuring and, 63

Cognitive outcomes, decision
making and, 122

Color, of classrooms: intelligence
quotient and, 255; performance
and, 253–55, 274, 283; pleasing,
effects of, 253–55, 283, 285–86

Comfort zone, 243

Commission on Instructional
Technology, 181–82

Communication: management
strategies and, 147; theories of,
147

Community: administrative roles

and, 18; politics of education
and, 159; psychologists' contact
with, 91; teachers and, 297;
values of, educational, 17

Community, participation in
education, 314–16, 319–32;
achievement and, 315–28,
330–35, 338; conceptual
framework for, 323–28;
governance-related, 323–25;
policies for, 323; research on,
315–16, 319–38; systems
approach to, 326, 332

Comparative media studies, 185–87;
research design of, 195–96

Compensatory education programs,
parental involvement in, 324

Competency-based education, 112

Computers, as media, 181, 185

Computer-assisted instruction
(CAI): costs of, 196; reading
achievement and, 193

Conceptual framework: of
community participation, in
education, 323–328; of teacher
effectiveness, 72

Conflict management, 148

Content coverage, as instructional
dimension, 81–82

Context variables, instructional
strategies and, 163

Coopersmith Self-Esteem Inventory,
263

Coordinated classroom concept, 235

Counseling: as career guidance, 99;
as personnel service, 86;
programs, 5; research on, 86,
92–95, 99–105

Counseling, elementary: discipline
and, 93–95; and goal setting, of
students, 93–94; group, 92–96;
group, and behavior of students,
94–95; self-esteem and, 94–95;
and socioeconomic status,
improvement of, 93–95

Counselors: and achievement,

effects on, 6, 101–02, 106; administrative roles and, 17; background of, 107–08; characteristics of, 100; and decision making, of students, 103–04; education programs for, 100–01; parent-child relationship and, 102; and self-concept of student, effects on, 102–03; special education and, 107–08; teacher training and, 107–08; as therapists, 100. *See also* Guidance; Psychologists

Council of Education Facility Planning, International, 238

Creativity: open classrooms and, 117; as teaching strategy, 284

Criterion-referenced measures, of basic skills, 331–33

Criticism, performance of students and, 69–71

Crowding, and achievement, effects on, 260–61, 275

Cultures: evaluation of different, 115; personality and, 16

Curriculum: administrative roles and, 17; agency impact on, 229–30; classroom climate and, 296; citizen advisory committees and, 335; development of, 128; district size and, 141; extracurricular activities and, 226, 228–29; and instructional television, effects of, 189–90; media and, 185–194; objectives of, 53; policy and, 229–30; school size and, 271; small-group learning and, 128; standards for, 342; year-round schooling and, 143

Decision Involvement Index, 25

Decision making: administrative, 14, 23–28; citizen participation and, 323–25; cognitive outcomes and, 122; democratic, 137–39; group participation in, 24–27; group vs. individual, 336; laissez faire, 139; management and, 133; management teams and, 138–39; media and, 213; open space schools and, 263; outcomes and resources and, 1; parental, role in, 232; research on, 23–28; shared vs. autocratic, 138–39; student outcomes of, 5; student role in, 116–20, 124, 232; of teacher, and artistry in teaching, 167–69, 173; of teacher, power of, 272–73; theory of, 23–25

Decision making, of students: achievement and, 116–18; career goals and, 103; citizen participation and, 323; counseling and, 103–04; open classrooms and, 263

Defense, Department of, and underground schools, 265

Delinquency, athletics and, 224

Delphi Technique, planning and, 150

Democratic decision making, 137–39

Democratic leadership, 29

"Descriptive-correlational-experimental loop," 164

Dewey, John, 124–25, 228–29

Direct instruction: achievement and, 55–56, 79, 169–71; basic skills acquisition and, 55; concept of, 79; socioeconomic status and, 55–56. See *also* Indirect instruction; Instructional strategies

Discipline: citizen advisory committees and, 335, counseling effects on, 93–95; teacher maintenance of, 62

Division of Education Replication, 178

Effectiveness: of leadership, productivity and, 43; of schools,

1–2; of teachers, 47, 62, 72; of
teachers, research on, 49–70. *See
also* Teachers, effectiveness of;
Management
Engineering, educational:
administrators and, 44–45; as
instructional strategy, 178
Environment. *See* Climate,
classroom; Climate, educational;
Instructional environment
Equal educational opportunity, 332
ERIC Clearinghouse on Educational
Management; and climate, of
schools, 146; conflict
management and, 148; decision
making and, 138; and
documentation, of personnel
services, 86; management and,
134
Ethnography: and climate, of
classroom, 166; instructional
strategies and, 7; as research
methodology, 40; teacher
effectiveness and, 40, 46
Evaluation: achievement and,
114–15; of administrators, 136;
and administrators, view of, 115;
of culture, effects on, 115; of
education, 342–44; government
funding of, 3; of learning
environments, 90, 291; of media,
213–15; procedures of, 114–16,
124; strategies of, achievement
and, 114; of students, 66,
114–15; of teachers, 134–36
Evaluative feedback: performance
and, 59–61; research on, 60
Expectations: research on, 125–30;
self-fulfilling prophecy and,
125–26; of student learning,
125–30; of teachers, student
intelligence quotient and, 68
Extracurricular activities:
achievement and, 223–29; and
attitudes, effects on, 218–224;
career achievement and, 223–25;

curriculum and, 226–29;
long-term effects of, 217,
224–25; minorities and, 217, 226;
performance and, 217–29; policy
and, 7, 232; research on, 217–26;
222–27; and skills, interpersonal,
224–25

Facilities: achievement and, 237–76;
and buildings, age of, 239; and
classroom, color of, 253–55, 274;
design of, as instructional tool,
286; as instructional tool, 281-86;
learning and, 48; maintenance
of, 268, 275; noise levels and,
256–59, 274; open space
classrooms and, 262–64, 275;
research on, 237–76, 282–85; site
size and, 267, 273; thermal
factors and, 242–48, 274;
underground, 265–66, 275;
windowless, 264–65, 275
Facilities, support: achievement and,
269–73; input-output studies of,
269; library as, 269–70; school
size and, 270–73
Facilities, planning of, teaching
methods and, 284
Federal programs, participation in,
35–36, 315–16
Field-based research, facilities and,
238
Follow Through project, 51, 56, 63,
64, 66–67, 304, 316
Footcandles, visual factors and,
248–50
Futurism, planning and, 150

Gates-McGinnitie Reading Test, 262
General Anxiety Scale for Children,
265
Georgia State Department Project
on Public School Standards, 34;
rationale behind, 341, standards
for, 342
Goals, educational, conflict

management and, 148
Governance: achievement and,
323–25; parent participation in,
323–25, 336
Government, research findings of,
42
Group counseling, 92–96
Group instruction, achievement and,
65. *See also* Instructional
strategies; Teaching
Group participation, decision
making and, 27
Guidance: as personnel service, 68;
rural schools and, 96–97. *See also*
Counseling; Psychology

Head Start Programs, 51
Health, Education, and Welfare,
Department of, 143
Hearing factors, in education:
achievement and, 285; behavior
and, 286; instruction and, 283.
See also Facilities
Home climate, achievement and,
300, 321
Home experiences, achievement
and, 164

Illuminating engineering, 248, 251
Illuminating Engineering Society,
238
Indirect Instruction, 55–56, 79. *See
also* Direct Instruction;
Instructional Strategies;
Teaching; Teaching, strategies of
Individually guided education
(IGE): administrative teams and,
157; as a management strategy,
157–58
Inner-city schools, student
motivation and, 118
Input-output analysis: and
buildings, age of, 239; and
buildings, utilization of, 267–68;
and expenditures, of students,
157; facilities and, 269; as

management strategy, 157;
productivity and, 150–51
Instruction, group, achievement
and, 65
Instruction, individual: achievement
and, 65–66; 127; class size and,
141; decision making and, 26;
efficiency of, 80–81; open
classrooms and, 121–22. *See also*
Instructional strategies; Teaching
strategies
Instructional environment:
achievement and, 316; effects of,
264, 289–303, 304–10, 336. *See
also* Climate, classroom; Climate,
educational; Facilities
Instructional management:
achievement and, 139–146, 173;
class size and, 140–41; curriculum
and, 141; as instructional
strategy, 173; school year and,
143–44; time spent in learning
and, 143–44
Instructional strategies: achievement
and, 176, 322; and behavior, of
teachers, 163–69; classroom
management and, 162; and
engineering, educational, 178;
management and, 173;
motivation and, 4; student
involvement in, 162; research on,
161–73, 177–78; resource
allocation and, 177; and tutoring,
of students, 158. *See also* Media;
Teaching, strategies of
Instructional tactics, resource use
and, 177–78
Instructional technology. *See* Media
Instructional Television (ITV),
189–90
Intelligence quotient (IQ): and
background music, effects of,
257; and color, of classroom,
255; and expectations, of
teachers, 68
International Association for the

Evaluation of Educational
Achievement, 50–51
Intuition, art of teaching and, 168
Iowa Test of Educational
Development, 241–42, 247,
262–63, 265, 272

Job satisfaction: psychologists and,
89; of teachers, 21–22, 41–42
Juvenile delinquency. *See*
Delinquency

Laboratory-derived research,
climate of classroom and, 296
Laboratory research, facilities and,
238, 274
Laissez-faire teaching climate, 292
Laissez-faire decision making, 139
"Laws of learning," and
instructional strategies, 177
Leaders: organizational climate and,
113; styles of, 113. *See also*
Administrators; Management;
Principals
Leadership: achievement and,
45–46; administrators and,
28–33; communication and, 45;
management and, 133; research
on, 31–34; and satisfaction, of
staff, 32–33; student outcomes
and, 5, 14; theory of, 29–30
Learned helplessness, achievement
and, 119–20
Learning: and noise, impact of, 256,
274; psychological climate and,
289. *See also* Achievement;
Performance; Productivity
Learning efficiency, psychologists
and, 91
Learning environments, evaluation
of, 291. *See also* Climate,
classroom; Climate, educational;
Educational environments;
Instructional environments
Learning Environment Inventory,
293, 295, 296; as an index of

curriculum, 296
Learning, freedom of, 220–23
Learning, long-term, teacher
authority and, 6
Learning, observation of, 73
Learning outcomes,
social-psychological
environments, 4, 8, 293
Learning productivity. *See*
Achievement; Performance;
Productivity
Libraries: as media centers,
198–201; as support facilities,
269–70. *See also* Facilities,
support
Likert, Rensis, 42
Lorge-Thorndike Intelligence Test,
263

Mainstreaming, of handicapped
children, 348
Management: achievement and,
133–34; as administration, 133;
communication and, 147; of
conflicts, 148; decision making
and, 133–36; and learning,
research on, 133–52; as media,
182; as science, 40; research on,
134, 146–49, 155–56; standards
for, 155. *See also* Administrators;
Principals; Supervisors
Management, instructional. *See*
Instructional management
Management by objectives (MBO),
136; planning and, 149–50
Management strategies: and ability,
of students, 155; and attitudes, of
students, 155; child development
and, 155; classroom size and,
156–57; input-output analysis
and, 151–57; mastery learning
and, 158–59; outcomes and, 155;
policy development and, 6, 151.
See also Management
Management teams, 137–39
Mastery learning, 6, 158–59

Mathematics: achievement and, 263, 316, 320; counseling and, 102; instructional television and, 189–91; and noise, impact of, 257; optimal building temperature and, 242; programmed instruction and, 193; and questioning, by teachers, 57; time spent on teaching of, 53, 232

Mechanistic organization, of schools, 20

Media attributes, research on, 184–85

Media: achievement and, 183–213; appropriateness of, 197; attributes of, 184–85; audio materials and, 185, 192, 212; communication and, 181; costs of, 213–24; curriculum and, 185–94; decision making and, 214; design of, 182; and development, educational, 182; effectiveness of, 183, 214; evaluation of, 213–14; film as, 181, 185, 212–13; guidelines for, 203–04; history of, 183–85; management of, 182; and objectives, educational, 182, 204; research on, 183–96; programmed instruction as, 185, 192; and research, design of, 195–96; as a resource, 182; school board members and, 211; and teachers, needs of, 181–87, 205, 212; as technology, 181–82, 211–15

Mediating-process, and behavior, of learner, 166

Memory, and noise, impact on, 256

Mental ability, and learner characteristics, 164

Mental health, psychologists and, 91

Mental performance, classroom size and, 261. See also Achievement; Performance; Productivity

Mill, John Stuart, 213

Minimum competency tests, 333

Minorities: achievement and, 332; aspirations of, 220–21; community participation and, 330–31; and effectiveness, of schools, 330; extracurricular activities and, 217, 226; self-fulfilling prophecy and, 125–26

Morale, of staff: organizational theory and, 19–20; student outcomes and, 297–98

Morale, of students: and participation, in education, 116; and teacher leadership, styles of, 113–14

Morale, of teachers, and productivity, 42–43

Motion pictures, as media, 189–90, 195

Motivation: instructional strategies and, 4; external, 115; open education and, 117; and praise, by teachers, 59

Multimedia instruction, effectiveness of, 194. See also Media

National Advisory Commission on School Libraries, 198

National Defense Education Act, 184

New Stanford Achievement Test, 249

New York Commission on Ventilation, 244

Noise, achievement and, 256–57. See also Facilities

Norm-referenced tests, 333

Objectives, instructional, management and, 173

Observation, of behavior, 37

Open classrooms: achievement and, 116–17, 145–46, 261–64, 274; creativity and, 117; decision

making and, 263; defined, 261;
individualized education and,
121–22; peer relations and, 263;
research on, 120–22, 145–46;
self-concept and, 263–64
Open climates: achievement and,
298; decision making and, 263;
defined, 261; peer relations and,
263; self-concept and, 263-64
Opportunity to learn, 169
Organic organization, 30-31
Organization: classroom
environment and, 260;
management and, 133; research
on, 21–23, 41–44, 238, 274; of
schools, 19–20, 22–23, 238, 274
Organizational adaptiveness, school
structure and, 21
Organizational climate, 41–44;
group morale and, 113;
productivity and, 113. See also,
Climate, classroom; Climate,
educational
Organizational theory, efficiency
and, 19
Otis Self-Administering Test of
Mental Ability, 249, 262
Outcomes: cognitive, 122;
educational, 155; learning, and
social-psychological
environments, 4, 8, 293;
measurement of, 322; student, 5,
14

Parents: achievement and, 270,
329–36; advisory councils of,
235–36; authoritative, and
self-concept of students, 229; as
decision makers, 314, 325; and
psychological climate, as part of,
289; and tutoring, of students,
326, 336; year-round schooling
and, 143
Parents, involvement in education
of: case studies of, 328; and
climate, of classroom, 304–05;

compensatory education
programs and, 324; federal
programs requiring, 315–16;
governance and, 336; and
self-concept, of students, 319
Peers, involvement in classroom,
305
Peer group expectations,
achievement and, 220, 225
Peer relations, open classrooms and,
263
Performance: and classroom, color
of, 59–61; criticism and, 59–61;
delinquency and, 224; light levels
and, 248; open education and,
117, 263, 275; standards for
improving, 342; and teachers,
feedback of, 61, 80; and teachers,
role of, 309. See also
Achievement; Learning;
Productivity
Performance-based criteria, 342
Permissiveness, 124; achievement
and, 112, 122; classroom
management and, 162;
delinquency and, 122
Personality: acoustical conditioning
and, 259; culture and, 16
Personnel: administrative roles and,
17; economic constraints on, 88;
functions of, 85–97; guidance
and, 86; objectives of, 88; as
parents, 313–14; ratio of, to
students, 96, 105–07; research
on, 86–87. See also Counselors;
Psychologists
Phenomenology, as a research
methodology, 40, 46
Physical environment, achievement
and, 282–85. See also Climate,
classroom; Climate, educational;
Instructional environment
Planning, educational: Critical Path
Method (CPM), 149–50;
Planning, Programming,
Budgeting System (PPBS),

149–50; futurism and, 150; input-output analysis of, 150–51; management by objectives (MBO) and, 149–50; management strategies and, 149–51

Planning, Programming, Budgeting, System (PPBS), 149–50

Policy: curriculum and, 229–30; extracurricular activities and, 7, 232; school board members and, 211, 332–39

Policy development, 151; community participation in, 338–39; parental involvement in, 314; research on, 151–52

Politics, educational: conflict management and, 159; policy development and, 151, 159

"Portrayal," teaching and, 165–66

Praise, by teachers, achievement and, 45, 129

Principals: individually guided education and, 157–58; leadership of, 32–33, 331; management teams of, 138; and morale, of staff, 297–98; successful, 45–46; teacher contact with, achievement and, 297–98; and tutoring, by students, 158

Problem-solving skills, and self-perceptions of students, 120–21

Process variables, 163

Productivity: accomplishments and, 232; administrators and, 4, 13–35; adult accomplishments and, 232; input-output analysis of, 150–51; measurement of, 10; and morale, of teachers, 42–43; organizational theory and, 19; resources and, 2, 9; supervision and, 42. *See also* Achievement; Instruction; Learning

Programmed instruction, 192–97

Project Talent, 240, 272

Psychologists: background of, 107–08; community and, 91; evaluation of, 88–91; and motivation, of students, 4; teachers and, 308. *See also* Counselors

Psychological climate, learning and, 289

Psychological measurement, 9

Psychological reactions, thermal factors and, 244

Psychology: models for, 91; policy and, 1; research on, 88–91; role of, 290–91; schools and, 88–99

Public Law 94–142; and climate, of classroom, 308; and counselors, role of, 108; personnel specialists and, 87

Reading achievement: and background music, effects of, 257; building age and, 240, 273; computer-assisted instruction(CAI) and, 193; lighting levels and, 248–49; open classrooms and, 262; parents and, 317–20; and teachers, questioning by, 58; and time spent on reading, 52, 53

Reinforcement, achievement and, 173

Research on: achievement, of minorities, 332; academic learning time, 75–78; behavioral science, 34; classroom size, 140–41, 156; climate, educational, 292–99, 304–10; community participation, in education, 315–16; 319–20, 322–38; counseling, 92–95, 99–105; counselors, 99; facilities, 237–78, 282–85; instructional strategies, 161–73, 176–78; leadership, 31–33; management, 134, 146–49; 155–56; management teams, 138–39; open classrooms, 120–22,

145–46; organization, of schools, 21–23, 41–44, 238, 274; parents, 318–19; perceptions, of student, 296; personnel, 86–87; policy, development of, 151–52; psychology, 88–92; school year, 143–44; students, 116–20, 125–26; success rates, 73–74; supervision, 136–37; teaching, 49–70; 166–69, 112–15; teachers, evaluation of, 134–35

Resources, educational: and organizaton, of schools, 21–23; policy and, 4. *See also* Media

Resources, management of, 133; achievement and, 134, 240; availability of, to teachers, 137; media and, 182

Rural education: facilities for, 237; school size and, 142

Rural School Guidance programs, 96–97

Sarason's Test Anxiety Scale for Children, 265

School board members, 211, 332–39

School buildings: achievement and, 258, 260–61, 267–68; age of, and achievement, 239–42; and behavior, effects on, 260; as a learning environment, concept of, 266; maintenance of, 268. *See also* Buildings; Classrooms; Environments

School climate. *See* Climate, classroom; Climate, educational

School-community relations, 326–30, 336

Schools: criticism of, 111–12; as open systems, 14–15; organization of, 19–22; policy and, 112; as social settings, 127

School district size, 141; and instructional management, 140–41

School planning, research on, 282

School size: achievement and, 297; curriculum and, 271

Self-concept, of students: achievement and, 263; and administrators, role of, 17; career guidance and, 105; classroom environments and, 298–302; counselor effectiveness and, 6, 102–03; and decision-making style, of teachers, 293; Follow Through project and, 56; governance and, 323; who are handicapped, 308; open vs. traditional classrooms, 117, 263–64, 301; organizational structure and, 22; parental involvement and, 319; and perceptions, of students, 305, 307; standards for improving, 342

Self-estrangement, psychological causes of, 223

Self-fulfilling prophecy, 60, 126–26; minorities and, 125–26

Skills, interpersonal, and extracurricular activities, 224–25

Social-psychological environments: and climate, of classroom, 293, 296. *See also* Climate, classroom; Climate, educational

Social systems theory, administrators and, 15–17

Socioeconomic status (SES): achievement and, 297, 305–06, 317; community involvement and, 328; counseling and, 73; direct teaching methods and, 55–56; extracurricular activities and, 222; management strategies and, 155; school buildings and, 241–42, 272–73; and teachers, effectiveness of, 54, 330

Sociometric evaluation, 307

Socrates, 212

Special education, counselors and, 107, 108; minorities and, 330–31

Spectra Spot Brightness Meter, 257
Staff, educational. *See*
  Administrators; Counselors;
  Personnel; Psychologists;
  Teachers
Stanford Achievement Tests, 265
Still pictures, effectiveness of,
  research on, 191–92
Structuring: of classrooms, 81; open
  vs. traditional, 120–22; 124
Students: and behavior, of teachers,
  59–62; decision making and, 263;
  communication and, 64;
  expectations of, 128;
  responsibilities of, 1, 112; success
  in school and, 64; tutoring, 3,
  158. *See also* Achievement;
  Performance, Productivity
Students, behavior of: and building,
  effects on, 268, 274; and climate,
  of classroom, 290;
  communication and, 64; parent
  effects on, 291; public policy and,
  290; self-control and, 122; and
  teachers, effects of, 299
Student, involvement in education:
  and behavior, of teachers,
  170–71; in decision making,
  116–20, 124; discussion and, 167;
  learning and, 53, 60, 111–29,
  162–63, 167, 170; outcomes of,
  116–18; teacher assessment of,
  167
Student, perceptions of: ability, 120;
  achievement and, 118; and
  climate, of classroom, 292,
  306–07; learned helplessness
  and, 119–20; learning and, 128,
  290; measurement of, 291,
  293–96; of psychological climate,
  289–90; of self-control, 118–20;
  teacher influences on, 120
Success rates: attitudes and, 77;
  instructional design and, 73–75;
  self-esteem and, 73–75
Supervisors: learning process and,

4, 13–35, 136–37; qualifications
  of, 342. *See also* Administrators;
  Leaders; Management; Principals
Support facilities. *See* Facilities,
  support
Systems approach, community
  involvement and, 325, 332
Systems models, 14, 34
Systems theory: administrators and,
  14–17; impact of human
  resources on, 5
Task structuring, 63
Team approach: to personnel
  services, 87; of teaching, vs.
  traditional, 21
Teacher: behavior of, 15, 137, 259;
  communication of, 63–64;
  community contact with, 297;
  curriculum development and,
  128–29; decision making and,
  167–69, 292–93; evaluation of,
  134–36; evaluation, of student
  performance, 66, 114–15; job
  descriptions for, 43; leadership,
  styles of, 113, 124; media and,
  212; motion pictures vs., 187;
  perceptions of, 297, 304, 307;
  psychological climate and, 289;
  research on, 49–70, 112–15,
  166–69; role of, 112–14, 309
Teacher, effectiveness of:
  achievement and, 49–70;
  conceptual framework of, 72;
  ethnographic analysis of, 47;
  research on, 49–70
Teacher training: counselors and,
  108; media centers and,
  199–200; instructional strategies
  and, 172–73
Teaching: academic learning time
  and, 50–53, 78; as an art, 40,
  166–69, climates of, 299–301;
  research on, 49–70, 163–69; and
  self-concept, of student, 66–69.
  See also Achievement;
  Instructional strategies;

Performance; Teaching,
strategies of
Teaching, strategies of: achievement
and, 302, 155; artistry as,
167–69; creativity as, 284; direct
instruction as, 5, 171;
encouragement as, 220;
expectations and, 125–29;
facilities and, 284; feedback as,
171–72; intuition as, 168;
motivational devices and, 172;
and praise, of teachers, 58–59,
67–68, 129, 172, 290;
questioning of teachers as, 56–68,
79–80, 172. *See also* Instructional
strategies
Technology, educational. *See* Media
Temperatures, optimum, for school
room, 244
Territoriality, personal space and,
260
Test of Academic Progress, 241
Testing, by educational
psychologists, 89, 107
Test scores, ability of students and,
170
Theory base, teaching and, 64
Theory, of leadership, 29–30; policy
formation and, 125
Thermal factors, 274; achievement
and, 243–48, 282; efficiency and,
243–48; psychological reactions
to, 244
Time, instructional, 5, 8, 10;
achievement and, 50–54, 67, 73,
156, 322; budgeting of, 231–32;
content coverage and, 82;
curriculum and, 53; decision
making, parents'role in, 232;
economics of, 231–32;
extracurricular activities and,
230–31; management of, 143–45;
mathematics achievement and,
156; reading achievement and,
156; and students, participation
of, 116

Time-on-task, 170
Title I of the Elementary and
Secondary Education Act, 316,
324, 334; parental involvement
and, 336
Title IX, 226
"Tracking," achievement and, 127
Traditional classrooms. *See* Open
classrooms; Open education
Tutoring, parental, 326, 336
Tutoring, student-to-student:
achievement and, 6, 65, 158; as
instructional strategy, 158

United States Navy, research on
thermal factors, 245
United States Office of Education,
178

Validity, of research, 92
Validity: of psychological measures,
research on, 3, 5, 9; of observer
judgments, 72–73
Values, educational, 16–17
Variables: behavior of teachers and,
82–83; effective teaching and,
82–83
Visual factors, 248–53; guidelines
for, 251; and learning, 283;
performance and, 274
Visual Task Photometer, 252

Waetzen Self-Concept as a Learner
Scale, 264
Wide-Range Achievement Test
(WRAT), 51
Windowless classroom, student
learning and, 265–66

Year-round schooling: attendance
and, 143–44; curriculum reform
and, 143; as a management
strategy, 143

ABOUT THE EDITOR

Herbert J. Walberg is professor of human development and learning and research professor of urban education at the University of Illinois at Chicago Circle. He was formerly at the Educational Testing Service and held faculty positions at Harvard University and the University of Wisconsin.

Dr. Walberg received his Ph.D. from the University of Chicago in 1964. Since then he has served as consultant to a wide variety of private and public institutions and agencies in the areas of program and curriculum design and evaluation research. He is author of more than ninety research papers, is editor of *Educational Environments and Effects* (McCutchan, 1979), and coeditor of *Evaluating Educational Performance* (McCutchan, 1974) and *Research on Teaching* (McCutchan, 1979). He has contributed as author or editor to several other books and recently planned and coordinated a series of worldwide broadcasts for Voice of America.